Reflective Practice for Renewing Schools

Third Edition

We wish to dedicate this book

To our parents and grandparents—they were our first teachers

*To the teachers who supported us learning
during our formative years in school*

*To our educator colleagues who have been gracious enough to invite us
to learn alongside them now*

*And to our children, all of whom are now grown-ups who continue to inspire
us by how they show up in the world*

Reflective Practice for Renewing Schools

An Action Guide for Educators

Third Edition

Jennifer York-Barr
William A. Sommers
Gail S. Ghere
Jo Montie

Foreword by Arthur L. Costa

CORWIN
A SAGE Publishing Company

FOR INFORMATION:

Corwin

A SAGE Company

2455 Teller Road

Thousand Oaks, California 91320

(800) 233-9936

www.corwin.com

SAGE Publications Ltd.

1 Oliver's Yard

55 City Road

London EC1Y 1SP

United Kingdom

SAGE Publications India Pvt. Ltd.

B 1/I 1 Mohan Cooperative Industrial Area

Mathura Road, New Delhi 110 044

India

SAGE Publications Asia-Pacific Pte. Ltd.

3 Church Street

#10-04 Samsung Hub

Singapore 049483

Program Director: Dan Alpert

Senior Associate Editor: Kimberly Greenberg

Editorial Assistant: Katie Crilley

Production Editor: Melanie Birdsall

Copy Editor: Janet Ford

Typesetter: C&M Digitals (P) Ltd.

Proofreader: Theresa Kay

Indexer: Sheila Bodell

Cover Designer: Michael Dubowe

Marketing Manager: Charline Maher

Printed in the United States of America

ISBN 978-1-5063-5051-6

This book is printed on acid-free paper.

SUSTAINABLE FORESTRY INITIATIVE

Certified Chain of Custody
Promoting Sustainable Forestry
www.sfiprogram.org
SFI-01268

SFI label applies to text stock

16 17 18 19 20 10 9 8 7 6 5 4 3 2 1

Contents

Visit the companion website at
http://resources.corwin.com/YorkBarrReflective
for downloadable resources.

List of Figures, Tables, and Practice Examples

LIST OF FIGURES

LIST OF TABLES

LIST OF PRACTICE EXAMPLES

Foreword

Making meaning is not a spectator sport. It is an engagement of the mind that transforms the mind. The brain's capacity and inclination to find patterns of meaning are keys of brain-based learning. Human beings are active, dynamic, self-organizing systems integrating the mind, body, and spirit. Their natural tendency is to organize experiences into greater levels of complexity and diversity. We never really understand something until we can create a model or metaphor derived from our unique personal world. The reality we perceive, feel, see, and hear is influenced by the constructivist processes of reflection. Humans don't get ideas, they make ideas.

Furthermore, making meaning is not just an individual operation. The individual interacts collaboratively with others to construct shared knowledge. There is a cycle of internalization of what is socially constructed as shared meaning. Constructive learning, therefore, is viewed as a reciprocal process in that the individual influences the group, and the group influences the individual.

Children come fully equipped with an insatiable drive to explore, to experiment, and to inquire. Toddlers are in a constant state of exploring everything that they can detect with their hands, eyes, and lips. They live in a state of continuous discovery: dismayed by anomaly, attracted to novelty, compelled to mastery, intrigued by mystery, curious about discrepancy. They derive personal and concrete feedback from their sensory adventures. Their brains are actually being transformed with each new experience.

Unfortunately, the educational process often is oriented toward controlling rather than learning, rewarding individuals for performing for others rather than cultivating their natural curiosity and impulse to learn. From an early age, a fragmented, compartmentalized curriculum may teach competitiveness and reactiveness. We may be trained to believe that deep learning means knowing accepted truths rather than developing capacities for effective and thoughtful action; acquiring knowledge is for passing tests rather than accumulating wisdom and personal meaning. We may be taught to value certainty rather than doubt, to give quick answers rather than to inquire, and to know which choice is correct rather than to reflect on alternatives. Learning may be perceived to have little or no relevant application beyond the school to everyday living, further inquiry, or knowledge production.

Schools and classrooms today are busy, active places where students and teachers are pressured to learn more, to learn faster to be more rigorous and to be held accountable for demonstrating to others their achievement of specified standards and mastery of content. For that reason, classrooms are much more present and future oriented than they are past oriented, and it is often easier to discard what has happened and simply move on. Thus children, whose natural tendency is to create personal meaning, may be gradually habituated to think that they are incapable of reflecting and constructing meaning on their own. Eventually, students may become convinced that knowledge is accumulated bits of information and that learning has little to do with their capacity for effective action, their sense of self, and how they exist in their world. Later, as they mature, they may confront learning opportunities with fear rather than mystery and wonder. They seem to feel better when they know rather than when they learn. They defend their biases, beliefs, and storehouses of knowledge rather than inviting the unknown, the creative, and the inspirational into their meaning making. Being certain and closed provides comfort whereas being doubtful, ambiguous, and open causes fear. Life experiences and actions are viewed as separate, unrelated, and isolated events rather than as opportunities for continuous learning. Psychologists refer to this syndrome as an *episodic grasp of reality*.

Schools' and districts' improvement efforts may also signal an episodic approach. Proudly striving to keep abreast of educational improvement practices, some schools adopt an array of innovations (project-based learning, flipped classrooms, instructional technology, interdisciplinary instruction, STEM/STEAM, mentoring, Common Core State Standards, Personalized Learning, and so forth). Whereas a great deal of time may be spent in planning, limited time is spent in reflecting. As a result, teachers and administrators soon become impervious to integrating all the disparate pieces. In such an intellectually barren school climate, some teachers and administrators understandably grow depressed. Their vivid imagination, altruism, creativity, and intellectual prowess soon succumb to the humdrum, daily routines of unruly students, irrelevant curriculum, impersonal surroundings, and equally disillusioned coworkers. In such an environment, the likelihood that staff members would value reflectivity would be marginal.

The authors of this richly documented and valuable book provide a brighter vision. They believe that the organization that does not take time to reflect does not have time to improve and that reflective organizations view school improvement from a broader perspective, as a process of revealing and emancipating human and organizational resourcefulness. They make a strong case for the *less is more* principle and believe that to take the time, to set the tone, and to provide the opportunities for group and individual reflection prove beneficial not only for students but also for entire faculties. The time and effort invested in reflection yield a harvest of greater student learning, higher teacher morale, enhanced feelings of efficacy, and a more collaborative professional community.

The authors propose that a major, but often overlooked, goal of education should be habitual reflection on one's actions so as to maximize the autonomous, continual, and lifelong construction of meaning from those experiences. They offer compelling evidence that

- Reflecting on one's own work enhances meaning
- Constructing meaning from experiences enhances the applicability of that knowledge beyond the situation in which it was learned
- Reflecting on one's experiences results in insights and complex learning
- Reflecting on experiences is amplified when done with partners and in group settings
- Reflecting by individuals is signaled and encouraged when reflection is implicit in the organization's values, policies, and practices

Maximizing meaning from life's experiences requires enhancing and amplifying the human capacities for reflection. To be reflective means to mentally wander through where you have been and try to make some sense out of it. Reflection involves such habits or dispositions as

- Thinking about thinking or metacognition and conducting an internal dialogue before, during, and after an event
- Connecting information to previous learning
- Drawing forth cognitive and emotional information from several sources, such as visual, auditory, kinesthetic, tactile
- Acting on and processing the information—synthesizing, evaluating, self-modifying, goal setting
- Applying insights to contexts beyond the one in which they were learned

As individuals, staffs, and organizations reflect on their learning, they gain important information about how they perceive the efficacy of their planning, experimenting, data gathering, assessment, and self-modification. These experiences provide opportunities to practice the habit of continuous growth through reflection. The authors refer to this as the "reflective practice spiral." Individuals, groups, and schools begin to learn how to become a continuously growing and learning professional community by seizing opportunities to reflect individually, in partnerships, and in group situations within an atmosphere of trust.

Reflection is not just kid stuff. The authors make a strong case for habitual reflection throughout the learning community—in students, teachers, administrators, and parents—as well as for integrating reflectivity in organizational practices. Because imitation is the most basic form of learning, impressionable students often need to see adults—parents, teachers, and administrators—reflect on their practice. Adults are not only facilitators of meaning making, but also models of reflection. Their role is to help learners approach an event in a thoughtful and strategic way, to help monitor their progress during the experience, and to construct meaning from the content learned as well as from the process of learning it, and then to modify one's actions and apply those learnings to other contexts and settings. Educators in reflective schools and classrooms seek to ensure that all the inhabitants are fully engaged in the making of meaning, organizing experiences and activities so that stakeholders are the producers of knowledge rather than just the consumers of knowledge.

If the goal is to engage in deep reflection on one's work so as to make life experiences meaningful and to acquire the humility of continuous learning, then potent strategies must be employed in all quarters of the organization—for students, teachers, and administrators—and at all levels of the school community—in the classroom, in the school, in the school district, and in the community. Developing habits of continuous growth requires not only the capacity to be self-reflective; time also must be regularly scheduled to reflect on learning. Opportunities must be seized; strategies must be experimented with and evaluated for their productivity. And that is what this book so abundantly furnishes: clear directions for engaging in reflection individually, with partners, and in small and large groups; creative techniques for engaging in meaning making, clever ways to find the time, and practical strategies for deliberately setting an organizational tone of reflectivity.

We must vow to serve and maintain this natural tendency of humans to inquire and experience, and then, through reflection, find patterns, integrate meaning, and seek additional opportunities to satisfy the human propensity for learning. A goal of education, therefore, should be to recapture, sustain, and liberate the natural, self-organizing, learning tendencies inherent in all human beings: curiosity and wonderment, mystery and adventure, humor and playfulness, connection finding, inventiveness and creativity, continual inquiry, and insatiable learning through reflection.

The school that commits its resources of time, energy, and talent to reflection makes a clear statement of its valuing of the continuous intellectual growth for all its inhabitants and its desire to make the world a more thoughtful place.

Arthur L. Costa, EdD
Granite Bay, California

Preface

We begin this third edition with a new title, *Reflective Practice for Renewing Schools*. We substituted *renewing* for *improving*. We were searching for a more energetic and empowering term. We were also inspired by John Goodlad who prefers the term *renewal* to *reform*. He explains,

> [Reform suggests] somebody is trying to do something to somebody else who it thought to be wrong and who will be reformed if he or she follows these directions. By contrast, in renewal, [insiders] want to change and to do so in the light of knowledge, in the light of inquiry into what is needed. It's the difference between digging up a garden to replace all the plants with something else and nurturing the garden. (Ferrace, 2002, p. 31)

As with the first two editions, we are drawn to images of nature, nurture, and growth . . . and bristle from images of fixing inadequacies or remediating deficiencies. Learning environments differ from machines with interchangeable components. Authentic and lasting change is motivated internally and continues to grow in creative workplaces. This book is about tapping internal hopes and desires that inspire continuous learning by educators who, in turn, inspire and nurture continuous learning by today's young people in schools.

In the fifteen years since our first edition was published there has been an increasing stream of literature on the topic of reflective practice. Still dominant is literature about reflection in preservice teacher education and ongoing learning improvement for experienced professionals. Adding to this core is literature from the fields of nursing, adult education, and professional development for practicing educators. Emergent emphases include use of technology to support reflection, engaging students in reflective practice, and using reflection to foster cultural proficiency. Further, there are even more accounts of meaningful, ongoing, and collaborative reflective practice among educators in the context of instructional teams, observed schoolwide, among schools, and both districtwide and across districts. Importantly, there is a sharper focus on reflection as a means for advancing teaching and learning practices with the explicit intent of increasing student achievement. We view the expanding literature base on reflective practice, including research on its effectiveness, as a sign of hope and encouragement that more reflection and learning is and can be happening in the lives of educators to the ultimate benefit of students.

At its core, we believe that reflective practice is about tapping into things deeply human: the desire to learn, to grow, to be in community with others, to contribute, to serve, and to make sense of our time on earth. We believe the vast majority of educators have chosen this most noble of professions in hopes of making a positive difference in the lives and development of young people, consequently making a difference in societal life for years to come. We know this work is enormously challenging given complex contexts of practice, the wide variety of individuals and communities with whom educators engage, and the unrelenting pressure to perform and to be accountable. We believe that effective teaching involves both the hard focus on standards, instruction, and outcomes and the softer focus of relationships, intuition, and emotion. Students remind us that both caring and competence are necessary teacher attributes. Without care, there is no connection to the competence. Without competence, there is no respect.

We are concerned when structures and cultures in schools impede our natural tendencies to learn, to connect, to create, and to contribute. Working in schools can feel like living in a container, limiting space, time, and access to nutrients. Plants in such environments eventually wither and die. People who work in isolating cultures and who are cut off from essential nutrients also can lose energy and wither. It is way too hard to go it alone as educators. Edward Deming asserted many years ago that much of the reason for moving away from the work and not doing work as well, lies in the culture and the structure of the environment. Fortunately, much has been learned about how to initiate and sustain the process of re-creating culture, structure, expectations, and support such that educators are renewed in their development work with children. We are grateful for the work of Peter Block and Edgar Schein who continue to provide renewed thinking about our cultures and community.

Reflective practice is at the root of renewed life and energy in schools. Trust is at the root of collaborative cultures that sustain growth. Reflective practice is the vital and largely untapped resource for significant and sustained effectiveness. Experience by itself is not enough. Reflection on experience with subsequent action is the pathway to renewal and continuous improvement. Reflection is a means for examining beliefs, assumptions, and practices. It can lead to encouraging insights about instructional effectiveness. It can also result in the discovery of incongruities between espoused beliefs and actual actions. Either way, the self-awareness gained through reflection can motivate individuals to initiate changes in practice to enhance student learning. Effective implementation of reflective practices requires continuous development of both individual and organizational learning capacities. The hectic pace and rigid structures in many schools makes it difficult to take time out to reflect and learn. The learning demands, however, continue to escalate for both students and staff.

For readers of this book, our desired outcomes are to understand the positive potential, and perhaps even the necessity of reflective practice to improve teaching and learning in schools; to initiate or extend individual commitments to reflective practice as a way to continuously learn and improve educational practice; and to support implementation of individual and collaborative reflective practices within schools. Implied is the assumption that in order for students to learn well in school, so, too, must the community of educators who encircle them. In the words of Art Costa, who wrote the foreword for all three editions of this book and who is renowned for his work in cognitive coaching, "If we don't provide intellectually stimulating environments for teachers, why do we think they will provide that for students?"

This book offers a framework, strategies, and practice examples for thinking and doing as reflective educators. It is organized into eight chapters. In Chapter 1, we define reflective practice, provide a rationale for its potential to improve schools, describe characteristics of reflective educators, and present the reflective practice spiral as the organizing framework for the book. This framework asserts that the place to begin implementation of reflective practices is with oneself. From that base, reflective practice can expand to include colleagues throughout the school and organization. In Chapter 2, we identify and describe fundamental considerations for the design and development of conversations in which reflective practices are embedded. The learning, as always, is in the conversation. Skilled facilitators of reflective practice have learned ways to tailor learning structures, processes, and practices to both invite, and sometimes compel, community members to listen, speak, and learn together. Chapter 2 offers principles of adult learning, including findings from brain research that inform the design of conversational space. Also identified in Chapter 2 are practices for listening, thinking, promoting trust, along with conversational norms that when enacted result in every voice being heard. Chapter 2 closes with a new practice example that offers the short version of a five-year process of growing a more interdependent community of diverse practitioners with the focus of improving equitable opportunities for students who are traditionally at risk for being removed from general education. Chapter 3 is new to the book and specifically focuses on leadership understandings and practices aimed at growing more reflective communities of practice.

In Chapters 4 through 7, we offer strategies and examples for supporting reflective practices for individuals (Chapter 4), for partners (Chapter 5), for small groups and teams (Chapter 6), and school- and districtwide (Chapter 7). Finally, in Chapter 8, we share lessons learned from our experiences working with educators and schools to implement reflective practices. We also offer ideas and strategies for remaining hopeful about possibilities in our work. At the end of every chapter we include a reflection page for you to write down your own reflection with an aim toward application.

New to this third edition are greater attention to reflection for fostering equity and cultural competence and for being more mindful about ways our brains work to either be open to learning or to shut down. There are more strategies for individual reflection as a means of continually clarifying, grounding, and refining both purpose and practice. There are new and more robust practice examples, including more administrator and school-wide examples. And, as mentioned above, there is more attention to ways to lead this work. In the accompanying website at http://resources.corwin .com/YorkBarrReflective, there are numerous resources that can be easily accessed and printed for use to design and guide reflective practices.

As with the first two editions, the primary audiences for this book are teacher leaders, staff development specialists, program coordinators, site administrators, and other educators who assume responsibility for renewal, improvement, and staff development in their school communities. Faculty involved in preservice, in-service, and ongoing service in the development of teachers and administrators should also find this book a useful resource as it offers foundations, strategies, and examples for continuous learning and development of the professional educator. To this list, we add "positive deviants" as an intended audience. Since the first edition, when we introduced the concept of positive deviance (grounded in the work of the late Jerry Sternin, an international development specialist for Save Our Children), the term has taken root in some educational circles (described more in Chapter 1). Briefly, positive deviants are individuals who thrive in situations that others do not, and situations where individuals would not necessarily be expected to thrive. In the context of education, positive deviants are those individuals who "Just do it!," to borrow Nike's slogan, mindfully and with a deep understanding of context and culture. They are the seemingly innate reflective practitioners. They just continue to reflect and learn and grow, despite what seem to be constraining forces and conditions around them. We intend this book for the positive deviants among us who we hope will feel affirmed and supported in extending their enviable and attainable propensity for growth and renewal. Maybe this book can serve as a boost for those who continue to see possibilities and who do their part, every day, striving to create positive futures. We believe that now more than ever before, educators must continuously and meaningfully reflect on their practice—by themselves, and with their colleagues. We look forward to more learning about reflective practice and the results on learning for years to come. We are convinced of the extraordinary talent, good intentions, and steadfast commitments demonstrated by the vast majority of practicing educators in K–12 schools. We are equally convinced that without significant advances in opportunity and the capacity of individuals and schools to foster continuous renewal and improvement, the demands on educators will exceed their capacity to promote high levels of learning for all students. We offer this book as encouragement and reference for individual and collective efforts to create schools where both students and adults continually learn. We cannot be like the Nike slogan and do it alone. We must go together. A commitment to reflective practice is a journey toward realizing our potential as educators to move beyond humans just doing to become humans being.

Acknowledgments

All works with intention to benefit and serve a broader community are grounded in a web of relationships inclusive of the many and varied humans who have touched our lives and shown us, through modeling, what matters most and how to strive to be our best selves at home, in our communities, and through our work with young people and educators whose work both humbles and grounds us. As we all know about ourselves, some days we manage to show up well, other days not so much. We are blessed to have family, colleagues, and friends who encourage us along and love us anyway.

Family first. Our parents, Jim and Barbara, Bill and Frances, Howard and Kathy, Len and Carol, were our first teachers. And even though not all of them continue to walk with us on earth, their teachings and memories stay with us and guide us still. They taught us to care about our communities and the variety of people within. We are forever grateful for the enduring love and support of our spouses, Dean, Dave, in spirit, and Carl. Our children, Jason, Justin, Sam, Temple, Perry, Erin, Aaron, Chris, Alex, Shannon, Emma, and Amelia . . . they remind us what matters in life and also in the lives of younger people: creating their own lives, contributing their energy and talent to our world, and growing within communities of neighbors, friends, and colleagues. Each of them contributing in his or her own beautiful way.

This book would not have been possible without the invaluable insights, learning, and examples provided by our friends and colleagues: Barb, Jane, Jenny, Catherine, Shelly, Sharon, Laurie, Donna, Doug, Jeff, Jim, Lisa, Ty, Kari, Tom, Mary, Tim, Jim, Dick, Ron, Jill, Elizabeth, Jennifer, Taylor, Matt, Diane, Skip, and Marney. Without you, there would have been very little authentic learning in practice. We are grateful that you have trusted us enough to enter your community of practice as partners in learning and creating. To Art Costa, we offer our heartfelt thanks for your enduring support of our work and extraordinary insights and modeling of what it means to be a lifelong reflective leader. We extend our appreciation to Pat Wolfe for teaching us about the implications of brain research on learning and how modifying the learning context supports reflective practice. Recognizing that many of the practice examples in this third edition are from within the Saint Paul Public Schools, we wish to acknowledge Superintendent Valeria Silva for her leadership and innovation on behalf of students. Without a doubt, each of you are among the best humans ever, who care about young people more than words can fully express.

Finally, we could not be more grateful to our Corwin colleagues, Dan, Melanie, Kim, Katie, Janet, and undoubtedly others, who have stood with us and continued to cheer us on, despite some significant challenges that slowed our momentum for this third edition. Each of you is a caring, collaborative, competent partner in every way. We are your fans for life!

PUBLISHER'S ACKNOWLEDGMENTS

Corwin gratefully acknowledges the contributions of the following reviewers:

Michele R. Dean, EdD
Coordinator, Ventura County Indian Education Consortium
Ventura Unified School District
Ventura, CA

Cindy Harrison
Independent Consultant
Broomfield, CO

Pat Roy
Educational Consultant
Learning Forward
Madison, VA

Donnan Stoicovy
Principal
Park Forest Elementary School
State College, PA

About the Authors

Jennifer York-Barr, Professor Emeritus, Organizational Leadership, Policy and Development, University of Minnesota, Twin Cities, received her PhD from the University of Wisconsin–Madison. Her development, research, and teaching have been grounded in partnerships with educators in schools and school districts. Her early worked focused specifically on creating classroom communities that included students with various exceptionalities. That work grew into a broader focus on growing school communities grounded in conversations that support ongoing reflective practice and learning. She has been honored with several college- and university-level teaching awards and has authored or coauthored more than 100 publications, most of which are focused on instructional collaboration, inclusive schooling, teacher leadership, or professional learning. In 2014, Dr. York-Barr retired from the University of Minnesota, in part because she wanted to finish her career working in partnership with school and school district colleagues.

William A. Sommers, PhD, continues to be a learner, teacher, principal, author, leadership coach, and consultant. Bill has come out of retirement five times to put theory into practice. He was on the Board of Trustees for five years and president for the National Staff Development Council now called Learning Forward. He is the former executive director for Secondary Curriculum and Professional Learning for Minneapolis Public Schools, and a school administrator for over 30 years. In addition to being an adjunct faculty member at several universities, he has been a program director for an adolescent chemical dependency treatment center and on the board of a halfway house for 20 years. Bill has coauthored eight books and coauthored chapters in several other books. In January 2016,

Bill and his colleague Skip Olsen launched a website called www .learningomnivores.com that includes educational blogs, new rules, and book reviews. Dr. Sommers has continued to be a leadership coach for over twenty-five years to school administrators, and is a practitioner who integrates theory into leading and facilitating schools.

Gail S. Ghere, PhD, Special Education Supervisor, Saint Paul Public Schools, received her PhD from University of Minnesota in educational policy and program evaluation. She has a master's degree in Special Education with practice experience as a related service provider. Over her career, she worked in PreK–12 education in rural, suburban, and urban school districts. She also has served as a program evaluator for K–12 education, higher education, and private foundations. She is the coauthor of several publications on collaboration, program evaluation, and paraprofessional development. Her belief in equitable outcomes and inclusive learning opportunities for students has guided her work throughout her career whether she was working directly with students, supporting adult learning, or developing programs that met the needs of diverse learners.

Jo Montie, faculty, Special Education Department, University of St. Thomas, Minnesota, received her MA in Educational Psychology from the University of Minnesota (1996) and a BS in Behavioral Disabilities from the University of Wisconsin–Madison (1984) when she started her work in schools as a special education teacher. She has been teaching at the University of St. Thomas since 2003 where she also contributes leadership in the areas of teacher education program development and online teaching and learning. Jo's over 25 years of teaching and her work in schools continues to stress the need for more collaboration, reflective practice, and greater access and equity for all learners.

1

Reflective Practice for Renewing Schools

Life must be understood backwards. But it must be lived forwards.

—Søren Kierkegaard, *Journals*, 1843

Each school has its own unique culture, its own vibe. Just listen and observe the interactions among students, administrators, teachers, and the rich variety of additional staff who serve young people in schools. In schools that are moving forward, you can see, hear, and feel the hum of student learning. You see in action the foundational beliefs that all students are learners, that established rituals and routines provide the structure that lead to enhanced student engagement, and that strong relationships among adults and students are the bridge for access to learning for all. When the desired outcomes are not evident, staff members dig into their data to collaboratively determine what is working well; what is showing promise, but needs more time to grow; and what needs to be changed. Blaming is not useful. In fact, it's destructive, often creating divisions among staff. Reflecting together on what happened and why is the foundation for continuously improving teaching and learning. Educators have no illusions that everything always works out or that there are not issues to be unpacked and addressed. The culture of the school (i.e., how we do things around here) sends the message that learning is important for both students and adults and that we, collectively, commit to supporting and learning together to do our best on behalf of students. In these schools, the renewal process is continually internally driven.

In other schools, a culture of learning for staff and students is absent or waning. The traditional norm of school culture, isolation, is visible and tangible in how teachers work and how they talk with one another. Collective commitment around the "what" and "how" a school will achieve its mission is absent. Such schools are not necessarily "broken." In fact, many have a history of being successful schools. Often structures, processes, and relationships that previously served to support reflective learning conversations have gradually dissipated. Staff and administrative changes, along with an increasing array of new initiatives with inadequate support for reflection, learning, and implementation, result in staff members managing as best they can on their own. Whenever key people leave a school, a void can appear because their subject matter knowledge, as well as tacit knowledge about the organization, exits with them. Without a plan for rekindling communal commitments around purpose, shared practice with reflection, learning and collective knowledge is challenging to bolster or rebuild. In other schools, changing student demographics drives the need for staff to revisit their focus and determine changes in practice that will sustain growth in achievement. Establishing structures and processes that create regular opportunities for members to design, reflect, and learn together must be priority within school schedules. It is in the context of conversation that members learn and grow their practice and their community of practice. When the sturdy fabric that once created a sense of interdependence dissipates, it must be intentionally rebuilt.

Much can be learned about the culture of a school by observing and listening in classrooms, hallways, common areas (e.g., libraries, cafeterias, gymnasiums, and outdoor contexts), as well as in both whole staff and smaller team meetings. Sometimes this is done through a formal walk-through process, but it can also be done through casual visits and observation in different school settings. The resource shown in Table 1.1, Walking, Watching, Listening, Learning, offers some guiding questions to focus on during casual observations. The insights gained can help create a deeper understanding of current context, culture, and conversation that grounds reflection and provides direction for renewing conversations, teaching and learning practices, as well as the overall school climate and culture of the school. Culture is the subconscious driver of behavior. When what is happening is not what is needed to continuously grow both adults and young people in schools, changes in learning structures and processes are often necessary. Conversations in which staff reflect back on practice to examine what happened and why, and then reflect forward to generate ways to improve practice the next time, are a pathway for creating a culture of continuous learning and improvement for everyone. The central aim of this book is to offer a variety of ways to accomplish this.

Table 1.1   School Culture Observation Tool: Casual Observation of Teaching and Learning in School

Walking, Watching, Listening, Learning: A Menu of Questions to Guide Casual Observations of Teaching and Learning in School

Before starting your walk, (1) clarify for yourself a particular purpose or focus for your casual observation; and (2) skim questions on this tool, highlighting items aligned with your particular areas of interest.

Observation Focus: I want to learn more about . . .

Guiding Questions . . . some possibilities to consider

In classrooms

. . . who is doing most of the talking, adults, or students?

. . . are all students receiving "first best instruction" in their home class?

. . . do students seem clear about what and how they are learning? How do you know?

. . . to what extent are learning rituals and practices in place for student engagement?

. . . when teachers introduce new material, do they model practices expected of students?

. . . what do you see and hear that affirms students' race and cultures, including home languages?

. . . in what ways do students talk with each other to make sense of their work?

. . . who receives high levels of attention from the teacher and for what purposes?

. . . as students work, in what ways are effort and perseverance reinforced?

In meetings

. . . are meeting purposes pertinent to teaching and learning?

. . . are meeting purposes clarified and additional priorities invited for consideration?

. . . is a guiding question used to move participants to the present and to hear each voice?

. . . in what ways do members reflect on connections between teaching practice and student learning?

. . . when current instructional routines and practices are not resulting in growth or success for particular students, how do team members think together about ways to improve?

. . . overall, how reflective and generative is the "conversational space"?

. . . to what extent do structures and processes support reflection and deliberation?

. . . is it apparent that members listen well and are respectful of other perspectives?

. . . when decisions are made, what types of follow-up actions are generated and agreed on?

. . . in what ways do meetings conclude such that learning is made visible, collective work is affirmed, and follow-up is agreed on?

. . . overall, was a conversational culture of openness and inquiry about practice present and supported?

Most schools are somewhere on the continuum between being highly collaborative and interdependent, and being highly autonomous and disconnected. The results for students and staff in the latter schools are fragmentation and a lack of coherence. Learning, and the good energy it unleashes, diminish for everyone. There may be thriving learning cultures in some grades or departments, but in other parts of the organization there is little reflection and learning happening. What was once a thriving learning organization is thriving only in isolated pockets so there is no collective wave of momentum for the good. These circumstances are, in part, why this edition of our book is titled *Reflective Practice for* Renewing *Schools*. We believe in every school there are seeds, if not roots and a maturing ecosystem, that are poised or on their way toward revitalization. Revitalizing the adult learning cultures that underlie the growth of learning cultures for students is at the core of creating our next generation of young people poised to care and contribute in our rapidly changing global context. What could be more important than that? Hats off to you!

A steady stream of research over the past couple of decades offers evidence for what common sense always told us: student learning is linked with staff learning (Garet, Porter, Desimone, Birman, & Yoon, 2001; Ingvarson, Meiers, & Beavis, 2005; Lambert, 2003). Essentially, if the adults are not learning, neither are the students. Successful schools are communities in which ongoing learning and reflection on learning practices and results are core practices for students and staff. Established learning cultures show evidence of embedded structures and processes for learning in multiple ways: partners, small groups, large groups, groups with "alike" staff members, and groups that have members with different perspectives and roles (Wahlstrom & York-Barr, 2011). The significance of creating opportunities for staff learning across role types cannot be overstated. Learning together and understanding the varied ways staff members contribute to student learning goes an enormous distance toward creating a cohesive staff. Absent such learning opportunities and perspective taking, factions and hierarchies form and subtly tear at the fabric of a school. Nothing good happens when this occurs.

High levels of student learning require high levels of staff competence. The dominant culture in many schools is one of doing, with little or no time for reflection and learning. It is not unusual for teachers to put aside carefully constructed lessons due to unanticipated events, circumstances, or responses. It is also not unusual for those same lessons to become fragmented as a result of the comings and goings of students and staff in classrooms. Disruptions rupture the process of learning . . . of going deep and making connections, of growing new insights. Educators routinely juggle multiple tasks, process information on many levels, manage a continual stream of interruptions, and make on-the-spot decisions to meet the changing needs and demands in the teaching environment. Who has enough time or a settled mental space to reflect? Yet, put succinctly, "where there is no reflection, there will be no learning" (Wahlstrom & York-Barr, 2011, p. 32).

Learning from practice requires reflecting on practice. From an individual perspective, "It can be argued that reflective practice . . . is the process which underlies all forms of high professional competence" (Bright, 1996, p. 166). From an organizational perspective, reflective practice is considered a powerful norm for schools to achieve high levels of student learning (Kruse, Louis, & Bryk, 1995; Senge, Cambron-McCabe, Lucas, Smith, Dutton, & Kleiner, 2012). Reflective practice is also a powerful means for propelling individual and organizational renewal. It plays a central role in supporting learning and growth throughout the development of career educators (Steffy, Wolfe, Pasch, & Enz, 2000). It is a critical element for individuals and organizations to learn for and from their actions (Marzano, Boogren, Heflebower, Kanold-McIntyre, & Pickering, 2012). Reflective practice underlies learning from practice in ways that inform and improve on future actions.

This chapter presents a grounding for the *why*, *what*, and *how* of reflective practice that renews schools and that anchors reflective practice in the reality of schools today. It lays the foundation to go deeper with the *what* and *how* of leading reflective practice and also the particularities of individual, partner, small group, schoolwide, and systemwide reflective practice. In this book, there is a chapter dedicated to each of these contexts of practice.

THE POTENTIAL OF REFLECTIVE PRACTICE TO RENEW SCHOOLS

At its core, reflective practice is about improving teaching and learning, which over time leads to advancing and deepening the culture of learning in schools. Reflective practice is not a new concept. The roots of reflection and reflective practice germinated many centuries ago through both Eastern and Western philosophers, including Buddha, Plato, and Lao Tzu. John Dewey, an influential 20th-century educational philosopher, is frequently recognized for applying the principles and practices of reflection to the field of education. Dewey emphasized not just rigor in practice, but the importance of incorporating scientific knowledge into reflection (Dewey, 1933; Fendler, 2003; Rodgers, 2002). He valued equally external knowledge, such as educational research, and internal knowledge that emerged from practitioners when they mindfully examined the impact of their practice, and what likely accounted for the impact, with the aim of advancing, altering, or exiting a practice that does not yield enhanced outcomes. Focusing only on internal or external knowledge, however, creates an incomplete picture. Donald Schön, a grand elder in the field of organizational learning, clearly associated learning as the foundation of individual and organizational improvement (Schön, 1983, 1987). His work validated the explicit (directly taught) and implicit (learned through experience, observation, modeling) learning that comes from professional practice. As is often the case, the answer is not "either/or" for Dewey and Schön, but "both/and." Each of us perform better by tapping both internal and external resources to inform decisions. To summarize this body of work, reflective practice can be viewed as an active thought process aimed at understanding current realities of practice and considering multiple possibilities for improvement. Reflective practice

- occurs in different ways and for different purposes, yielding different results;
- is influenced by both personal and contextual variables;
- considers social, moral, and ethical perspectives;
- impacts community conversation and action; and
- heightens morale and collective efficacy brought about by effective practice.

The key takeaway is that reflective practice leads to informed action, not "mindless following of unexamined practices or principles" (Sparks-Langer & Colton, 1991, p. 37). Located in the accompanying website (http://resources.corwin.com/YorkBarrReflective) is a resource, Significant Contributions to the Thinking About Reflective Practice, that identifies practitioner scholars who have contributed significantly to conceptualizing and operationalizing useful applications of reflective practice in the field of education, including John Dewey, Max van Manen (1977, 2002), Georgea Sparks-Langer and Amy Colton (1991), and Karen Osterman and Robert Kottkamp (2004).

In schools today, the adults are in continuous motion. At times the pace feels frenetic. Anyone who does not know this has not been inside a school recently. Days are packed with plentiful "to dos" that vary from the ground-level work of supporting individual students, to reflecting and planning with colleagues, to refining implementation plans for new practices and the use of technology. Teachers and administrators continually feel the heightened and accelerated demands of their work. In the 1950s, studies conducted by Harvey (1967) revealed that air traffic controllers manage the greatest number of mental tasks and that teachers are number two in this regard. Things have not changed. "Teachers make thousands of decisions a day, and they don't do it about an abstract idea, they do it about the life of a child. You can't imagine anything harder" (Jupp, 2012).

Despite all of these "to dos" being completed at a fast pace, we ask, "Are schools and teams realizing the benefits of all that they are doing?" The fast pace of organizations should not mean "random acts of improvement" or action, but rather "aligned acts of improvement" and action (National Education Goals Panel, 2000). In schools where collaboration and reflection have grown to be a cultural norm, the pace does not necessarily feel slower, but actions are more mindful, aligned, and collective, thereby creating a more coherent learning experience for students.

School culture has a significant impact on teacher and student behaviors. Culture can be thought of as the norms and expectations, often unwritten, that individuals implicitly learn and follow in order "to fit" within an organization. Deliberate monitoring and attention to culture helps to identify what to celebrate and continue to grow, as well as what to intentionally work at removing (Gruenert & Whitaker, 2015). If a robust positive culture of adult and student learning has been created, school members become more adept at accepting and adapting to the challenges, as well as continually reflecting on and improving both practices and outcomes. If school culture is dominated by norms of isolation, not only does the potential for collective learning suffer, but destructive cultures of isolation, competition, and blame often grow. Members feel unsupported, unappreciated, and unable to gain traction for improvement. As we discuss at greater length in Chapter 3, growing *learning-full cultures* is the core work of administrator, team, and teacher leadership.

However, the shift from idiosyncratic to coherent learning and reflective practice is not work that happens in the fast lane. The Chinese proverb "Go slow to go fast" applies here. Starting small increases the likelihood of success because it is easier to design and sufficiently support the learning of new practices. For example, consider a school learning and using cooperative routines to increase student talk. Using common language for teaching the routines and identifying common places within instructional sequences to practice the routines more quickly results in teachers forming the habit of embedding routines and in students learning them, thereby reflecting more on their content area learning. "Talk" is a big part of making sense of new content. After giving initial instructions, teachers can model and then invite students to turn and talk with a partner about what they will be learning and doing. At the end of a lesson, students might be asked to find a new partner and talk about what each learned, and perhaps, to share a question they have. This type of focus and coherence increases the likelihood of successful acquisition. Success creates energy and momentum, for staff and students.

Chapter 3 introduces an example of how one school supported teacher learning and reflection on use of cooperative routines. Developing effective reflective learning practices eventually allows everyone to focus more energy on learning content. Practitioners who learn "how" to learn well can accelerate "what" they learn. Learning content continually evolves and changes. With the aim of continuing to improve practice, learning processes, which typically follow a cycle of reflective practice (i.e., learn–do–reflect–act), inform what's working well and what is not. Even though the press for teacher learning is often focused on learning content, this is more effectively done among teachers who have become adept at reflective learning processes.

Embedding and protecting regular times for teams to meet creates an essential and ongoing space for colleagues to engage in reflective conversations about the ways that students are engaged and respond to instruction, and also ways to move each student forward. There are other times when conversation is necessary, but has to be done asynchronously. For example, a top-notch co-teaching team in an urban middle school saw steady growth for almost all of their general education, English language, and special education students. This team could not accomplish everything during their common Professional Learning Community (PLC) time that was built into the master schedule. They relied heavily on Google Docs (a free online file development and sharing system that provides for synchronous, real time or asynchronous collaboration) to develop their lesson plans, determine flex groups, and delineate differentiated teacher roles for the upcoming lesson. The co-teachers accessed the Google Doc at different times of the day or evening and left recommendations for ways to differentiate instruction, meet Individual Education Plans (IEP) goals, and enhance understanding of key vocabulary and concepts. The online reflective practice component was extremely successful as an extension to their face-to-face time. It also anchored the on-the-fly conversations that happened during their fast-paced days.

Administrators and teachers learn from "on the fly" conversations and decisions, as well as conversations that occur in more calm, grounded, and mindful periods. Especially in times of turbulence, learning while flying means gaining the knowledge and skills while improvising and shifting to make sense of sometimes seemingly unrelated episodes. Learning while grounded connects people to their roots, clarifies their identity in the work, and seeks a stable knowledge base to draw on in other situations, whether flying or grounded (Fenwick, 2006). Simultaneously learning while flying and grounded seems paradoxical. Educators have described this as "hot action" in schools where they must be adaptive and develop the habits and routines to respond appropriately when there is no stopping the action to consider what happened and to figure out next best steps (Eraut, 1985). In fast-paced environments, adults must make spur-of-the-moment decisions. These moments need to be anticipated because making the best decision for each situation is important. "Workplace learning in these circumstances will need to be contextually sensitive" (Beckett, 2001, p. 75).

Designed well, reflective practice integrates grounding knowledge with contextual knowledge as both inform possible next actions. Here is an example. A school had an incident involving a safety concern that rippled into the community. At that moment, administrators and school staff needed to make immediate decisions based on the known facts, district procedures, and the systems within the school. The morning after the incident, building administrators convened to an after-action review. This practice was different than in the past when the team would handle a situation and then move on to the next situation. The key people involved in the event came together and asked: What were the facts? When did we know them? What did we do? Why did we do this? What can we learn from this incident? What is needed to prevent a similar incident?

The facts were listed in one column on the whiteboard. The technical decisions made by each person made were listed in another column. The dialogue then shifted to reflecting on what worked, what did not work, and what was confusing or insufficient. Areas in need of refinement were immediately identified, along with roles and responsibilities for next steps. Changes related to safety procedures were addressed immediately. Additional steps that required more time to develop were rolled out over the next few weeks. This process of collective reflection on practice took 45 minutes. In addition to coming up with new procedures and protocols, there were other positive results. The strength of the team and school were enhanced. There was an openness to consider what had been effective and not effective. The staff felt supported. There was recognition that these incidents do not belong to just one person, but to everyone. By allocating just 45 minutes to engage in a reflective process, the team learned and improved their practices for future incidents.

CORE COMPONENTS OF THE REFLECTIVE PRACTICE CYCLE

There is no universally accepted definition of reflective practice. There is not a recipe for how it is done. No one person, no one team, no one school embeds reflective practice in the exact same ways. Reflective practice is a thought process that both challenges and supports individuals, teams, and school communities to consciously embed opportunities to learn from practice to inform how to improve practice. It is adaptive and nuanced work to figure out what, specifically, will advance practice in particular learning contexts. Reflective practice is an active process that continually seeks to assess, understand, and adjust practices. Growing a reflective practice community means that at each level and point of the system, members listen and observe practice. Reflective practitioners listen well and are open to multiple perspectives, interpretations of events, and possibilities for improvement. From the possibilities generated, they take mindful actions that lead to either continuing the direction, tweaking the direction, or changing direction.

The reflective practice cycle (refer to Figure 1.1) helps to visualize the components of the cycle and how they build on one another, ultimately leading to action. The cycle, as shown here, begins with being *grounded in purpose*, followed by being actively *present* to observe and learn, being *open* and participating in the *inquiry*, gaining insights from the learning and adding to the dialogue so others gain new *insights*, taking informed *action* based on the knowledge that is generated, and ends with routinely asking "Are we seeing the *results* that we want to see?" If yes, then the team asks "Now what?" And, if no, then the team asks "Now what?"

Figure 1.1   Reflective Practice Cycle

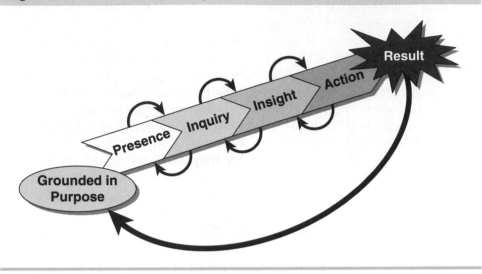

This is not a linear process, but a continual cycling forward and backward to challenge thinking and produce deeper practice knowledge. In between the purpose and results are thought cycles that regularly circle back to previous steps to assess, challenge, and fine-tune the cycle so that however it re-cycles, it remains grounded in the purpose. Core elements of the reflective practice cycle are . . .

Being grounded in purpose: you must be grounded in the "why" to reach results that matter. Simon Sinek (2009) asks if you know the *why* behind what you do. He emphasizes that great organizations and great leaders are grounded, first and foremost, in *why* they do something, not *how* or *what* they do. The all-encompassing *why* speaks to the core beliefs and values we hold about learning for all students. It is the driver of all decisions that are made at every level of the system. Often we jump to *what* and *how* without being clear about *why* we care and *why* we are investing time and energy into the work. When the *why* is clear, people are much less likely to lose their way or their motivation to push forward when things get messy. When the *why* is clear, it is easier to invest oneself fully in work, despite the demands and energy required to teach and lead in schools. In education, the details about the purpose may continually unveil themselves through practice and be reinforced by data, but ultimately they are linked with our deep beliefs and aspirations for all students to learn well and be successful as they transition to post-school life. When educational staff understand and are compelled by the *why* of their journey, the energy required to figure out what, specifically, matters most for students and how, specifically, to move in that direction is more readily generated and sustained. The *why* anchors the vision that compels continuous learning and improvement on our own and with our colleagues.

Presence is a combination of being present by pausing, being open to listen and learn, and being actively engaged. It means remaining present both in mind and body during conversation. When you watch people in conversation, you can tell much by listening to verbal behavior, and especially by observing nonverbal behavior, such as body language and facial expressions. What are some indicators that people are open? Are they listening? Are they interested? Are they encouraging others to share, to speak their truth? In some respects, nonverbal behavior is more telling of presence and participation (or lack thereof) than verbal, spoken language. Particularly telling of a person's stance is to watch and listen when differences of opinion arise. What happens? In what ways do the verbal and nonverbal behaviors of the speaker and others in the group change? Honoring this openness and asking probing questions to fully understand, particularly when you are not sure you understand, or when you view the subject differently, can foster not only clarity, but trust. Authentic inquiry promotes connection and understanding. It makes learning happen.

Inquiry is both a cultural norm in reflective practice communities and a skill that individuals and teams can develop. When people are present and open to learning then the possibility exists for inquiry. Inquiry is a state of mind in which questions and wonderings about practice are invited, embraced, and, at times, compelled. Questions are generated to help clarify, probe for deeper understanding, and make connections among various perspectives and observations . . . all of which expand and challenge thinking, which, in turn, creates new understandings and insight. Designated time and space, along with intentional efforts to deepen the conversational skills of team members, creates the possibility of insight that leads to refined action, deeper connection, and even momentum. John Maxwell (2007), a leader in the area of organizational leadership, is clear that momentum, the act of getting things moving forward, is more important than having every detail determined in advance. In short: *momentum is more important than precision.*

The purpose of inquiry is to learn. Inquiry stems from wondering about and questioning the impact of one's own practice. What did I specifically do and what did I notice in how students responded? As Albert Einstein said, "The important thing is not to stop questioning." Asking questions that prompt inquiry is a skill that develops through practice, and ultimately has the potential to deepen understandings about practice.

From inquiry comes *insight* that can both affirm and call into question particular practices and their impact. This results in deeper understandings about the nuance and "fit" of practices in particular situations. Insights emerge from active, deliberate, and conscious processing of thoughts for the purposes of examining goals, beliefs, and practices. *Goals* are the aims, outcomes, and intentions for yourself, for students, and collectively for the school. *Beliefs* are the mental models through which we view the world. They encompass people's values, visions, biases, and paradigms that inform possible directions. *Practices* refers to one's dispositions, knowledge, and skills across a wide range of performance domains. In schools, this includes *building* relationships with students, *designing* instruction, *providing* instruction, *discerning* the impact of instruction, *collaborating* with colleagues and administrators, and *connecting* with families.

Action means movement. This element is essential in the reflective practice process. Thought and related learning without subsequent action are mere musings. Reflective practice is not a bystander sport. It is not for the faint of heart. It is for actively committed professionals who intentionally learn and change and create improved outcomes for students. Without application, who cares? Action and then reflecting on the action and its impact is the whole point. What happened and why? The phrase "Ready, Fire, Aim" captures the nature of high performing companies (Peters & Waterman, 1982) and schools (Fullan, 2010). Move to action then mindfully observe and discern what is significant from the results. The action period (i.e., "fire") is also a learning period. Learning informs the fine-tuning of practice such that improvement occurs. *Results* are the outcomes, our impact. Actions lead to results. Both our actions and results are fed back into the cycle of reflective practice to inform future practice. What did we learn from what happened? Is this something to do again? If so, in what situations and with which students? Reflective practice leads to improvement and renewal only when these deeper understandings inform improved actions that are subsequently enacted.

Table 1.2 provides an example of a schoolwide behavior support team and how they engaged in problem solving to address the particular needs of a group of students. The team process encompassed the elements of the reflective practice cycle. They all knew their purpose, came ready and prepared to participate, had current data ready to consider, and expanded on the data by adding the relevant context to individual student situations. They also used data to identify the trends and needs for the school. Based on their analysis, they collaborated to proactively add support for students who were showing signs of escalating behavior. They wanted to intervene early to interrupt this pattern in order to keep students in school. The results showed that working with these students in small groups, building student skills to handle conflict and frustration, and developing positive relationships with a staff member were effective interventions for many students. This prevented further escalation of behaviors and helped improve class attendance. It also provided a more robust "toolbox" for the whole school when other students needed additional supports.

Table 1.2   An Example of the Reflective Practice Cycle in Action

Purpose	The schoolwide behavior intervention team's goal was for all students to be learning in school. They strongly believed that they could make a difference in educational outcomes for all students, even those with higher needs, if they could match the interventions to a student's needs.
Presence	The team, consisting of representatives from counseling, social work, special education, behavior specialist, and administration, met weekly. They were engaged and collaboratively sought solutions for all students. Their specific roles or department affiliation was not an issue. They shared their expertise willingly to achieve the overall goal. Their openness to learning for each other was readily visible.
Inquiry	The team considered the office referrals and suspensions and dismissal data. They unpacked the data, looking for patterns, as well as outlying incidents. Team members offered varied perspectives with the aim of better understanding the context and specific variables that might be underlying the referrals.
Insight	To gain further insight, the team used a brief functional behavior assessment process to understand what was being communicated by each behavior. They also looked across multiple data sources to identify needs for the system. The team determined that there was an absence of direct instruction to teach self-awareness and replacement strategies to students whose behaviors regularly escalated.
Action	The team selected a social-emotional curriculum that focused on the strategies they felt were needed by the students, especially when a student was in the "zone" that led to confrontation. They accessed the resources, and met to review the curriculum and how to teach/reinforce the replacement strategies. They developed a schedule for teaching these strategies to small groups of students who had been identified based on the school data.
Result	School personnel felt better equipped to respond to student needs because they had a more complete set of interventions in their "toolbox." Also, they could intervene earlier to meet the needs of students who were showing signs of escalating behaviors. Staff began using common vocabulary to help students understand their feelings and behaviors. In turn, students learned the language to tell staff which "behavior zone" they were in so that they could verbally process their concerns before the behaviors escalated. As a result of collaboratively analyzing the data and selecting the social-emotional curriculum to teach the replacement strategies to students, there was an overall decrease in office referrals and improved class attendance, as well as suspensions and dismissals.

As we focus our actions and link them to our learning, the intent is to see improvements in student learning. Learning is broadly defined to include students' capacities to think, their motivations to learn, their effectiveness utilizing these capacities constructively with others, and their contribution to the world around them, along with more traditional measures of student learning (e.g., formative assessments about ongoing learning and annual testing around state-determined student learning practices). Further, the results must be considered through an *equity lens* to determine if all, or only some, students are learning. Enhanced student learning must be equitable. The education system in the United States is more inclusive, but is it equitable? Do students of all races and ethnicities see themselves in the curriculum? Can they identify with the texts they read? Are they engaged by the instruction? If yes, what can we learn that can be shared more broadly? If no, then how do we challenge our beliefs and practices to interrupt or put aside some of what we do to create new practices that lead to improved outcomes for each learner?

These six elements of the reflective practice cycle are important regardless of the level or place in the system at which they are implemented—in a classroom, a team, the school, or the district. There is a logical flow to the elements. If one is missing or weakened, then the impact of the cycle is diminished or even absent (refer to Table 1.3). If the process is not grounded in purpose, then the *why* is not sufficiently powerful to compel commitment to engage and sustain the work. If participants are not present and open, then dialogue is stifled and multiple perspectives are not heard. If there is no inquiry, then possibilities for improvement do not emerge. Without possibilities to try, then nothing will change. If the process does not generate new insights by considering both internal and external knowledge, then challenging thinking patterns that leads to new action does not occur. If no action is taken that leads to different results, then participants question why their time is being spent reflecting in an attempt to address problems by making changes in practice. Ultimately, they will opt out of the process even if they are present at the table. If the results are unknown because they are not measured or they are stagnant for all or some groups of students because the known data are not used, then schools will not reach their goals of achieving a high level of learning for all students.

The reflective practice spiral (Figure 1.2) presents one way to think about initiating and expanding efforts to embed reflective practices as a cultural norm throughout schools and districts. It reflects an assumption that the place to begin is with oneself and that learning occurs from the inside out. The reflective practice cycle is the core learning process within each of the nested layers within the system. Beginning with the innermost level of individual reflective practice, reflection with partners, in small groups and teams, throughout a school, and extending across a school district, reflective practice can have an

Table 1.3 The Impact of Missing Elements of the Reflective Practice Cycle

Reflective Practice Cycle Elements	What Happens When the Element Is Present?		What Happens When the Element Is <u>Not</u> Present?
Purpose	• Clarity about the *why* • The *why* anchors the work and leads to greater commitment	⬆	• A lack of understanding about the work and the direction • Minimal personal investment. Staff go through the steps of the process because they are required to participate • A lack of commitment to achieving different results
Presence	• Participants are present in mind and body • They actively participate in the process • Their actions foster greater trust	⬆	• Decisions are made by a few members • There is a lack of trust, so the openness needed for dialogue never develops • There is less buy-in by various parties about the decisions that are made • Staff who are committed to the work opt out of the group to avoid superficial commitments
Inquiry	• There is an openness to multiple perspectives • Multiple perspectives are invited and respected • Space is created to promote inquiry • The sharing of ideas leads to coherence	⬆	• The information that is being considered is narrow and limited • There is an inability to explore data through multiple perspectives • Dialogue is closed down. Teams do not have the norm or the skills to question ideas and open up new possibilities • Actions are based on narrow and shallow interpretations of the issues and data

(Continued)

Table 1.3 (Continued)

Reflective Practice Cycle Elements	What Happens When the Element Is Present?		What Happens When the Element Is <u>Not</u> Present?
Insight	• New and deeper understandings of data emerge • New perspectives are used to challenge beliefs and existing paradigms • The new insights provide opportunities for meaningful action	⬆	• Beliefs about students and effective instruction are not unpacked and challenged • Teams continue to implement current practices even when the desired outcomes are not evident • Teams jump between strategies without understanding why they are making these decisions, hoping that "something will work" • Progress monitoring the results does not happen, so data are not available to gain new insights
Action	• Movement forward to change outcomes is evident • There is a joint commitment for action across a team or school • Individuals and teams "walk their talk"	⬆	• There is no change in the results that lead to beliefs being challenged • Opting out by group members because the process does not lead to meaningful action • Individuals pull away from the group and take action on their own regardless if it is aligned or not aligned with the work of the group
Results	• The data that were collected are used to enhance student learning • The impact on adult and student learning is evident • When the data are disaggregated, the impact on learning is equitable across all students • Reflective practice becomes a larger part of the culture of the organization	⬆	• There is little to no change in student learning • Individuals wonder if what they are doing is making a difference and if their time is well spent • Sustaining reflective practice is challenging because change is not evident or measured

entire systemwide impact. The spiral reinforces the interconnectedness among levels and layers in the system.

Each of us has a scope of influence within our system. It starts with colleagues with whom we work directly and influence indirectly. It expands outward through the professional relationships that we have through our horizontal connections among teams and vertical connections across the levels of the system. As the scope of influence increases, the power of alignment increases across the levels of the system. Reflective practice is at the center of this alignment.

Lived experience is perhaps the most powerful influence on the formation of beliefs, which are the driving forces behind actions. The learning and positive growth that an individual experiences from engaging in reflective practices provides an informed, experiential foundation from which to advocate and commit to expanding the practice of reflection beyond themselves. As we develop our individual reflection capacities, we can better influence the reflection that occurs with partners, in small groups, or in teams where we are members. As more groups become reflective in their work, the influence and potential of reflective practice spreads throughout the school. A critical mass of individuals who have experienced positive outcomes from their own reflective practice and from reflection within groups and teams can better support widespread adoption. Each level in the reflective practice cycle is described below, along with the respective potential benefits. Specific considerations and examples for reflective practices at each level are addressed in Chapters 4 through 7.

Figure 1.2   Nested Levels of the Reflective Practice Spiral

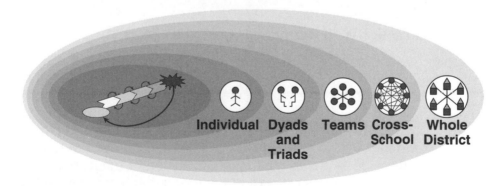

Individual   Dyads and Triads   Teams   Cross-School   Whole District

Individual Reflective Practice

This is the level where, as educators, each of us has full responsibility and control. We can choose to be reflective in our work and life. Reflection on our own provides each of us with a renewable resource that we totally control. Committing to growing as reflective practitioners creates an opportunity to realize the following benefits:

- Improvements in our professional practices, given greater awareness of personal performance, practice dilemmas, possibilities that emerge from divergent and creative thought, and effects of our practices;
- Enhanced student learning and learning capacities, given improvements in our practices;
- Increased personal capacities for learning and improvement, as the knowledge, skills, and dispositions for reflective practice become embedded in our way of thinking and doing;
- Restored balance and perspective, given the space created for reflection and learning; and
- Renewed clarity of personal and professional purpose and competence, given a sense of empowerment to align our practices with desired intents.

As we learn about reflective practice and its potential through personal experience, we begin to increase our capacity to effectively support others in developing their reflective capacities. Some ways to reflect alone include journaling, reviewing a case, reading literature, developing a teaching portfolio, exercising our bodies to free our minds, taking a personal retreat, and observing or listening to one's own practice through use of videotapes or webinars. Chapter 4 offers additional considerations and specific examples of reflective practice with oneself.

Reflective Practice With Partners

Joining with another person in the process of reflection can result in greater insight about one's practice, especially when trust is high and the right combination of support and challenge is present. When reflecting with others, we realize the truth in the adage, "What goes around comes around." Partner reflection can also introduce an element of fun. Humor, when appropriately interjected, reminds us not to take ourselves too seriously and that mistakes are an inevitable dimension of the learning process. In addition to the gains realized at the individual level of reflection, adding one or two partners to the reflection process can result in

- Expanded learning about our own practice, given the different perspectives of another person and, when coached through the process of reflective inquiry, our learning can be even deeper when we reflect with individuals who are of different cultures and back-grounds than our own;

- Increased professional and social support, decreased feelings of iso-lation at work and increased competence and confidence given the presence of a strengthened collegial relationship;
- Increased sense of who we are and how things work in our school, given the connection and exchange with another person who prac-tices in our place of work; and
- Greater commitment to our work and our work environment, given an increased sense of competence, confidence, and connection to another person in our place of work.

Some ways that two or three people can reflect together include interac-tive journaling, cognitive coaching, conversing about instructional design possibilities, talking through steps of an inquiry cycle related to specific events or dilemmas, peer observations, reading and talking about articles or case studies, examining student work, and planning with your co-teacher and online dialogue. Chapter 5 contains additional considerations and specific examples of reflective practice with partners. The increased sense of competence, support, and connection that can emerge from reflec-tion with a partner positions us on more solid ground to extend the prac-tice of reflection to teams.

Reflective Practice in Small Groups and Teams

There is a big shift from reflecting alone or in a small partnership to reflecting in a small group. While the potential impact of reflection increases as the number of people who are involved increases, so too does the personal risk. Because more people are in a group, the sense of safety and connection between individuals is different than with partner reflec-tion; it is often more variable and diffuse. Groups and teams also are fre-quently appointed or mandated, whereas partner reflection is often voluntary and self-organized. In appointed or mandated groups, there is frequently less control over who joins the group and their desire to partici-pate. Composition and commitment affect interactions and outcomes.

Despite the risks involved in expanding reflective practice to such groups, good reasons exist to venture forth into this domain. When reflec-tion becomes part of educational practice within small groups or teams, its members can realize the following gains:

- Enhanced learning and resources for learning about practice, given more people, each of whom brings varied experiences and expertise in life, learning, and education;
- Increased professional and social support (including fun), given the expanded and more varied network of collegial relationships;

- More effective interventions for individual students or groups of identified students, given shared purpose, responsibility, and expertise among members of a group;
- An emerging sense of hope and encouragement that meaningful and sustained improvements in practice can occur, given group members committed to working and learning together; and
- Improved climate and collegiality, given greater understanding of our own and others' experiences and perspectives about our shared place of work.

Some ways to reflect in small groups include action research, study groups, regular grade-level or content area meetings to review and design instruction and assessment procedures, examining student data and work, and case-study reviews and problem-solving sessions. Reflective practices can also enhance committee work by intentionally reflecting about past practices and future possibilities and by soliciting multiple perspectives of people representing broad interests in the work. Refer to Chapter 6 for more considerations and specific examples of reflective practice in groups or teams.

At the small group level of reflective practice, the potential to influence educational practices throughout the school gains momentum. Small ripples of change frequently become the impetus for much broader changes, even when that was not an original intent (Garmston & Wellman, 2013; Wheatley, 1992). The potential to improve educational practices significantly increases when greater numbers of groups and teams embed reflective practices in their work. A culture of inquiry and learning begins to take hold on a grander, schoolwide basis.

Schoolwide Reflective Practice

The greatest potential for reflective practice to improve schools lies within the collective inquiry, thinking, learning, understanding, and acting that result from schoolwide engagement. Isolated efforts (e.g., initiatives taken on by individual teachers, grade levels, or content areas) typically result in only isolated improvements, with few cumulative gains realized once students or teachers move on from those experiences. Furthermore, effects do not spread to other groups of students without intentional efforts to design and implement new practices with those students. When reflection becomes part of educational practice on a schoolwide basis, the following gains are possible:

- Significantly expanded learning opportunities and resources for achieving schoolwide advances in practice aimed at student achievement;
- Enhanced sense of common purpose and shared responsibility for all students;

- Greater shared knowledge, planning, and communication about students among teachers throughout the school, resulting in greater instructional coherence;
- Increased professional support realized from the expanded network of relationships and the extensive expertise revealed within the network;
- Enhanced understanding of school culture, specifically what influences policy and practice and how schoolwide improvement efforts can be successful;
- Increased hope and possibility for meaningful and sustained improvements in practice given an expanded awareness of the commitments and talents of staff throughout the building and given the strengthened network among staff members; and
- Lessened sense of vulnerability to external pressures, and paradoxically, more reasoned consideration of opportunities that might result from external partnerships.

Reflective practices at the schoolwide level can take many forms. An entire school staff may be involved in study groups on a common topic, such as reading in the content areas, instructional strategies, or performance assessment. There might also be groups or teams across the school with varied purposes. For example, interdisciplinary groups could form to share disciplinary expertise and to create a set of integrated student outcomes that would be addressed within each of the content areas. Cross grade-level teams might explore the best practices for effective student transitions between grades or schools. Some issues require schoolwide attention and participation, so group composition should be intentionally designed to connect people across grade levels or curricular areas to bring forth different perspectives and relationships between individuals who may not typically cross paths during a school day. It is neither possible nor essential to include every staff member in every learning or shared work initiative. What matters is that staff members are involved in some type of collaborative learning that coheres and contributes to overall educational goals and experiences for students. Chapter 7 describes additional considerations and specific examples of schoolwide reflective practices, along with examples of reflective practice among participants from multiple schools.

District-Level Reflective Practice

Moving districtwide is extremely challenging because of the complexity and particularity of the work in different school settings. It is challenging given the lack of proximity and easy access between school and district-based personnel, particularly in urban districts. District administration sets annual priorities for its schools based on aggregated data and coordinates its leadership and resources to support schools in implementing these priorities. The priorities are determined based on the multiple demands placed on a district, including external mandates, such as aligning instruction with state standards and addressing equitable outcomes for subgroups of students. District administrators determine the tight and loose aspects for implementing their priorities, and aligning professional development with these priorities. It is challenging for staff who are "singletons" in their work environments, such as a principal or a district coach, to remain focused on these priorities when there are so many demands on their time. Staff in these situations benefit from constructive opportunities to reflect with others in similar roles to consider and learn as they work through complex issues. When reflection becomes part of educational practice on a districtwide basis, the following gains are possible:

- Enhanced sense of common purpose and shared responsibility for all students across the whole system;
- Greater coherence for students across their PreK–12 experience;
- Focused communication with the district and community regarding what influences policy and practice decisions to positively affect districtwide improvement;
- Alignment of resources for achieving districtwide advances in practice aimed at equitable student achievement;
- Shared knowledge and planning through cross level groups so issues are deeply understood and the insights gained guide the next steps;
- Coordination and collaboration across departments to align their work and professional development; and
- Increased professional support realized from the expanded network of relationships and sharing of expertise within the network.

Moving districtwide is the most complex. To achieve it takes a concerted effort by district-level administrators to work collaboratively across departments to integrate at the district level what we ask schools and teams to integrate at their respective levels. Reflective practices at the districtwide level can take many forms. District level departments are linked by the common commitment to support graduation for all students and for students to learn their state content and grade-level standards. Engaging district leaders to work across departments to create a coherent approach for supporting school-level practitioners to reach these goals could go a long way toward achieving more connection and coherence, not to mention better coordination of resources, for both district-based and school-based practitioners. For example, the Curriculum and Instruction department could co-design and co-present professional development with the English Language Learner and Special Education departments to support schools in integrating these disciplines to align instruction. And, the special education department could support its subspecialty staff (e.g., speech language pathologist, psychologists, coaches) at all levels of the system to work together to eliminate racial disparities in referrals to special education.

Moving Outward

There is greater potential to achieve schoolwide and districtwide improvement in practice as reflective practices take root and grow across all levels of the system, from the individual level through the district level. The potential realized at the outer levels is based on the premise that individuals continue to enhance their individual reflection and learning. Resources, information, perspectives, ownership, commitment, relationships, along with shared responsibility and leadership increase substantially at each progressive level given greater numbers of staff members learning together. For most teachers, the greatest opportunity for impact will be within their school. For principals, the greatest opportunities for impact also will be within their schools. In both groups, some will have opportunities to influence through reflective practice at the district level, as well, depending on the size of the district. For district administrators, the opportunity comes from supporting the capacity for reflective practice at each level of the system by facilitating cross-level teams and developing the capacity of its district staff to move practices to each level of the system.

One of the greatest influences is success. Schools in which members are reflecting on their practices to align and bolster their efforts and, as a result, see progress in student achievement learn that what they do matters. Seeing positive outcomes from our individual and collective practices increases our individual and collective efficacy. Efficacy is the *belief* that what we do matters. It fuels the energy to keep on figuring out how best to serve each student. The strongest beliefs we hold are the ones grounded in our experience. Being successful in our work builds our sense of confidence that we can figure out ways to support students well in their schooling.

As reflective practices extend outward from the individual level to being more inclusive of others, as partners in teams and schoolwide, the design challenges of implementation are greater. Complexity is dramatically increased due to the greater number and, often, variety of people involved along with the corresponding variation in work and scope of the work. Because the load and variety of work is significant for each person in the system, it is easy for participants to conclude that their work has little or nothing to do with the work of others. Logistics, such as scheduling time for reflection, become more difficult. Individual risk is greater because an individual's perspectives are exposed to a greater number of people with whom there may be varying degrees of trust, respect, and commitment. The context and climate of a school also have a greater effect as practices expand to include more people. There are long-standing structures that reinforce isolation among participants, which exacerbates the sense that work is differentiated or specialized and not shared. The history and established cultures within and across groups create invisible barriers to interaction. Multiple and often competing priorities for time and professional development can fragment focus, effort, and people. In short, as the individual moves out in the spiral, there is more potential for success, but also more complexity and less control.

Recognizing the presence of significant, complicating variables at the school level can raise serious doubts about the feasibility of reflective practice. The inherently complex nature of schoolwide change can easily feel overwhelming. This is one of the reasons for proposing the reflective practice spiral as a guiding framework. Each of us can choose to remain committed to our own professional learning and improvement by embedding reflective practices in our own work. We can at least engage in reflective practices at the individual level. Choosing to assume a responsible, proactive stance toward our own development adds positive energy to our lives and to the environments in which we work. As individuals, we reap the benefits of continuous learning and we increase our professional competence. Learning also renews our spirit. Our human needs to learn and grow can be met, in part, through reflective thinking. A commitment to individual reflective practices benefits us as individuals and also has an indirect effect on others.

Beyond the individual, the potential for improvement in schools increases with each additional person who chooses to make a commitment to professional learning and improvement. "Those who work in schools know that influence happens at every level of the system, with collegial influence being perhaps, the most powerful means of aligning and accelerating effort for the good of children" (Wahlstrom & York-Barr, 2011, p. 23). Understandings about how organizations or systems evolve suggest that significant positive changes can happen when members learn more about ways the work of others can inform, complement, and support their own work, resulting in more nuanced support and better outcomes for students. Each person and her or his arena of practice exists because it is intended to contribute to the greater good of the organizational purpose. Mining and sharing the learning and insights of each participant turns the aspiration of doing good for young people into reality. It is the web of relationships among organizational members that enhances the collective knowledge and bolsters the energy to sustain effort around the work (Garmston & Wellman, 2013; Wheatley, 1992). Another significant understanding is to know that change happens in ways we cannot always predict or control. As each of us continues to learn, and as we reach out to connect and learn with others, relationships form and strengthen, thereby increasing the potential for larger scale improvement. Gradually, we come to understand that we are part of a much larger whole that has the power and momentum to positively affect the lives of students. Schoolwide engagement helps keep energy high and hope alive.

Combinations of different groups of staff members learning together throughout the school result in expanded and strengthened relationships among all staff members. In effect, a web of relationships forms to facilitate communication and connection throughout the school community (see Figure 1.3). This web of relationships serves several very important functions:

- *A safety net is created for students* who are less likely to feel anonymous and fragmented because staff members are in better communication about students, especially those who are struggling in school;
- *A rich network of resources,* people, and information is formed and any member of the school community can tap it; if someone in our immediate network does not know something, we are likely to be connected to someone in another network who may know; and
- When we are more tightly coupled with others in our work, there is a greater likelihood of more *comprehensive, effective, and rapid response* to schoolwide issues, ranging from safety concerns to adoption of new curricula.

To enhance the web metaphor for school improvement, consider that the threads of weaver spiders are one of the strongest organic materials that nature produces. In laboratories, scientists harvest the threads and weave them into bulletproof vests. Thus, the web is an apt metaphor for the durable and protective community that emerges and spreads from the spinning of many individuals being reflective practitioners.

Figure 1.3   Visual Representation of the Relationship Web Among Staff Members, Strengthened by Reflective Practices

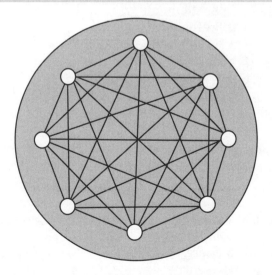

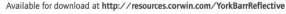

WHO IS A REFLECTIVE EDUCATOR?

What does a reflective professional look like? We believe that person looks like or can look like any of us, perhaps, all of us. This is important because to be an effective professional is to be a reflective professional. One of the distinguishing characteristics of reflective educators is a high level of commitment to their own professional development (Zeichner & Liston, 1996). They are lifelong learners who have a sustained interest in learning. Inquiry, questioning, and discovery are norms embedded in their ways of thinking and practice. Their inquiry focuses not only on the effectiveness of their instruction or leadership but also, personally, on the underlying assumptions, biases, and values that they bring to the educational process. Reflective educators consider issues of justice, equity, and morality as they design and reflect on their practice. They create ways for students' cultures and voices to enter the classroom (Lindsey, Roberts, & CampbellJones, 2005). Their interest in learning is continually sparked by triggers of curiosity about some aspect of practice. Instead of blindly accepting or rejecting new information or ideas, they carefully examine, analyze, and reframe them in terms of specific context variables, previous experiences, and alignment with desired educational goals. They rely on both external knowledge from research and experts as well as internal knowledge from their own and colleagues' experiences. They are decision makers who develop thoughtful plans to move new understandings into action so that meaningful improvements result for students. These elements of reflective practice provide a lens into colleagues who are reflective.

The relationship of what we do and what we experience leads to the question of "How did each of us contribute to creating our current realities?" (Block, 2009). Our impact in the world and on the world is shaped by our identity (Forde, McMahon, McPhee, & Patrick, 2006). Every person is the creator of their world as well as a product of that world. Personal identity is the fusion of one's beliefs, values, attitudes, and understandings. It is strongly influenced by individual, racial, ethnic, and cultural experiences. Personal identity contributes significantly to the core of one's professional identity. In addition, professional identity develops overtime by our roles, education, experiences, and connections with professional groups.

Reflective educators recognize that much of the knowledge about effective practice is tacit, meaning that it is learned from experience within the practice context. To learn in and from dynamic, unpredictable, and sometimes ambiguous contexts, reflective educators are keenly aware of their surrounding context, are open to and seek feedback, and can effectively distill the information that should be considered in a reflective process (Bright, 1996). We offer the profile of a reflective educator as one who

- stays focused on education's central purpose: student learning and development;
- is committed to continuous improvement of practice;
- assumes responsibility for his or her own learning—now and lifelong;
- demonstrates awareness of self, others, and the surrounding context;
- develops the thinking skills for effective inquiry;
- takes action that aligns with new understandings;
- holds great leadership potential within a school community; and
- seeks to understand different types of knowledge, internally and externally generated.

Given prevailing school and societal norms that fly in the face of slowing down to think, question, and then demonstrate the courage and conviction to act, reflective practitioners represent a countercultural phenomenon. In effect, they can be considered "positive deviants." Positive deviants are people whose behavior and practices lead to solutions to problems that others in the group who have access to exactly the same resources have not been able to solve. We want to identify these people because they provide demonstrable evidence that a solution for the problem exists within the community (Richardson, 2004). Reflective educators often serve as leaders, formal and informal, who attract others. In doing so, they influence practice beyond their immediate teaching domains. They attract others because they embody the profile characteristics listed above: a focus on student learning; the commitment, responsibility, awareness, thoughtfulness, thirst for inquiry; and finally an action-orientation. Given the importance of formal and informal leadership in schools, Chapter 3 focuses on core leadership practices for growing reflective practice.

Our list of reflective educator qualities also includes a valuing of different forms of knowledge. Distinctions have been made between reflective educators (or reflective practitioners) and experts, in terms of how knowledge is viewed, generated, and valued (Schön, 1987; Webb, 1995). In addition to the historical, political, and sociocultural knowledge bases that surround us and influence how we think and live (Kinchloe, 2004), generally speaking, there are two sources of knowledge that educators bring to bear on practice: externally generated knowledge and internally created knowledge. Externally generated knowledge comes by way of the research community and usually offers generalized findings, directions, and strategies to be considered by practice communities. Internally created knowledge comes by way of educators learning by reflecting on their practice and by customizing application of externally generated knowledge to unique contexts of practice, that is, specific schools, classes, and students. This is sometimes referred to as tacit or experiential knowledge (Schön, 1987).

Reflective practitioners draw largely from an experiential or contextual knowledge base in which "it is impossible to disentangle knowing from doing" (Webb, 1995, p. 71). Content experts draw largely from a technical-rational knowledge base (Schön, 1983). They are masters of content, but may not have the practice background that generates tacit knowledge about how to apply, use, or teach content in the classroom. They can share research findings, but cannot necessarily model or demonstrate application in authentic settings. This perspective explains some of the disconnect that educators may sense when learning from experts of content who cannot make the application to the classroom context. It also speaks to the frustration or cynicism that can arise among practicing educators when content experts assume an easy transfer of technical-rational knowledge to contexts of practice.

For some aspects of practice, educators draw on a technical-rational knowledge base, such as disciplinary expertise. However, for many other aspects of daily practice, educators draw on their experientially and contextually derived knowledge from practice. It is unnecessary and perhaps even counterproductive to differentially or exclusively value one type of knowledge over others. It is the job of educators to adopt a reflective stance, to continually learn and expand their understanding and repertoire of practice. In doing so they realize a paradox—both humility and joy—vested in lifelong learning: "Significant learning generally involves fluctuating episodes of anxiety-producing self-scrutiny and energy-inducing leaps forward in ability and understanding" (Brookfield, 1992, p. 12). Such is the journey of a reflective educator.

CLOSING

Education is about learning—not only student learning, but also staff and school community learning. Learning is a function of reflection, as depicted in Figure 1.4. "Adults do not learn from experience, they learn from processing experience" (Arin-Krupp as cited in Garmston & Wellman, 1997, p. 1). Dewey asserted years ago that experience itself is not enough. Ten years of teaching can be ten years of learning from experience with continuous improvement, or it can be one year with no learning repeated ten times. Learning and improvement can no longer be optional. Reflection, therefore, must be at the center of individual and organizational renewal initiatives.

Reflective practice offers one powerful way for educators—individually and collectively—to stay challenged, effective, and alive in their work. When educators in a school join together to reflect and learn, they make a difference by harnessing the potential of their collective resources: diverse experience and expertise, shared purpose and responsibility for students, expanded understanding of students throughout the school, professional and social support, and hopefulness about meaningful and sustained improvement. Despite the hectic pace and the steady demands, increasing

Figure 1.4   Learning by Reflection on Experience

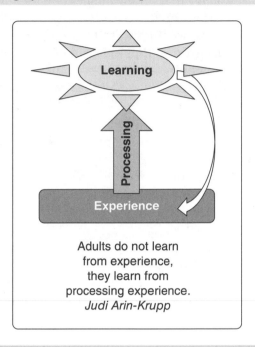

Learning

Processing

Experience

Adults do not learn
from experience,
they learn from
processing experience.
Judi Arin-Krupp

Source: Inspired by Judi Arin-Krupp.

Available for download at http://resources.corwin.com/YorkBarrReflective

numbers of educators are making it a priority to create space in their professional lives to ground their reflection and learning, as well as to learn while flying. In doing so, they are being nurtured to grow and are expanding their repertoire of effective instructional practices. They are moving from a culture of doing to a culture of learning with doing.

In Chapter 2, we describe and offer examples of fundamental skills for learning reflective practices and growing reflective practice communities. In Chapter 3, we identify practices and offer examples for leading the development of reflective practices in schools and districts. Chapters 4 through 7 focus on specific considerations and strategies for advancing reflective practices at each level (e.g., individual, partner, small group or team, and school or districtwide) of the reflective practice spiral. In this edition we offer many new examples from practice that offer ways that many schools and educators are grounding the learning and development through intentionally designed learning structures and processes, tailoring their focus on the particular learning aims for students.

Peter Block (2002) shares, "the value of another's experience is to give us hope, not to tell us how or whether to proceed" (p. 24). By offering examples from practice we hope to inspire ideas, energy, and action. We realize, however, that our examples cannot tell you how, specifically, to proceed in your particular place of practice. Gather with your colleagues, listen and learn from one another. You will figure out how to start. From there, your ongoing reflection on and for practice will guide your next moves forward. Hats off to you! Connect. Reflect. Learn. Grow. Get better. Celebrate. Renew.

2

Fundamentals for Reflective Practice

Be brave enough to start a conversation that matters. Be intrigued by the differences you hear. Trust that meaningful conversations can change your world.

— Margaret Wheatley, *Turning to One Another: Simple Conversations to Restore Hope to the Future*, 2009

A s described in Chapter 1, at the heart of the reflective practice cycle (Figure 2.1) is meaning-*full* conversation that results in learning from practice, which, in turn, informs and advances both teaching practice and student learning. Ways that school community members talk, think, and learn together is one of the strongest influences on the quality of teaching and student learning. A core principle for growing reflective practice communities is understanding that *the learning is in the conversation*. This means that the strongest norm of traditional school culture, *isolation*, must go away. For sure, there is evidence this is happening. Staff members in many schools gather regularly to learn with and from each other, in learning structures that are small enough to support participation, ensuring that *every voice is heard*. They also gather more regularly as a full staff, which makes it possible for staff members who do not work closely on a daily basis to be together in mixed groups, learning ways the variety of staff members in a school contribute to student growth and can support one another.

Figure 2.1   Reflective Practice Cycle

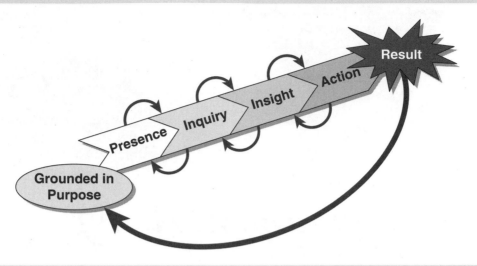

The old days of staff meetings for the purposes of disseminating information are increasingly repurposed to advance practice and to grow more
interdependent communities of practice. Many schools have decidedly
entered a new era in which planning alone, reflecting alone, and even teaching alone is fading away. Collaborative school cultures are increasingly
recognized as essential for growing communities of *shared* practice that
thrive in service to do good for the young people therein.

Intentionally designed small group learning is good for grown-ups,
just as we know it is good for students. As new teachers learn in their
preparation: *whoever is doing the talking is doing the learning.* Smaller structures provide more opportunities for each member to talk and to hear their
thinking. Adults, as well as students, often need to be taught *how* to have
meaningful conversations around content that matters and how to ensure
that each person participates.

Communities of practice grow from the collective, mindful work of
individuals who are open, listen to understand, and both describe and
reflect on practice to learn and then make commitments to improve.
Consequently, there are times when talking about mindful practice in
order to make it visible to peers can elicit a sense of vulnerability. As these
conversations continue, however, and nothing "bad" happens to members, trust grows. Participants learn through experience that "we are all in
this together." They learn that there are many opportunities to gain knowledge and grow right where they are with their colleagues at work. Trusting
and respectful relationships create a learning context in which members
can learn, thrive, improve, and deepen collective commitments to skillfully

teach well the young people in front of them. For many years, an adage that we have espoused and been mindful of in our practice is: *Go-eth not alone!* Together, we learn more and are able to sustain the energy required to do our collective work well.

Facilitators who teach and guide the growth of reflective practice conversations become proficient at observing nonverbal behavior, as well as listening to the words and intonation of verbal behavior that occurs in conversations. Both verbal and nonverbal behavior influence the ways that participants talk, learn, and create together . . . or not. If conversations are frequently interrupted verbally, or if dismissive nonverbal behaviors (e.g., rolling one's eyes, looking absently around the room, sighing audibly, doodling on the agenda) become norms, members lean away from the conversation and are less likely to contribute, biding their time until at last they can leave.

When individuals and groups are relatively new to reflective practice it is wise to be proactive about teaching skills that support reflecting both *on* and *for* practice. Remember—*Go slow to go fast*. Learning new practices rarely happens in the fast lane. Allocate sufficient time for modeling, teaching, and practicing skills of listening, speaking, inquiring, and responding. Additionally, even when participants are just learning the skills of reflective practice, design this work around content that matters. A specific way you might begin practicing such conversational routines in dyads and triads is shown in Practice Example 5.1, Learning Conversations, on page 166. Initially, teaching specific ways to reflect on and for practice builds understanding and confidence in the usefulness of these practices, and also averts "do-overs" that can cause frustration and slow momentum. Do-overs also can feel like an intervention, even though the real culprit may be that the group never received their "first best instruction" on how to have a reflective practice conversation. The language of reflective practice is foreign to many educators. It is more open, more inquisitive, and more personal than many of the conversations that occur in schools. Go slowly. Scaffold the learning and the language. Provide many opportunities to practice. Notice and acknowledge progress, just as we do with young people. Know that reflective practice is, in effect, a culture shift for many, and probably most, educators. The pace and language and personalization of the reflective learning conversations are substantially different from traditional staff learning. They have not experienced, *yet*, the rich learning and interpersonal support available from a different kind of conversation.

In the words of Linda Lambert, "the quality of the school is a function of the quality of the conversations within the school" (Lambert, 2005, p. 40). Facilitators of reflective practice aim to engage the hearts and minds of community members, who can then engage the hearts and minds of the young people they serve. As with all other arenas of practice, it is through practice with reflection that we get better at our craft. Through practice we begin to habituate norms of reflecting forward to plan for instruction, reflecting in practice to monitor and adjust instruction as we go, and reflecting back on practice to discern what seemed to support student engagement and what was less effective for doing so.

Most of this chapter is dedicated to introducing a framework for growing skills, practices, and dispositions that become norms in reflective practice communities (see Figure 2.2). First, however, we offer a succinct summary of ways that brain research, along with what is known about how adults learn, inform reflective practice. Toward the end of the chapter, we offer a robust practice example that describes structures and processes used to guide conversations that shaped the growth of an adult practice community over five years (2011–2015). The members had varied practice backgrounds (e.g., special education administrators and coaches, school psychologists, behavior intervention team members, counselors, and social workers). Prior to these ongoing learning opportunities, these individuals worked in relative isolation from one another. As they began learning together and began realizing the value of that fusion, they became increasingly interdependent, their outreach and impact cascaded throughout the system, resulting in more equitable learning opportunities and outcomes for students with disabilities, and also for students who did not formally qualify for services. Ongoing observation of student practices and reflection on staff practices continues to inform ways to sustain and deepen the relationships and collective work among this community of practice professionals.

Like a rubber band, stretched from its relaxed state of rest, tension is required to sustain and continually strengthen the form, function, and results that are possible within a practice community. Based on the work of Robert Fritz (as described in Peter Senge et al., 2000), this is referred to as "creative tension" that exists between the current state and the desired future state. Without sufficient tension, momentum slows and can even reverse. Upholding the vision and continuing to make progress requires ongoing reflection to determine what is contributing to movement toward the vision, what is deterring progress, and then to make adjustments accordingly. A central idea here is that school community members, by thinking together, can figure out ways to create and sustain momentum for achieving the vision in their particular practice context. *What's happening? What might be some reasons this is happening? What are some instructive learnings from this happening? What could be some shifts that are likely to increase progress toward our goals?* Then, do it. Observe what happens. Consider why it's happening. Mine your learning. Refine your practice. Repeat. Finally, the chapter closes with a table that offers a summary of perspectives related to designing and facilitating reflective practices that grow and strengthen communities of shared practice in schools.

> If teachers are to help student learners who begin and proceed differently, reach similar outcomes, they will need to be able to engage in disciplined experimentation, incisive interpretation of complex events, and rigorous reflection to adjust their teaching based on student outcomes. (Darling-Hammond, 2006, p. 3)

Sustainability and deepening of practice communities cannot be taken for granted. Ongoing mindful design of conversations and ongoing reflection on practice to inform next refinements in practice are required. There is no shortcut for deepening expertise or growing interdependent communities of practice. Next, we offer a summary of pertinent findings from brain research and adult learning that offer insight and considerations for the design and facilitation of reflective practices.

WHAT ARE SOME WAYS BRAIN RESEARCH AND ADULT LEARNING PRINCIPLES INFORM REFLECTIVE PRACTICE?

There is an extensive research base about contexts and processes that foster learning for young people and adults. Many learning principles apply equally for both age spans. Recent research on how the brain functions also has contributed substantially to understanding conditions that engage learners and learning. One significant finding is that neuroplasticity, that is, the ability of the brain to create new neural connections with greater complexity in response to new experiences and environments, "exists from the cradle to the grave; and that radical improvements in cognitive functioning—how we learn, think, perceive, and remember—are possible even in the elderly" (Doidge, 2007, pp. 46–47).

Learning occurs when new information is taken in through multiple sensory systems, followed by activation of neural networks in the brain linking this new information with prior knowledge. Presenting information through multiple modalities (e.g., sensory, auditory, kinesthetic), designing ways for active engagement with the content, and encouraging multiple ways for "showing what you know," also aligns with how the brain makes sense of new information (Rappolt-Schlictmann, Daley, & Rose, 2012). This "owning and making sense of" new information, in turn, stimulates growth of neuron dendrites. Dendrites are the sending and receiving tentacles that extend from the body of neurons and create the starlike structures often depicted in diagrams. Increasing connections among dendrites from different neurons creates networks of neurons, thereby extending connections and deepening learning, understanding, and memory retention. When students have little prior learning or experience in certain areas, it is important to create a foundation of experience on which to build and extend understandings. The same is true, of course, for grown-ups. Strong background knowledge from prior experiences creates a web of meaning that is a resource for making sense of new material. By nature, our brains are wired to learn, making learning a pleasurable experience. When learning happens, the neurotransmitter, dopamine, is produced. Dopamine creates a feeling of pleasure within the brain. This pleasurable response reinforces seeking new learning experiences (Wolfe, 2015). When students are involved in setting their own goals, they often do so by identifying goals in domains where they already have a sense of competence. Goals situated in positive belief systems also release the same neurotransmitter (Jackson, 2011).

Emotions have a powerful impact on the brain and, ultimately, strongly influence how learning takes place. When learners trust that no harm will come from stepping into new learning (meaning the learning environment feels psychologically safe), there is more openness to learning. When a potential threat is sensed, protective emotions predominate. This can result in withholding one's own perspective, watching how others respond, and even affirming what others share despite holding a different view. In short, participation and multiple perspectives often decrease. The overall impact is impeded learning potential for everyone (Wolfe, 2015). "Accuracy and efficiency of thinking processes, perceptions, and effort all are influenced by affective states, while motivation and emotion substantially predict learning behavior and outcomes" (Rappolt-Schlictmann et al., 2012, p. 57).

When situated in psychologically safe environments, people can be seen, literally, leaning into the conversation with their body and zooming in to make eye contact. There is a thoughtful, measured pace of conversation, sharing of thoughts and opinions, and respectfully challenging ideas and providing feedback to improve collective work. This type of engaged conversational culture creates a context in which participants become more intrinsically motivated to listen, inquire, and learn. The focus is on the conversation and learning, instead of what is safe to say or do here. Such intrinsic motivation generates more self-directed learning and self-actualization (Jackson, 2011). When fear is absent, engagement deepens and learning grows.

Much of what we know from brain research also aligns with what we know about best practices for supporting adult learning. Adult learning is enhanced when

- colleagues have opportunities to listen to each other in open, caring, and respectful ways;
- discussions are not based on assumptions, but on data and observations that inform and sometimes challenge one's thinking;
- dialogic contexts invite sharing of multiple perspectives that spark productive deliberation and inform shared purpose and direction; and
- feedback is recognized and appreciated as having the potential to support growth, instead of as a threat. (Drago-Severson, Blum-DeStefano, & Asghar, 2013)

Malcom Knowles (1994), an esteemed elder in the field of adult learning, described how individuals mature their shift in self-concept *from* being dependent *to* more interdependent; *from* being externally motivated to learn *to* being more internally motivated; *from* having relatively few experiences from which to draw on *to* having a wealth of experiences to guide decision making;

and *from* using subject-specific material *to* drawing from multiple subject areas to solve problems. He recommended four principles for supporting adult learning: (1) include participants in the planning and evaluation of their instruction; (2) include experiences that did not turn out as expected, as therein lies much to be learned; (3) focus on topics or issues that have immediate application in the professional or personal lives of participants; and (4) maintain a problem-oriented focus (Knowles, 1984; Pappas, 2013).

Considered together, adult learning and brain-based research have several implications for designing ways to effectively reflect on practice. *First*, learning environments must be safe. Learning happens in environments that present *low* or *no* psychological threat. This makes it possible to process new information and to consider perspectives different from one's own. *Second*, educators must be respected as learners and have a voice in ways to apply new learning to their particular practice contexts. *Third*, context provides meaning that both motivates practitioners to learn and influences the shaping of knowledge and skills to be effective in the particular practice contexts. *Fourth*, opportunities to examine underlying beliefs, values, and assumptions create learning opportunities to achieve deeper understanding of teaching and learning processes. *Fifth*, when introducing new information or perspectives, opportunities to compare, contrast, link, and integrate old and new perspectives deepen understandings about practice. Reflecting on experience creates learning opportunities that take advantage of integrating information across multiple neural pathways. In sum, significant learning for educators involves an active process of knowledge construction that draws from experience and other knowledge sources to make sense of new experiences, thereby advancing understanding about context-specific practices.

Ronald Brandt (1998) drew from several sources (e.g., American Psychological Association, 1997; Caine & Caine, 1997) to present a succinct informative summary of conditions that promote what he referred to as "powerful learning." Such learning, he asserts, happens when *what* individuals learn about is meaningful and requires some degree of challenge to understand. Brandt also emphasized the significance of *how* learning is supported. Opportunities to make choices, to construct new knowledge, to engage with peers, to make connections with one's own experience, and to receive strategic feedback all contribute to a successful learning experience. Brandt also emphasized the significant influence of context, or *where* people learn. Learning contexts that are positive and that invite and inspire learners to think, reflect, and come up with multiple possibilities offer fertile territory for learning to happen.

We have referred to Ron Brandt's work in each of the previous editions of this book. His perspectives are no less relevant today, 20 years later. We also include his work as one small way to honor Ron, a remarkable human who, in particular, gave so much and grew so much good in the field of education. May we all serve so long and well.

A FRAMEWORK FOR GROWING REFLECTIVE PRACTICE COMMUNITIES

Thinking together implies that you no longer take your own position as final. You relax your grip on certainty and listen to the possibilities that simply result from being in relationships with others—possibilities that might not otherwise have occurred. (Isaacs, 1999, p. 19)

Growing school communities in which reflective practice is a dominant cultural norm creates the potential for cultivating context-relevant learning among colleagues who share responsibility for teaching well a community of students. This ground level *knowledge* is extraordinarily valuable for adapting and advancing practices that are nuanced for particular staffs and students. In Figure 2.2, we offer one way of thinking about growing the skills, dispositions, and capacities for becoming a community of reflective practitioners. Please note that the framing of each "chunk" in a box erroneously suggests degree of separateness and linear sequencing among the "chunks." We used boxes to bring clarity to particular areas of development. The sequence in which they are ordered suggests one way to set about learning or deepening reflective practice skills and capacities, knowing there is much interconnectedness among these areas.

Thinking is, of course, integral to each component in Figure 2.2, A Framework for Growing Reflective Practice Communities. Theory and research abound on the topic of thinking. What is thinking? How does one think? What prompts thinking? What supports thinking at higher levels that results in concept formation? What shuts down thinking? Alan Raelin (2002) proposed a thinking framework based on the classic works of Vygotsky and Piaget, two eminent cognitive psychologists, and provided a synthesis of findings from studies in which the framework was utilized. Specifically, he identified five skills of reflective practice: *being, speaking, disclosing, testing,* and *probing.* He describes *being* as "the most unusual yet potentially powerful of the skills, with the purpose of opening up to experience and to our interpersonal environment" (p. 70). Being present is a state of mind that allows for consideration of multiple perspectives. It requires hearing different views as valid ways of thinking not as threats. We now describe more fully the significance of each "block" in Figure 2.2, along with offering ideas about how to learn and practice.

Be Present

Being present is to be aware of oneself, of others, and of the surrounding circumstances. "To be aware is to allow our attention to broaden and expand to include more and more of our immediate experience. The central idea here is that we are capable of coming to understand what is

Figure 2.2   A Framework for Growing Reflective Practice Communities

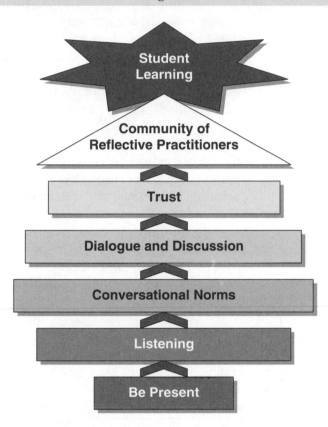

happening as it is happening" (Isaacs, 1999, p. 144). Being aware of and paying attention to others is an acknowledgment of value and presents an opportunity to learn and understand more fully one's context and the people therein. It is also an example of reflection in practice. Decades ago, Kahn (1992) described how individuals who are psychologically present can bring themselves more fully to their work and to interactions with others at work, resulting in higher levels of productivity. He explained that

> The long term implication of such presence is that people who are present and authentic in their roles help to create shared under-standings of their systems that are equally authentic and respon-sive to change and growth. This process is what allows social systems . . . to become unstuck and move toward new and productive

ways of working. When individuals are open to change and connecting to work with others and are focused and attentive and complete rather than fragmented, their systems adopt the same characteristics, collectively. Individual and systemic wholes, in these respects, are intertwined and complementary. (p. 331)

Being present underlies each of the components in the *Framework for Growing Reflective Practice Communities*. Being present is being mindful of one's own thoughts as well as paying attention to the verbal and nonverbal behaviors of others. As mentioned above, it is related to the five skills of reflective practice identified by Raelin (2002), where he identifies *being* as "the most unusual yet potentially powerful of the skills, with the purpose of opening up to experience and to our interpersonal environment" (p. 70). *Being open* is a state of mind that allows for consideration of multiple perspectives. It requires hearing different views as valid ways of thinking, instead of viewing them as threats. This phrase is similar to Zeichner and Liston's term, *open-mindedness*, which they describe as "an active desire to listen to more sides than one, to give full attention to alternative possibilities, and to recognize the possibility of error even in beliefs that are dearest to us." (1996, p. 10). Being open demonstrates a belief that you can learn with and from others, people of all ages, races, cultures, abilities, genders, religions, sexual orientations, and socioeconomic circumstances. "It also means you can suspend certainty, meaning how you view things, and be open to exploring the tensions of opposites" (Raelin, 2002, p. 70).

To be fully present and learn from conversation, one needs to be open and to see the value in understanding differing views among the variety of people who gather to reflect, learn, and create. *Being present* matters because it signals engagement around the task at hand. When members disengage (e.g., withdraw or withhold their perspective) learning and results are potentially diminished for everyone. When members withdraw, there is also the possibility of resentment and judgment of those who chose not to contribute. Being open and mindful requires more energy than one would think. Tracking, making sense of, and connecting with the views of others is valuable, and sometimes exhausting. Through reflective practices, learning is not only possible, but useful in that it informs future conversation and potential action.

REFLECTIONS ON BEING PRESENT

What are some ways I can keep myself engaged and mindful in conversation with my colleagues?

How can I support others in sharing their views so that we all understand and benefit?

Listening

Related to presence and openness is the ability to listen well, without judgment and with empathy. Agreement is not necessarily the objective. The objective is to understand the perspectives of others. To listen well requires not only being present but also being *open*. Being open is a state of mind that allows consideration of multiple perspectives. It doesn't require agreement, but it does require hearing different views as valid and not as threats. If, as leaders, we do not listen well, we will not connect well, and therefore, we limit the extent to which we can influence others. Listening demonstrates respect. Without respect, there is no relationship, no pathway for influence. Listening builds trust. Trust fosters relationships. Relationships provide the context for shared reflection, learning, development, and leadership, all of which are closely linked. If we do not listen well, we do not learn well, and we do not connect well with others. If, as leaders, we do not learn and we do not connect, we also do not influence (lead) others. We can assert positional authority, but without engaging the hearts and minds of others, professional and organizational practices will not be advanced.

Our tendency is to listen from memory, screening and interpreting what is said through our own filter of experiences, values, and beliefs (Carlson & Bailey, 1997; Isaacs, 1999). When we listen this way, a speaker's intended meaning may be misinterpreted. Listening well requires an awareness and suspension of our own thoughts so the focus is on the speaker's experience and intended meaning. "To suspend is to change direction, to stop, step back, and see things with new eyes. This is perhaps one of the deepest challenges that humans face—especially once they have staked out a position" (Isaacs, 1999, p. 135). This explains, in part, why it can be so difficult to listen well. The listener's own ways of thinking or acting are at risk of being changed or influenced (Rogers, 1986).

Stephen Glenn, noted author, family psychologist, and educator, said years ago, people want three things: they want to be listened to, to be taken seriously, and to know that a person has a genuine interest in what they are saying. Suspension is a thinking skill that fosters listening. We invite you to read the excerpt about suspension from the work of Garmston and Wellman (1999) in Figure 2.3. As you read this excerpt, underline, highlight, or make notes in the margin about words, phrases, and ideas that resonate for you. After reading, share with a partner what you identified as significant and why it resonated with you. Some of the words and ideas that stand out for us are: *notice our own thinking . . . suspension is a way of emptying the cup . . . choosing to temporarily put aside your views . . . others have opinions that are true for them . . . as challenging as it is, it increases our learning.*

When initially learning suspension, the idea that we can be more aware of our thoughts but choose *not* to engage around them is often an "aha" experience. That we can choose to let our feelings and thoughts pass, or at least be set aside temporarily, is a freeing notion. Hard to do, but worthy of

Figure 2.3   Suspension: An Internal Skill of Dialogue

SUSPENSION

Suspension is the essential internal skill of dialogue. Suspension draws on mental, emotional, and values-based resources. Within conversation and dialogue, there inevitably come points of personal conflict. These often occur when we feel we are not being heard or that our points of view are being distorted by others. Our anger or uneasiness at these times can be on the edge of our own awareness, yet our discomfort influences our listening and can influence our overt responses, which in turn influence the internal and external behaviors of others in the group.

As we increase our skill in dialogue, we come to recognize these moments as points of choice. The first choice is whether or not to allow the feelings to surface. The second choice is whether or not to trust the feelings. With increased awareness and experience, we come to realize that these feelings are based on our perceptions—on our internal experiences and interpretations. We then start to notice our own listening and start to listen as we listen to others.

The next choice we face is whether or not to check out our perceptions with others in the group or whether to listen further to observe how others are responding and how further dialogue shapes the meaning of the moment. The danger in confronting perceived distortions is that this can polarize the conversation or narrow the dialogue to a few issues and a few people.

To suspend means to set aside our perceptions, our feelings, or judgments, and our impulses for a time and listen to and monitor carefully our own internal experience and what comes up from within the group. "Ultimately, dialogue achieves a state of knowing one's thought as one is having it" (Schein, 1993).

Source: Garmston & Wellman (1999).

 Available for download at http://resources.corwin.com/YorkBarrReflective

attempts to do so. Sometimes there is no particular need to engage passing thoughts or feelings and make them bigger than they are or allow them to take over our thinking, thereby moving in tangential directions. They can be put aside, allowing space to attend more fully to others. As you engage in reflection with others, pay attention to your thinking and practice the skill of suspension. *Suspension* is a core skill that grounds our ability to listen, learn, and understand. Our tendency is to listen from memory, screening and interpreting what is being said through our own filter of experiences, values, and beliefs (Carlson & Bailey, 1997; Isaacs, 1999). When we listen this way, a speaker's intended meaning may be lost or misinterpreted. Listening well requires an awareness and suspension of our own thoughts so that the focus is on the speaker's experience and intended meaning (Garmston & Wellman, 1999; Lee, 1995). "To suspend is to change direction, to stop, step back, and see things with new eyes. This is perhaps one of the deepest challenges faced by humans—especially once they have staked out a position" (Isaacs, 1999, p. 135). This explains, in part, why it is so difficult to listen well. The listeners' ways of thinking or acting are at risk of being changed or influenced (Rogers, 1986).

Empathetic listening involves an even deeper sense of genuine connection with another person, a feeling of strong connection not only to the words, but also to the emotion felt and expressed by that person. "Empathic relationships generally confer the greatest opportunity for personal, and thus professional, growth in educational settings" (Rogers as described by Butler, 1996, p. 265). Listening is perhaps the greatest gift we can offer one another, and in the process, we extend the potential for being in community with others. This is definitely a skill that can be practiced at home, often with positive results. The attitude, knowledge, and skill around empathetic listening is further elaborated in Chapter 5.

Understanding is an outgrowth of listening well. Understanding does not require agreement, although full understanding often lays the groundwork for identifying points of agreement. Seeking to understand other people's thoughts and actions leads to a better appreciation of who they are, how they view their circumstances, and the ways in which they contribute or hope to contribute in the world. Further, when engaged in authentic inquiry, both the speaker and listener experience increased depths of understanding. Understanding is one of the most respectful and powerful ways of connecting with another person (Covey, 1989). Being open is a state of mind that allows consideration of multiple perspectives. Learning to hear different views as valid ways of thinking, not as threats. "Open-mindedness is an active desire to listen to more sides than one, to give full attention to alternative possibilities, and to recognize the possibility of error even in beliefs that are dearest to us" (Zeichner & Liston, 1996, p. 10).

Exposure to different views fosters inquiry by providing additional information, which may contrast with one's own views (Hatton & Smith, 1995; Levin, 1995). In the absence of openness, reflection merely validates and perpetuates one's current views. At the core of being open is a belief that there are multiple ways of experiencing, making sense of, and acting in the world. Also recognized, if not anticipated, is the complexity that often results from remaining open and seeking a richer understanding of phenomena. In our fast-paced daily lives, we often make hasty decisions or accept superficial (sometimes incorrect) explanations or understandings. Being open guards against such tendencies. Listening and suspension matter because pausing to consider what is being said can change your thinking and the thinking of others. Even though you may not agree, consider what happens if statements in a conversation are true. Pause and ask a question rather than making assumptions and closing the dialogue too soon.

Located in Figure 2.4 are ways we sometimes listen, or more accurately, *fail* to listen, that impede our ability to hear what others are saying. These *12 listening blocks* were originally located on the Listening Leader website at http://onmymind.areavoices.com/2011/11/05/the-12-blocks-to-listening/. We often introduce these blocks as a fun and nonthreatening way to acknowledge how difficult it can be for *each* of us to truly listen with the intent to understand a speaker. When listening to others speak, most of us can easily slip into judging, contrasting, or in other ways comparing ourselves and our thoughts to what another person is saying, which means we are not really listening for the meaning or message. Listening matters not only so that we become informed about and learn to consider other perspectives, but also because listening creates the possibility of relationships with others. When listening stops, rapport is broken. When listening stops, learning often comes to a halt as well. No one person holds *the one best way* for moving forward in a community of practice. Better decisions often emerge from broader consideration of perspectives.

Figure 2.4 Blocks to Listening

Comparing

Comparing makes it hard to listen because you are always trying to assess who is smarter, more competent, more emotionally healthy—you or the other.

Mind Reading

The mind reader doesn't pay much attention to what people say. In fact he or she often distrusts it and is always trying to figure out what the other person is really thinking and feeling.

Rehearsing

You don't have time to listen when you are rehearsing what to say. Your whole attention is on the preparation and crafting of your next comment.

Filtering

When you filter, you listen to some things and not to others. You pay attention only enough to see if someone is angry or unhappy or if you are in emotional danger. Once assured that the communication contains none of those things, you let your mind wander.

Judging

Negative labels have enormous power. If you prejudge someone as stupid or nuts or unqualified, you do not pay much attention to what they say. You have already written them off.

Dreaming

You are half listening. Something the person says suddenly triggers a chain of private associations. And, you are off in la la land.

Identifying

In this block, you take everything a person tells you and refer it back to your own experience. They tell you about a toothache, but that reminds you about the time you had oral surgery.

Advising

You are a great problem solver, ready with help and suggestions. You don't have to hear more than a few sentences before you begin searching for the right advice.

Sparring

This block has you arguing and debating with people. The other person never feels heard because you are so quick to disagree.

Being Right

Being right means that you will go to any length (twist the facts, start shouting, make excuses or accusations, call up past sins) to avoid being wrong. Your convictions are unshakeable.

Derailing

This block is accomplished by suddenly changing the subject. You derail the train of conversation when you get bored or uncomfortable with the topic.

Placating

Right, right, right. Absolutely. I know. Of course. You are incredible. Yes. Really? You want to be nice, pleasant, and supportive. You want people to like you. So you agree with everything.

Source: Adapted from On My Mind [Web log post]. *The 12 Blocks to Listening.* Retrieved from http://onmymind.areavoices.com/2011/11/05/the-12-blocks-to-listening

 Available for download at **http://resources.corwin.com/YorkBarrReflective**

Another concept, *Thought Systems*, introduced by Richard Carlson (1997) also bolsters our understanding about how thinking and learning happen, or not. Our thought system is the way that we view the world, the lens through which we see each new experience. Each of us has a unique thought system.

> Your thought system contains all the information you have accumulated over your lifetime. It is past information that your thought system uses to interpret the relative significance of everything that happens in your life. In this sense, a thought system is the source of *conditioned* thought. When you rely on it, you are thinking in a habitual manner, your usual way of seeing things. Here is where your habitual reactions to life are formed.
>
> Thought systems contain our view of "the way life is." They are psychological mechanisms that convince us when we are right, accurate in our understanding, or justified. Thought systems by nature are stubborn and do not appreciate being tampered with. They are absolutely self-validating. (Carlson, 1997, pp. 20–21)

Our thought system influences how we learn and work with others, as well as how much energy and commitment we invest in creating a school community that supports all learners. Thought systems can either open us to understanding ways of thinking where multiple perspectives are included, considered, and integrated, or they can close us to hearing and seeing different perspectives. Being aware that we have thought systems and that we continually monitor our thoughts is helpful to understand, in part so that we can be mindful about our thinking and intentionally try to remain open to new ideas. This is, of course, a precursor to both listening and learning. As one of us is known to say, "God gave us two ears and just one mouth for a good reason." Hearing (listening) requires *at least* twice as much effort as talking!

Here is an example of how our thought systems can alter interpretation of another person's meaning. In public schools with a high percentage of students from low-income neighborhoods that receive additional Title 1 funding, some staff members "reflect a *lack* of belief in the capacity of these students, focusing instead on identifying and targeting weaknesses" (Jackson, 2011, pp. 28–29). Jackson asserts that this focus on perceived deficits requiring remedial approaches to instruction fails to recognize the breadth of student capabilities and their full potential. In contrast, thought systems that recognize the attributes of adaptivity and resilience often demonstrated by such students are open to creating learning opportunities tailored to these strengths.

Resilience requires persistence. Persistence is one of the most significant positive influences on learning capacity. It is a characteristic of many people viewed as successful in life. Educators can choose to recognize resilience as an asset, and therefore encourage and reinforce persistence as an asset for growth and successful engagement around higher level concepts. Conditioned ways of thinking strongly influence how and what we teach. Often it is the people with the power, the educators, for example, who grow when they realize the limitations on their own perspective have delimited the potential of their students. Surely this is an extremely important arena for reflection so that educators can become more aware of the blind-spots and biases firmly lodged in their own thought systems, in order to make intentional strides forward to build on the assets of students to support their growth.

REFLECTIONS ON LISTENING

As I listen to others, what "blocks" to listening readily emerge in my mind?

How might I get better at settling my thoughts so I maintain rapport and learn?

When I am talking, what nonverbals from my partner suggest that I am not being listened to?

What types of paraphrasing supports communicating to a partner that I heard and understand her message?

Conversational Norms

Establishing and then adhering to conversational norms in group learning situations supports mindfulness, and even vigilance about behaviors and dispositions that facilitate thinking, learning, and working together. Observation of the ways that group members talk provides a window into understanding the learning potential of a group. Do you notice listening, inquiry, and shared contributions? Such conversations indicate the potential for deepening understandings about practice. Or, does the conversation serve primarily to reinforce the status quo (Heifetz, Grashow, & Linsky, 2009)? Frequently, we begin group sessions with the verbal or visual reminder that "we are all in the same room, but not in the same place" (anonymous as quoted by Garmston & Wellman, 1997, p. 29). This serves to acknowledge the differences among individuals and to support the assumption that members are likely to have different perspectives around the topic of conversation.

Norms and expectations can be provided, generated, or a combination of both. We offer one caution about generating norms. Experience has taught us that when groups are invited to generate their own norms, members often come up with norms that are *procedural*, such as the desire to begin on time, end on time, appoint a facilitator and recorder, and identify dates and times for the next meeting. Members also often generate norms that are considered *higher order ways of being*, such as norms that involve respect and trust. There is nothing inherently wrong with either of these types of norms; however, they are often not sufficient for increasing the likelihood of enacting respect or trust.

We suggest that the likelihood of norms being understood and practiced requires that they take the form of *verbs*, meaning words and actions that can be heard and seen. Higher order ways of being, such as respect or trust, typically emerge when words and actions are aligned with these behaviors and are regularly practiced. What does respect look like and sound like? What types of actions and words can lead me to feel I can trust another person?

For many years we have used the *Norms of Collaborative Work* originally identified and developed by Bill Baker (personal communication at Cognitive Coaching Advanced Training, South Lake Tahoe, CA, 1993) and later formally articulated in the *Adaptive Schools* work of Bob Garmston and Bruce Wellman (2009). Figure 2.5 illustrates one way that we have configured these norms to be visibly accessible in group learning situations. Further, it is worthy to note that the original set of these norms advanced by Bill Baker included one additional "*p*" norm: *providing data*. Given the abundance of data that is useful, many teams have adopted this additional norm as well.

When learning and practicing these conversational norms, it is useful to teach and learn ways to inquire and respond such that participants do not become defensive. We offer here some examples of conditional language that can assist. *I am really interested in what you just shared, what are some ways you teach students to do that?* This inquiry takes the form of affirm then inquire. *How would you suggest I try out using that and what should I watch for as I do it?* This invites support for trying something new. For more in-depth information about modes and norms of conversation, and a whole host of other facilitation and learning skills, we suggest taking a look at the book *Unlocking Group Potential* by Bob Garmston and Valerie von Frank (2012). Another set of norms that have served as an important complement to *Norms of Collaborative Work* are the *Four Agreements of Courageous Conversations* developed by Glenn Singleton (2012) of the Pacific Education Group. These norms are *stay engaged, experience discomfort, speak your truth, and expect* and *accept nonclosure.* These norms are most often learned and practiced by educators to reflect on their teaching mindsets and practices, with a heightened focus on ways students from varied racial and cultural backgrounds engage with instructional content and learning processes.

Habituating use of productive conversational norms is significantly advanced if they are kept visible *and* are integrated into the structure and process of all learning meetings. Visual reminders help prompt their use. The depiction in Figure 2.5, which we call Tabletop Collaborative Norms,

Figure 2.5   Tabletop Collaborative Norms

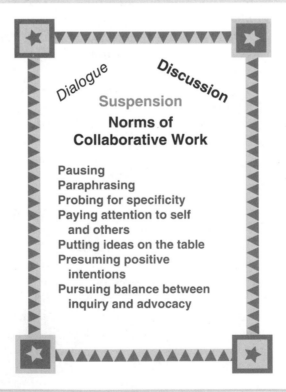

Source: Based on Garmston & Wellman (1999).

 Available for download at **http://resources.corwin.com/YorkBarrReflective**

can be sized for insertion in 5-by-7-inch self-standing acrylic picture frames for placement on tables where teams meet. We also have sized the norms to print on firm 8 ½-by-11-inch paper to either lay flat on the table or be posted in meeting areas. Sometimes we supersize and then laminate the norms as posters. You never know when you might find yourself in a meeting where the norms can help keep the conversation going in productive ways! ☺

Most important and worthy of overemphasis is the recognition that to be effective, norms and expectations must be regularly and intentionally practiced. Especially early on in their introduction and in the development of teams, we invite group members to identify, individually or as a group, a norm on which to focus at the start of each meeting. Sometimes, this is one of the grounding questions that launch each gathering and include "every voice in the room." At the end of meetings, members are then invited to reflect on individual and collective use of the norm(s) during their conversations, along with their sense about how norm use supported the conversations.

Experience has taught us that becoming proficient in use of conversational norms (that is, verbs, practices) leads to higher order ways of *being in community* with others, which consequently generates *respect, care, trust,* and *high regard.*

REFLECTIONS ON CONVERSATIONAL NORMS

In what ways are these group norms similar to and different from norms used in your groups?

Which of the norms do you view as especially important for growing shared understandings?

What are one or two norms that you would like to get better at using?

Which norms might help you to stay mindful about the impact of varied student cultures on teaching and learning?

Dialogue and Discussion

David Bohm, now deceased, has been recognized as one of the greatest physicists and foremost thinkers of this century. In 1989 he wrote *On Dialogue*, one of the most widely read books about dialogue. Here is an excerpt from his book that helps to clarify meanings of dialogue and discussion.

I give meaning to the word "dialogue" that is somewhat different from what is commonly used. "Dialogue" comes from the Greek word, dialogos. Logos means "the word," or in our case we would think of the "meaning" of the word. And, "dia" means "through"—it doesn't mean "two." A dialogue can be among any number of people, not just two. The picture or image that this derivation suggests is of a stream of meaning flowing among and through us and between us. This will make possible a flow of meaning in the whole group, out of which may emerge some new understanding. It's something new, which may not have been in the starting point at all. It's something creative, something created. And this shared meaning is the "glue" or "cement" that holds people and societies together.

Contrast this with the word "discussion," which has the same root as "percussion" and "concussion," which means to break things up. It emphasizes the idea of analysis, where there may be many points of view, and where everybody is presenting a different one—analyzing and breaking it up. That obviously has its value, but it is limited and it will not get us very far beyond our various points of view. Discussion is almost like a ping-pong game, where people are batting ideas back and forth and the object of the game is to win or to get points for yourself.

In dialogue, however, nobody is trying to win. Everybody wins if anybody wins. There is a different spirit to it. In dialogue, there is no attempt to gain points, or to make your particular view prevail. Rather, whenever a mistake is discovered on the part of anybody, everybody gains. It's a situation called "win-win," whereas the other game is win-lose—if I win, you lose. But, a dialogue is something more of a common participation in which we are not playing a game against each other, but with each other. In a dialogue everybody wins. (pp. 6–7)

The power of dialogue to promote reflection and learning has been widely claimed for generations (Bohm, 1999; Garmston, 2012; Isaacs, 1999). Dialogue has been described as a "conversation with a center, no sides" (Isaacs, 1999, p. 19) and as a "living experience of inquiry within and between people" (p. 9). It is a process of sharing and thinking together for the purposes of expanding thinking, promoting understanding, making connections, and generating possibilities. It is a way to get unstuck as you uncover assumptions and beliefs. "Thinking together implies that you no longer take your own position as final. You relax your grip on certainty and listen to the possibilities that simply result from being in relationship with others—possibilities that might not otherwise have occurred" (Isaacs, 1999, p. 19).

Dialogue is frequently contrasted with discussion (Garmston & Wellman, 2009). As depicted in Figure 2.6, dialogue can be thought of as an inclusive and opening-up process in which participants discover new perspectives and arrive at fresh understandings, insights, and connections. There is no pressure to come up with one answer or one point of view.

Dialogue holds and reveals many possibilities without constraint. Discussion can be thought of as a narrowing and eliminating process. The purpose of dialogue is to increase understanding and possibility; the purpose of discussion is to narrow options and make decisions. Both processes are useful ways of conversing, each with a distinct aim. Moving to discussion (i.e., narrowing options) and decision making before adequate dialogue (i.e., generating possibilities) often leads to decisions that lack sufficient deliberation, and accordingly, to decisions that are not followed. Underlying the premise of dialogue is a theory that shared meaning leads to shared thinking, which leads to aligned action.

Figure 2.6   Illustrated Comparison Between the Processes of Dialogue and Discussion

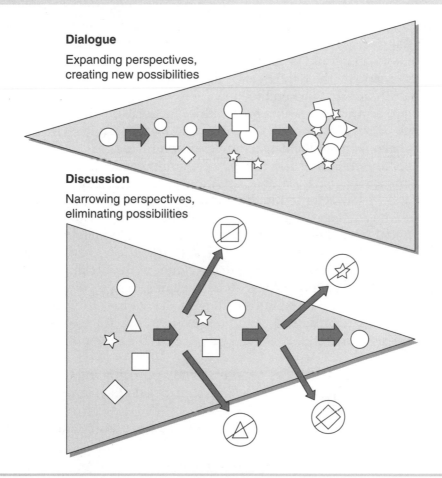

Dialogue

Expanding perspectives, creating new possibilities

Discussion

Narrowing perspectives, eliminating possibilities

Some decisions are not important enough to warrant the energy required for a group to engage in an extensive, participatory process of dialogue before decision making. For example, the color of copy paper or the contents of the pop machine would not be worthy of extended periods of conversation. But, important and complex decisions that affect students and staff call for consideration of many diverse perspectives. For example, what are some ways to warmly welcome new students and families to our school? How might our schedule be revised to allow more time for team learning? What might be our schoolwide practice priorities for the upcoming year to support more coherent learning experiences for students? From both a buildingwide resource perspective, as well as from a team-based perspective, what do we need to consider as we move toward creating opportunities for flexible instructional groups? In what ways might we rethink counseling and course options and sequences to ensure equitable access for all our students? What principles will best ground decision making about dealing with financial cutbacks in our district? For these types of substantial decisions that have long-term impact, a broad constituency of people resources should be tapped for at least two reasons. First, decisions should be made on the richest set of information. Second, people can usually live with decisions when they feel their viewpoint has been heard and considered, and when reasons for an ultimate decision are communicated and understood. Most grown-ups can live with decisions that they view as having arisen from an inclusive, deliberative process.

For an illustration of the difference in outcomes that can be realized when using an inclusive dialogue (instead of a focused discussion) prior to making a decision, refer to the diagram of two groups in Figures 2.7a and 2.7b. Each diagram shows a group of 12 people, each of whom is indicated by a different circled letter, seated in a circle. In the top circle, only person A and person H share their respective views with the rest of the group (represented by the letters A and H in the center of the circle). In the bottom circle, each of the 12 individuals share their respective perspectives with the group (represented by all the letters in the center of the circle). Now, consider that each group makes a decision about how to proceed based on the perspectives shared (i.e., the perspectives in the center of each circle).

- Which group had more people actively participating?
- Which group is likely to have learned the most during its conversation?
- Which group had a richer set of perspectives from which to base a decision?
- Which group might have discovered several new possibilities for moving forward?
- Which group's members are more likely to honor and abide by the decisions made?

This simple example illustrates two different ways that groups can converse and the likely consequences of each type of conversation. The group in the bottom circle could be thought of as having engaged in a dialogue. The group in the top circle is more likely to have moved quickly to discussion and thereby limited the number of perspectives shared.

Figure 2.7a   Group Considering the Perspective of Just Two Members

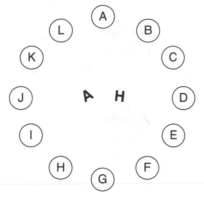

Figure 2.7b   Group Considering the Perspectives of All Members

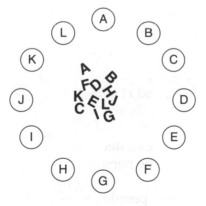

Sometimes, conversations about important topics look like that of the top group in Figure 2.7a. Only a few perspectives are shared, which can result in lower quality decisions and in decisions that are not honored by all group members. Not surprisingly, therefore, some topics appear repeatedly on group agendas. Often groups will argue there is not enough time to dialogue before making decisions. These same groups, however, out of necessity allocate time to revisit "decisions" that have been made but not honored. Often, we end up spending time addressing the same issues over and over and over again. A proactive stance that allows time for dialogue about important issues on the front end may ultimately be more efficient and effective.

One more way for thinking about the potential of dialogue, especially helpful for the visual learners among us, can be seen in the quilt blocks located in Figure 2.8. For those of you who are not quilters, we will explain. At quilt festivals all over the country, there is often an open competition for anyone interested in participating. Here is how it works. Each participant is given a plastic bag with exactly the same materials—same patterns and same size cuts of fabric. From those exact same materials, each participant makes one quilt block of a designated size (often 16" × 16"). At the festival, all of the quilt blocks made by participants are mounted on a wall and judged. And so, what do the final products look like? Without fail, the many blocks displayed are different from one another (see Figure 2.8). There is not one duplicate—at least not that we have ever seen. So, what does this have to do with dialogue? The unlimited variations in the block patterns represent the variety of possibilities that can emerge when groups engage in dialogue. Dialogue creates possibilities. The greater the participation, the richer the array of resulting options.

Figure 2.8   Quilt Blocks as Dialogue

Source: Images courtesy of MaxCab/iStock/Thinkstock

Available for download at http://resources.corwin.com/YorkBarrReflective

REFLECTIONS ON DIALOGUE AND DISCUSSION

What stood out for you as significant differences between dialogue and discussion?

In what ways do they both serve the purpose of making well-grounded and informed decisions?

How might each of these modes of conversation be useful in growing our school community?

In what ways could the norms of collaboration support us as we learn dialogue and discussion?

Questioning and Response Strategies

Questioning and response strategies are part of most conversations. Ways we inquire and ways we respond in conversation significantly influences ways we listen, learn, and contribute. *What* we say and *how* we say it matters. The tone, choice of words, and nonverbal behaviors present in our conversational talk can support conversations that are inclusive and yield useful results, and also can shut down conversations when questions become pointed and responses become terse or dismissive. Along with thinking, questioning and responding also occur in each of the components in Figure 2.2, A Framework for Growing Reflective Practice Communities. In this section we describe strategies for asking questions and offering responses.

Questioning Strategies

Because language constructs everyone's reality, the language chosen when asking questions has a significant impact on emotion, the learning environment, and ultimately personal identity as a learner. *Intonation, syntax*, and *presuppositions* are key linguistic elements in posing effective questions (Costa & Garmston, 2015). Each element is described briefly here.

The nonverbal quality of *intonation* refers to how the message sounds and is experienced by the recipient of the communication. Intonation, what the question *sounds like*, tends to be a more accurate discriminating variable than the content of a question. An *approachable voice* invites genuine inquiry and should be used when posing questions intended to prompt reflection. Consider these two questions. Read them aloud, emphasizing the italicized words: (1) *Why* did *that* happen? and (2) What *might have been some* reasons the students responded in that way? The first question sounds like an interrogation. The second is more open, inviting more reflection and possibilities. The first seems more accusatory; the second more curious.

A second element of asking questions is *syntax*, or how the question is structured. The nature of responses provided depends on the nature of the questions asked. If questions ask for recall, answers tend to be short and to the point. For example, *"What is the life cycle of a mosquito?"* There is no elaboration. If the syntax of questions suggests making comparisons, contrasting different events, analyzing multiple options, or some other means of active processing of thoughts, answers are longer, with greater breadth and depth. If the syntax is structured to engage consideration of positive potential, such as *"What might be some best possible results when doing this presentation?"* or *"If you taught a lesson in which all the students were curious and engaged, what would that look like and sound like?"* participants start to construct a positive future. When the mind is actively engaged in constructing responses, the likelihood of behaving in congruent ways is increased. Constructing a response in our mind is similar to creating an initial draft of a paper. It requires energy *and* focus and results in ownership of the material. We tend to align our actions with what we understand. People grow ownership of their thoughts and actions. Further, in non-threatening contexts, consideration of the others' perspectives is more likely. If people cannot internally or verbally construct positive outcomes, they encounter difficulty with moving forward to accomplish their desired goals.

What we think will happen before it actually happens, that is, our *presupposition*, often influences what actually happens. Similarly, the way we ask questions can either promote reflection or shut down reflection. Presuppositions are powerful because individuals and groups act as if presuppositions are true. Presuppositions can work whether they are negative or positive. The old adage "watch what you say" holds true. Words matter. They are indicators of what people believe.

Statements tend to spark analytic thinking and judgment. Questions, on the other hand, tend to spark creative thinking and generate either a search for answers, a negotiation of meaning, or a continuation of dialogue. Inquiry helps people to construct their own meanings and become partners in helping others to construct the same. "Our educational system focuses more on memorization and rote answers than on the art of seeking new possibilities" (Vogt, Brown, & Issacs, 2003, p. 2). The rush to find quick answers that rely on black and white statements and either/or thinking blocks us from asking the questions that truly opens up reflective thinking and innovation (Vogt et al., 2003). Organizations that grow their ability to sustain change regularly explore questions, such as, *"How is our external environment changing? What internal challenges are mirroring those external changes? What are the gaps between where we are . . . and where we want to be?"* (Heifetz et al., 2009).

Albert Einstein is identified as saying, "If I had an hour to solve a problem and my life depended on the solution, I would spend the first 55 minutes determining the proper question to ask, for [because] once I know the proper question, I could solve the problem in less than five minutes." Inquiry, an active search for understanding, is facilitated by carefully constructed questions. Perkins (1992), in his book *Smart Schools*, wrote, "Learning is a consequence of thinking" (p. 8). Our corollary is: *thinking is a consequence of questions.*

Reframing. Reframing is one of the most powerful tools in a reflective educator's toolbox, which often is sparked in the form of questions. Reframing offers one strategy for challenging our values, beliefs, and assumptions and paving the way for considering alternative explanations and achieving more thorough understandings. Every learning opportunity for each of us can turn into a learning opportunity for all of us. When we close ourselves off to learning from others, we close ourselves off from the experts in the room, thus we close ourselves off to hearing multiple perspectives and to enriching our own skill set.

Peter Block (2002) in his book *The Answer to How Is Yes: Acting on What Matters* suggests a shift in paradigms for reframing questions by moving away from "how" questions and toward "what" and "why" questions. Or, at least, achieving a better balance between these types of questions and "how" questions. He explains that *how* questions carry the risk of passing quickly over what and why questions that are questions that give our lives and our work purpose. *How* questions often presume the answers are "out there," vested in the external world around us, not inside us. *How* questions reinforce our cultural propensity for doing more and more and more! Block explains,

> We live in a culture that lavishes all of its rewards on what works, a culture that seems to value what works more than it values what matters. I am using the phrase "what works" to capture our love of practicality and our attraction to what is concrete and measurable. The phrase "what matters" is short hand for our capacity to dream, to reclaim our freedom, to be idealistic, and to give our lives to those things which are vague, hard to measure, and invisible. (p. 4)

Although it is true that *how* questions can grow from a genuine desire to understand and support something new; *how* questions can also be a defense from taking action and serve to deflect individual responsibility, ownership, and the commitment to address presenting situations.

Block, when interviewed by Sparks (2003), captured the essence of his reframing as "trying to shift the focus from skills and methodology to issues of spirit, of will, of courage" (p. 52). Block does acknowledge that *how* questions, in the right context, are valid and useful. But, too often "they become the primary questions, the controlling question, or the defining questions" (p. 24). Instead he urges questions that are more inviting of our own human deliberations and more empowering of our own free will.

He provides examples of reframing *how* questions to *what* questions such that reflections about personal meaning, purpose, and responsibility are elicited. When someone asks, "How do I get others to change?" the intent is external. How do I get someone else to do something differently? Often this search is in vain because we have very little control over the behavior of other people. Reframing can prove adaptive when the focus shifts to what we can do. More specifically, when the focus shifts from changing something or someone out there (an external focus), to changing something internal (which we can control), there is more possibility of change. Here are some examples Block offered to show ways that subtle changes in questions have the potential for a more productive yield of responses.

From . . . How do you do it?	To . . . Is it worth doing?
From . . . How long will it take?	To . . . What commitment am I willing to make?
From . . . How much does it cost?	To . . . What is the price I am willing to pay?
From . . . How do you get those people to change?	To . . . What is the transformation in me that is required? What is my contribution to the problem I am concerned about?
From . . . How do we measure it?	To . . . What measurement has meaning to me?
From . . . Where else has this worked?	To . . . What do we want to create together?

Source: Block (2002).

Before rushing to *how* questions about reflective practice, such as "*How* do I engage in reflective thinking?" or "*How* can we find time to meet?" or "*How* will this improve my teaching?," try going deeper with *why* and *what* questions to ground the purpose of the work and the end goal you want to achieve. Here are some questions to prompt this type of thinking:

- What is valuable to me about being reflective and thinking about my practice?
- What kinds of questions do I have about my practice?
- What contributions might reflective practice make to our school community?
- What could our team learn if we were to think together in both designing and reflecting on practice?

In Raelin's (2002) model of reflective practice introduced earlier in this chapter, he identifies *being* as the skill that allows one to be in a framing mode. He describes framing as "how we think about a situation, more specifically, how we select, name, and organize facts to tell a story to ourselves about what is going on and what to do in a particular situation" (p. 72). Stories are typically recounted in one frame. Coming to understand stories more fully or in alternative ways often requires *re*-framing. Here are some sample questions to prompt reframing:

- How might I think about this situation differently?
- What am I not considering?
- What judgments and assumptions are blocking alternative ways of seeing this situation?
- Why am I holding onto this view, what function does it serve, what might I be defending?

Tightly held views block us from considering different explanations and from learning new ways of thinking and practice. For learning to occur, firmly entrenched views must be relinquished, or at least, loosened up a bit. "Learning is and should be, on some occasions, a disturbing and unsettling process . . . deep learning involves frame breaking and discomfort" (Butler, 1996, pp. 275–276). It is not unusual, therefore, to enlist another person to coach different ways of thinking about specific situations.

What we assume before something occurs—our presuppositions—can influence the way we ask questions and can either promote reflection or shut down reflection. Presuppositions may work whether they are negative or positive, and are powerful because individuals and groups act as if presuppositions are true. Jay and Johnson (2002) introduce comparative reflection as a way to "reframe the matter for reflection in light of alternative views, others' perspectives, research, etc." (p. 77). They offer specific questions intended to support the reframing process:

- What are alternative views of what is happening?
- How do other people who are directly or indirectly involved describe and explain what's happening?
- What does the research contribute to an understanding of this matter?
- How can I improve what's not working?
- If there is a goal, what are some other ways of accomplishing it?
- How do other people accomplish this goal?
- For each perspective and alternative, who is served and who is not? (p. 77)

When reframing, Jay and Johnson continue, "we can only begin where our thinking tendencies bring us. In other words, we start with where we are. We may even stubbornly hold onto these views for a while convinced that the problem or issues are 'out there.' We blame what is external to us, defending what we know or believe that we know" (p. 77).

They offer three types of reframing that educators could invoke in their practice: "reframing with a lens on relational and human dimensions; reframing that widens the cultural proficiency lens; and reframing that shifts from *how* questions to *what* and *why* questions." They explain, "relational reframing, involves shifting from a dominant academic or cognitive focus when working with students to being more inclusive of relational and human dimensions" (p. 77).

Max van Manen, widely recognized for his technical, practical, and critical reflection typology, writes about the pathic dimension of teaching. Pathic knowledge refers to a "teacher's personal presence, relationship perceptiveness, tact for knowing what to say and do in contingent situations, thoughtful routines and practices" (van Manen, 2002, pp. 216–217). He reminds us about the significance of pathic knowledge in pedagogical effectiveness, which underscores what most educators already know and what accounts for many of their decisions to teach. Relationships and connection are precursors to teaching and learning. Instruction is mediated by personal and relational factors (van Manen, 2002).

Yvette Jackson (2011) offers, "These reflections help us recognize that we all have a cultural frame of reference through which we perceive the world, and it affects how we respond to all of the experiences we encounter" (p. 46). This applies directly to the work of educators with students when there are differences between the race of the students and the teachers. Nationally, the teaching profession is largely populated by Caucasian teachers, although in the past decade the teaching force has become more diverse. Many teachers struggle with discussing culture and race because of the history and legacy of race in the United States (Jackson, 2011). In teams where trust is present and conversational norm includes dialogue that in earnest is intended to deepen understanding and lessen judgement, there is fertile ground to engage in conversations about race and culture. Milner (2003) explains

> . . . introspective behavior could lead teachers to better understand and relate to their students of color because they better understand themselves as racial beings . . . Many White teachers do not see themselves as racial beings and often (idealistically) dismiss notions of race. Reflection in cultural contexts could prove effective as they grapple with ways to better meet the needs of diverse learners. (p. 180)

When we understand and appreciate how our culture influences our thinking and behavior, among staff and with students, we open ourselves to hearing, and learning, and most importantly, understanding multiple perspectives.

Journaling has been recommended as a strategy for adults to privately think through and question themselves about these complex and challenging issues in order to increase awareness of themselves as racial beings before they are ready to discuss them in a group. Milner (2003) poses the following questions to support reframing of culturally grounded conflicts.

- How will my race influence my work as a teacher with students of color?
- How might my students' racial experiences influence their work with me as the teacher?
- What is the impact of race on my beliefs?
- How do I, as a teacher, situate myself in the education of others, and how do I negotiate the power structures around race in my class to allow students to feel a sense of worth?
- How might racial influences impact my interest and my students' interest in the classroom? How might I connect lessons to those interests?
- To what degree are my role as teacher and my experiences superior to the experiences and expertise of my students, and is there knowledge to be learned from my constituents?
- How do I situate and negotiate the students' knowledge, experiences, expertise, and race with my own?
- Am I willing to speak about race on behalf of those who might not be present in the conversation both inside and outside of school, and am I willing to express the injustices of racism in conservative spaces? (Milner, 2003, p. 178)

Response Strategies

Finally, ways we respond to a situation are sometimes more important than the event that happens. Given the number of people, adults, and students, and the multiple ways they show up in school, sometimes, there is little control over what happens. We do, however, have control over how we respond to what happens to us. The more repertoire available to us on how to respond, the more influence we will have in the moment. Having lots of repertoire provides choices, which builds competence and confidence, and can also support remaining mindful and calm.

Henry Ford is reported to have said, "Whether you think you can or think you can't, you are right." Paying attention to the questions we ask and having questions grounded in positive presuppositions helps us to reach positive results. The way we ask questions is one consideration for expanding our inquiry and overcoming the tendency to respond to new or conflicting information in familiar and comfortable ways.

Using the mnemonic SPACE, defined below, can be a supportive structure for inquiry that involves attitudes, knowledge, and skills to respond in productive ways. Respond with SPACE. The way in which a person responds to another person influences thinking and inquiry just as much as questioning does. Costa and Kallick (2000a) use SPACE as an acronym for the response strategies described here.

S	Silence
P	Paraphrase
A	Accepting nonjudgmentally
C	Clarifying
E	Extending

Silence. If the intent of responding is to promote reflective thinking, time must be provided to think and oftentimes requires silence on the part of the listener. A fitting Estonian Proverb says, "Silence is sometimes the answer." We tend to want answers quickly. But, for reflection to occur, less is frequently more. There are skills and strategies to try to help yourself create silence. For some cultures, a person's eyes may look up or move while thinking, and when done thinking, the eyes come back to center and refocus on others. If people are interrupted with more questions or information while in the midst of thinking, they never have a chance to complete their thoughts. Silence allows people to think. Some people may offer clues on this if their eyes follow this pattern and you will know when it is OK to respond when the speaker pauses and her attention and eyes have turned back toward you. Silent counting is another strategy that can help take longer pauses, although it is hard to listen when counting. One teacher hangs up reminder notes in her classroom that say "less talk, more visuals." We can each find ways to remind us that silence is sometimes the first best response.

Paraphrasing requires listening. When listeners paraphrase, the speakers know that they have been heard. Paraphrasing is not *parrot-phrasing*. In other words, listeners should not say exactly the same thing the speakers just said. Such responses can be interpreted as mocking restatements or as lacking sincere interest, which damages rapport. Paraphrasing is taking the main concepts or ideas and saying them back to check out whether or not you have correctly interpreted the meaning and intent of the speaker. Some sentence stems to use are

- Let me see if I understand; you said . . .
- I want to make sure I got all the points; you said . . .
- You said [this], and then you said [this], and then . . . Is that right?

Paraphrasing communicates a genuine attempt to try to understand. If listeners have the wrong meaning, the speaker can correct through restatement.

Accepting nonjudgmentally is the third response strategy. If listeners want a stream of meaningful thoughts from speakers, they must accept what is being said. Interrupting with one's own viewpoints or responding with apparent disagreement will inhibit thinking and sharing. Listeners can accept nonjudgmentally without adhering to the same views. Acceptance and disagreement are communicated not only through words, but through body language and facial expression. Nonverbal communication accounts for the majority of communicative intent. A relaxed body posture, relaxed facial expression, and head and eye orientation toward the speaker provide nonverbal cues that what is being said is being heard and accepted without judgment.

Clarifying is the next response behavior that can increase reflection and metacognition. If a teacher says, "I want students to know the times table," a principal might respond, "How will I know when a student knows the times table?" By asking clarifying questions, teachers can distill in their own minds the desired student responses and indicators of learning. This kind of reflection happens only when people take the time to ask naive questions that internally illuminate the meaning. When asking clarifying questions, be sure to use proper intonation such as approachable voice so clarifying does not sound like interrogating or accusing.

Extending is the last response strategy of the SPACE acronym and one that is easily and frequently used. The following sentence stems, for example, call for an extension of thinking:

- Say more about . . .
- Tell me more about . . .
- Some other possible connections are . . .

Using these stems gives people a chance to extend their thinking beyond what they have already considered and discussed. Another strategy for extending thinking is to ask takeaway questions. For instance, "As we end our conversation, what are the possible connections to the team goals?" Or, "I wonder if we were to ask the students what they thought, how they might respond?" Takeaway questions frequently cause continued thought and reflection. It is not unusual for people to show up the next day and say, "I have been thinking about our conversation and. . . ." This is a sign that people are actively participating in a reflective process.

Trust

A culture of high trust and collaboration among staff members has been identified as one of the cultural norms in schools that have "beat the odds." A study of professional community in 248 elementary schools in Chicago found that, from an interpersonal perspective, "by far, the strongest facilitator of professional community is social trust among faculty members. When teachers trust and respect each other, a powerful social resource is available for supporting the collaboration, reflective dialogue, and deprivatization characteristics of professional community" (Bryk, Camburn & Louis, 1999, p. 767).

Bryk and Schneider (2002) explain that relational trust develops through the day-to-day interactions with people who share some common experience. From an *organizational* perspective

> Specifically, we see relational trust operating as a resource for school improvement in four broad ways. *First,* organizational change entails major risks for all participants . . . *Second,* the transaction costs associated with decision-making are reduced in environments where individuals are predisposed to trust one another . . . *Third,* contexts with strong relational trust benefit from clear understandings about role obligations that are routinely reinforced in day-to-day behavior . . . *Finally,* relational trust sustains an ethical imperative among organizational members to advance the best interests of children. Participants in schools with high relational trust enact an interrelated set of mutual obligations with one another. (p. 33)

Trust is an essential ingredient for humans to work and learn together, especially when in conversations around challenging and complex practice contexts. Miller (2002) reminds us that "Trust is fragile. It is hard to build and easy to destroy" (p. 77). The presence of trust creates a safe, respectful, nonjudging emotional space that holds potential for people to risk being both honest and vulnerable. This should not be confused with someone being told "just trust me." Trust grows over time through repeated interactions with people whose demonstrated behavior indicates that they are trustworthy.

School cultures are created by the networks of relationships within the school. The interconnectedness of the social networks signals how information flows within organizations (Lindsey et al., 2005; Reeves, 2006). Trust fosters relationships that build strong social and learning networks. Listening, without judgment and with empathy, builds trust. A growing body of research offers evidence of how trust is an essential requisite for learning and improvement in schools. A widely cited study of professional community in 248 elementary schools in Chicago found that "by far, the strongest facilitator of professional community is social trust among faculty members. When teachers trust and respect each other, a powerful social resource is available to support collaboration, reflective dialogue, and deprivatization characteristics of professional community" (Bryk, Camburn, & Louis, 1999, p. 767). Why is that the case? Because trust is a cultural norm in learning organizations. In trusting environments we create psychologically safe spaces to learn personally and professionally.

Further, in trusting environments, sharing thoughts, ideas, and feedback is far riskier than keeping ideas to oneself. As we open ourselves to greater risk, the opportunity to realize greater gains increases. When we trust less, we risk less. And, the potential for gains are greatly diminished (Fisher, Ury, & Patton, 2011).

> Trust is perhaps the essential condition needed to foster reflective practice in any environment. If the reflective process is going to flourish in an organizational setting, the participants must be confident that the information will not be used against them—in subtle or not so subtle ways. (Osterman & Kottkamp, 1993, p. 45)

More specifically, Osterman and Kottkamp assert that in order to have open conversations people need to "feel safe, secure, and able to take risks" (p. 45). In essence, they must trust that no harm will come to them if they participate.

Despite realizing the importance of trust and being able to sense when trust is absent, trust is also difficult to define. Megan Tschannen-Moran in *Trust Matters* (2004) defines trust as "one's willingness to be vulnerable to another based on the confidence that the other is benevolent, honest, open, reliable, and competent" (p. 17). Vulnerability is about taking risk, hoping that it results in support and insight. Change and new learning involves risk. Benevolence is experienced when we sense that another person truly cares about us and is trying to make the right decisions based on our needs, shared interests, along with the common good. Trust means being honest and authentic in terms of recalling decisions that were made and agreements that were acted on. It also means feeling safe to disclose when you do not know something or when an error was made. These behaviors lead to greater trust because vulnerability is evident. Trust is also connected to competence. Just wishing to be viewed a certain way by others is not enough, in our teams, we need members who can demonstrate competency in their teaching and ways of working with children and families. Experiencing the competent actions of our colleagues engenders trust toward them.

Trust requires constant attention. Trust and respect need to be operationalized through the practices of group norms. When we act in consistent reliable ways, others can trust us because we show that we are trustworthy. "To get extraordinary things done, people have to rely on each other. They need to have a sense of mutual dependence—a community of people in which each knows that they need the others to be successful" (Kouzes & Posner, 2007, p. 233). We call this interdependence, which is a defining element of authentic practice communities. Without trust, there is no foundation for a relationship focused on learning. Relationships influence the emotion with which one approaches reflection, and as we learned from brain research, emotion controls the gateway to learning (Wolfe, 2010).

What can you do to foster trust? To be in trusting relationships requires acting in trustworthy ways. Bryk and Schneider (2002) explain that *relational trust* develops through interactions with people who share some common experience. Relational trust evolves from social exchanges between and among members of a school community (e.g., teachers, students, parents, and principals). Further, they explain, it is through daily interactions that individuals discern whether or not relational trust exists. Criteria for discerning such trust are identified as respect, competence, personal regard for others, and integrity.

Rob Bocchino, a consultant, facilitator, and teacher (2015, personal communication), explains, "Trust is a combination of trusting and being trustworthy." Trusting someone who is trustworthy is positive. Trusting someone who has violated your trust may not be a smart thing to do. When working with schools in which trust is not a cultural norm, we have often used an activity developed by Bocchino that invites members to reflect on what it means to be *trusting* and also what it means to be *trustworthy*. He then invites participants to identify ways to advance trust in their practice context. We often use this activity as a way to "put the elephant in the room" (metaphorically speaking) in schools where communication has broken down and various groups compete in various ways, with the elephant symbolic of low trust in the school. This is a way to engage staffs in talking about trust using Bocchino's activity. Located in Figure 2.9 is a picture of two intersecting circles, one identified as trusting, the other identified as trustworthy. At the intersection of each of these circles is the word trust, suggesting that trust is a combination of being trusting and trustworthy. To begin, participants are shown a diagram suggesting that trust emerges from the intersection of being trustworthy and trusting, and then they are asked to identify what it means to be *trusting* and *trustworthy*.

The first step in this reflection process is to invite participants to individually write what is means to be *trusting* and what it means to be *trustworthy* (Figure 2.9). Often we then ask that each table group write their collective "definitions" on large poster paper. The papers are then posted so all groups can see what was written. The next step in Bocchino's process is to ask members to reflect on the question, "Which is harder, being trusting or trustworthy? And, what are some reasons for that?" Often for this step we ask that members find two other people, each from a different group, to form triads to talk about this. Being in a group with people who are not typically part of your interaction can feel like a safer context for conversation. As the conversation lulls (or time begins running short), invite the mixed groups to share the essence of their interpretations. Typically participants indicate it is easier to be trustworthy because that is their responsibility, and harder to be trusting because others need to be relied on to not break trust. The final step in this process is for participants to come up with ways they can foster more trust among their team and

Figure 2.9   Trust Activity

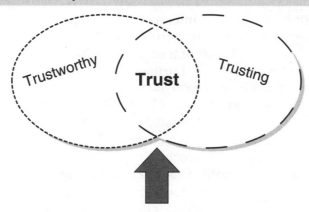

What does it mean to be trustworthy?

What does it mean to be trusting?

Which is easier and why?

In what ways can we further trust?

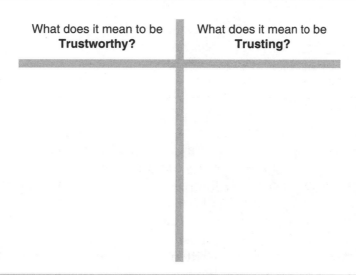

What does it mean to be **Trustworthy?**	What does it mean to be **Trusting?**

Source: Framework and questions from Rob Bocchino, at http://www.heartofchange.com.

 Available for download at **http://resources.corwin.com/YorkBarrReflective**

school colleagues. In some schools, the result has been posting of the strategies in order to serve as a reminder of the shared aspiration and collection of strategies that they can apply to grow a more trusting and trustworthy context of practice together.

Learning increases when trust is present. This is a powerful reason to be intentional about conversational design such that trust deepens within communities of practice. Educators want to make a difference in the lives of young people. That is what drew them to the field of education, and for the most part is why they choose to stay. Continuing to create and refine ways to learn and teach is more probable in trusting cultures. This is especially important in times of uncertainty, which some scholars would suggest is our present period in time. Henry Cloud, in his tweet as cited in Wiseman (2014, p. 150), said "Certainty is one of the weakest positions in life. Curiosity is one of the most powerful. Certainty prohibits learning, curiosity fuels change." We think certainty results in status quo and resists learning. Curiosity, on the other hand, helps seek out answers to new and old problems. Trust and openness aids curiosity. We want to stimulate learning. Stanley Marcus Jr. (2011), also quoted in Wiseman (2014), said "The stimulation of learning is more rejuvenating than any mythical fountain of youth" (p. 217). This is true for staff, students, and community. Trust stimulates learning. Enough said.

Community of Reflective Practitioners

Many years ago, Tom Sergiovanni (1992) wrote about leadership in the context of community. He offered a compelling vision of how, as educators, we could be our best as colleagues and in service to students. He offered this idea: change the metaphor of the school to be a vision of community. Specifically, he wrote,

> We view schools as formal organizations, so we think of leadership in terms of the hierarchical bureaucracy. In communities on the other hand, people are bonded together in different ways, and a different kind of authority compels them to behave as they do . . . ideas are key . . . something a person believes in and feels passionately about is that person's source of authority. (1992, pp. x–xi)

Individual learning begins when a person chooses to be physically and psychologically present in the here and now. Community develops when there is a sense of belonging. Teaching and learning can be very isolating because the physical environment reinforces isolation, and because educators often choose to or by default must work alone because they take their work home at night. Peter Block (2009) has identified a significant challenge in the quest to create an authentic community. Specifically, he wrote,

> The essential challenge is to transform the isolation and self-interest within our community into connectedness and caring for the whole. The key is to identify how this transformation occurs. We begin by shifting our attention from the problems of community to the possibility of community. (Block, 2009, p. 1)

The premise of this book on Reflective Practice is that *learning, which largely grows from reflection on and for practice, is most important*. Growing an interdependent community of practice also is a goal. Strong communities attract others who share the desire to belong in a group whose members are growing, learning, and sharing together. Here are some questions to consider when growing a practice community:

1.   How do we invite others into a learning community?

2.   Who is not in the room who needs to be?

3.   What is the best use of our time together?

4.   What is keeping me from making a full contribution to this group?

5.   How can we keep building trust in order to build an authentic learning community?

Student Learning

Each of the prior sections of this chapter purports to inform and advance practice so that members of school-based communities can successfully guide students to high levels of learning that position them to be successful once they leave our charge. The assumption is that the more adults learn, including the more they learn how to tap the wisdom and support of one another, the more that students will learn. Findings across many research studies have supported the view that when adults learn from practice such that practice improves, the more likely it is that students will realize the benefits. As craftspeople of one of the most complex crafts that exists, teaching and teachers increase student learning. Referring back to Figure 2.2, student learning is, intentionally, at the top. As schools grow to be communities of practice in which ongoing reflective practice is a habituated norm, continuous improvement happens. Students learn more.

CLOSING

We close this chapter with an inspiring practice example that illustrates how the type of transformation Peter Block urges can happen. The growing or renewing of a collaborative culture in schools and districts is not a single event. It requires using both a long leadership lens focused on the larger goal, while also taking shorter steps to build alignments that assure movement toward the final goal—student learning. The skills described in Chapter 2 serve as the foundation for developing and supporting reflective practices at each level of the system.

This practice example, Cascading Equitable Practices in an Urban District, was chosen as the first practice example for this book for two reasons. First, creating systems that lead to equitable student outcomes is morally, ethically, and legally grounded in the work of PreK–12 schools. This is complex work because districts are complex systems and the larger the district, the greater the complexity. There is no one way or one answer to reach this outcome. It requires a laser focus on the desired outcome, our beliefs about students and their potential, a commitment to continually peeling back the layers of the system to identify barriers to equitable outcomes, and a continual leveraging of technical change to create sustainable adaptive outcomes.

Second, as you read the example, consider how the design of the multi-year process illustrates ways that intentionally cascading implementation of changes in structures, strategies, processes, and the use of resources are supported by professional development that integrates reflective practice that results in learning throughout. Notice how the impact on the system is designed to compound over time to change the system's culture and outcomes. This is accomplished by continually reinforcing collaborative norms; grounding the work in the data; supporting individuals to challenge their beliefs and assumptions; focusing on the *why* as well as skill development of the *how* and *what* to facilitate change; and varying the professional development designs based on the goals and movement toward the goals, for example, determining when and whether to have homogeneous versus heterogeneous work groups, introducing new material through articles and videos, then processing individually and collectively, and analyzing complex problems using tools that go beyond the immediate event to identify system needs.

PRACTICE EXAMPLE 2.1

CASCADING EQUITABLE PRACTICES IN AN URBAN DISTRICT

Contributed by Dr. Elizabeth Keenan, Assistant Superintendent,
Office of Specialized Services, Saint Paul Public Schools, Minnesota

Context

The Saint Paul Public Schools (SPPS) is a midsize urban school district in Minnesota. The district is diverse in many ways (refer to Table 2.1) with its students representing multiple races, ethnicities, home languages (students speak over one hundred languages and dialects), and income levels. In 2011, an evaluation of the Special Education department that was completed by an external agency became our call to action. The evaluation findings included that 18.8 percent of SPPS students were identified as having disabilities, while the average in the United States was 12.8 percent and the average in Minnesota was 13.2 percent. SPPS demonstrated a higher special education referral rate (13 percent) than the national rate (6.7 percent).

African American and American Indian students were overrepresented in the referrals for special education evaluations. A disproportionately high percentage of the referred African American students were identified as having emotional behavioral disabilities. The longer that African American and American Indian students with disabilities (SWD) were in special education, the lower their academic proficiency. And, African American students, both with and without disabilities, had the highest suspension and dismissal rates in the district.

Table 2.1   Saint Paul Public School District Demographics (2015)

Student Demographics (N = 37,844)	Percentage of Student Population
Asian	31.9%
African American	30.3%
Caucasian	22.1%
Hispanic	13.8%
American Indian	1.9%
Student Demographics (N = 37,844)	**Percentage of Student Population**
English Language Learners	31%
Free and Reduced Lunch	71%
Special Education	16%

While the issues of racial disproportionality in special education is a national concern, these were *our* data. As a new leadership team, both personally and professionally, we needed to face the issues, ask hard questions, and reflect on our practices to understand the *why* that led to these outcomes. Without beginning by reflecting on *why, what,* and *how,* whatever we did would not lead to lasting change. This meant having deep, critical discussions about the story that our data told us about how students of color were being impacted by district practices. It meant challenging systemic practices to determine what was perpetuating racial inequities. It meant collaborating with other departments in the school district to reflect on the current practices and how they came to be, and then identifying structures and strategies that would build the capacity of both the general education and special education systems to confidently teach a wider range of learners. It meant committing to a new ideal and continually problem solving as we moved forward in making it a reality. It meant an unwavering commitment to equity.

(Continued)

(Continued)

Process

During the 2011–2012 school year, the Office of Specialized Services (OSS) Leadership team (along with administrators from all district departments) participated in *Beyond Diversity*, a two-day training led by the Pacific Educational Group (PEG) to delve into courageous conversations about race (Singleton, 2015). We shared, discussed, and reflected on our personal experiences and beliefs about race. Throughout the year, we continued to discuss issues related to race and equity in our OSS Leadership meeting, using the Courageous Conversation norms to guide our conversations and our work. During our summer data retreat, we committed to a new mission statement: *The Saint Paul Public Schools Office of Specialized Services is committed to reducing the disparity of our most marginalized students, primarily our African American males, by bringing the inequity to the forefront. We will be achieving excellence through equity for all students with disabilities by providing access to culturally responsive curriculum, environment, and instructional practices.* Our goal was to significantly and positively impact the academic and behavioral outcomes for all students with disabilities. We recognized that if we improved the outcomes for our most marginalized students, our African American students with disabilities, we would positively change the system for all students.

With our mission in the forefront, we began a multi-year journey to implement change throughout the district. We knew the end point we wanted to achieve and described it in terms of quantitative goals. While the plan would take multiple years to implement, we expected to see some evidence of progress within one year. We knew that we had to challenge beliefs in order to change practices while simultaneously changing practices in order to challenge beliefs. We had a plan to move forward, but we did not let the planning process paralyze the change efforts. We continually reassessed our data, engaged groups, identified next steps, and allowed the plan to evolve. Over the five years, the changes touched all facets of our system . . . from the purpose of each part of the system; to the people and their roles; to the structures and processes that supported education; to the strategies and skills of the administrators, teachers, and paraprofessionals. The more we understood the downstream impact of some of the current practices, the clearer the next steps became. Figure 2.10 provides a sample of the key changes we made districtwide between 2011 and 2015 to address high priority issues. Access the resource Sample of System Changes That Were Implemented by the Office of Special Services (OSS) to Increase Equitable Outcomes Districtwide at http://resources.corwin.com/YorkBarrReflective to see a detailed explanation of the key changes depicted in Figure 2.10.

Between 2012 and 2015, the OSS leadership team met every other month to revisit our mission and goals; consider new data; and collectively perform school walkthroughs with assistant superintendents, principals, and coaches where we observed both general education and special education service provision. The purpose

Figure 2.10 Sample of Districtwide Changes to Cascade Equitable Outcomes

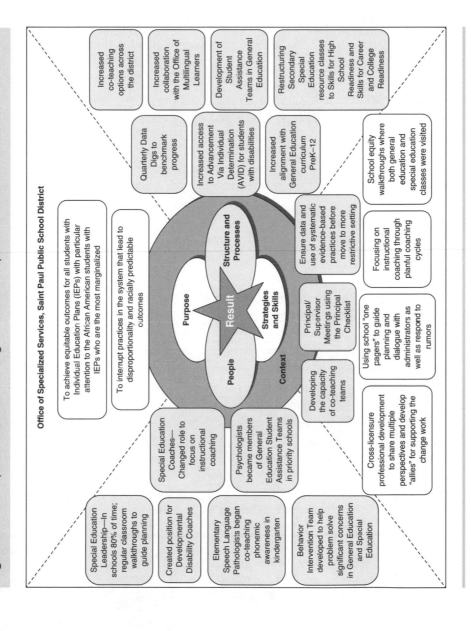

Office of Specialized Services, Saint Paul Public School District

(Continued)

(Continued)

was to identify what was working or not working and build our toolbox to lead the work. Many sessions were facilitated by Deborah McKnight, PEG Special Education Consultant, who previously had been the Executive Director of Special Education in the San Francisco Unified School District. We reflected individually on our priority schools and shared how we were adjusting our supports during the following month. During 2013, we also completed a book study on *The Practice of Adaptive Leadership* (Heifetz, Grashow, & Linksy, 2009) as part of our regular, bimonthly OSS leadership meetings. We read a chapter in advance, then rotated which administrator would summarize the chapter and facilitate the discussion of the text. We continually considered how we were moving away from only making technical changes (e.g., changing the schedule, adding more staff) to making adaptive changes where problems were reframed and patterns identified so more systemic issues were addressed.

We strategically brought personnel groups into the equity professional development (PD) to develop a cadre of equity leaders who touched all levels of the system (see Figure 2.11). Each staff member attended *Beyond Diversity* training to begin conversing more explicitly about race. Starting in 2012–2013, we

Figure 2.11 Cascading Equitable Outcomes Through Strategic Professional Development

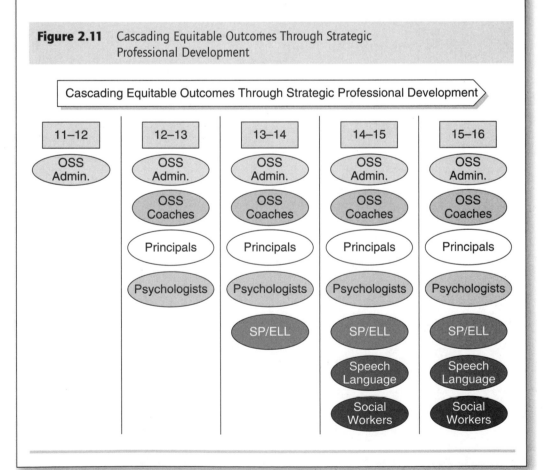

held monthly equity PD for the OSS Coaches. We collaboratively worked with the coaches to shift their responsibilities from being resource coordinators who supported student placement and provided resources and due process support to primarily instructional coaches who coached teachers to deepen their academic and behavioral skills. The equity meeting agendas followed a similar flow that we could duplicate whenever we brought in new groups to the equity PD. Portions of the agendas included:

- Beginning each session with a unique quote that captured the essence of the work as well as reflective questions to connect personal commitments to the participants' actual work in the schools;
- Celebrating successes. The agenda included time for sharing and celebrating the "small wins" where coaches interrupted predictable practices that led to inequitable placements and outcomes;
- Teaching new information and then processing it in small groups so the information was applied to each person's work with schools. For example, participants read journal articles or watched a topical video. Through reflection, they integrated the new information with their experiential knowledge to consider next steps;
- Holding quarterly data digs in which updated district data and trends were shared. Participants then received their individual school data. During weeks following the data digs, OSS administrators met with their coaches to adjust school action plans based on the new data;
- Developing skills in the art of questioning. Learning to ask the right questions that were phrased to promote reflection at the right times was effective for challenging assumptions and perceptions, as well as for deepening the dialogue about race and its impact on decisions. Previously, such conversations tended to shut down talk and options. To support development of dialogic talk, we developed tools to guide question selection and question stems for staff to reference as needed;
- Asking participants to share the challenges they faced and how they addressed the challenges. As peers listened, they learned from the experiences and reflected on the question, "What might I have responded if I were in a similar situation?"
- Having teams reflect using the *Iceberg Model* (Senge, 2012) to dig deeply into issues that tend to remain hidden when isolated events are the focus. Events are at the top of the iceberg . . . the part that is easily visible. Yet, it is what lies below the surface that reveals deeper, often unconscious patterns and trends, systemic structures, and mental models. Digging deep offered the possibility to gain understanding about the reasons for current practice and results, along with insight about what to change. Similarly, Senge's *Ladder of Inference* (2012) is a powerful tool for understanding the ways that individuals quickly move from data to action without making their

(Continued)

(Continued)

thinking conscious or visible. When the process is slowed down, individuals and teams can consider each step of the ladder and refrain from accepting quick conclusions as inevitable. Both tools have facilitated adaptive changes for systems rather than perpetuating systems that simply respond to isolated events;

- Creating heterogeneous table groups during each reflection and learning session, increased the likelihood of learning from a variety of colleagues and understanding multiple perspectives. We followed this by asking "What are some ways you will support one another when you are at meetings in your schools?"; and

- Closing each meeting with a reflective question. First, each participant would write a response, which is to the question prompt. This was followed by a round robin sharing of responses within each table group. The process involved each person sharing her or his response without others interrupting or asking questions until each person at the table had responded. Here are some examples of closing questions: *What are some ways you will continue to model your equity commitments? How will you isolate race in your everyday work? What seems to help you stay engaged in the work? When do you find yourself reaching out to your allies for support?*

About halfway through the 2011–2012 school year, we began including the district psychologists in monthly equity meetings. Their roles were expanding from being exclusively involved in special education evaluations to being involved in evaluations and supporting school-level Student Assistance Teams (SAT). From an adaptive leadership perspective, using OSS expertise to impact systems for early intervention was critical for reducing the percentage of students referred for special education evaluations. The new role of psychologists on the SATs in high priority schools was to support teams in developing a problem-solving approach to student learning concerns, identifying research-based interventions that matched the identified concern, and providing fidelity checks on whether interventions were being implemented. Within six months, we merged the monthly equity sessions to include the Office of Special Services coaches and the psychologists' equity sessions to expand the collective perspectives around complex issues, as well as to develop allies who could support each other during school-based meetings.

In 2013–2014, we continued meeting with the coaches and psychologists and extended our collaborative work to include specialists from the Office of Multilingual Learners (MLL). Our data showed that 30 percent of the students who were found eligible for special services were also eligible for English language services, but rarely were these departments collaborating to align instructional supports. With our MLL partners, we unpacked district data and jointly expanded the co-teaching professional learning sessions for General Education and Special Education co-teachers and General Education and English Language (EL) co-teachers focused on differentiating instruction in the content areas. We also moved to have MLL and OSS teams within schools meet to develop collaborative structures that supported student learning.

In 2014–2015, we cascaded our equity work further to include speech language pathologists (SLP) and school social workers (SSW). Our data analysis indicated that referrals for special education evaluations for students who were EL were high in some schools in comparison to the whole district. These students were referred for speech-language (SL) evaluations. The students who were found eligible for SL often were considered for additional disability categories when re-evaluated. From an equity perspective, the question that needed to be explored was whether these students truly had SL concerns or whether the concerns were typical of English language acquisition for emerging bilingual students. In addition, we shifted the elementary SLPs responsibilities to co-teach in one kindergarten class to strengthen phonemic awareness. This is a critical intervention strategy to reinforce preliteracy skills.

Our SSWs often were involved with students with emotional behavioral concerns. Understanding the SSW role in implementing culturally responsive and research-based interventions, modeling and teaching de-escalation techniques, and building relationships with students and families was central for moving forward with a proactive positive behavioral approach. During 2015–2016, we started the year with the same PD groups as we solidified the changes and assured sustainability. At the midpoint in the year, we combined all four groups (coaches, psychologists, SSW, and SLPs) into a single session. The tables were strategically developed so those working on the same teams sat together. They would collaboratively apply new information to their schools as well as build their relationships in order to support each other when they challenged practices that could lead to inequitable outcomes.

Across the years, we developed various tools for sharing targeted information about priorities, gathering current information, and guiding conversations with school administration and staff. For example, early in the change process, we created "one-pagers" for all of the schools and updated them quarterly. Each one-pager provided the trend data about key indicators for individual schools, including enrollment by disability, enrollment by federal level, state achievement trend data for students with and without disabilities, suspension and dismissal trend data by quarter, special education referral rates, and special education staffing allocations. These one-pagers grounded our actions in current data. While a technical tool, we used the data in adaptive ways to open new conversations, take different perspectives on concerns, and dig deeper into issues. In meetings, we were able to access current data to identify areas of growth or decline, as well as provide facts to counter any rumors. Another tool used in the process was the equity protocol for school walkthroughs. Questions on the protocol included: What did you see? What were your expectations? Given what was seen, what are some next steps in the action plan? A central focus was determining if something was working, whether it was working for all students, or only for some students. If it was the latter, then deeper reflection was needed to understand why this was true and what needed to change to achieve more equitable outcomes for all students. The Principal Checklist for Special Education

(Continued)

(Continued)

provided a list of guidelines for achieving structural and resource alignment across general education and special education services in the school to achieve the priorities. Some items were straightforward on paper, such as assuring that all special education teachers had access to online student databases and had the same curricular resources and technology as their general education peers; but, as we frequently learned, each item required working through other "hidden steps" in district processes. For example, to have access to online class data, special education co-teachers needed to be correctly entered in the student management system and master schedule database. These steps had not necessarily been implemented previously. Others items were more complex and required changes in school processes, including co-teachers having common planning and/or PLC time being built into the master schedule and ensuring that leadership assigned responsibility for the special education paraprofessionals so that their schedules were not idiosyncratic, but well integrated in the system to achieve student outcomes.

Results

Our work continues to be a work in progress. We continue to strive to achieve our mission of equitable outcomes for students with disabilities by staying focused, using data to determine current realities, and reflecting on our work to build a sustainable system. As we learn, we adapt our plan while maintaining the moving parts. Our data are showing positive changes. In 2015, the special education percentage in SPPS was 15.8 percent, a decrease of 3 percent since we started focusing on equitable outcomes. We have seen a 40 percent decrease in the initial referrals to special education. Within this, the referral rate of African American students decreased 41 percent. Within special education, we have reduced the percentage of students identified as having emotional and behavioral disabilities who were in the most restrictive programs from 30 percent to 11 percent, which is a 19 percent decrease. This decrease has occurred concurrent with a focus on increased student engagement, greater access to the general education curriculum that is aligned to higher standards, and a culturally relevant curriculum. We have focused on developing co-taught classes in early childhood through high school. We have increased the number of co-teaching teams from twenty-six in 2011 to over 550 in 2015, a 2000 percent increase. There are issues that continue to challenge us, such as fluctuating suspension and dismissal rates and inadequate academic growth. As we continue on this journey, we remain focused on examining race in all aspects of our work, using data to ground our work and reflecting on the next steps, identifying key areas that can leverage the changes that are needed, and continually challenging the beliefs and systems that support inequities in student outcomes.

 Available for download at http://resources.corwin.com/YorkBarrReflective

We close this chapter with Table 2.2 that offers some key perspectives on designing and facilitating reflective practice. At the end of the next chapter, Chapter 3, we offer a table of considerations for those leading the development of reflective practice communities.

Table 2.2   Perspectives on Designing and Facilitating Reflective Practice

1. **Why would you know how to do this?**
   Teaching started with a teacher in a room with students. It was very isolating. Now the goal is to get professionals together to talk about student learning and practices that advance student learning. This has been an ongoing process for the past twenty-five years. With every opportunity to thoughtfully design, facilitate, reflect on, and receive feedback about our teaching design and facilitation practices, we get better. Growing practice is a team sport!

2. **Create learning experiences where YOU would be an enthusiastic participant.**
   Consider carefully the context, content, and processes that are likely to inspire active engagement and reflection. Time is our most valuable nonrenewable resource. If professionals are going to spend their time in learning conversations, it has to be worthwhile. Professionals must be active participants, not curious bystanders.

3. **The learning is in the conversation.**
   Or, as Susan Scott (2002) offers, "The conversation is the learning." Teach and model conversational norms that create a mindful, listening, reflective space in which every voice is heard and that results in insights that inform continuous improvements in practice. So a question we have is "What are you talking about?" Are the conversations about learning, teaching, and applications to life? If so, the learning is likely to be rich and applicable. Enjoy!

4. **No reflection, no learning.**
   Judi Arin-Krupp stated, "We don't learn from experience, we learn from processing experience." This is the difference between one year of experience twenty-five times over and twenty-five years of cumulative experience that grows and deepens expertise. We learn from those who went before us, from colleagues among us, and from new ideas, technology, and creative uses for our learning.

5. **Less is often more.**
   Reflective practice does not happen in the fast lane. To implement new practices requires re-creating or tailoring existing practice routines. This is mind-FULL work. For each of us, learning happens at a speed that allows us to think about what we are trying to accomplish and also how we do it. Think of the "Goldilocks Theory." Not too fast to overwhelm the learner, not too slow to bore the learner. The learner knows. The encourager or coach, observes carefully and tries to help nudge success along, always reinforcing how challenging it is to un-learn old practices and re-learn new practices. This is the challenge that educators face. We are better off learning about and implementing deeply a few things that have the potential to matter for students.

(Continued)

Table 2.2   (Continued)

6. **Context matters. Implementation is particular.**
   Each person, team, school, and district has similarities *and* differences. Tailoring practices for each unique context is required. Relationships are extremely important. If learners do not believe the learning will be of benefit, they tend to give it less attention and not take it seriously. One of our goals as educators is to make the case, help learners see the context, and know there are applications to their learning.

7. **Structure is your friend, along with a whole lot of nurture.**
   Learning designs for moving forward new practices require intention about the structures in which participants learn and the processes that support participants as they learn about and learn how to do new practices. The *why*, *what*, and *how* all must be addressed. Kids and adults need boundaries. In student surveys, they tell us they want the teacher in control. Structures provide safety—both physical and emotional. Within safe structures great learning can occur by practicing some of the foundational strategies addressed in this chapter. Note: Because this is such a significant understanding we address it again in the next chapter as well.

8. **Almost always: smaller is better and less is more.**
   The smaller the group (three to five) the more pressure and opportunity there is for each member to speak and be heard. Fewer agenda items also hold potential for rich learning conversations. Be sure members sit facing one another and invite each to write their thoughts before sharing. This helps to both clarify one's own thinking and to be present when others speak. It is better to have space for all to contribute than have a jam-packed agenda to hurry through. This is one of the reasons decisions that are made do not stick. People want to be heard. When they are not heard, they leave or stay away from the conversation physically and/or emotionally.

9. **Go visual!**
   A picture of some kind, well sketched, can help clarify the inherent complexity and messiness of practice. Yes, a picture is worth a thousand words. Going visual also helps discuss the ideas instead of the person presenting the idea.

10. **Celebrate success!**
   Let's face it, we don't do this very well. We are suggesting we celebrate each and every success. Successes are hard-won evidence that who we are, what we do, and how each of us perseveres matters. Onward kindred spirits!

Figure 2.12 Chapter Reflection Page

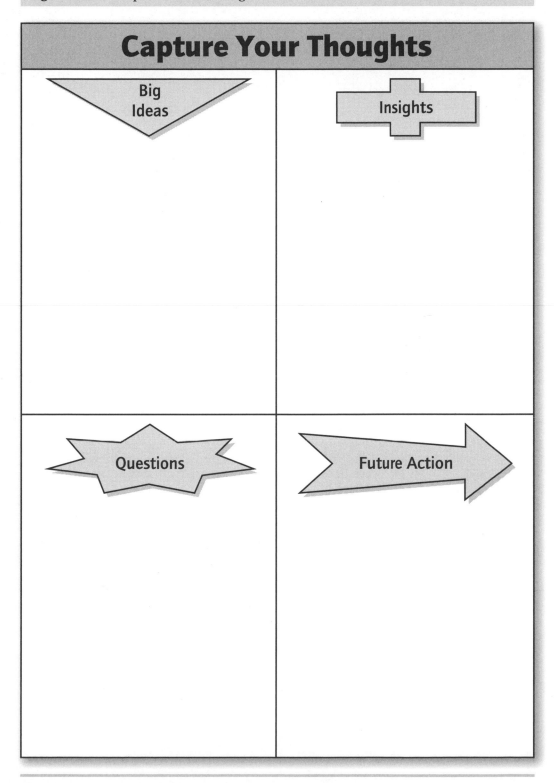

3

Leading Reflective Practice

We are a community of possibilities, not a community of problems. . . . We currently have all the capacity, expertise, programs, leaders, regulations, and wealth required to end unnecessary suffering and create an alternative future.

—Peter Block, *Community: The Structure of Belonging*, 2009

The opening quote by Peter Block serves as an inspiration for all of us who aim to "do good" in service to children, families, and communities by advancing teaching, learning, and an ethic of care in schools. This quote also can invoke questions and doubts about our capacity to do so.

We firmly believe that the "collective we," that is, the educators, family, and community members along with the young people themselves are enough—situated together in a shared community of practice, we *can* and *do* create the conditions that enrich the learning lives of our students. By doing so, we strengthen our surrounding communities at large. All of us learning and working together are investing in a brighter, more inclusive, and more equitable future for everyone. What could be more compelling, inspiring, gratifying . . . and challenging than that?

Authors' Note: We wish to acknowledge the contributions of Dr. Audrey Murray to this chapter. Her doctoral theses significantly informed and enriched our understanding of boundary spanning as a core leadership practice.

The work of leading reflective practice and growing reflective school communities is collective work that doesn't happen in the fast lane. A commitment to continuous improvement requires ongoing cycles of reflective practice: design → practice → reflect → learn → adjust → get better, and repeat. Part of the work of leaders is to weed out practices that no longer satisfactorily serve the learning mission of schools, and to plant, nurture, and grow practices likely to advance student learning. Gardening serves perfectly as a metaphor for Leading Reflective Practice.

Designing and facilitating processes that support continuous adult learning in schools is no less mindful or challenging than the work of facilitating student learning. Learning and becoming comfortable and effective with new practices takes much cognitive fuel, whether you are five years old or fifty years old. Reflecting on what works well and why something works deepens our understanding of practice and grows our effectiveness. This is not work done in the fast lane or alone. There is an African proverb that applies here: *If you want to go fast, go alone. If you want to go far, go together.* Our view? Let's grow together.

This chapter, Leading Reflective Practice, is new to this third edition of *Reflective Practice for Renewing Schools.* Previous editions focused almost exclusively on the core work of designing structures and facilitating reflective practices to figure out which seemed to hold strong potential to advance, even accelerate, both educator practice and student learning. We did not emphasize sufficiently the ways that this work is led and who shares in the leading.

We use the term "leader" as inclusive of both formal leaders, including administrators and teachers who serve as curriculum leads, instructional coaches, site leadership team members, and also informal leaders, including teachers and other service staff who directly support students.

As a field of practice, we have grown in our understanding about why and how teachers are one of the most powerful sources of influence. They are situated in horizontal networks among comparable colleagues in their schools. Every day they associate with other teachers who teach similar students or similar subject areas. Together, they mine and share their tacit knowing about what seems to work and why. Horizontal influence is more powerful than hierarchal influence (Reeves, 2006), in part because practicing peers are viewed as credible sources of ground-level wisdom. They are also more accessible to one another on a daily basis.

In field studies, we also have learned more about ways that teachers, who are formally identified as leaders, serve as effective partners for improving practice. A comprehensive review of two decades of research on teacher leadership (York-Barr & Duke, 2004) offers some useful, although not surprising, findings. Teacher leaders who were valued by their peers and administrators were identified as learning-oriented, effective with students, and able to see both the big picture and the micro level of practice. Beyond their value as excellent teachers, they understood the impact of school culture and leadership on teaching and learning. Teacher leaders also were viewed as effective at establishing trusting and collaborative relationships with teaching peers. These characteristics made them both valued and credible learning partners. Clearly, administrators and teachers both must share the differentiated work of leading the ongoing growth of reflective practice communities.

We have organized this chapter around ten *Guidelines for Leading Reflective Practice*. They are offered as anchors for leaders charged with advancing teaching and learning. Practice contexts, of course, vary significantly among schools, grades, and subject areas. This makes for nuanced work in the growing reflective practice communities, requiring leaders to continually reflect "on," "in," and "for" action to monitor, adjust, and sustain momentum for continuous learning within their respective communities of practice. After each principle is identified and described, related reflection questions are offered.

GUIDELINES FOR LEADING REFLECTIVE PRACTICE COMMUNITIES

Stay Grounded in the Why

As mentioned in Chapter 1, teaching is among the most intense "hot action" of professions. A diverse community of young people show up every day in school, each with her or his learning strengths, interests, challenges, and aspirations. Each influenced by the guidance, care, and expertise of teachers and other direct service staff members to learn well and grow confident in their capacity as learners.

Understandably, so much energy is directed toward the "what" and "how" of teaching and leading, that the "why" can fall off the radar. It is the "why," however, that likely inspired most of us to become educators, and it is the "why" that sustains us in this challenging vocation. Our collective work is rich with meaning and inspired by visions of a more equitable world. This is why most of us continue to show up in schools.

In a 2013 TED Talk, Simon Sinek asserted that inspired leaders stay vigilant about *why* they do what they do. He argued that we are motivated by purpose. What are some reasons you chose to work with young people in schools? As you reflect back on your day, what were some interactions that energized you? What keeps you grounded in that deep, meaning-*full* space that affirms who you are as an educator and why you do what you do? When we see students engage, make connections, and develop a sense of power in their lives, we cheer them on and feel grateful and honored for the opportunity we have been granted to do good in the world, to be integrally involved in growing the next generation of grown-ups. Staying grounded in the "why" energizes us to sustain the effort required for the "what" and "how" of teaching and leading.

REFLECTIONS ON YOUR "WHY"

What's your *why*?

What are some ways to stay grounded in your *why*?

What do you see in your work with young people that affirms your *why*?

Go-eth Not Alone

If ever there was a shining example of the fallacy of rugged individualism, it would be attempting to grow reflective practice communities on your own. The work is too complex and too demanding to go it alone. Each of us needs partners to support us as we plant, nurture, and continually reflect on the growing of our communities of practice. Trusted partners create a space for authentic reflection and learning . . . a relational space to be who we are and to not be judged. A thinking space with people who care about us and the work we do . . . people who will listen to our thinking, share back what they hear, and when invited, offer their thoughts and ideas so that we can reflect and plan together. Partnerships energize us through conversation and shared reflection. Partnerships calm us down because we are not alone. We are not supposed to be.

REFLECTIONS ON POSSIBLE LEARNING PARTNERS TO SUPPORT YOUR LEADERSHIP

Who are or might be reflective practice partners for you in this work?

What are your greatest areas of learning interest?

What would be some times, places, and ways to regularly connect around your growing work? Ways to talk about what you are growing, how you are growing your community of practice, and what you are learning about this significant work?

Leadership Is Influence . . . for the Good

Leadership is not simply about getting people to do things, it is about getting them to want to do things . . . It is about achieving influence, not seeking compliance. (Haslam, Reicher, & Platow, 2011)

Specifically *what* and *how* to influence for the good, once again, depends on the specific contexts of practice. Leaders continually scan their contexts to know what is being taught, how teaching happens, ways that students engage and learn with adults and peers, and also ways that adults interact with and support one another. In some ways, every classroom, team, and school is similar, and in other ways, very distinct. What educators observe in their particular learning spaces with their particular group of young people informs next targets for growing their learning communities. Look back at Table 1.1 in Chapter 1, also available on the companion website (http://resources .corwin.com/YorkBarrReflective), for a series of questions to guide observations about student, teacher, and team interactions that can assist in grounding your understanding of current practices and inform next areas for growth.

When considering *how* to influence for the good, Lunenberg (2012), drawing on the original work of French and Raven (1960), offers insight about sources of power for influencing organizational members. Of particular relevance were findings that *personal power* (relationship) was more influential than *organizational power* (hierarchy). One significant source of personal power was identified as *expert power.* This refers to "a person's ability to influence others' behavior because of recognized knowledge, skills, or abilities" (Lunenberg, p. 3). In other words, the more credible a person is in terms of their knowledge and practice expertise, the more likely he or she is to be effective influencing others to join in the work. Another source of influence is known as *referent power*, which is described as "a person's ability to influence others' behavior because they like, admire, and respect the individual" (Lunenberg, p. 4). Knowledge about content and adeptness at relationship pave a pathway for influence.

REFLECTIONS ON ORGANIZATIONAL AND PERSONAL POWER SOURCES

Consider Lunenberg's findings about two sources of leadership influence, organizational and personal power. Reflect on recent school improvement or professional learning work in your school that you view as having been reasonably successful.

- How did organizational power support this work?
- What were some ways personal power supported this work?
- What are some areas related to these two forms of power that you would like to learn more about? How could you make this happen?
- Who among your colleagues could support you in growing your means of influence?
- Knowing how you learn best, how might you get started?

Relationships Are the Influence Pathway

In organizations, real power and energy are generated through relationships. The patterns of relationships and the capacities to form them are more important than tasks, functions, roles and positions.

—Margaret Wheatley, *Leadership and the New Science*, 1992

The quote above reinforces the perspective that the quality of relationships is one of the strongest determinants of whether and how well communities of practice learn, grow, and serve the young people in their charge. Shared purpose attracts members to join together. Relationships form the community in which ideas for continuous improvement are vetted and continually shaped to "fit" particular learning contexts. We are blessed when we find ourselves in this type of open, generative space, and inspired to create such a community when it does not exist . . . *yet.*

The terms "influence" and "relationship" strike some leaders as too soft or too subtle an approach, especially when there is so much to improve and so little time to do it. "Get going, already! Just get it done!" For us, it recognizes the autonomous nature of humans. Mutual respect and shared interests go a long way toward enrolling participation. Mostly, we cannot make others behave in ways we view as more effective just by telling or asking them. Instead, it is incumbent on leaders (e.g., administrators, teacher leaders, community leaders) to articulate *why* changes are warranted, along with ideas for *what* is likely to make a difference and *how* we might go about this together . . . just as we do with students.

REFLECTIONS ON STRENGTHENING RELATIONSHIPS WITH STUDENTS AND STAFF

In what ways do you show up with students that draws them to you?

As you reflect on your practice life with colleagues, in what ways are you an attractive force?

What might be some areas of growth in your collegial relationships to continue building and strengthening your community of practice?

How do you create and sustain your energy for teaching, learning, and leading both young people and colleagues? What are sources of renewal away from your work?

Listening Is the Relationship Pathway

Speech is a joint game between the talker and the listener against the forces of confusion. Unless both make an effort, interpersonal communication is quite hopeless. (Weiner, 1998, p. 92)

Weiner's assertion makes it clear that successful communication requires joint effort from each person who is part of the conversation. He states that reflection is also a joint effort, even if it is internal. Individually, we have to listen to our internal thoughts and draw on our experiential resources to make adjustments.

Casual observation of conversation often suggests that listening is both an undervalued and underpracticed skill. Too often we hear verbal interruptions and see nonverbal dismissals, such as looking away, rolling eyes, and even physically moving away. Our nonverbal actions are powerful sources of communication about our interest or lack thereof in both the person communicating and his or her perspectives.

When we look at research on listening by Burley-Allen (1995), we find that communication is 9 percent writing, 16 percent reading, 35 percent talking, and 40 percent listening. Undoubtedly, each of us could benefit from deepening our heart and mind presence to ground better listening. If we listen, we understand more, the other person feels understood at a deeper level, and clarity of the issue improves. Moreover, listening causes us to ask better questions, clarify ambiguous terms and meanings, and consider more possibilities because of deeper thinking.

David Perkins (1992) from Harvard said, "learning is a consequence of thinking." We propose two corollaries: (1) thinking is a consequence of questions; and (2) thinking is a consequence of listening. Listening creates possible questions to clarify, understand, and create patterns. Listening and questions save time by illuminating areas of possible misunderstanding before making snap judgments. Listening is a core relationship practice, which also makes it a core leadership practice. Listening does not infer or require agreement with what a person is saying, but it does require respect and interest. Listening, done well, is an active interpersonal space of connection and care. When people feel heard, they feel valued. Listening creates a bridge between people. In words attributed to the Dalai Lama, "When you talk, you are only repeating what you already know. But if you listen, you may learn something new."

REFLECTIONS ON HONING LISTENING SKILLS

In what types of situations is it especially important to hone your listening abilities?

What are some things you listen for that offer insights about leading learning and development work in your context of practice?

What are some ways you support yourself to remain present and attentive?

How do you know when it is appropriate and helpful to verbally engage? For example: paraphrase or offer an open question?

When, despite your desire to do so, you cannot take the time to listen, how do you gracefully and with care express your dilemma?

Culture Is the Work

Culture is both a dynamic phenomenon that surrounds us at all times, being constantly enacted and created by our interactions with others and shaped by leadership behavior, and a set of structures, routines, rules, and norms that guide and constrain behavior. (Schein, 2004, p. 1)

Edgar Schein, now a distinguished elder, has been one of the most influential leaders in the field of organizational leadership and culture. He explains how leadership and organizational culture are inextricably linked. Specifically he writes,

When we examine culture and leadership closely, we see that they are two sides of the same coin; neither can really be understood by itself. On the one hand, cultural norms define how a given nation or organization will define leadership. On the other hand, it can be argued that the only thing of real importance that leaders do is to create and manage culture; that the unique talent of leaders is their ability to understand and work with culture; and that it is an ultimate act of leadership to destroy culture when it is viewed as dysfunctional. (Schein, 2004, pp. 10–11)

Often, culture is described simply as *the way we do things around here.* When we notice that we are not getting desired results, we reflect on what we have been doing and identify changes to "how we do things around here." That is, we begin to shift culture. Such re-culturing is not easily done, no matter how obvious and important it seems to leaders. Change disrupts existing, subconscious expectations, structures, routines, practices, and thought systems. It makes daily routines, temporarily, more mindful and effortful. As Richard Carlson (2006) has taught us, "thought systems do not like to be tampered with. They reflect the way an individual or a collection of individuals, see the world" (p. 31), and, by extension, how they see themselves in the world. Changing how we think often takes more than a nudge.

So, how do cultures shift to become more collaborative, generative, and effective? Learning together in new ways is one way forward. Initially this requires intentionally designed conversational structures, processes, and norms that essentially teach members new ways to reflect, learn, and practice . . . new ways to think and talk together, such as those described in the previous chapter.

When educators think and learn together, they become exposed to a wider array of perspectives (i.e., thought systems) and a wider array of practices from which they may choose to add or deepen their own thought systems and practice repertoires. Further, they deepen their understanding and appreciation for learning together and mining collective wisdom of practice. Together, they learn and grow their practice repertoire for more effectively engaging the minds and hearts of students. When students learn well, teachers grow in their sense of efficacy, that is, knowing what they are doing is making a positive impact on student learning . . . knowing that who they are and what they do as teachers makes a difference.

Reflecting on practice provides feedback about effectiveness of particular learning practices in particular learning contexts. This, in turn, informs decisions about staying the course, making adjustments, or seeking different approaches for creating and sustaining momentum for student learning. Changing how we "do things around here" is not easily accomplished and often not welcome work, especially in education where tight schedules constrain opportunities to reflect, learn, and adapt accordingly, or to learn new replacement practices.

In this chapter, we describe two ways for thinking about changing "how we do things around here." First, we summarize findings from a study by Tom Guskey (1986) from almost 30 years ago, but the results hold true today. Second, we draw from a more recent source, the book *Switch: How to Change Things When Change Is Hard* (2010), written by the Heath brothers, Chip and Dan. Finally, we offer a recent example from a middle school principal and literacy coach.

The Guskey study sought to determine the order by which change in practice was likely to occur. He reviewed a substantial body of research on changing ways of practice and ways of thinking, most of which studied the relationship between three elements of the change process: teacher practices, teacher beliefs and attitudes, and change in the learning outcomes of students. Some of the studies, wisely, also considered the professional development that supported teacher learning of new practices.

Guskey grounded his study in two different theories of change, each with the same three elements. One theory of change was that changes in *teacher practice* would create changes in *student learning*, which would, in turn, impact *teacher beliefs* about the effectiveness of the practices used. The second theory of change posited that *changes in beliefs* would alter *changes in practice*, which would *impact student learning*. Results of the study showed that when teachers used new practices that resulted in improved student learning there was a change in teacher beliefs about the value of the practices employed. Guskey concluded, "The point is that evidence of improvement (positive change) in the learning outcomes of students generally precedes and may be a pre-requisite to significant change in the beliefs and attitudes of most teachers" (p. 7).

He also offered implications for professional learning that have, almost 30 years later, stood the test of time: "(1) recognize that change is a gradual and difficult process for teachers; (2) ensure that teachers receive regular feedback on student learning progress; and (3) provide continued support and follow-up after the initial training" (pp. 9–10). Although the implications of the Heath brothers' and Guskey's work may seem like common sense, often it is not common practice.

One useful assertion about change articulated by the Heath brothers (2010) in their book *Switch: How to Change When Change Is Hard* is that "Clarity dissolves resistance" (p. 72). Although this statement might sound oversimplified, it does make a significant point for reflective practice leaders to clarify, as much as possible, what, how, when, and where specific new practices will be learned and used. A well-articulated plan for change offers some reassurance that there has been considerable thought about how best to guide teacher learning aimed at improving student learning. And also remain cognizant that specifics of learning about and learning how to implement practices will vary somewhat across application contexts, such as elementary versus secondary schools, primary versus intermediate grades.

To teach about their change theory, the Heath brothers use the metaphor of a *person* riding an *elephant* that is navigating along a *path* (see Figure 3.1). The rider symbolizes our human *analytical system* that needs a strong rationale for *why* change is necessary. The *elephant* symbolizes our human *emotional system*, which recognizes that mostly humans don't like to change,

Figure 3.1   Visual Depiction of a Heath and Heath (2010) Change Metaphor: A Person Riding an Elephant Along a Path

Source: Adapted from Heath & Heath (2010). Images courtesy of clipart.com.

 Available for download at **http://resources.corwin.com/YorkBarrReflective**

preferring the comfort and ease of existing ways of doing things, sometimes regardless of how effective those ways are. The *path* represents the surrounding *context or culture* that holds both supports and constraints for change. In a School Briefing Interview in the *Audio Journal* about *Switch*, Chip Heath stated, "Very often when people look like they are resisting change, it may be that they are just clueless about how to change."

Similar to the assertions from the Guskey (1986) study, the Heaths suggest that leaders must make clear *why* change is necessary, acknowledge the challenges of changing practice, and ensure support for learning and implementing new practices, including reasonable clarity about *why*, *what*, and *how.* An image drawn from the natural world about the power of culture was written by Peter Senge and his colleagues Scharmer, Jaworski, and Flowers (2004, p. 2) and shared in Figure 3.2.

Figure 3.2   An Image From Nature About the Power of Culture

It's common to say that trees come from seeds. But how could a tiny seed create a huge tree? Seeds do not contain the resources needed to grow a tree. These must come from the medium or environment within which the tree grows. But the seed does provide something that is crucial: a place where the whole of the tree starts to form.

As resources such as water and nutrients are drawn in, the seed organizes the process that generates growth.

In a sense, the seed is a gateway through which the future possibility of the living tree emerges.

Source: Senge, Sharmer, Jaworski, & Flowers (2004, p. 2). Image courtesy of clipart.com.

 Available for download at **http://resources.corwin.com/YorkBarrReflective**

REFLECTIONS ON CREATING
CULTURES THAT ADAPT TO CHANGE

As you think about the statement by Edgar Schein that "leadership and culture are two sides of the same coin," how do you make sense of this assertion in your own practice?

(Continued)

(Continued)

What are some cultural norms, that is, "ways we do things around here" in your practice context that are advancing practice in ways that are good for students? And, what are some cultural norms that interfere with the improvements in practice you know to be important?

Implementation Is Particular to Context

Arguably, the work of everyone in a school district is in some way intended to support the mission of reaching and teaching each student who shows up. Each of us does our part, doing our best to ensure a meaningful and productive educational experience that grounds a successful path through life. The overarching purpose is shared, but the specific type of work varies among "levels" or "communities" in the system.

Shown in Figure 3.3 is a hierarchal representation of a school district. Leaders in the central office aim to align resources, including fiscal, personnel, space, and equipment, to the needs of individual school sites. Administrative leaders at the school level determine how best to allocate resources to support ground-level teaching and student learning. Site learning leadership teams, whose members represent varied parallel groups in the school, identify site development priorities and create clarity around focused practices: the what, how, where, and when of student learning. Smaller teams form around designated groups of students, for example, grade levels, language learning emphases, or special services. These are considered "affinity" groups because members have in common similar work, and are therefore appropriately positioned to support one another.

Each district, school, classroom, teacher, and student has similarities and also differences. Nuanced practice is required. Specific to the arena of teaching and learning, translation and tailoring is almost always required. Decisions about curricular resources, for example, are made centrally, although often with input from school-based personnel. With new resources in hand, school-level practitioners must become familiar with the resources *and* figure out how to use and adapt the resources given variability in class size, staffing to support small strategy or language-alike groups, and availability of special education and language teachers to co-teach.

Our point that implementation is particular to context is apparent in an exploratory study by Audrey Murray (2013). The purpose of the study was to gain insight into the work of instructional leaders who are based in central offices, and serve as links between layers and places in the system by partnering with school-based administrators and teachers to

Figure 3.3 Hierarchal Representation of Leading and Learning
Layers Within Schools Systems

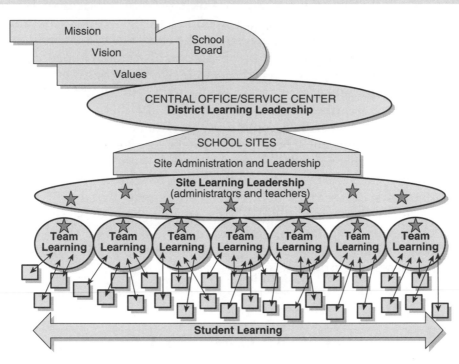

support work with students. Participants in Murray's study perceived themselves as sensemakers who help others understand new ideas and practices in teaching and learning. Their leadership practice varied widely, according to the level or place of the work.

Using two non-probability sampling methods, Murray's study included twelve participants distributed across five Midwestern school districts, four males and eight females. Data for the study were gathered through in-depth interviews with study participants. Overall, the participants perceived themselves as teachers who influence other district educators by helping them make sense of new ideas in teaching and learning and what is going on in various parts of the school district structure. They served as both sensemakers and information brokers. Among the leadership practices the participants valued most were the continuous deepening of their own expertise, the gathering and sharing of information across levels or places in the system, and maintaining an unwavering focus on making sense of teaching and learning.

Murray grounded her study in two related concepts: boundary spanning (Tushman & Scanlon, 1981) and information brokering (Burch & Spillane, 2004; Wenger, 1998), to understand the work of participants in her study. Boundary spanning describes the use of informal communication networks across formal organizational boundaries. Boundary spanners perform the essential function of linking levels or places within the system. Information brokering is embedded in the work of boundary spanners. Information brokering refers to the exchange of information for the purpose of professional learning. Examples of boundary spanning and brokering from Murray's research include working between different communities of practice, serving as a bridge to new ideas and understandings, collecting and disseminating information about change, translating information into terms that community members may be particularly likely to use, and linking schools to information and expertise in the central office or in other schools.

Next, we offer an in-depth example that describes one way school administrators can remain relatively up-to-date with current instructional practice by participating in a Learning Lab process. Specifically, instructional leaders who are based in their central office engage in the boundary spanning work to deepen their own expertise through an authentic teaching opportunity.

PRACTICE EXAMPLE 3.1

BOUNDARY SPANNING INCREASES LEARNING BY CENTRAL OFFICE LEARNING LEADERS ABOUT MIDDLE SCHOOL LITERACY PRACTICES

Contributed by Dr. Tyrone Brookins, Principal, and Ms. Mary Green, Literacy Coach, Saint Paul Public Schools, Minnesota

Context

Several years ago the Saint Paul Public School District in Minnesota created a school support structure referred to as Vertical Teams. Each Assistant Superintendent created a team of central office-based teaching and learning personnel whose work was to tailor support to specific schools based on particular school interests and needs. Vertical team members had varied practice backgrounds and were resources to support staff in a designated number of schools in the district. Learning teams included staff with experience in areas such as special education, English learning, behavior, and school psychology.

We were receiving numerous requests to visit our middle school to observe our approach to literacy workshop, which was only recently introduced in our middle school, but seemed a promising practice. We discussed options for fulfilling this request and decided that interested persons coming to "watch" wasn't a strong teaching strategy

Table 3.1   Student and Staff Demographics for This Middle School

Student Demographics (*N* = 771)	Percentage of Student Population
African American	30.6%
Asian American	43.2%
Hispanic American	16.6%
Native American	1.2%
White	8.43%
Staff Demographics (*N* = 115)	Percentage of Staff Population
African American	20.0%
Asian American	6.1%
Hispanic American	3.5%
Native American	0.0%
White	70.0%

for the visitors. It also had the potential to feel evaluative instead of collaborative. If the intent was for the Vertical Team members to learn the practices, then they would learn best by first observing the practices in a real classroom of students, and then by partnering with another Vertical Team member to co-design, co-teach, and then collectively debrief their authentic learning experience. A "Learning Lab" model was chosen for use.

Participants

In this instance, the Vertical Team members who participated were the Assistant Superintendent, Special Education Supervisor, Assistant to the Superintendent, Coordinator of Teacher Development and Evaluation, District Literacy Coach, and Director of Peer Assistance and Review.

Learning Lab Process

Orient → Observe → Reflect → Prep → Teach → Reflect

1. **7:30A Orientation**: We met with the Vertical Team members in our school conference room. The area superintendent and an external coach also were

(Continued)

(Continued)

present to partner in the facilitation of this process. Using words and graphics on poster size papers, we described the purpose of the session as an opportunity to learn about Literacy Workshop by means of background knowledge, observation, authentic practice, and reflection on both the process and the learning that emerged.

More specifically, we described the mini-lesson purposes and structures, commonly referred to as the "architecture of the mini-lesson": connection → teach → active engagement → link. Key points for each component of the mini-lesson were illustrated on large poster paper, including use of sticky notes that provided specific language cues that demonstration teachers and eventually the Vertical Team members would likely use when it was their turn to teach.

We emphasized six qualities of the demonstration for observers to notice:

- Teaching points include the skill (what to learn) and strategy (how to learn)
- Demonstrating for students what the teaching points are
- Thinking aloud during the demonstration
- Repeating the teaching point with consistent language
- Presenting a predictable problem (the students often have) and model how to get out of the problem
- Setting up the students to watch for a specific learning point using language like "Watch as I . . ." and wrap up at the end with "Do you notice . . ."

Because the Vertical Team members would be co-teaching a mini-lesson after their observation, they paired up prior to the observation and decided which of the four mini-lesson structures each would plan for and then teach.

2. **8:15A: Observation**: Transition to the middle school reading teacher's classroom. Observe and take notes on the mini-lesson.

3. **8:45A: Reflect and Prep:** Return to conference room. Vertical team partners reflected on what they observed and learned from the observation. Each then drafted plans for how they would teach their respective components of the mini-lesson in the same classroom, but with a different group of students.

4. **9:30A: Team Teach:** Vertical team partners return to the reading teacher's classroom. Each pair goes to a different table of students. Vertical Team partners teach the mini-lesson.

5. **10:00A: Overall Reflections:** Vertical team members return to the conference room to debrief their experiences and to talk about potential uses for this approach to learning for Vertical Team members.

Sampling of End of Session Reflections by Vertical Team Members

Learning Content Reflections

Question 1: Overall, what were some of our key "learnings" about the architecture (structures and processes) of the mini-lesson? Draw from your observation notes and your opportunity to teach the lesson.

- Breaking down the architecture of a mini-lesson was helpful to understand what should be covered in the ten minutes of the mini-lesson
- Key parts of the mini-lesson: transitions, intentional language, common language that should be used in all classrooms
- The importance of sticking to one focus. It helps in keeping the lesson tight
- I've not had Reader's Workshop PD in many, many years. So the orientation helped to prepare me for the observation
- Organization of architecture of the mini-lesson, timing, transitions between sessions

Question 2: Consider specifically the "watch for" items identified in the table. Which were most evident? Are there some that prompted your questions or wonderings?

- I wonder more about the predictable problem and how to bring that out further in the mini-lesson
- The specific key language to "look for" triggered me to be watching for the "look fors"
- "Connect" was relevant to students' lives and allowed them to be engaged right from the beginning
- I think all four components were evident
- Thinking through the demonstration aloud. Hearing key phrases before observing the mini-lesson gave me specifics to look for that assisted in strengthening my understanding of the four components

Question 3: What questions are circling around in your mind about the design and implementation of mini-lessons? And/or questions about how, as an instructional leader, you might learn more about the content focus of this experience?

- I am ready to see the next portion of how this applies to the student practice, strategy groups, conferencing, etc.
- I understand the design fully now. I am thinking about how to implement this in other content areas
- How to help teachers bridge old pedagogy with this means of instruction
- I would like more PD on Reader's/Writer's Workshop as a whole

(Continued)

(Continued)

Learning Process Reflections

Question 1: In what ways did this particular "Learning Lab" process deepen and sharpen your understanding of the mini-lesson architecture?

- It gave me the opportunity to ask my questions, have specific "look-fors" while observing, and then a structure to practice
- I have not had professional development on the mini-lesson. So the components of orient, observe, and reflect/prep were very informative
- In all ways through experience
- The breaking down of the architecture, getting to see and practice it was very informative as to what the teachers go through
- It was great to be able to see the mini-lesson dissected and to see how it works together to lead students to the purpose. It was important for me to experience teaching it, not merely observing. The co-teaching aspect added another layer of audience, accountability and partner in reflection
- The model can be applied to all content areas in the school. The model is an easy one to follow
- Model of PD: orient – observe – reflect/prep – do – reflect
- It helps with the moves and what it looks like
- I appreciated all the tools to help me deliver the mini-lesson
- I appreciate special education being at the table for this

Question 2: What might be some ways to improve the "Learning Lab" process? Your feedback is very much appreciated!!

- Debrief the observed lesson before planning our own teaching
- Share materials ahead of time that could be reviewed
- Front load with curriculum goal and guiding questions
- Option to create all artifacts beforehand if desired
- A bit of feedback after the teaching as to how well the mini-lesson was taught would be helpful to understand how to coach the teachers, what to look for in the teacher's teaching
- I would appreciate the ability to connect with the text and the learning target beforehand
- I am game for doing the entire mini-lesson
- Have ALL content areas participate in a learning lab. The model will make teaching any content easier
- This becomes how we do things: leadership team → grade-level team → whole group/staff

 Available for download at http://resources.corwin.com/YorkBarrReflective

**REFLECTIONS ON SPANNING
ORGANIZATIONAL BOUNDARIES**

How does the practice of "boundary spanning" make sense to you?

What are some ways you have seen this done masterfully? And, why was that the case? What was it about the practice or person or context that are likely to have had a positive impact?

As you think about your current development priorities, are there ways that "boundary spanners" . . . you or someone else . . . might positively support your priorities?

Grow Ownership Around the Work

Just telling them to do it, doesn't work. When leaders talk about trying to persuade educators to change their practices, often the term "buy-in" shows up. This is a term that makes us bristle as it suggests that a type of manipulation or pay-off needs to happen before teachers are willing to try something new.

As reinforced in the preceding example on boundary-spanning, despite research that supports many of the practices used to teach students, there are always particularities within specific practice contexts that require some nuanced design for "goodness of fit" for individual or groups of students.

Yukl and Fable (1990) found that consultation tactics, "seek[ing] participation in decision-making or planning how to implement a proposed policy, strategy or change" (p. 133) and rational persuasion "use[ing] logical arguments and factual evidence to persuade you that a proposal or request is viable and likely to result in the attainment of task objectives" (p. 133).

Shown in Figure 3.4 is one way to think about how to respectfully engage teachers around learning new practices. One overarching idea is that something new (e.g., a new teaching practice) is at least somewhat unfamiliar to those expected to learn and implement it. It can be thought of as currently existing *outside* the teacher (or other participant). This brings attention to the double-sided arrow at the bottom of the figure, showing movement from outside to inside. Overall, learning about a new practice is a process that, figuratively, moves the practice from *outside* the participant to *inside* the participant.

The progression of ovals in the figure offers a theory of change from little or no connection with the new practice, through opportunities to become more familiar with and practice use of a new practice, through increasing understanding of how it supports student engagement and learning to reaching a point at which the practice (assuming it is successful) is incorporated into the teacher's repertoire. A more specific description of each oval is offered next.

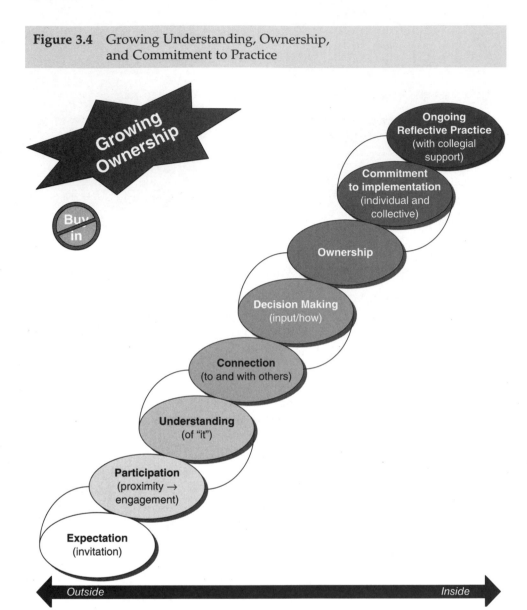

Figure 3.4   Growing Understanding, Ownership, and Commitment to Practice

First, an expectation is set for learning something new. This actually can be done gently and without suggesting it means current practices are inadequate. The introduction can feel more like an invitation. *Second*, participants are provided with an opportunity to become familiar with the new practices . . . what does it look like and sound like? This can be done by means of video or a live demonstration. Before the video, it is helpful to suggest "look fors" and "listen fors" as participants watch. These serve as reflection prompts after the viewing. *Third*, from the examples offered, teachers now better understand what the practice is and how it looks in practice. What follows—the *fourth* bubble—is that they now have a stronger *connection* with it. *Fifth,* participants can now begin thinking about and then deciding when specifically they might try it out. *Finally,* an outgrowth of being involved in decisions about use, is *ownership.* Ownership increases commitment to use, especially with collegial support. Done well this type of approach to learning leads to growing ownership, which can grow the combined benefits of learning that makes a difference in practice, and learning that deepens an appreciation for the opportunity to learn with colleagues.

Joyce and Calhoun (2010) offer the following insight that helps deepen understanding about the central influence of competence for commitment. The message is that if leaders want members to commit to new practices, members must grow in their understanding and competence.

> Teachers move from a position of initial skepticism to a position of pragmatic acceptance of practices that were new to them as they became more competent in the use of those practices. The implication for staff development organizers is to put less energy into trying to persuade teachers that they will like a new practice and more energy into helping those practitioners master the new strategies. (p. 79)

PRACTICE EXAMPLE 3.2

GROWING SCHOOLWIDE COOPERATIVE ROUTINES AT PHALEN LAKE HMONG STUDIES MAGNET SCHOOL, SAINT PAUL PUBLIC SCHOOLS, MINNESOTA

Contributed by Catherine Rich, Principal, and Michelle Brown-Ton, Instructional Coach, Phalen Lake Hmong Studies Magnet School, Saint Paul Public Schools, Minnesota

So, how did we set about planting and growing schoolwide practice? A full day schoolwide learning event was created for the teachers. The "why" of the day emphasized research informed assertions about strong connections between intentionally directed student talk and greater student reflection, understanding, and ownership of learning. Teachers were organized in grade-level teams for this learning opportunity, in part to support use of common routines throughout each grade level, thereby creating greater coherence and practice for students.

The "what" included use of video to show use of cooperative routines with students who were very much like the students in this school. After viewing the video,

(Continued)

(Continued)

each grade-level team had a dialogue about possibilities for when and how to teach "turn and talk" to students. They identified specific parts of the day and also sketched language they would use to model and teach "turn and talk" to students.

As mentioned above, initially teachers worked in grade-level, team-based groups. Toward the end of the learning event, however, teachers were reconfigured into standing mixed grade-level groups to share and learn what, when, and how other grade-level teams planned to teach and use the routines.

It is significant to note the value of ensuring opportunities for staff members to talk with colleagues from other grade levels and varied teaching assignments in their schools. This generates a broader range of possibilities for the use of practices, and equally valuable is recognizing that sharing across "home" teams helps to increase a greater sense of connection among school members and decrease subtle forms of comparison-contrast-competition that frequently arises among teacher groups.

Another "how" of this example was the intentionally scheduled and designed follow-up opportunities for grade-level team members to reflect on ways each teacher used routines, the ways that students responded, and any adjustments made to increase student conversation for learning by use of cooperative routines.

So what does this example have to do with leading reflective practice? To realize the positive potential of learning events, they must be intentionally and specifically designed by people who understand the learning contexts (e.g., priority student needs, staff members, teams and their respective conversational cultures). As all effective teachers know, each student and every group of students has its own culture and teaching must be nuanced accordingly. The same can be said about teacher groups.

 Available for download at **http://resources.corwin.com/YorkBarrReflective**

Typically this design work falls to principals and teacher leaders who are situated in the specific contexts of teacher practice (e.g., schools). Powerful learning rarely just happens, therefore know this reality: it is not unusual for sketching the learning design and developing the learning resources to take much longer, sometimes a multiple of four, than the learning event itself. Tending to the details of design, development, facilitation, and reflection demonstrates care and the respectful use of participants' time. It also dramatically increases the likelihood of engagement and learning. When the effort of intentional design results in high engagement, it is exhilarating! And, when it doesn't, there is even more to reflect on and learn for use the next time. (Chapters 4 through 7 offer numerous authentic examples of this work done well.)

**REFLECTIONS ON GROWING
OWNERSHIP FOR NEW PRACTICES**

Are there recent learning opportunities where you were a participant that approached learning in this way? If so, what were parts of the process that made the biggest positive influence on you?

Think about an upcoming learning focus for either students or staff members. How might the "growing ownership" process shown in Figure 3.4 help you design and develop the learning for growing the focus? What changes would make it fit better for your practice?

Structure and Nurture Around an Organizing Force

One way to overall frame the *what* and *how* of leading reflective practice is shown in Figure 3.5. Leading reflective practice requires structure and nurture around an organizing force.

Figure 3.5   Leading Reflective Practice: Structure and Nurture . . . From Here to There . . . Around an Organizing Force

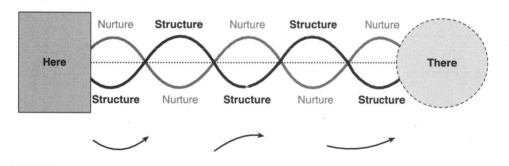

The "organizing force" is the "what" of reflective practice, and the learning is represented in the figure by the dotted line that begins in the "here" and moves to the "there," and represents a common goal, such as deepening our understanding about how race and culture impact instructional practice and student access, or learning how to use data to more specifically tailor instruction for students, or working together across grade level or content areas, or revisiting tiered interventions of support.

The elements of *structure* and *nurture* are woven together around the organizing force. Together they are the *how* of growing reflective practice. The "structure" part of the weave includes specific ways to organize people to reflect, learn, and support one another. Depending on the *what*, designers might decide to use alike groups or mixed groups, for example. Or they may choose smaller structures such as dyads or triads to increase both a sense of safety and participation.

The "nurture" strand of the weave brings attention to interpersonal and conversational elements, such as care, inquiry, listening, norms of collaborative work, and other ways of being together that support reflection and conversation. A safe place for speaking one's truth is ultimately required in order to realize outcomes with the great potential to create the conditions that will enrich the current and future lives of young people in our schools.

Leading reflective practice is an artful and mindful craft of organizing people around important goals and aspirations and creating a safe and constructive space to share, reflect, learn, and create possibilities for enriching student learning and lives.

It's All Practice. And, With Reflection, We Learn and Keep Moving Forward

At the end of the chapter and on the book's accompanying website at http://resources.corwin.com/YorkBarrReflective we offer a one page listing of the Guidelines for Leading Reflective Practice presented and described in this chapter (see Table 3.2). This resource might serve well as a useful at-a-glance resource for reflection, individually, among partners, or in group settings. Specifically, it could be offered as the focus of the grounding process that begins learning meetings.

CLOSING

To close, we once again draw from the insights and grounded perspective of Peter Block (2009). The following are the shifts in context that signal a transformation into authentic community:

- We are a community of possibilities, not a community of problems.
- Community exists for the sake of belonging and takes its identity from the gifts, generosity, and accountability of its citizens. It is not defined by its fears, its isolation, or its penchant for retribution.
- We currently have all the capacity, expertise, programs, leaders, regulations, and wealth required to end unnecessary suffering and create an alternative future.

Community is fundamentally an interdependent human system given form by the conversation it holds with itself. The history, buildings, economy, infrastructure, and culture are products of the conversations and social fabric of any community. The built and cultural environments are secondary gains of how we choose to be together. (pp. 29–30)

Table 3.2   Guidelines for Leading Reflective Practice

1. **Stay grounded in the why.**
   K–12 public education in the United States is mandatory and aims to be inclusive. It is not equitable . . . yet. This aspiration is inspiration that grounds why we show up every day in school.

2. **Go-eth not alone!**
   No one can do this work alone. Each of us needs practice partners: trusted colleagues with whom we can speak and be our truth. Partners who will help us get better and keep going.

3. **Leadership is influence . . . for the good!**
   Each interaction creates an opportunity to influence for the good . . . of the young people in schools, the good of the educators who care about and inspire them . . . and the good of the community.

4. **Relationships are the influence pathway.**
   Caring, authenticity, and trust lay the groundwork for growing reflective practice partnerships. Rarely can we agree with all perspectives that are shared; but always we can listen respectfully.

5. **Listening is the relationship pathway.**
   When people feel heard, they feel valued. Listening creates a bridge between people. Sometimes, just listening is enough. Listen with sensitivity and tolerance, even when you don't necessarily agree. Listen with the intention to understand. Sometimes just listening is enough.

6. **Culture is the work.**
   Culture is described as "how we do things around here." Reflecting on how we do things around here informs us about practices that are working well and also those that need to be *retired.*

7. **Implementation is particular to context.**
   Each person, class, team, school, and district is the same and different. Implementation is nuanced work, particular to each human who shows up and to the specific context of practice.

8. **Develop shared ownership of the work.**
   Teachers and other direct service folks who spend their days ground level with students must understand and own the *why, what*, and *how* of implementation work relating to the students. It is their work to do! Talking about, drawing, showing, and teaching a partner requires owning the work.

9. **Be humble and be first.**
   You first! Humility is an attractive force. Each of us is a piece of work. Model being a piece of work *in progress.* Take the risk of trying something new. It's all practice. Learning is the payoff. And, by taking the lead, you likely muster the courage of a colleague to try it too.

10. **Be gentle with yourself, body, mind, and spirit.**
    Breathe. Laugh. Move. Play. Rest. Imagine. *Forgive.* Tomorrow always holds the potential for you, and everyone else, to become your next best self.

Available for download at http://resources.corwin.com/YorkBarrReflective

We offer the following questions as prompts for reflection on your work as an educator and also as a leader of reflective practice and learning. And, if we embrace the perspective that leadership is influence for the good and influence is everywhere in our communities, the message calls on each of us to show up in communal space so that we can both influence others and allow ourselves to be influenced . . . *for the good.*

REFLECTIONS ON LEADING
REFLECTIVE PRACTICE AND LEARNING

In what ways is your context of practice a community of possibilities? How might the possibilities within your community be expanded?

What are some ways you remain mindful, or would like to be more mindful of possibilities amidst the daily intensity of leading, teaming, and teaching?

What might be some ways to inspire the vision and practice of possibility among your colleagues—the young people whose lives you help shape?

Figure 3.6   Chapter Reflection Page

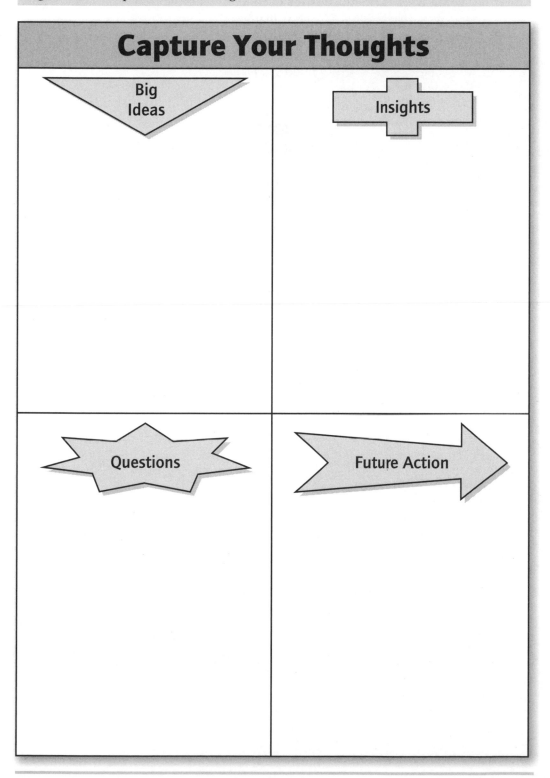

4

Individual Reflective Practice

> *From the perspective of the individual teacher, it means that the process of understanding and improving one's own teaching must start from reflection on one's own experience.*
>
> —Kenneth Zeichner, *Connecting Genuine Teacher Development to the Struggle for Social Justice*, 1993

You may be asking yourself, how does reflective practice relate, specifically, to me in my life as an educator? Reflection offers great potential for illuminating meaning, purpose, and learning in your professional life. By being more reflective, you have the potential to increase your own effectiveness and also to positively affect the thinking and practice of others. When we choose different behaviors, those around us might also change. We use a metaphor taken from the airlines: put on your own oxygen mask before assisting others. In this chapter we focus on ways to grow and deepen individual reflective practice, knowing its potential to influence others to do so as well.

To be reflective means choosing, with intention, ways of thinking, being, and doing. To be reflective means being aware of our thoughts and actions, which leads to choosing enrichment around our day's activities. It means committing oneself to continuous growth as a person and as a professional. Each of us interacts with people with whom we can connect and together create new and improved realities for the children in our charge as educators. We also come into contact with people who we would not necessarily want to spend more time around. Either way, reflecting on the experience increases our ability to act differently.

REFLECTIONS ON PERSONAL INSPIRATION

Think for a moment:

- Who do you spend time with that inspires you?
- What do you think about that activates your creativity?

In our work lives, each of us encounters circumstances, both planned and unplanned, that can be better learned from and understood when our commitments to personal reflection are honored. Gary Klein (1998), in a book called *Sources of Power*, discusses reflection in action. Professionally, educators spend most of their day in this frenzied fast-paced learning mode. Klein investigated three professions that can be related to teaching and administrating in a school.

Firefighters, staff in operating rooms, and EMTs all have "in the moment" quick decisions to make. When studying these professionals, he suggests two things that help make better decisions on the fly. One, pattern recognition, explains why experience can help make better decisions. A new teacher does not have years of trial and error developing multiple patterns that work in the classroom, with peers, and in leadership roles. As more patterns are developed, it is easier to determine what is working, what isn't working, and more importantly, how to effectively use that information.

The second form of help for making better decisions on the fly was mental simulation. Yes, simulation, not stimulation . . . arguably, in these professions there is an overabundance of stimulation. So, reflecting internally about how an upcoming lesson, presentation, meetings might go— what the goals are, and how we will assess success—increases our preparedness. We have essentially, mentally rehearsed the upcoming event, including consideration of unexpected turns and the ways we could respond. Discussing this simulation with colleagues also can be supportive, as we address in the next chapter.

The greater your personal reflective capacities and practices, the greater your potential to influence colleagues in your school to become more reflective . . . to help them put on their oxygen masks. Colleagues respect and are drawn to individuals who are thoughtful, who strive to continuously learn and improve, who are flexible in their approaches to teaching and leading, and who stay clearly focused on what matters most: students being included and learning well. Self-development is the core of professional development, or "more profoundly, [it is the process of] personal being and becoming" (Butler, 1996, p. 265).

This chapter, Individual Reflective Practice, and the following three chapters (Chapter 5, Reflective Practice With Partners; Chapter 6, Reflective Practice in Small Groups and Teams; and Chapter 7, Schoolwide Reflective Practice) focus more specifically on the "how" of reflective practice, including offering practice examples. Each of the chapters is also organized in a parallel way. First, there is a brief review of the respective configuration (e.g., individual, partner, team or small group, school or districtwide) or context of reflective practice. These considerations are followed by a presentation of examples from the authentic practice contexts, and then a menu of additional ideas to consider for use. In reviewing some of the examples and ideas, you are likely to see potential for application in other configurations. Each chapter closes with questions to guide getting started with reflective practice at that particular level.

One note of caution: Many of the examples and ideas in Chapters 5 through 7 offer structures or protocols intended to foster reflection. The structures, however, will not result in reflection, learning, or improvement *unless* inquiry, deliberative thinking, and action result. Changes in structure provide only the *opportunity* for reflection, learning, and advances in practice. Positive, discernable results depend on the quality of the reflection and conversation within the respective structures, from which insight and possibilities for improvement emerge. In order to support your practice, some of the reflection guides presented in our book can be located in the companion website for this book (http://resources.corwin.com/YorkBarrReflective). You are welcome to print and use them to support your work of growing reflective practice on your own, with partners, in groups, and throughout your school or district.

SPECIAL CONSIDERATIONS FOR INDIVIDUAL REFLECTIVE PRACTICE

One of the first considerations for reflecting on our own is finding and *guarding* time and space in our lives for significant pauses. The cultures in which we work and even the cultures in which we live can make this exceedingly difficult. Creating space in which to think conflicts with the norms of doing, and the value placed on being decisive and quickly responsive. Given the pace and complexity of educational practice, being reactive easily becomes the norm, leaving more deliberative proactive work to fall by the wayside. Personal uncertainty about whether the benefits of reflective practice will outweigh the costs also makes it difficult to give ourselves permission to claim time to reflect. When you find yourself wavering, consider the following reassurance, "It is in the quiet and solitary times of reading and writing that the insights from life take on a more systematic form" (Webb, 1995, p. 76). How powerful it would be if more of us—teachers and administrators—adopted and modeled reflective ways of practice thereby lending value and credibility to this pursuit. A first step in claiming time for reflection is making a personal commitment to grant yourself time to reflect and make sense of practice because it has the potential to re-ground and renew your spirit as an educator. The outgrowth of this claim on time for reflection is likely to prove its worth, time and time again. Margaret Wheatley (2009) offers this question for consideration by each of us: "Am I willing to reclaim time to think?"

REFLECTIONS ON CLAIMING TIME TO REFLECT

Am I willing to make time for me to reflect?

How might I help others to take time to reflect?

Assuming that a commitment to yourself—your all alone self—is important to you, the task becomes one of finding your own way to claim space for reflection. Some people mark time on their weekly calendars. Others build thinking space into daily routines . . . going for an early morning run, turning off your phone and claiming space to listen your thoughts along your daily commute, closing your door and turning off the lights during a prep period, hanging out a bit longer in the shower (or laundry room), walking right after work, or settling in with a cup of tea and your journal after putting the children to bed.

A discussion of honoring time for oneself is not complete without also stating the importance of living a balanced life, which includes attending to basic needs like good sleep, good nutrition, and the importance of family, friends, relaxation, and play. Like most people, we lay no claim to having figured out how to do this. We just know that when we do allow ourselves a break, our breathing slows, our thinking deepens, and we can more calmly reflect on the day's events, mining the good as well as considering ways to get even better, and envisioning potential for good to happen tomorrow. For sure, this makes for a more restful night's sleep. Like exercise, rest, nutritious food, and fun, we know that reflective practice is good for us, but commitments to healthy personal practices are not easily sustained.

We now share several additional considerations that influence individual journeys as reflective educators. We view these considerations as serving to deepen personal inquiry and thought that leads to greater learning about ourselves and to grounded actions as a professional educator. We begin with a substantial examination of *identity*, the ways in which who we are in our work, consciously and subconsciously, drives both our thoughts and actions. A framework for considering issues of identity is

Table 4.1 Special Considerations for Individual Reflective Practice

Identity . . . clarifying our identity

Ethics . . . asking ethical questions and considering moral dilemmas

Courage . . . examining what it means to be courageous

Caring for others and for self . . . seeking balance to keep us centered

Voice . . . strengthening our own and being open to others

Practice, reflect, learn, improve, repeat

offered as a reflection tool and may offer support in considering other ideas within the chapter. Next, we raise consideration of *ethics* embedded in our daily work. The essential place of *courage* is then considered. To engage seriously in examining our thoughts and practices, big and small, is not an endeavor for the faint of heart. The importance of *care* is addressed next, followed by a discussion of *voice*. Finally, we emphasize again the place of continuous practice to improve and embed our reflection capacities in daily life. These considerations for individual reflection, summarized in Table 4.1, will now be explored.

Identity

Identity encompasses how a person understands his or her relationship to the world, how that relationship is constructed across time and space, and how the person understands possibilities for the future. (Norton, 2000, p. 5)

Who am I in this work as an educator? How do I hope to contribute in my school community and in other parts of my life? In what ways are the school and other learning environments shaping the identities of our children? Each of us assumes multiple roles in our daily lives—teacher, parent, son, principal, granddaughter, friend, sibling, and colleague are just a few examples. Roles are the labels used to define certain functions, relationships, or classes of responsibility. Identity and role are not the same thing. Identity and culture are not the same thing, even though identity is shaped by the various cultures of which we are part, such as race, gender, class, and work cultures. Identity is more personal and individual than either role or culture. Our identity is who we are and how we see ourselves as a person in particular contexts. "For an individual, identity is a framework for understanding oneself" (Garmston & Wellman, 1997, p. 162). Why is this important to our discussion of reflective practice? There are at least two reasons. *First*, our individual identities are operative influences on what we believe, how we think, and how we behave in the context of our practice. *Second*, because identities are shaped by social interactions and forces around us, we are compelled to consider the effects of our school and classroom environments on both children and adults in schools. We begin by sharing a model that offers a way of reflecting on how our identities influence our beliefs, thinking, and behaviors.

Identity Intertwined With Development and Action

We are not suggesting that identity is the exclusive focus in learning work, only that it be addressed along with matters of why, what, and how. Typically emphasized in learning work are the lower levels, the "doings." We have found this model to be instructive and compelling for many educators seeking to understand who they are in their work and how they can contribute to the growth in others. The model offers insight about the interconnectedness of identity, beliefs, strategies, and skills. It helps to explain why low-level instruction or development activities sometimes fail to produce generative gains. It provides a structure for understanding our thoughts and actions and gives permission and encouragement for engaging in questions of meaning and purpose in our work and our lives. Feel free to check the website that accompanies this book (http://resources.corwin.com/YorkBarrReflective) for a protocol (similar to Table 4.2) to guide individual thinking about each level. Our thoughts, interactions, and work every day are deeply rooted in our personal identity, our sense of who we are.

Social Influences on Identity Construction

A second reason to examine identity in our work as educators involves the social influence on identity construction. Since identity is shaped by social forces around us, it is critical to consider the types of learning environments in which children and adults live, work, and play. For children, place in the classroom's social order affects both their identity and their access to learning opportunities, especially social learning opportunities with other children. This creates a formidable challenge for children who are not native English speakers as they attempt to negotiate participation and position in classroom communities (Hawkins, 2004). Lacking subtle language finesse the children are at risk for being marginalized from or by their English speaking peers. Hawkins explains, "Identities are, thus, deeply linked to the positioning work that is always operant throughout social encounters and interactions, and possibilities and constraints are determined, in large part, through the power and status relations of the participants in the interaction" (p. 19). One does not freely choose an identity.

Social exchanges and discourse have a strong influence on the identity shaped in particular contexts.

According to Hawkins, implications for educators include reframing the essence of their work from

> teaching English to offer[ing] students access to the range of knowledge, abilities, and forms of languages (discourses) that will enable them to lay claim to the social identities that afford them a participant status in the social communities of their choice, and to provide scaffolding (and a truly support environment) for the attainment of these. (p. 23)

Such reframing work (e.g., a shift from "teaching English" to empowering life outcomes for young people) may be prompted by looking at children's learning environments through a reframing tool like the Personal Reflection Model for Professional Practice lens (Table 4.2), or using other reframing tools.

The extension of social influence on identity formation applies equally well to grown-ups in schools. Each new teacher, just like each new student, walks through the door with an indeterminable amount of potential to both learn and contribute in valuable ways in the school community. The ways in which newcomers are socially acculturated significantly influences their identity formation within the community, and consequently their learning and contribution. In Etienne Wenger's (1998) social learning theory published as *Communities of Practice*, identity is inseparable from practice, community, and meaning. In the particular case of newcomers, they must find and claim their identities. He explains,

> . . . theories of identity are concerned with social formation of the person, creation and use of markers of membership (e.g., ritual, rites of passage, social categories); address gender, age, class, ethnicity; learning is caught in the middle. It is the vehicle for the evolution of practices and the inclusion of newcomers and the vehicle for the development and transformation of identities. (p. 13)

According to Wenger, both participation and nonparticipation in a community shape our identities, which in turn influence how we locate ourselves in a social landscape: what we care about and what we neglect, what we attempt to know and understand and what we choose to ignore, who we seek connections with and who we avoid, how we engage and direct our energies, and how we attempt to steer our trajectories. Reflective questions then arise about how we intentionally welcome, socially support, and professionally acculturate newcomers to our practice communities in ways that are likely to maximize participation and contribution.

Table 4.2   Personal Reflection Model for Professional Practice
With Sample Responses

Level	Reflection Question	Response
Mission or Overarching Purpose	What am I working toward? What are we creating or aiming to achieve?	Equity in schooling; ensure opportunities, access, and support so that all children have a sense of belonging in their schools and are successful in their learning; foster academic, social, and emotional growth
Identity	Who am I in this work? How do I hope to contribute?	Facilitator of teacher and student learning; connector of people and resources; lifelong inquirer, learner, and practitioner
Values and Beliefs	What do I believe about or value in this work? Why should we proceed in this way?	Inclusivity is the foundation for constructive growth; learning alone and together foster positive interdependence; humans want to learn, grow, and contribute; competence builds confidence
Capabilities, Strategies, Mental Maps	How do I or will I accomplish this work? What strategies will guide my actions?	Relationships must be established as the pathways for learning; students must be understood as individuals and viewed in life context; opportunities, expectations, and instruction all must be intentionally provided
Behaviors and Skills	What do I do to advance this work?	Observe, listen, inquire; identify individually relevant zones of proximal development; adapt expectations and strategies to create and build on success; introduce the plan, design, implement, and reflect cycle
Environment and Structure	What structures and surroundings support this work?	Proximity; intentional mix of whole group, small group, individual work; flexible time structures; time to confer with instructional colleagues

Source: The levels (column 1) and questions (column 2) in Table 4.2 are adapted from Dilts (1996) and Garmston & Wellman (1997).

 Available for download at **http://resources.corwin.com/YorkBarrReflective**

Ethics

Teaching at its core is a moral profession. Scratch a good teacher and you will find a moral purpose. (Fullan, 1993, p. 12)

What does it mean to be a moral profession? How do issues of right and wrong come into play in the lives of educators? What does one do when conflicts arise between one's own ethics and the ethics of others around them? Are there universal ethical standards or are all ethics relative? There are no singular agreed upon answers to these questions. Indeed, philosophers and ethicists have engaged around these types of questions since the beginning of humankind. Despite the continuing ambiguity, Rockler (2004) reminds us that "On any school day, professional educators face a myriad of problems that contain moral dilemmas. For [educators] to act responsibly, they constantly must examine ethical questions" (p. 15). Further he asserts,

> The study of ethics has become more urgent as people seek to determine ways to live ethically meaningful lives in the most complex times in human history. Persons now face the most destructive forces to ever confront humankind. Professional educators need to engage in the process of moral reflection more than ever before. (p. 46)

We bring up ethics in the context of reflective practice not to offer any absolute resolutions, but to affirm the presence of moral dilemmas in everyday educational practice and to affirm the struggle that one engages in reflecting on best courses of action when faced with such dilemmas. Drawing from Michael Rockler's *Ethics and Professional Practice in Education*, we present just a few of the ethical issues that he raises, along with some related questions. (As a point of clarification, Rockler uses the terms *moral* and *ethical* interchangeably.)

- *Ethics and political decisions.* Do vouchers diminish a sense of connection among people that is necessary for a democracy? On the other hand, what about individual rights to choose? What are the effects of educational outcomes being determined primarily by single measure performance on standardized tests? What should be the priorities for allocating public resources? Under what conditions is it appropriate to increase individual taxation to achieve a greater societal good?
- *Ethics and diversity.* What ethical conflicts might exist between commitments to cultural diversity and adopting standardized curricula? How are tensions between cultural assimilation and cultural difference resolved so that identity is not threatened and so that underclass status is not reinforced? What are the effects of teaching only English to children whose first language is not English? Should all students learn the same things? If not, how do we decide and who decides?
- *Ethics and relations with students.* What discussions between educators and students are kept in confidence? What circumstances warrant conversation among educators or educators and parents regarding individual students? What are appropriate boundaries in relationships between educators, students, and their families?

Courage

Angeles Arrien (1993) writes about courage in her book, *The Four-Fold Way*. She says that one part of leadership is being a warrior. As leaders for education, we have to fight for what is most important in schools. We must stand up for what matters most regarding the health, well-being, and well-learning of the children we serve. How do we show up and stay fully present in our daily pursuit of meaningful and substantial learning? How do we summon the courage to do what we know is right? A principal colleague, Michael Huerth, once explained that in his culture, Native American members have a spear to put in the ground when deciding on an issue of major importance. The spear symbolizes the final stand on what one views as important, the point at which one is not willing to concede without engaging in conflict and standing up for one's values and beliefs. Educators are called on to advocate for learning as the central focus in schools. Knowing what to stand for and the willingness to advocate for those values is becoming more important for leaders.

In Ira Chaleff's (1995) *The Courageous Follower*, he describes the interdependence of formal leaders and their organizational colleagues, whom he refers to as followers. He explains that leaders and followers orbit together around the purpose of the organization and that followers do *not* orbit around the formal leader. One of the essential roles for all members of an organization is to keep practices aligned with purpose and to keep formal leaders grounded in purpose. To serve effectively in this role, members must be courageous. Chaleff explains, "Courage is the great balancer of power in relationships. An individual who is not afraid to speak and act on the truth, as she perceives it, despite external inequities in a relationship, is a force to be reckoned with" (p. 18). Also consider what effective leaders know, that to be good leaders, they must be willing to follow.

In Chaleff's newest book, *Intelligent Disobedience* (2015), he suggests that blind obedience is not a good thing. We train guide dogs to intelligently disobey when the blind person cannot see a danger, like stepping off a curb to an oncoming car. He quotes David Nyberg and Paul Farber in an article titled "Authority in Education," with this quote,

> This Question of how one shall act in role of authority is the foundation of educated citizenship: Its importance cannot be overemphasized. Teachers, we believe, have a special obligation to teach about authority while they act as authorities in supervising education. (Nyberg as quoted in Chaleff, p. 136)

When a teacher knows what is needed for a student to learn, and does not meet the mandated prescribed action, we think professional judgment should be an option, assuming reflection on practice with particular emphasis on student impact is explicitly embedded. Often this is referred to the "plan-do-reflect-act" cycle of learning. Most current literature states that making decisions closest to the point of acting with the client's best interest maximizes positive results.

Parker Palmer (1998) has written extensively about the *Courage to Teach* in his book by the same name. He states that his book is built on a simple premise:

> good teaching cannot be reduced to technique, good teaching comes from the identity and integrity of the teacher ... The connections made by good teachers are held not in their methods but in their hearts—the place where intellect and emotion and spirit and will converge in the human self. (Book jacket)

We extend this premise to administrators as well. We teach who we are based on our identity, which is built on our values and what we hold significant. So, what are your values? Stan Slap (2010) in his book *Bury My Heart in Conference Room B* asks people two questions. First, what are your values? The second question we think is the most important and will cause deeper internal reflection. How did you get that value? What you will hear is a story that was profound and personally meaningful. So, we ask you the same two questions. What are your answers? How do those answers affect your teaching, your learning, and your leadership?

As an educator, authentic pursuit of a conscious and reflective life requires strong hearts and minds. Like the lion in *The Wizard of Oz*, the capacity to be courageous is within each of us, but is not always summoned. Chaleff (1995) contends that "Our 'courage muscle' will develop to the degree we exercise it" (p. 20). The will to continue strengthening our courage muscle comes from an inner knowing that good teaching and good leading come from within. As we continue through the seasons of our work and continue our commitments to learn and improve, we can take heart in Palmer's reassuring message that we teach and we lead who we are.

REFLECTIONS ON MY VALUES AND THEIR ORIGINS

What are my deepest values for learning? For schools? For others?

What in my past assisted me in getting those values?

How did I behave in alignment with those values?

Caring for Others and for Self

Caring is the greatest thing. Caring matters most. (von Hügel, as cited in Manser, 2001, p. 29)

Many would agree with Baron von Hügel's words: when looking back at our lifetime and considering what matters in our time on earth, caring may be what matters most. The importance of caring and compassionate responses to others is a theme shared by people, cultures, and religions around the world. And, when considering our work in schools, it is clear that a teacher's caring and pathic responses are critical aspects of a student's experience in school.

Like nurses and other direct care professionals, as educators we are considered part of the caring professions, professions in which much energy is spent in care and support of other human beings. This sentiment incorporates with it the inherent reward of building connections and promoting growth. It also carries the inherent challenge of feeling overwhelmed by the many human needs faced on a daily basis. On some days, as we drive away from work, our thoughts turn to the children or grown-ups for whom we wish we could have done more. Especially today during times of increased demands, increased diversity of student needs, and an overall tone of doing more with less, educators can easily move into feeling overly responsible, overwhelmed, and undernourished. Left unchecked, these thoughts can easily turn to feelings of guilt and inadequacy.

In some respects it seems odd that people who care so much may also be the ones who feel guilt so much. Only partially in jest, Andy Hargreaves (1994) suggests that the degree of burden educators feel is proportional to the size of their tote bag carried to and from work each day. He explains that educators are particularly susceptible to feelings of guilt due to a combination of factors, including a commitment to care and nurture, the open-ended nature of teaching, pressures of accountability, and a persona of perfectionism. The ever present cycle between expectations and constraints further exacerbates the feelings of not doing enough for those about whom we care. Perhaps twinges of occasional guilt or certainly feelings of discomfort are not harmful as it engenders responsible, compassionate, and caring responses. Moments of guilt or disequilibrium may be a catalyst for further reflection and learning. But, ongoing (excessive) guilt is an emotional trap, unhealthy, and a direct path to burnout. And, in many cases excessive guilt is a sign that a teacher has lost balance in caring for his or her own needs in some way. Guilt can be a clue to step back and redefine one's responses. We're not saying don't care, rather we're suggesting that as you care deeply about your students, your colleagues, and your work, don't forget to care for yourself. Guilt and shame can too quickly move us to despair. Such thoughts do no good for anyone and have no place, especially not in a caring learning environment. Guilt reduces efficiency and effectiveness.

The ways to attend to this balance of care of others and care for self vary from person to person. Here is how Carl, a second-grade teacher in an urban school, helps thoughtful colleagues keep feelings of guilt in check. When he hears extremely hard-working colleagues begin to spiral downward with feelings of being ineffective in this way or that, when he feels that a colleague is being too hard on himself or herself, he has a mantra:

"You are a good enough teacher. You are good enough." Basic to this mantra is the idea of letting go of perfectionism. Often, guilt and inadequate feelings come from expecting everything from oneself, expecting to be perfect. So Carl has found this a useful construct to apply when competent teachers are beating up on themselves. Angeles Arrien calls this "inner terrorism." He also has a strong personal orientation on the "here and now," in his teaching and life. He seeks to be fully present with his students when he is with them, and to be focused on his students when he is planning for them. Likewise, he seeks to be fully present with his family when he is not at work. He attempts to be mindful and present in all of his relationships.

Relevant for our purposes here is the realization that work in a caring profession provides us with both human rewards and struggles. Such work can be a source of great joy and also great angst. We intend that by putting issues of care, guilt, and balance on the table, educators will not feel alone in this struggle and may over time come to better understand these dilemmas, and potentially choose constructive responses. Such responses include enlisting the support of trusted colleagues to reflect on what is reasonable, possible, and most productive so that we sustain the energy and health required to engage in this caring profession. In moving more into reflection and examination of one's teaching and teaching practice, we suggest that teachers strive for a healthy tension around care about students and care for oneself. It doesn't need to be a win/lose or either/or dichotomy in which either we care for our students or we care for ourselves. We believe that a "both/and" paradigm can be useful here—both care for students and care for oneself.

Voice

Another example of "both/and" thinking involves keeping tension around both clarifying one's own voice and opinions on educational issues, and continuing to stay open to other people's perspectives. Both are important. Some educators have difficulty finding their own voice as they engage in reflective practices (Canning, 1991; Costa & Kallick, 2000b). It is easy to fall into routine ways of doing things without much consideration of how we really think or feel. We can also become accustomed to others telling us directly or implying indirectly what is expected and what we should do. The busier and less present we are, the more likely these incidents happen. Our hierarchical orientation in education can seem to privilege expertness from the top or from outside, and as such can diminish the recognition and value of our own wisdom. "Self-knowledge involves what and how you are thinking, even unconsciously. Many people are not used to engaging in the 'self-talk' that is necessary for hearing their inner voice" (Costa & Kallick, 2000b, p. 60). For example, consider the following questions.

- What do I think about this?
- If I were to make the decision, what would I identify as important and why?
- What would be the most productive way for me and my colleagues to move this issue forward?

Finding our own voice is an asset because we come to know our innermost thoughts, questions, and desires regarding our work. We can also tap and share our knowledge of practice. By sharing these discoveries with others, we enrich the conversations, deliberations, and collective action with our colleagues. To keep our own voice in check, we must also be intentional in our efforts to remain open and consider other perspectives. Our past experiences inform our present thoughts, and can therefore limit, as much as inform, our perceptions of present realities. Our own view of the world is so much a part of who we are that it serves as a filter for our thinking. "We see the world as we are, not as it is" (Zen proverb). We must become aware of our biases and make a conscious effort to attempt to see things from another perspective. In an effort to remain open, we can ask ourselves the following questions:

- What are some other ways of thinking about this?
- Has this always been the case, or have there been times when something different has happened? Why?
- What influences on thinking and behaving have I not considered?
- How do my beliefs guide me to think this way, and how might other beliefs alter my thinking?
- If I trusted people's intentions, would I interpret their responses differently?
- Are there other people who could help me see this differently?
- Why do I hold on so strongly to this one view?

Practice, Practice, and More Practice

Finally, like every other set of skills and dispositions, with practice reflection capacities develop, strengthen, and become more integrated into how we think and behave . . . lots of practice . . . lots of consciousness . . . lots of intention . . . and lots more practice and reflection on practice. We can practice all of these capacities on our own, then carry them with us into learning conversations with others.

INDIVIDUAL REFLECTIVE PRACTICE: PRACTICE EXAMPLES

In this section, we offer several frameworks (i.e., mental models) for use in fostering reflection with ourselves. Such frameworks may be especially helpful to reflective practice newcomers in guiding intentional reflection experiences.

Eventually, all of us develop our own ways of prompting inquiry and reflection about our practice. The first example offers a big picture organizer for thinking about how reflective practices might be more present throughout your day. The remaining examples offer a variety of reflection processes and sample protocols that we encourage you to adapt to your needs.

Insert Reflective Practices Everywhere!

One evening while listening to a colleague, RoAnne Elliott, encourage a new generation of professional learning facilitators, we heard her advice, "Insert learning processes everywhere!" This idea is both simple and profound. By closely examining our daily routines and activities, we can undoubtedly identify opportunities to insert reflective practices. As we prepare for the day, we can insert reflection prompts like: What dispositions do I want to model today for my students? How can I keep my mind open to different viewpoints? At the end of the day, what will I have hoped to accomplish? At the start of committee meetings, participants could be asked to think about the dispositions or behaviors that will foster productive use of the meeting time. Administrators and teachers could begin faculty meetings with partner shares about an unexpected instructional success or challenge and the thinking it prompted. They could end with a take-away question, likely to prompt continued thinking after the meeting ends. Walks to the faculty lounge or around the school during lunch could be filled with free-flowing observations about how teachers are enriching their curriculum to foster equitable practices.

When does reflection happen, or more to the point, when could it happen throughout an already full and often hectic day? How can we reframe our hectic days as opportunities to learn, and importantly opportunities to re-prioritize our time and then make good on these opportunities so that our own reflection, learning, and development serve as the cornerstone of our practice? We see many more teachers engaging in reflective practice, not only with their colleagues but also with their students. What can students teach us about our practice? When teachers create an inclusive, caring, and inquiry-based learning classroom, students are well poised to contribute by offering feedback, without the fear of repercussions. One teacher we know opens the door to this type of conversation by explaining to her students, "By giving me your feedback, I keep getting better as a teacher." Then she asks questions like "What helped you learn today?" . . . "If something happened that interfered with your learning, what was it and are there ways that we can prevent it from happening again?" . . . "How did you help yourself stay focused and engaged in your learning today?"

In Figure 4.1 we offer a framework for taking inventory of your current state of reflective practice and for considering possibilities for embedding more reflection and learning opportunities. Our point is not to elicit reflection fatigue, a state of mind brought on by obsessive questioning and thought. Rather, it is to recognize the many opportunities for reflection and

Figure 4.1   Personal Inventory of Reflective Practice

Reflective Educator . . . Take Inventory

	Current Realities	Reflection Prompt	Possibilities
	In what specific situations do you find yourself	How much reflection and learning is going on?	How might reflection and learning be advanced?
	. . . on your own?		
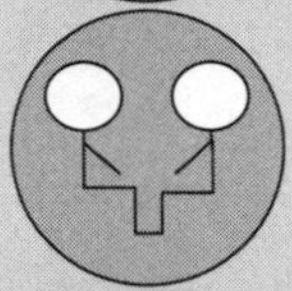	. . . in dyads or triads?		
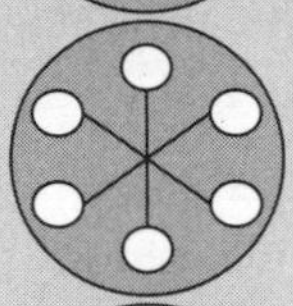	. . . in small groups or teams?		
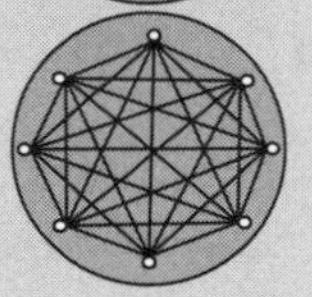	. . . in large groups (e.g., school or organizational level)?		

Available for download at **http://resources.corwin.com/YorkBarrReflective**

learning that already exist in our daily practice. By reframing some of our daily experiences as opportunities to reflect and learn, we exercise the potential to increase both the meaning and effectiveness of our practice, without necessarily allocating more time. There are opportunities daily to reflect by ourselves and with others.

REFLECTIONS ON EMBEDDING REFLECTIVE PRACTICE

Where can I insert reflection into our meeting structure?

How can I take a few minutes at the end of the day to reflect on events and what influenced those events?

4-Step Reflection Process

The 4-step reflection process outlined in Table 4.3 guides reflection-on-action and reflection-for-action, both focused around a specific event or circumstance. It is similar to a reflective process introduced by Smyth (1989). It brings the reflector through a sequenced process of thinking: description (what?), analysis and interpretation (why?), overall determination of meaning (so what?), and projections about future actions (now what?). This sequence of thinking is easily embedded into a personal reflection repertoire. This 4-step reflection process and the example that follow, *Letting Your Reflections Flow*, were used in a reflective practice initiative in a high school. They were formatted on single pages and placed in faculty mailboxes. These mailbox prompts, as they were called, served as gentle reminders to take a time-out for reflection and offered a structure for engaging in reflection. We have found that some educators still appreciate having a piece of paper as the place to write ideas, instead of always having to fire-up their computers to write. Offering both modalities allows for choice.

Letting Your Reflections Flow

David Bohm (1989) refers to dialogue as "a stream of meaning flowing among us and through us and between us" (p. 1). Although dialogue is often used to refer to interactions among people, it can also refer to a person's internal exploration of various viewpoints and assumptions—an *inner dialogue*. Most of us must learn how to dialogue with ourselves. It is not an intrinsic skill to any of us, although we each have the potential. A recommended mode for dialogue with yourself is writing. However, be careful not to pressure yourself to write in technically correct ways. The purpose is expression of thought, not coherent and carefully sequenced articulation. Select a prompt, and let the dialogue begin.

Have a Written Dialogue With Yourself About What It Means to Be a Teacher

When did you first think about being a teacher? What influenced your thinking in this way? Did particular teachers or other people influence your thoughts about becoming a teacher? How do you want to contribute to the lives of children? What are your hopes and visions? What do you want students to learn from you and with you? What do you need to continue learning from them? What are some underlying beliefs and values that guide your teaching? Where do you struggle with alignment between beliefs and values and actual behavior? What might be some reasons for this? Explore potential reasons for this. How do you want to be as a teacher? What do you want to learn more about that will enhance your teaching? How can you remain true to these desires?

Table 4.3   4-Step Process for Guiding Reflection-on-Action

Think about a significant event or interaction or lesson that occurred in your classroom or school, with students or adults, that you feel is worth further reflection. You might choose a positive and encouraging experience, or you might choose a more unsettling and challenging experience.

Now consider the following series of questions to prompt your thinking about the experience. You may wish to write down your thoughts. You may even want to share your thoughts aloud with another person.

1. **What happened? (Description)**

   - What did I do? What did others (e.g., students, adults) do?
   - What was my affect at the time? What was their affect?
   - What was going on around us? Where were we? When during the day did it occur? Was there anything unusual happening?

2. **Why? (Analysis, interpretation)**

   - Why do I think things happened in this way?
   - How come I chose to act the way I did? What can I surmise about why the other person acted as she or he did? What was going on for each of us?
   - What was I thinking and feeling? Or was I thinking at the time? How might this have affected my choice of behavior?
   - How might the context have influenced the experience? Was there something about the activities? Something about the timing or location of events?
   - Are there other potential contributing factors? Something about what was said or done by others that triggered my response? Are there past experiences—mine or the school's—that may have contributed to the response?
   - What are my hunches about why things happened in the way they did?

3. **So what? (Overall meaning and application)**

   - Why did this seem like a significant event to reflect on?
   - What have I learned from this?
   - How might this change my future thinking, practices, and interactions?
   - What questions remain?

4. **Now what? (Implications for action)**

   - Are there other people I should actively include in reflecting on this event? If so, who and what would we interact about?
   - Next time a situation like this presents itself, what do I want to remember to think about? How do I want to behave?
   - How could I set up conditions to increase the likelihood of productive interactions and learning?

Identify a Specific Event or Experience and
Write About It From as Many Perspectives as Possible

What happened from my viewpoint? What happened from the view-point of others? How might someone in the balcony look down on and interpret the event? How can I view this as understandable differences instead of trying to identify winners and losers? Does there have to be a right way and wrong way?

Select Any Topic and Do Some Freewriting

You may want to think metaphorically. Learning to reflect is like plant-ing a seed, patiently watching it, and hoeing away the competing and unwanted weeds. For example, Bohm's depiction of dialogue as a stream of meaning could be envisioned as a river. Dialogue is like a river. Or teaching is like planting and tending a garden. Write down your thoughts, feelings, beliefs, and observations about the selected topic. Write about connections between your topic and other things. Don't evaluate or judge thoughts as they pour out. Just let them flow! Later, look back at all your thoughts. Ask yourself, "I wonder what this means? What are the connec-tions between this and that? Are there new insights or perspectives I hadn't really thought about before? How did this experience of freeing up my mind expand my thinking? What additional questions are raised?"

Reflection Directions

Reflection has direction. Figure 4.2 depicts four different directions that guide reflection. As you begin or extend your process of individual reflection, practice these different ways of reflecting. You can reflect within to inquire about personal purpose and why you are the way you are. Why are you a teacher? How did you come to be here? What are your inten-tions? How do you stay centered? What nurtures your creativity and zest for teaching? How do you want to be with your students and colleagues?

You can reflect back on circumstances or events that have already occurred, referred to as reflection-on-action (Schön, 1983; Webb, 1995). This is one of the most frequently employed forms of reflection. It occurs after an event, when you are removed from it, and the doing is done (tem-porarily). The mind is then freed up to reflect on the action.

> During [reflection-on-action], personal experiences are reflected on, a reevaluation occurs. . . . During this activity, new data are linked to what is already known, relationships within the data are established, ideas and feelings are tested for their authenticity, and

thus new personal practical knowledge and understanding are established. The outcome of this is the state for the design of future action; in other words, it is the input for reflection to action. (Butler, 1996, p. 274)

You can reflect in the present as events are occurring, referred to as reflection-in-action (Butler, 1996; Schön, 1983). This is one of the most difficult, but potentially powerful forms of reflection. It is difficult because of the "hot-action" nature of teaching (Eraut, 1985, chap. 1). It is powerful because it is the means for making adjustments in the process of teaching, based on a keen awareness of what is going on in the present.

Figure 4.2   Reflection Directions

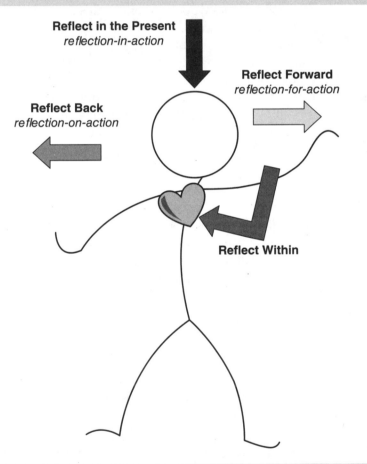

Source: York-Barr et al. (2006) based on Donald Schön's reflection framework (1983).

 Available for download at **http://resources.corwin.com/YorkBarrReflective**

> Reflection-in-action . . . is possible if and only if there is mental processing capacity available to get outside the act of generation of the performance and to watch its effects and evaluate them. This means being able to accumulate and evaluate immediate feedback within the performance context . . . it allows modification of the performance plan to make it more efficacious. (Butler, 1996, p. 273)

The abilities to reflect-in-action and to make adjustments accordingly are readily apparent in master educators, teachers, and administrators. The mind of master teachers, for example, are not totally consumed with delivering instruction and keeping students engaged. Their minds are freed up to observe student responses, to notice subtle indicators of confusion, to identify unusual responses. Reflection-in-action requires a high level of consciousness. High-performing athletes also offer salient examples of reflection-in-action, making minor adjustments as they perform. Teachers consider, *how are students responding? Who is not responding? When did student engagement trail off? What might be some reasons for this?*

You can reflect forward, referred to as reflection-for-action or reflection-to-action (Butler, 1996). In this type of reflection, you envision the effect of specific interventions or actions on a group of students, the classroom as a whole, a group of colleagues, the learning environment, and the school as a community. Reflection-for-action has the potential to identify future ways of thinking or behaving that are likely to produce desirable results. As mentioned above, reflection-on-action is the major input source for considering reflection-for-action.

Journaling

Journaling makes invisible thoughts visible, and actually audible. Often as we write, we are saying the words internally, sometimes even aloud. This provides a means of describing practice as well as identifying and clarifying beliefs, perspectives, challenges, and hopes for practice. It is a way to put your thoughts on paper. It offers a private place for honest accounting and review. You can go back and read entries many times. It sometimes helps to recall thoughts and different times in your life. If you have journaled about past problems, when you face another, you may be able to find references, analogies, and problem-solving strategies that have worked previously. Journaling can be a quiet or energizing time of reflection, and both states can elicit nurturing. A middle school principal once explained that journaling was a way to dump thoughts and feelings, which helped him get rid of old problems. He was able to write about an issue, to think about it, and then to let it go. He also used his journal as a way to document events.

Here we share three varied examples of how high school teachers engaged in a schoolwide small learning community's literacy project, journaling each in her own way. Later in the chapter we share specific ways that journaling has been used with student teachers at the preservice level of teacher development.

Visual Diary

Monica, a high school art teacher, shared her way of journaling—a visual diary. She uses the visual diary to record her daily reflections on teaching. But, instead of sticking with words, she depicts meaning with a variety of visual representations that capture the meaning of her day. She drafts sketches, diagrams, and mind maps. She uses pictures from magazines or that students have drawn that have particular meaning. She finds sayings in articles or magazines or she creates words and phrases from letters cut out of the newspaper. She includes poetry that students write, or poems she finds meaningful. She sometimes also includes topics she wants to share with her colleagues. Monica shares her visual diary with her students as a model for reflection and as a model for the kind of journaling she expects in her classes from her students.

Monica shared this method of reflective journaling with other teachers and the idea has spread. Some use this technique of reflective journaling to record their thoughts for the monthly faculty table talk, a monthly time for faculty to sit with peers from other departments and share what they are learning and working on. Other teachers have taken the visual diary idea as a technique to use with their students to encourage student reflection.

Calendar Prompts

Another journaling technique was created by Susan, a science teacher, and is incorporated into her planning book. At the beginning of each month she creates a monthly calendar with question prompts to which she wants her students to respond. Susan then uses these same prompts to reflect on ideas she wants to share with her students, as well as to help clarify her own thinking on topics prior to responding to her students' reflections.

Lesson Plan Sticky Notes

A math teacher, Leslie, developed yet another way to prompt reflection through journaling. Keeping a notebook or journal did not fit her style of learning, but she did want to record her ideas, successes, challenges, and questions that surfaced as she implemented new literacy strategies into her classes. Her way was to keep sticky notes on her lesson plan book. As she practiced new teaching strategies or noticed changes in the behavior or learning patterns of students, she would jot on the sticky notes. To track her thinking and observations, she then used her collection of sticky notes to support her evaluation of the success and failures of the week and to ground her plans for implementation the next week. Leslie also used the sticky notes from her lesson plan book when reflecting with another math teacher. Since this was the first time both math teachers had taught the new curriculum, they met weekly to plan together, discuss student behaviors and concerns, evaluate student work, troubleshoot potential challenges, and create their embedded weekly literacy lessons. The sticky notes assured that Leslie's insights were not forgotten, but used for reflection-on-action and for-action.

Five States of Mind

The five states of mind described by Costa and Garmston (2015) offer a rich framework or mental model for guiding reflection on your own, and also with others, such as in the context of groups and teams. Briefly described here are the five states of mind, with related questions that prompt reflection.

Efficacy involves having an internal locus of control and knowing that you can make a difference.

- Am I thinking efficaciously in this situation?
- How am I assuming responsibility for my role in this situation?
- As I think about what happened, what are things I did that I want to make sure that I do in the future?
- How did I decide to make that change in plans?
- What might I tell a colleague about my learning?

Flexibility involves thinking outside the box, choosing to look at things from a different perspective.

- Am I thinking flexibly? Or, am I limited to only one way of thinking?
- How might I do that differently the next time?
- What are some different outcomes I might want to incorporate into my aims of practice?
- What new ideas am I learning about that can increase my impact?

Craftsmanship is a focus on continuous improvement and use of data, a desire to always get better at what you do.

- Is this better than what we or I used to do?
- How can it be improved?
- What did I see or hear that tells me the goals were reached?
- What are some of the elements that I would plan more specifically next time?
- How will I assess the students'/colleagues'/parents' performance?

Consciousness is being aware of your own process of thinking; the contexts or environments around you; and the relationships among various thoughts, actions, and circumstances.

- What am I aware of?
- What is not here that needs to be?
- What don't I know? As I planned this activity and think about what happened, what were the most important lessons I learned?
- What do I want to pay more attention to and learn more about?
- How do I know when and how to make midcourse corrections in the moment?

Interdependence recognizes that you are never working alone, because you are always involved in an interdependent relationship whether you want to be or not.

- Who else might help? Who else is or might be involved?
- What would my friend do?
- Who else could I talk with about this activity?
- How do I plan together for future applications?
- What are some of the lessons I have learned from my mentors?

Thinking through this framework prompts internal reflection that can assist getting unstuck when what we are doing isn't working. One of the authors of this book has the five states of mind posted on the wall in his office. When stuck, he looks at the posted states of mind and goes down the list, one by one, thinking about the problem, his actions so far, and what he may have forgotten to try. Sometimes, it is important to look for what is not there as much as what is there. Thinking about the questions posed above prompt reflection-on-action and reflection-for-action.

Internal Reflections From a Principal

To say that the daily life of a principal is continual in-action work is perhaps an understatement. From the moment you arrive at school until you hit the pillow at night, you can never be too sure what will come your way. Over the years, I have accumulated strategies and mental maps to guide my thinking and action. Here are some examples.

What Are Your Non-Negotiables?

A personal reflection question for principals is: What are your non-negotiables? What is it that you will not negotiate away for yourself, your staff, your students, your parents, and so forth—these are things, ideas, principles you feel so strongly about that you would be willing to go to the wall for. What would you be willing to be fired for? With more and more demands, and fewer and fewer resources, priorities get very clear because you cannot do everything for everybody. So, before you are tested, and you will be tested if you have not been already, what are your non-negotiables?

It May Not Be Easy, But Is It Right?

The life of a principal regularly places you in conflict situations. We create some of these situations ourselves, but most are created by others. As decision makers, many times you will have someone unhappy with your decisions, thus you will incur criticism. In the final analysis you must do what you think is right. It may not be easy, but is it right?

JIT Worrying

An acronym borrowed from the business world, JIT, short for Just in Time, has been useful in school leadership work. Bill Sommers, one of the authors of this book who has served as an administrator, explains that if he worries too soon, he has to worry twice—once about what might happen (reflecting forward) and then again when the issue actually does happen (reflection-in-action). He does, however, create scenarios ahead of time. Creating actions to take if the results are good or bad provides more options for consider. In the end there is probably no benefit in worrying twice, if at all. Worrying twice drains your energy.

Can You Live With the Critics?

Angeles Arrien provided this question to ask of yourself: Is your self-worth as strong as your self-critic? We can terrorize ourselves by what we think about. Stop the inner terror. Self-reflection can create possibilities or put you into a downward spiral. Spend time answering the question and thinking of the possibilities before assuming the worst-case scenario.

No Deal Is an Option

Peter Block (1987) said there are five possible outcomes in any negotiation: Win-Lose, Lose-Win, Lose-Lose, Win-Win, or No Deal. In the first three, there is a loser and normally that means an emotional loss and damaged relationships. Of course, we all want the fourth option of win/win. But, Block introduces a fifth option: No Deal. Sometimes it is better to walk away rather than agree to something that you will be unhappy with later. No Deal is a powerful option.

How Do You Manage Up?

Dee Hock (1996) said you should spend 40 percent of your time managing yourself, 30 percent of your time managing up, 15 percent managing your peers, and 15 percent managing your direct reports. It is doubtful that these percentages hold in education like they do in business. Nevertheless, the concept of managing up is a good one to consider. If there is a mismatch of supervisory styles, how do you react? Let's say you are very concrete and your boss is a free thinker, you probably just want the boss to tell you what to do. Another possibility is that you are a creative person and your boss is a concrete sequential wanting to know every move you make. To manage up you must decide if you need to direct your boss in order to get your work done. For examples about how to manage up, visit www.fastcompany.com, and search for Boss Management, or go to Dobson and Singer's 2000 book titled *Managing Up*.

REFLECTIONS FOR MANAGING UP

What is your style?

What is your supervisor's style?

Are they a match? Does that mean there may be a blind spot?

Are they a mismatch? How will you work together in the most effective way?

INDIVIDUAL REFLECTIVE PRACTICE: MORE IDEAS TO CONSIDER

There are many creative ways to reflect that we sometimes discover all by ourselves. Not everyone benefits from prompts or prescribed processes, such as those described above. Some find that meditation and prayer open their minds and hearts to different ways of thinking. For others, exercise, yoga, or music have the effect of creating space for new thoughts and insights to emerge. Still others listen to audio books as a way to both ground and expand thinking about practice. We even know of individuals who simply go to sleep and let their unconscious minds take over the processing of problems or complexities of practice, resulting later in more conscious insights or understandings. Oftentimes, they wake up in the middle of the night with clear minds and new ideas. Undoubtedly, we are on the front end of discovering myriad ways to enrich and expand our thinking capacities, which will unleash exponentially our ways of doing. Below is a menu of ideas for reflecting on your own that may spark an interest for your reflection.

Self-Observing

Bergsgaard and Ellis (2002) introduce the practice of *self-observing* as a means by which educators become more conscious observers of their thoughts, feelings, and behaviors in order to gain insight into their teaching practices. They propose that mental activity in human beings takes three forms, which sometimes work independently of one another and other times work interactively. One form, *organic impulse*, is described as an immediate response like an emotion to a presenting stimulus. Another form, *idea generation*, refers to the thoughts that emerge consciously or unconsciously that result in meaning or interpretation. Often emotional responses and emergent ideas reinforce a thought-emotion cycle that can spiral and be difficult to control. The third form of mental activity is *self-observing* described as "the condition of consciousness characterized by awareness, objectivity, clarity, acceptance, and being in the present as well as by the absence of opinion, preference, prejudice, and attachment" (p. 56).

To illustrate, Bergsgaard and Ellis offer an example. A student gets up and leaves class. The teacher demands he stop and return to his seat. The student leaves despite the command. She follows him down the hall at which point he informs her he is feeling sick. Her thinking and behavior shifts instantly. The teacher acted on fear (an impulse) that was exacerbated by concerns (idea generation) of losing control. The authors offer commentary on this scenario:

> What is most remarkable . . . is that the strongest, most stressful feelings for the teacher were not based on the simple reality of one human being leaving a room, but issued out of ideas based upon assumptions and illusions that provoked emotion which provided a further acceleration of the idea development process. (p. 59)

The authors suggest that practice at self-observing could have resulted in the teacher recognizing she was feeling threatened and rather than acting on emotions might have demonstrated more informed and sensible actions.

Bergsgaard and Ellis suggest five strategies for developing the practice of self-observation. *Contemplative observation*, they explain, is derived from Buddhist meditations and has been described by Richard Brown (1998) as a method that

> synchronizes the observer with the learning environment; awakens and clarifies perceptions, thoughts, and emotions; and develops knowledge and compassion. In contemplative observation, we observe not only what is happening in the environment, but also what is simultaneously occurring within ourselves. (Brown, p. 70, as quoted by Bergsgaard & Ellis, 2002, p. 61)

A second strategy, *journaling* (introduced earlier in this chapter), the authors suggest can be used to gain insight about how organic impulse and idea generation are evoked within ourselves. The other three strategies are inter-related. *Breathing techniques* assist in quieting the mind and slowing down the pace of thought and action thereby allowing reconnection with authentic instead of perceived realities. *Relaxation responses* support the state of non-attachment, the ability to let thoughts through one's mind without attaching emotion. They explain:

> When this practice awareness of breathing and the Self is brought forward into the classroom, what appeared to be a charged, frantic and chaotic environment can be viewed by the objective, but compassionate observer as individual human beings all interacting out of their own needs in ways that make sense to each. (Bergsgaard & Ellis, 2002, p. 64)

Finally, *meditation* is posed as a way to "tap into the mindfulness and awareness that leads to the Self-Observing" (p. 64). The process of self-observing, in particular, reinforces the early steps of reflective practice cycles (e.g., pausing and openness) and lays the groundwork for later steps of gaining new insights that lead to improved teaching and learning practices.

Reflection in the Design of Web-Enhanced Lessons

Koszalka, Grabowski, and McCarthy (2003) developed the ID-PRISM protocol for assisting educators in the process of creating web-enhanced learning environments that integrate learning objectives and technology resources. Refer to their protocol shown in Table 4.4. The acronym stands for: Instructional Design: Possibilities, Realities, Issues, Standards, and Multi-Dimensional Views. Underlying the design of the protocol are five research-based characteristics of effective reflective practices:

- Inquiry, shown as the big picture framing questions;
- Recipes or tools that offer structured guidance for reflection;
- Strategic sequencing of the protocol's elements from unconstrained thinking to more focused planning;
- Contextualizing that engages teachers in consideration of web-enhanced instructional possibilities related to the specific learning constraints and opportunities in their classrooms; and finally
- Action planning that creates a bridge to implementation by specifying actions or steps.

Essentially, the ID-PRISM protocol serves as a scaffolding tool for teacher learning on embedding effective use of technology to enhance student learning. Readers are encouraged to consult this resource for an in-depth description and a rich set of examples.

Table 4.4   The ID-PRISM Reflection Tool for Web-Enhanced Learning

Possibilities

What are the possibilities for your ideal teaching and learning environment?

- The best strategies and resources I currently use in my classroom . . .
- Using real-world experiences during learning . . .
- Student activity during ideal learning events . . .
- Ideal informational and people resources available for learning . . .
- Based on my beliefs about teaching and learning, my ideal classroom . . .

Realities

What are the school infrastructure realities that impact the creation of your ideal web-enhanced learning environment?

- As I think about my current classroom . . .
- To move toward my ideal classroom . . .

Issues

How do teaching and learning issues impact the creation of your ideal web-enhanced learning environment?

- Internet access can support my teaching . . .
- Internet access can support student learning . . .
- Internet access would affect social interaction in my ideal classroom . . .
- An acceptable use policy (e.g., censorship, copyright) in my ideal classroom . . .
- Assessment and evaluation of my students in my ideal classroom . . .

Standards

How do educational standards and curriculum requirements impact the design of your ideal web-enhanced learning environment?

- My goals and expectations for learning in my ideal electronic learning environment . . .
- Resources that will support my goals include . . .
- Educational standards and curriculum requirements influence my teaching . . .
- Teaching consistency across grade levels is . . .

Multidimensional Perspectives

How do learning, learners, and the environment impact the learning design of your web-enhanced learning environment?

- The relationship among learning, learner, and the environment in my ideal classroom . . .
- Based on my beliefs about teaching and learning, to create my ideal classroom . . .

Source: Reprinted with permission from Koszalka, Grabowski, & McCarthy (2003).

 Available for download at http://resources.corwin.com/YorkBarrReflective

What Question Did You Ask Today?

Questioning is a powerful reflection tool. It positions us as active learners and can open our minds to new possibilities and ways of thinking. When Isidor Isaac Rabi, the winner of the 1944 Nobel Prize in physics, was young, each day after school his mother would ask him, "What question did you ask today in class?" Her question stood apart from the typical questions parents often ask their children, such as "How was your day?" or "What did you learn today?" Later when reflecting on his achievements, Rabi attributed his success to his mother's daily question and the stimulus it created for thinking creatively and moving beyond surface understandings (Bonder, 1999).

Questions emerge from our need for information as well as our curiosity to understand commonalities, discrepancies, and interrelations among differing ideas and perspectives. Pausing to craft a question sharpens our thinking about what we already understand, do not understand, and want to understand. As we reflect on both the question and what is learned, new knowledge is created. What we learn helps us discover breaks in our logic or discrepancies in our associations. Some questions do not have answers, but stretch our thinking as we consider the possibilities. Questions do not have to be asked of someone else. We may ask ourselves a question and then hold it in our thoughts to play with ideas. When we choose to ask questions of others, the potential exists not only to learn, but to create conditions that open up conversations for others to reflect and learn.

Reflecting on Race, Culture, and Equity

Cultural diversity and equity are primary considerations in the process of continuous renewal and improvement in schools. A significant challenge in our profession is the limited experiences of our predominantly Caucasian teaching force with culturally diverse populations. This does not mean that White teachers cannot be effective with students of color, as explained by Gloria Ladson-Billings (2000) in her book, *The Dreamkeepers*. Each of us, however, brings our lived experience as our underlying theory of how the world works and our cultural norms and expectations. If we lack experience interacting in diverse cultural contexts, our underlying theories for understanding and acting in the world are devoid of those influences.

In Chapter 2, we shared some of Richard Milner's (2003) work regarding reflection around race and culture. He recommends journaling as one way that educators could safely begin exploring their thoughts and examining their actions and interactions with students around the construct of race. You are referred back to the reframing section (Chapter 2, pages 57–61) which includes some of Milner's specific reflection questions on race and culture. Also recommended is direct interaction with Milner's full text (full citation located in the reference list) to add depth of consideration to racial influences on education generally, and teaching and learning specifically.

Mapping . . . Go Visual!

Mapping could be considered a form of journaling. Journaling is a linear or sequential presentation of written information—one sentence or thought after another. Mapping is a more fluid presentation, showing connections and relationships between ideas and information. Similar to graphic organizing, mapping is a way to visually represent an event, meeting, lesson, curricular unit, reading, or presentation. A map can clearly communicate the big ideas at a glance. For example, a presenter may have shared and expanded on three main ideas about classroom management: relationships, classroom expectations, and communication structures. Figure 4.3 illustrates a map of pedagogy skills identified as significant for emphasis related to how Engineering is taught to students. Notice that specific engineering content ("the what") is not the emphasis in this map. Instead, "the how" of engineering teaching and learning is emphasized and will show up across numerous units of engineering study. Mapping allows different emphases on information by altering the sizes, boldness, accents, and locations of words and pictures. It also easily depicts relationships among the main ideas as well as between each main idea and its respective subpoints. The process of constructing maps requires higher-order thinking about the content and creates a framework onto which future information can be added.

Teacher Narratives

Teacher narratives are "stories written by and about teachers that form the basis of narrative inquiry" (Sparks-Langer & Colton, 1991, p. 42); they are a somewhat more-disciplined form of writing than journaling. Journaling is more free-flowing. Teacher narratives usually have more structure and focus, because their intent is to communicate a story. Either keen observers or teachers themselves write real stories about teaching. The stories illuminate the realities, dilemmas, joys, and rewards of teaching. Reflecting on teacher narratives yields several benefits: insights about motivations for teacher actions, about the details and complexities of teaching, and about the teachers themselves (Sparks-Langer & Colton, 1991).

Teacher narratives can be specifically designed for use as case studies, in which specific problems of practice are presented that require reflection for analysis and solution finding. Case studies have the advantage of portraying realities of practice without requiring *in vivo* observations, which are time-consuming (Taggart & Wilson, 1998). Autobiographical sketches, also called personal histories (Sparks-Langer & Colton, 1991), are a specialized form of teacher narratives. The stories are of a more personal and in-depth nature, offering insight "into the past to uncover preconceived theories about teaching and learning" (Taggart & Wilson, 1998, p. 164).

Figure 4.3   Sample Reflection Map Used to Plan and Reflect

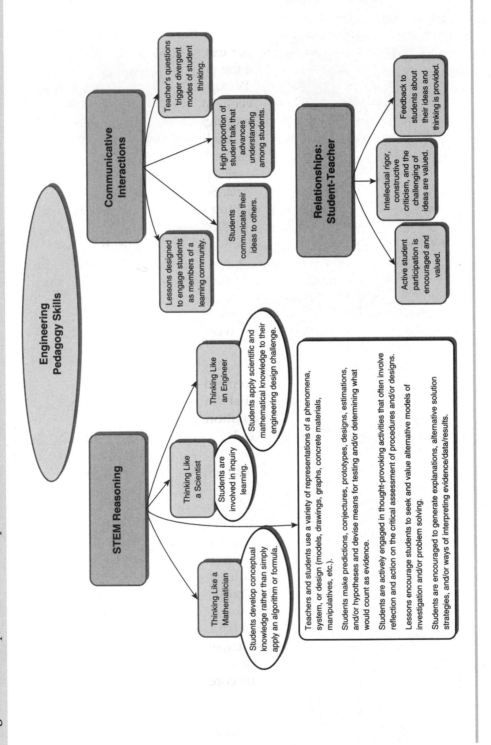

Weekly Journal Seeds for Student Teachers

As part of work with preservice teachers, a university instructor developed "Weekly Journal Seeds" as a structure to support student teachers in a more meaningful examination of the teaching competencies (which appeared all too theoretical), and to prompt deeper examination of the teaching context, including consideration of some of the unique and at times ambiguous aspects of their teaching situation. The *Weekly Journal Seeds* were e-mailed to student teachers on Monday of each week. Most weeks there were at least three seed questions with one question designed to prompt exploration of their teaching context, one question overtly linked to the teaching competencies identified for their licensure area, and one question framed around an inspirational quote from the supervisor's personal "quote collection."

To personalize the design of the *Journal Seeds,* the university supervisor considered the flow of the student teaching experience (including certain events that needed to occur, such as a midterm and final conferences), the parameters of the student teaching (what was required and what was flexible), and the wide range of student teacher backgrounds in the program (some already had licenses and years of teaching experience, others were brand new to teaching). The university supervisor brought her own experiences and creative intuition into the process as well. Following is a sample of the journal seeds sent during the first week of the students' practicum.

- What have been the highlights of your start-up week(s) so far? What success stories do you want to remember? What are some specific things that you did as a teacher that you believe contributed to some successful student and class situations? What have been the surprises, challenges, and headaches?
- As you anticipate this school year, what are your biggest hopes and dreams for your students? For yourself? For you and your teaching team that you work with?
- There is a lot of scheduling and adult communication that goes on in your position, especially at the start of the school year or new semester. Tons of effort, right? So far, how is it going with communication/consultation/collaboration (as described on the competency checklist)? What specific positive qualities and actions do you add to the collaboration in your classroom/school? Are there certain strategies or skills you'd like to learn more about? Do you have other noteworthy joys or concerns in the area of collaboration right now?
- Quote to ponder: "The one who teaches is the giver of eyes" (Tamil proverb). What does this quote mean to you? Does this or another quote resonate with some of your core beliefs as a teacher?

To date, student feedback on use of *Journal Seeds* suggests that the journal seeds are supportive of focused examination of their teaching week for teachers who are regular users of e-mail.

Teaching e-Portfolios

Teaching e-folios have been described as "a purposeful collection of any aspect of a teacher's work that tells the story of a teacher's efforts, skills, abilities, achievements, contributions to students, colleagues, institution, academic discipline or community" (Brown & Wolfe-Quintero, 1997, p. 28). Items that might be included in a teaching portfolio (Bailey, Curtis, & Nunan, 1998) are (a) a personal statement of teaching philosophy, strengths, interests, challenges; (b) a description of teaching goals and responsibilities (e.g., courses, specific assignments); (c) any materials developed by the teacher (e.g., lesson plans, syllabi, assignments, audiovisuals, tests); and (d) evidence about teaching performance and effectiveness (e.g., student feedback, student-performance data, colleague and peer perspectives, supervisor feedback) and the teacher's interpretation or analysis of the evidence. Today's world of electronic communications and storage offers a readily accessible and easily stored reflective space.

Teaching e-folios offer numerous assets in the process of reflection (Bailey et al., 1998; Brown & Wolfe-Quintero, 1997). First, the process of reviewing and selecting items for the portfolio is itself a reflective process. "The very process of developing a portfolio can help [teachers] gather together their thoughts about their professional strengths and synthesize them into a cogent collage" (Brown & Wolfe-Quintero, 1997, p. 29). Second, teaching portfolios contain multiple and varied data about teaching and its effects. Multiple perspectives add breadth and depth to the analysis process. Third, the time spent reflecting on the teaching portfolio as a whole "inevitably enlarges a teacher's view of what teaching is" (Brown & Wolfe-Quintero, 1997, p. 29). Finally, teaching portfolios provide one way of documenting the nature of one's teaching at one point in time. In reviewing portfolios over the years, one realizes one's growth. Use of teaching portfolios not only serves to document growth but also contributes to it.

Instead of creating a comprehensive portfolio that addresses an entire scope of teaching, smaller portfolios can be developed that focus on one specific area of teaching (e.g., one course or curricular area). This allows a focused review of specific areas and facilitates an easier revision process because the materials for each area are gathered together. Another idea is to include a partner in the portfolio's design and review process, the same way in which a teacher assists a student in portfolio design, selection, and review. Another person adds the invaluable dimension of an outside perspective and serves as coach to support reflection and inquiry.

Metaphors

Metaphorical thinking is a way to illuminate features through comparison. Orson Scott Card, a novelist, is quoted as saying, "Metaphors have a way of holding the most truth in the least space." Metaphorical thinking has been described as attending to likenesses, to relationships, and to structural features . . . identifying conceptual categories that may not be obvious or previously acknowledged . . . making knowledge in one domain a guide for comprehending knowledge in another, with some transfer or meaning taking place in both directions. . . . To be a metaphorical thinker is to be a constructive learner, one who actively builds bridges from the known to the new (Pugh, Hicks, Davis, & Venstra, 1992, pp. 4–5).

Developing metaphors requires creative thinking and has the potential to shift thinking in ways that analytic thinking cannot. Metaphors can be used to simplify and clarify problems, summarize thoughts, develop alternative ways of thinking about a topic or event, and communicate abstract ideas (Taggart & Wilson, 1998). Cross-cultural metaphors can have a powerful effect. Here are some examples:

- Not learning is bad, not wanting to learn is worse. (African proverb)
- Children need models more than critics. (French proverb)
- A poor person shames us all. (Gabra saying)
- No matter how far you are down the wrong road, turn back. (Turkish proverb)

Johnston (1994) described one example of the use of metaphor to promote reflection. She requested that each of three students completing a master's program "write a metaphor that described her experience in the program, paying particular attention to capturing ways in which she had changed or not changed during the two years" (p. 15). One student wrote about being a contractor, explaining that initially she followed predesigned plans, but that over time, she and the future homeowners worked together to create customized plans. Another student wrote about being a tree in a drought, whose roots system had to seek out new sources of nutrients. The third student captured her experience as an artichoke with each petal being an element of practice that can be understood only when peeled away and examined. (Use of metaphors to promote reflection in the context of groups is presented in Chapter 6.)

Reading With Reflection

Ideas for individual reflection would be incomplete without emphasizing the value of reading and reflecting on the information, although one emphasis of reflective practice is frequently on generating internal knowledge and making sense of one's teaching practice. External sources of knowledge are also important, if not essential. Given the isolating tendencies in the teaching profession, such as teaching in the same school or district for one's entire career, educators particularly must make concerted efforts to stay informed about findings from research and about practices occurring elsewhere in education. There are many ways to teach and learn. The greater one's repertoire, the greater the likelihood for success with all students.

Personal Reflections on Meaning in Life

Amid the *busy-ness*, which can often feel like *busy-mess*, of everyday life, there are times when we find ourselves deep in thought about who we are, how we contribute or would like to, what is important to us, and to whom we are especially grateful. There are also times when we are noticeably out of balance and must create the space to intentionally consider these life-meaning perspectives. Are we human doings or human beings? In what ways are we both doings and beings? Envision yourself high up on a mountain slope, looking up, down, and all around into vast open space. Or, maybe you are nestled in a wind-breaker seated on a cool sand beach watching the waves rhythmically rise and fall and then spread out across the sand. In both spaces, you are removed from the typical daily hustle and bustle and you are keenly aware of the natural world around you, a world with its own rhythms and energies that seldom grab your notice. You are small in comparison. You can just *be* in this place. You are not called to *do*. Here is a list of questions designed to help you select a few points to prompt reflection. And, of course, we encourage you to add to the list. We also invite you to consider with whom you might want to share some of your responses.

- What is it that I want to do with my most precious gift . . . the gift of life?
- If 80 percent of what I do has little noticeable impact and 20 percent provides me with the best results, what things in the 80 percent am I going to stop doing?
- Is my self-worth stronger than my self-critic and how do I know? Is my self-critic preventing me from moving toward my most valued life pursuits?
- How do I use my gifts and talents to foster caring, commitment, and interdependence in my work?
- What am I willing to get fired for?
- What words of wisdom would my parents or grandparents offer as I sort through what matters most, and how I can contribute?
- How do my children think of me, not only as a parent, but as a person? A citizen? What lessons do I hope to have taught them through modeling?
- Who are the people that bring joy to my life? And, to whose life do I bring joy?
- Who have been the most important mentors in my life? Have I thanked them lately? What is stopping me?
- If I had one week to live, what would I do?
- In one sentence, what would I want written in my obituary?

GETTING STARTED WITH INDIVIDUAL REFLECTIVE PRACTICE

The decision to be a reflective educator is a commitment to your own growth and demonstrates a high level of professional responsibility and personal leadership for continuous development of your practice. It is how you develop the expertise and insights that accumulate into wisdom. It is a commitment made in a life context that reluctantly yields space for thinking and creating. We are confident that it is a decision you will not regret. In fact, we believe that becoming more reflective is likely to heighten your awareness of the deep-seated yearning you have to make sense of your world and to become the best you can be. Webb (1995) describes the paradox of subtle urgency for reflection in our life of practice

> Reflection-on-action remains the endangered species of reflective practice. It is the most easily lost due to pressure of work and its loss has no immediate, transparent effect. My experience continues to tell me, however, that the quiet times of reflection-on-action are critical for the survival of my own reflective practice . . . this puts the onus on one's self to make the time and organize one's life in such a way that reflection-on-action can continue to have an impact on professional practice. (p. 77)

The longest relationship that you have is with yourself. Why not make the best of it! Becoming more reflective is a way to learn more about who you are, what is important to you, how you think, what you say and do, and who you are as an educator. Choosing reflection supports your desire for excellence and effectiveness in your work.

To further guide your thinking about developing your reflection capacities and your own preferred means of reflection, we invite you to contemplate the following questions:

- Thinking about your own development as an educator, what are you most interested in learning more about? Why does this seem important to you?
- What about the considerations of identity, ethics, courage, care, and voice? What of these issues seems most important to ponder further right now, and why? What are your thoughts on how you might step into examining such an area of your identity, and/or beliefs and values?
- As you reflect on your practice, what are your big questions? What parts of the curriculum are students missing? How can you maximize the learning strengths of all your students?
- What would be the best way to go about addressing these interests and questions? What ways of reflection are best aligned with your learning styles (e.g., journaling, exercising, reading, mapping)?

- How might you create space in your life to reflect and learn on a regular basis?
- Are there additional people you want to include in your process of reflection?

The Chapter Reflection Page (Figure 4.4) can be used to jot down your thoughts in response to these questions.

You can only teach and lead who you genuinely are (Palmer, 1998). In these demanding times, it is easy to slide to a place of feeling as if you are never enough. But, who you are every day, how you create meaningful learning experiences for students and colleagues, the positive energy you choose to bring to your work is enough. It is more than enough: it is an enormous gift to the world around you. By maintaining a focus on reflective capacities that expand and improve your personal practices, your influence on others expands as well. Just remember to place your own oxygen mask securely in place before assisting others.

Figure 4.4   Chapter Reflection Page

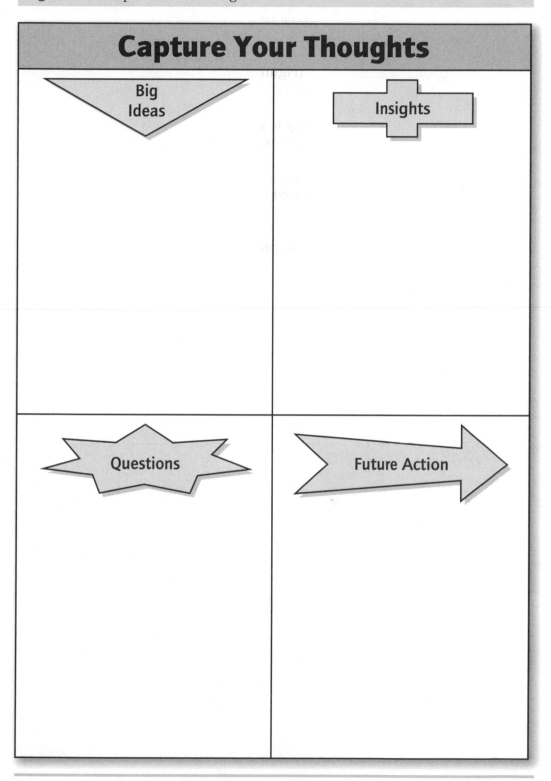

5

Reflective Practice With Partners

Awareness of one's own intuitive thinking usually grows out of practice in articulating it to others.

—Donald Schön, *The Reflective Practitioner: How Professionals Think in Action*, 1983

As human beings, we are drawn to interactions with others. These interactions provide a means of understanding who we are in our world around us, and in our professional and personal lives. Reflecting on educational practice with another person has the potential to greatly enrich our understanding and to support improvements in our practice. Because we filter our experiences through our own views of the world, however, reflecting alone can result in self-validation and justification (Bright, 1996; Butler, 1996; Levin, 1995; Zeichner, 1993). Reflection with another person offers a safeguard against perpetuating only our own thoughts. Bright (1996) explains,

> Because it is the practitioner's understanding which is the window through which a situation is understood and interpreted, an essential feature of "reflective practice" is the need for the practitioner to be aware of her own processes in the development and construction of this interpretation . . . to understand how she understands a

situation. . . . As intimated earlier, "reflective practice" is not easy, and the "self-reflexive" element of it makes it even more difficult. Paradoxically, this suggests the role of others in this self-reflective process because colleagues and clients may be very perceptive in detecting assumptions and bias present within a practitioner's practice. (pp. 177–178)

When reflecting, a partner can assist us in gaining awareness of fixed assumptions and viewing events from another perspective (Bright, 1996; Butler, 1996). Reflecting with a partner addresses the major concern about reflecting solely with ourselves, which is reinforcing only our own views and perceptions. Compared with reflection in groups, partner reflection offers the advantage of more privacy. Trust, therefore, often is more readily established. Trust and safety are always issues when interacting with others and especially when revealing one's practice, questions, and thinking.

Edward O. Wilson, in his book *The Diversity of Life* (1992), says, "diversity strengthens." Adding people's perspective to your own thoughts increases personal awareness of the effect on others, of implications outside your personal sphere of influence, and provides a wider world view. Bringing in outside viewpoints and experiences increases learning for us as individuals, and extends that learning to others.

Recall from Chapter 1 the potential gains that can be realized when configured as partners (i.e., dyads or triads). In addition to offering new insights, reflecting with a partner has the potential to strengthen collegial relationships, decrease feelings of isolation, and increase a sense of connection in and to one's place of work. We are not supposed to be alone in this complex arena of practice.

In this chapter, we focus on how to engage in reflective practices with partners. We use the term *reflective practice with partners* (or, reflection partners) to refer to two or three people (dyads or triads) who collaboratively engage in a reflective learning process focused on improving educational practice with the ultimate objective of enhanced student learning. We distinguish between reflection with partners and reflection in groups or teams (the next chapter) in the following ways. Reflective practice with partners (in contrast to groups/teams) is smaller and participation is often voluntary in that it is often practitioner (e.g., teacher, support personnel) initiated and self-directed. Partners often have connections through shared interests, areas of practice, or individual styles. Sometimes connections are sought with colleagues who have different roles and perspectives and can spark new ways of thinking about practice. In this chapter, we expand some of the how-to information shared in Chapter 4 (individual reflection) to include partners. Again, we offer considerations, examples, ideas, and suggestions for getting started with reflective practice with partners.

SPECIAL CONSIDERATIONS FOR REFLECTIVE PRACTICE WITH PARTNERS

It is not safe to assume that adults who learn well by themselves will learn well with others. Think about the specific and intentional support that teachers provide when students are expected to work together compared to when they work alone. Such intentional consideration of learning design is also helpful, sometimes even necessary, with adults. Reflective practice structures and processes are tailored based on the purpose of the reflection, the number of people involved, and the skills and dispositions they have acquired to reflect well together. A summary of considerations for partner reflection is offered in Table 5.1 for your reference, including relevant topics described earlier in the book. All these considerations interact with one another. The desired focus of reflection, for example, may influence who is selected as a reflection partner. Conversely, the choice of a reflection partner may influence the topic of reflection. Topical emphases for reflection are infinite; reflection partner options may be less plentiful. For some people, the choice of a partner precedes identification of a specific reflection focus. And, it is not unusual for partners to choose colleagues they view as good listeners who will support reflection by paraphrasing what they hear, but refrain from offering advice. Essentially, a well-crafted paraphrase offers the speaker an opportunity to hear and reflect on his or her own thinking. Often this, of and by itself, serves as a springboard to generate possibilities for moving forward. Practice Example 5.1 offers a robust example of this approach to reflective practice with partners and how it has transformed the culture of learning conversations in one school.

What Is the Purpose or Focus of Your Partner Reflection?

What do you want to learn about? As with any type of reflection, the overarching purpose of partner reflection is to expand thinking and understanding about practice in order to increase effectiveness as an educator. Partner reflection may focus on a specific area of teaching or leadership practice, a shared teaching or leading situation (e.g., co-teaching or co-facilitating), or a specific aspect of a partner's practice. It may also focus on external sources of knowledge or circumstances. Numerous factors influence what you and your reflection partner identify as a focus, some of which are described in this section.

To begin, the amount of teaching experience often influences reflection emphases. Early in one's career, the learning and development process usually concentrates on creating a supportive learning environment, becoming familiar with the curriculum, and establishing core classroom routines and instructional practices. Later on, learning and

Table 5.1   Considerations for Reflective Practice With Partners

Clarify Purpose and Process

- Something I would like to learn more about is . . . because . . .
- Things that help me to be reflective are . . .

Strengthen Listening

- Intentional pause: a requirement for both listening to oneself and listening to others
- Empathic listening: listening and understanding (from Chapter 2)
- Suspension: develop the ability to suspend beliefs in order to listen
- Increase awareness of listening blocks: comparing, mind reading, filtering, judging, dreaming, identifying, advising, sparring, being right, derailing, and placating

Expand Thinking and Inquiry

- Personal Inventory of Reflective Practice (Figure 4.1 from Chapter 4)
- Open questions, SPACE, Reframe, and Dialogue (from Chapter 2)
- A shift from *how* to *what* and *why* questions (from Chapter 2)
- Reframing and reexamining experiences through a new lens (from Chapters 2 and 3)
- Reiman's (1999) Guided Reflection Framework: apply "matching responses" to affirm and encourage; apply "mismatching responses" to challenge

Coach

- Reflection and inquiry embedded in practice context
- Direct support for knowledge development and skill transfer to practice
- Non-evaluative; judgment free data and inquiry (Sanford, 1995)

Available for download at http://resources.corwin.com/YorkBarrReflective

development expands to include more complex instructional issues (e.g., differentiating instruction to meet a wider range of abilities and interests), productive collaboration with colleagues, mentoring of new teachers, and contributing to school-level organizational and improvement work. As we enter middle and late adulthood, our interests typically shift to larger work and life issues, such as the effects of external state, national, and global events and trends on humankind, as well as issues and questions of our own contributions, and legacies to our families, profession, and communities.

Liz Wiseman in her 2014 book *Rookie Smarts: Why Learning Beats Knowing in the New Game of Work* advances the idea of including our less experienced colleagues in the process. She believes we make better decisions when those who are newer to the profession are asked their opinions. If enough trust exists to feel secure in stating their opinions, they bring new information, are willing to question what norms are in place, seek out answers to questions they cannot answer, and develop connections with more politically savvy veterans. Unfortunately, without this new perspective, we tend to rely only on what has worked in the past. While not wanting to rid ourselves of past successes, we will need to continue to look for additional ways to learn and teach a diverse group of learners.

In addition, the specific focus of reflection, such as a particular initiative or teaching practice, is influenced by the "stage" of implementation for an individual educator. Is this an instructional practice that I just started last week? Or, have I spent the past six months working with the practice and am now moving toward refining my understanding and use. Concerns and questions change over time based on the level of experience with a given practice or initiative.

As we think about implementing change, we reference the multiple editions of Gene Hall and Shirley Hord's *Implementing Change* (2014). The authors' seminal research, on how change happens, is meaningful. The Stages of Concern offers an emotional side of change.

Most consultants, salespeople, and supervisors initiate the conversations about change by reporting the research of the impact of a change. In our experience, this has not been very productive at implementation nor sustainable change. As suggested by Hall and Hord, the staff is thinking about *What do I have to do? What does this change mean for me and my classroom plans?* Once they understand what is going to be required, people start to focus on the task at hand: *Do I have the skills necessary to implement this change?* The final stage is that they then can focus on the impact the change is having in the classroom, school, or community.

Hall and Hord's research documents the following process from Self to Task to Impact:

- Awareness—I am not concerned with this change.
- Informational—I want to know more about it.
- Personal—How will this affect me? What do I have to do?
- Management—Adjusting my routines is taking a lot of time.
- Consequences—Is this making a difference for my students? Staff?
- Collaboration—How is this affecting my colleagues? School?
- Refocusing—How can I make this better? (Hall & Hord, 2014)

Trying to implement changing practices without paying attention to this research ends up in episodic, if not limited, positive lasting results.

Dyads and triads also offer an excellent opportunity to inquire about the process of learning through reflection. A focus of reflection may be shaped by questions partners have about their own reflective process (in a sense, meta-reflection). Partners may wonder:

- In what ways does the reflection process influence my thinking?
- What conditions are conducive to my reflection? What conditions inhibit my reflection?
- Why am I drawn to reflect on certain aspects of my teaching practice and routinely ignore other aspects?
- How do I increase my reflection as I am teaching or leading (reflection-in-action), instead of primarily afterward (reflection-on-action)?
- To what extent are my personal reflection capacities (being present, being open, listening) developing?

Such questions ground continuous refinement and are well suited for reflection with partners. Without a compelling purpose, time for partner reflection is not likely to be honored. If you are not learning or you are not learning something informative to your practice, the time allocated for reflection will soon become filled with other activities. Time spent learning together is too precious to be spent on issues of lesser importance, or worse, issues that detract from your growth, such as gossip or an obsession on circumstances beyond your influence or control. Reflecting on and for practice has great potential for not only learning, but also sustaining the energy we require to persist and get better at what we do for the young people in schools, for ourselves, and for the collective wellness of our staff.

Early in the process of reflecting together, partners are advised to articulate their learning interests (content), and also what helps them be present in a reflective space (process). Here are some specific ideas for deciding on topics and desired outcomes. One way is to take a few minutes individually and then share responses to the following prompts:

- Something I would like to learn more about is . . . because . . . ; and
- Things that help me to be reflective are. . . .

The first prompt identifies potential content emphases for reflection. It may also reveal areas or ways in which the individual would like to improve their reflection practices. For example, "I would like to get better at listening without feeling the need to respond." The second prompt gets at conditions that promote reflection, ranging from the surrounding environment (e.g., noise, light, temperature, seating) to ways of interacting (e.g., time to process before responding).

At the beginning of each reflective interaction, it is useful for partners to clarify what they hope to gain from the specific interaction. Is the primary intent to obtain insight, to identify a range of options, to make a decision, or to just get thoughts out in the open to begin clarifying issues?

At the end of each interaction, it is also helpful to recap the territory covered and to identify key ideas or outcomes that emerged. Sample formats and prompts for closing reflections are offered at the book's companion website at http://resources.corwin.com/YorkBarrReflective.

With Whom Might You Reflect?

We suggest that finding people who you trust, AND who may or may not agree with you, could be some of the best partners. When there is high trust, not necessarily agreement on all issues, more ideas are verbally on the table and dialogue ensues. With dialogue comes consideration of other perspectives that hold the potential to create new meaning, possibilities, and common purpose.

Initial reflection partners often are self-selected because the motivation to reflect in dyads or triads is inside-out (self-initiated), although partners or partnership are sometimes required, as in mentoring for early career teachers. Initial partners typically share an interest in some aspect of practice and may have similar experiences and viewpoints. In most schools, there is meeting time allocated in the schedule for alike groups, such as grade level teams or subject area teams. Partner conversations serve well as a focused and personalized launch in such meetings, helping participants to transition from where they just were (usually teaching) to being present among team members. Reflecting in partners serves to get every voice in the room early in the team time. In effect, reflection can serve as an activation activity. One prompt that might get this started can be something like: Last time we left our team meeting having identified specific literacy practices, we were going to teach students to bolster their focused independent reading. Let's return to that focus by turning to the person next to you and working through this reflection-in-action sequence:

- What were some ways you practiced using the strategy?
- What did you notice in terms of how students responded?
- How might their responses to the strategy inform future strategy use?
- As you think ahead to the next session with this group of students, what do you envision as ways to teach or re-teach use of this strategy?

There may also be times, however, when it could be informative to reflect and learn with colleagues who have different backgrounds of areas in which they teach. Sometimes, reflecting with colleagues who have the same students, but in different learning contexts, results in new insights for engaging students.

Choosing to reflect with partners who are not part of your "alike" grade level or subject area team can pose access challenges. Supported by the Internet, many teachers are holding face-time conversations, not just with local colleagues, but also with teachers locally, regionally, nationally, or internationally.

In seeking partners, choose people who produce energy rather than drain it. Negativity and cynicism are unproductive and diminish your spirit. Seek people who are open to growth, both yours and theirs. Be wary of people with expert tendencies. No one knows it all. Everyone can improve. Strong partnerships spark great growth potential. A checklist of considerations for partners is offered in Table 5.2. The list includes characteristics to continuously develop within yourself so that you, too, serve well as a reflection partner.

Table 5.2   Characteristics to Consider for a Reflective Practice Partner

Essential Characteristics

Characteristics that I would choose to be present in any reflective practice partner. Someone who

___ stays focused on student learning.

___ is committed to continuous improvement.

___ is trustworthy.

___ contributes positively to the overall climate.

___ is a good listener.

___ is curious.

___ is open to examining practice—his or hers and mine.

___ will inquire about and help expand my thinking.

___ will encourage and support changes in practice.

___ has integrity.

___ aligns actions and words.

___ is accessible enough to allow regular opportunities to reflect together.

Variable Characteristics

Characteristics that I may intentionally choose as similar to or different from me, depending on my learning needs and desires.

___ years of teaching experience

___ type of teaching experience (e.g., level, content area, school demographics)

___ teaching style and philosophy

___ life experience

___ age

___ gender

___ ethnicity, culture

___ personality

___ learning style

How Do You Reflect Together?

Listening, thinking, and coaching are central to fostering reflective practice with partners. We offer a quick review on key considerations related to listening and suspension, both of which are core practices for reflection. For a more robust review return to Chapter 2, pages 41–46. Coaching is elaborated more fully here as it is largely practiced in dyads or triads.

Listening

Listening seems simple enough. Beyond putting down the newspaper and physically orienting toward the speaker, how hard can it be to just listen? Turns out it is a lot harder than we might anticipate. It has been suggested that this is why we have two ears and just one mouth. Listening well is what enables us to hear and understand what someone says to us. Listening and being listened to create a sense of connection and trust between individuals and is a powerful means of establishing rapport. When we truly listen, we listen with our ears, our eyes, our body, and our heart. Deep listening is very honoring of a relationship. Stephen Glenn, author and family psychologist, said years ago that people want three things: to be listened to, to be taken seriously, and to know that a person has a genuine interest in what you are saying. Knowing that you are being listened to is the first step. Knowing the other person is taking you seriously and is interested deepens the trust in the relationship.

Suspension is a thinking skill that fosters listening. We invite you to review the suspension excerpt (Table 5.3) related to Figure 2.3 (page 42). As you read this excerpt, underline, highlight, or make notes in the margin about words, phrases, and ideas that resonate for you. Share with a partner what you identify as significant. Some of the words and ideas that stand out for us are: *notice our own thinking . . . suspension is a way of emptying the cup . . . choosing to temporarily put aside your views . . . dialogue as a finite game . . . others have opinions that are true for them . . . as challenging as it is, it increases our learning.* When initially learning suspension, the idea that we can be more aware of our thoughts, but choose *not* to engage around them is often an "aha" experience. That we can choose to let our feelings and thoughts pass or be set aside, at least, temporarily, is a freeing notion. Hard to do, but worthy of attempts to do so. Sometimes there is no particular need to engage passing thoughts or feelings and make them bigger than they are or allow them to take us, or our reflection partner, off in tangential directions. They can be put aside, allowing space to attend more fully to others. As you engage in partner reflection pay attention to your thinking and practice the skill of suspension.

Table 5.3   Thoughts About Suspension and Listening in Dialogue

The point of engaging in dialogue is to exchange ideas, opinions, and observations. The purpose according to David Bohm (1989) in his book *On Dialogue* is to create meaning from the flow of conversation. Dialogue is not analyzing, picking a side, or winning an argument. It is an ongoing sharing of views, and having a learning conversation with someone, or a group of people.

One of the first requirements of dialogue is to suspend judgment. To do so we must notice our own thinking. Garmston and Wellman (1999) refer to suspension as "the essential internal skill of dialogue" (p. 54) and explain that "to suspend means to set aside our perceptions, our feelings, or judgments and our impulses for a time and listen to and monitor carefully our own internal experience and what comes up from within the group" (p. 55). Suspension allows us to be open to others' views. Like the Zen master who overflowed the cup of the student, you must empty your cup (or mind) before more can be put into the vessel. Suspension is a way of emptying the cup.

John Dewey (1933), in his book *How to Think,* wrote about suspending judgment as a prerequisite to good thinking. We used to say to people, "be non-judgmental." This was problematic. How can you be "non" something? We now say, set aside judgment or suspend judgment while in dialogue. It does not mean giving up your opinions. It does mean choosing to temporarily put your views aside and be open to the views of someone else.

We like what John Carse (1986) says in his book, *Finite and Infinite Games*. A finite game is like Monopoly, Sorry, and Gin Rummy. The goal of a finite game is to win. When you win, the game is over. In an infinite game, the goal of the game is to continue the game. We like to think of dialogue as an infinite game, one in which the conversation continues over time, and supports extending and deepening our understanding and our learning.

To engage in dialogue requires acceptance of another person's point of view without responding in dismissal, disgust, or disengagement. Others can have opinions that are true for them. We can be aware of how other points of view create emotions in us. It is our responsibility to manage our own emotions. Keeping our breathing rates slow and deep can keep us from getting riled and from losing our ability to suspend. If we do not understand we can choose to inquire with the genuine purpose of understanding, *not* as an opportunity to challenge, tell, or teach. We can simply check it out, by asking questions, paraphrasing, or clarifying for understanding.

To have an exchange of ideas, we must listen. Be fully present and listen. Sometimes in workshops we ask, "What percentage of time are you listening and what percentage of time are you waiting?" Many times people are waiting to get a word in or are composing their own ideas rather than truly listening. Madeline Burley-Allen in her 1995 book, *The Forgotten Art of Listening*, says that in communicating we spend 9 percent of our time writing, 16 percent reading, 35 percent speaking, and 40 percent of our time listening. So, where in the curriculum do we teach listening?

As challenging as it is to suspend and to truly listen, when we do suspend, we have found it enhances our understanding and our learning in ways that would not otherwise have been possible. It is a gift we can give ourselves, as well as those with whom we engage.

Mastering suspension will also assist you in minimizing common blocks to listening. In Chapter 2 (Figure 2.4, page 44), we identified the 12 common blocks to listening: comparing, mind reading, rehearsing, filtering, judging, dreaming, identifying, advising, sparring, being right, derailing, and placating. (This list was originally located on the Listening Leader website. Most recently, we retrieved it from the onmymind .areavoices.com website.) Each block was described more fully in Chapter 2, with a "just right" dose of tongue-in-cheek humor. As you read this list, which blocks do you relate to? Typically, each of us has numerous ways that we unfortunately block our listening to others, thereby running the risk of breaking rapport. A break in rapport is instantaneously recognized by partners, which in turn interrupts thinking, and can disrupt relationships.

Thinking

Thinking, of course, is integral in the process of learning. Theory and research abound on the topic of thinking. What is thinking? How does one think? What prompts thinking? What supports thinking at higher levels resulting in concept formation? Alan Reiman (1999) proposes a reflection framework based on the classic works of Vygotsky and Piaget, two eminent cognitive psychologists, and then provides a synthesis of findings from studies that used where the framework. Our intent in summarizing Reiman's work is to further understanding about the complex processes involved in thinking and in supporting thinking in others.

According to Reiman, Vygotsky viewed knowledge construction as co-created through interaction with other people. His work emphasized the significant role of a "capable other" in providing appropriate types and levels of support to foster growth in others. Capable others are viewed as individuals who have a more in depth and complex understanding of the subject of interest. Vygotsky (2003, p. 50) also created the term Zone of Proximal Development (ZPD) to refer to the space in which learning is most likely to occur. In the ZPD, the task at hand is of interest to the learner (motivation); it is sufficiently complex to engage the learner (challenge), but not so complex as to be out of reach for the learner to engage.

In contrast to Vygotsky, Reiman explains that Piaget viewed knowledge construction as a process of individual adaptation. When faced with new information, an individual can choose to either dismiss or engage the information. If one chooses to engage, and the new information is similar to existing information, it is said to be assimilated. If the new information in some way extends or enriches existing information, it is viewed as being accommodated into existing cognitive structures. If new information is complex and challenging it causes a state of disequilibrium, which can feel uncomfortable and even stressful. This is resolved through a process of equilibration that requires changes in cognitive structures.

How do Vygotsky's and Piaget's theories apply to reflection and teacher learning? Reiman suggests that when teachers take on new and more complex roles or contexts of practice, disequilibrium occurs. He argues that disequilibrium presents an opportunity for cognitive growth, which is well supported by a capable other. The capable other determines the individual learner's zone of proximal development and the scaffolds for promoting growth. He explains:

> The instructor, hoping to guide reflection, must skillfully match and mismatch . . . responses according to the unique needs of the [learner] . . . Matching means "starting where the learner is." Conversely, "mismatching" implies providing additional challenge . . . The challenge for the instructor is knowing when to support (match) and when to challenge (mismatch). (p. 7)

Reiman refers to the process of matching and mismatching as *guided reflection*. He identifies seven categories of guidance that are differentially provided by a mentor (capable other) depending on the feelings, thinking, and behavior demonstrated by a mentee. The mentor response categories are accepting feelings, praising or encouraging, acknowledging and clarifying ideas, prompting inquiry, providing information, giving directions, and addressing problems. Some of these responses are considered matching responses in that their function is to affirm and encourage. Others are considered mismatching in that their function is to challenge. Here is an example. If a mentee is expressing self-doubt in a new situation, a mentor might choose a matching response of praise and encouragement, recognizing the impact of feelings on the ability to reflect. If a mentee is viewing a situation from only one viewpoint, a mentor may choose a mismatching response, such as prompting inquiry, to foster more divergent thinking.

Reiman synthesized the findings of numerous quantitative studies involving preservice teachers who were engaged in new teaching roles, and who, during that process, were required to use dialogue journals. The reflection framework was used to guide the instructor responses to student entries in the journals. The preservice teachers also were expected to use the framework to guide reflection with their peers (other preservice teachers). The result was "greater gains in cognitive-structural growth across conceptual, moral, and ego domains" (1999, p. 16). The requirement that teachers apply the framework with peers was indicated to be an important variable. "This element of the intervention studies appears to be a key aspect of the guided reflection process because it encourages the novice or experienced educator to empathize, clarify, and raise more complex professional and personal issues with his or her colleague or tutee. The role taking experience, by itself, would not guarantee social perspective taking" (p. 14).

Coaching

The previous discussion underscores the significant role of another person in reflective practice, especially someone skilled at listening and asking questions to expand thinking. In educational contexts such a person is often referred to as a coach. Schön (1987) speaks about the role and intent of coaching,

> The student cannot be taught what he needs to know, but he can be coached; he has to see on his own behalf and in his own way the relations between means and methods employed and results achieved. Nobody else can see for him, and he can't see just by being "told," although the right kind of telling may guide his seeing and thus help him see what he needs to see. (p. 14)

Also in support of coaching is recognition that knowledge construction is enhanced when learners are engaged in authentic, meaningful, and complex problems of practice (as opposed to being engaged in isolated contexts and made-up problems). Coaching, done in authentic contexts, mitigates the problem of knowledge and skill transfer.

Many published studies focus on promoting reflective thought in the context of hierarchal relationships, such as a novice being guided by an expert teacher. Reflective practice in the context of horizontal relationships, however, is equally and sometimes more powerful. Food service personnel can coach teachers, secretaries can coach principals. Coaching does not have to be just about professional staff. Coaching doesn't have to happen with like peers. Reflective practice coaches hold up the process of reflection, by listening well, offering paraphrases of what they hear, and then crafting and asking open questions that support the reflecting partner to hear and think about what she or he said. Coaching often occurs in horizontal relationships. Much evidence exists to support the claim that both partners learn, regardless of whether the relationship is horizontal, vertical, or bottom up. Ash and Levitt (2003), for example, demonstrated that teacher learning increases when teachers use formative assessment practices with students. They studied the trajectory of teacher change. First, teachers listened to students, observed students, or examined student work to identify current levels of understanding. Then, they identified discrepancies between current and desired levels of student understanding. Next, the teachers reflected on their own practices (subject area expertise, pedagogical knowledge) to determine ways for scaffolding student learning to the next reasonable target. Each step of the trajectory requires complex cognitive engagement (i.e., learning) on the part of the teacher. Teachers reported improving their capacity to listen to students and to move students to higher levels of thought and understanding. It could be argued that Ash and Levitt's trajectory explains a process of learning for any individual involved in deliberate reflective practices with partners.

Coaching grew from a realization that traditional approaches to staff development, such as isolated workshops, were largely an ineffective means of changing practice (Showers & Joyce, 1996). Whatever excitement or possibilities may have been created during a workshop were lost on returning to school unless there was regular follow-up back at school focused on continuously supporting implementation of and reflection on new practices (Joyce & Showers, 2002). Coaching is predicated on adult learning principles that emphasize development must be relevant to and embedded in practice, supported by collaboration among peers, and aimed toward generating and then implementing refined practices. (Recall the discussion in Chapter 2 on brain-based learning and adult learning principles.)

According to Joyce and Showers (2002), when the intent is transfer of knowledge and skills into daily practice (which, in education, would almost always be the case), the results of peer coaching far surpass workshops or even demonstrations. Further, they emphasize the importance of schoolwide commitments to coaching, including the involvement of administrators. In their work, they require of schools,

- Commitment to practice/use whatever change the faculty has decided to implement;
- Assistance and support of each other in the change process, including shared planning of instructional objectives and development of materials and lessons; and
- Collection of data, both on the implementation of their planned change and on student effects relevant to the school's identified target for student growth. (Joyce & Showers, 2002, p. 88)

From years of practice and research, they also conclude that feedback should be omitted from the coaching process because when viewed as providing feedback there is a tendency to fall into supervisory (hierarchal) or evaluative interactions. We qualify their assertion to suggest certain types of feedback are useful. Sanford (1995) explains that useful feedback results only when two conditions are met. First, feedback must be perceived as judgment-free data, and second that interactions around feedback must be perceived as judgment-free inquiry. In other words, constructive feedback is not evaluative. Another feature of Joyce and Showers peer coaching indicates that the person serving as coach is also the person doing the teaching, and the person who is being coached is also the person who is observing. Rarely do teachers have opportunities to observe colleagues teach for the sole purpose of learning. There is much to be learned from such reflection opportunities, as long as the observer does not revert to giving advice or interrogation.

In the best of all practice worlds, reflection and learning practices, such as peer coaching, would be embraced on a schoolwide basis, as reinforced by Joyce and Showers. Practice in an imperfect world suggests successive approximations are better than no approximation at all. So, while we like-wise encourage and support schoolwide development, we also applaud smaller efforts aimed at continuous development and renewal of professional practice. Reflection with partners is a valid and powerful means of achieving this aim.

REFLECTIVE PRACTICE WITH PARTNERS: PRACTICE EXAMPLES

Partner reflection may be one of the most commonly used supports for continuous learning. It holds much potential for increasing diverse thinking and fostering meaningful change in practice—in a relaxed context that is more easily scheduled into our daily lives than when more people are involved. We now share both formal and informal ways to reflect with partners.

Cognitive Coaching: Three Examples

Cognitive coaching is a way to expand the thinking capacity of individuals so they create their own best ways to address issues. Cognitive coaching has a much sharper focus on building capacity for problem solving and reflection than peer coaching. The five states of mind framework is core to cognitive coaching and includes the capacity building domains of efficacy, flexibility, craftsmanship, consciousness, and interdependence Costa and Garmston's 2015 work on states of mind referenced in Chapter 4, pages 133–134. When someone chooses to be coached, the coach poses thoughtfully constructed questions to elicit that person's thinking. This framework can be flexibly used to construct the questions and offer responses.

Throughout this book we offer numerous structures and protocols intended to support educators reflecting on and learning from their practice with the explicit aim of advancing practice so that students learn well. The value realized in any of these structures depends on the quality of the conversation.

Reflective Voice Mail Bridges the Time Crunch

Voice mail was probably not envisioned as a mechanism for reflective practice, but for two authors of this book it became a crucial channel for ongoing partner reflection. As is common with many educators, they found it exceedingly difficult to allocate time to meet regularly in person. Voice mail emerged as a productive and convenient communication and reflection link because it can be quickly accessed at any time to record or review messages. Over time, its use expanded beyond simple project or writing updates to sharing more lengthy perceptions, insights, and questions. Because the voice-mail modality is solely auditory, we were keenly aware of the intonation, affect, and emotional overtones. Because there is no need to respond immediately, we could listen with the intent of understanding first and responding later. The wait time in between messages allowed time to think in a more coherent and creative manner about our shared work. Voice mail offered more layers of meaning (e.g., words and intonation), as well as being easier and more readily accessible than e-mail, especially when traveling.

Next, we offer a practice example from Phalen Lake Hmong Studies Magnet School in the Saint Paul Public Schools in Minnesota. Reflective practice conversations in partners (i.e., dyads or triads) significantly deepened the culture of learning throughout the school. Three truths about reflective practice are clearly present in this example. First, *the learning is in the conversation.* Second, *the quality of the learning from a conversation depends on the quality of the conversations.* Third, *structure is your friend.*

PRACTICE EXAMPLE 5.1

LEARNING CONVERSATIONS AT PHALEN LAKE HMONG STUDIES MAGNET SCHOOL

Contributed by Catherine Rich, Principal, and Michelle Brown-Ton, Instructional Coach, Phalen Lake Hmong Studies Magnet School, Saint Paul Public Schools, Saint Paul, Minnesota

Reflecting *back on* past practice and *forward to* future practice creates a personal space of sensemaking. Before teaching, reflecting forward involves envisioning the upcoming instructional context, and, in particular, the students for the purpose of tailoring practice in ways likely to connect well for students. After teaching, reflecting *back on* what actually happened, both teaching practices and student responses, creates a thought space in which to mine the rich and contextualized learning available only in authentic practice contexts.

Shown in Figure 5.1 are two conversational maps we created to offer structure that guides reflective practice in dyads or triads. These were formatted by Michelle Brown-Ton, the Instructional Coach at Phalen Lake Hmong Studies Magnet in Saint Paul, Minnesota. These guides provided the scaffolding that successfully launched and grew a community of reflective practitioners throughout the School. (We refer you to the Phalen Lake Hmong Studies Magnet School example in Chapter 7 that describes core components of how, over the course of five years, our school focused our learning and development emphases and deepened that learning by creating multiple aligned structures and tailored processes to reflect regularly on our practice.)

Figure 5.1a Learning Conversations—Reflecting Forward

Learning Conversations—Reflecting Forward (Reflection-FOR-Action)

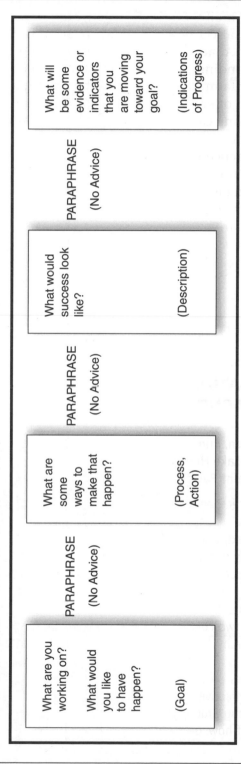

ROLES

Speaker Shares thinking around an idea being worked through.

Listener Asks questions to move conversation forward prompting the speaker to think through her or his own. Offers paraphrases that serve as brief summaries of key points made by speaker. Allows speaker to hear and reflect on her or his thinking.

Observer Observe the body language of the speaker and listener, tally paraphrasing, and other speaker/listener requests (not evaluating the conversation).

(Continued)

(Continued)

Figure 5.1b Learning Conversations—Reflecting Back

Learning Conversations—Reflecting Back (Reflection-ON-Action)

What happened? What was your plan and how did it go? (Description)	PARAPHRASE (No Advice)	Why do you think things went as they did? What might have caused this to occur? (Analysis, Interpretation)	PARAPHRASE (No Advice)	So what? What are some things you learned from this? (Overall Meaning, Learning)	PARAPHRASE (No Advice)

Now what? What are some likely next steps? (Implications for Action)

ROLES

Speaker Shares thinking around instruction that has already happened.

Listener Asks questions to move conversation forward prompting the speaker to think through what happened. Offers paraphrases that serve as brief summaries of key points made by speaker.

Observer Observes the body language of the speaker and listener, tally paraphrasing, and other speaker/listener requests (not evaluating the conversation).

Source: The structure of this reflection protocol was created by Michelle Brown-Ton, Instructional Coach at Phalen Lake Hmong Studies Magnet School in the Saint Paul Public Schools District, Minnesota.

The guides seem simple enough and make the reflective processes appear deceptively easy. How hard could this be, right? The challenge, however, as with many potentially valuable practices, lies with the quality of implementation. Here are a couple of key design features to keep in mind.

First, note the designation of roles at the bottom of each guide: speaker, listener, and observer. The *speaker* is the person reflecting back on or reflecting forward to a specific instructional context of her or his practice. The *listener* is the person asking open questions to prompt the speaker to reflect and respond. The listener also is the person who offers a paraphrase of the speaker's responses. The observer, an extremely important role in the early stages of learning these reflective practice routines, watches and takes notes on questions, paraphrases, and nonverbal behaviors of the listener that seemed especially helpful for the speaker; and also notes questions, paraphrases, and nonverbal behaviors of the listener that seemed to disrupt the reflection and thinking of the speaker. After the conversation, the observer offers descriptive feedback about what she or he heard and saw that supported and also that seemed to interrupt the reflection by the speaker. Early in the process of learning these routines, there were many intentionally created opportunities for practice (e.g., team meetings, classroom visits, and schoolwide gatherings).

Experience, personal and observed, has taught us it is extremely difficult for anyone listening to someone else speak, *not* to interject her or his own thoughts and *not* to offer unsolicited advice. You, too, can probably relate to this perspective. Interruptive conversation is a culture we know and have practiced well for many years at home, with our friends, and at work. In part because time is short and topics are (too) many and complex, interruptive conversation is the norm for many partners and teams. Members wait (or don't wait) to add their perspective or to ask a question that can change the course to become disruptive to the person speaking at the time. And then, a bell rings and it is time to scramble back to class. The students are waiting!

We have learned many times over that it is both a struggle and a gift to re-norm conversational habits such that listening, reflection, and generating one's own best ways to move forward are the norm. The effort required is well worth the conversational outcome. Insight can emerge from conversational space that allocates time and reflective support (e.g., paraphrasing, asking open questions) for making sense of one's practice and generating new ways of thinking about how to engage students. It is a rare opportunity to slow down long enough, and to have a skilled, mindful partner who offers the gift of uninterrupted reflection . . . someone who creates a space for you to put words to your thoughts, to inquire, and to learn.

As captured in the reflective practice cycle introduced in Chapter 1,

. . . without *presence,* there is no opportunity to reflect,

. . . without *inquiry,* there is no reason to reflect,

(Continued)

(Continued)

> . . . without *insight*, there is no new learning,
>
> . . . without *learning*, there is neither affirmation practices that seem to work, nor recognition of changes that could improve practice,
>
> . . . without refined *action*, no improvement in teaching or learning will occur.

So, find a partner or two, and grow your capacities to inquire and learn. Take turns creating a reflective space for another person and invite them to create a reflective space for you. Recall the sage advice of Judi Arin-Krupp: *"No reflection, no learning."*

 Available for download at **http://resources.corwin.com/YorkBarrReflective**

Here are some sample questions, some of which were used in the Learning Conversation templates in Figure 5.1 and some of which also were shared in Chapter 2.

REFLECTIONS ON A LESSON OR EVENT

How do you think the lesson went? What happened that likely caused it to go that way?

When you think about what you had planned and what actually happened, what were the similarities and what were the differences?

If there were differences, what were you noticing that initiated making changes in your plan?

As you think about the results you got, what were some of the ways you designed the lesson to cause that to happen?

As you reflect back, what elements would you keep the same and what might you change the next time you teach this lesson?

As you consider this lesson, what outcomes do you want to have happen again?

What are some of the professional goals that you are working on in your practice?

What resources are available as you work toward your professional goals?

Following are three examples of a principal coaching a variety of staff members.

Coaching for Interdisciplinary Instruction

One summer day, a biology teacher and an English teacher came into the office to talk to the assistant principal about team teaching. They wanted the same students during first and second hour so they could begin some two-hour instructional blocks. This was a very traditional school, organized around a traditional six-period day. Because the administrator had coached both of the teachers individually, he knew they were excellent teachers. Both were also very global thinkers and attending to details was not their strength.

After the teachers talked about their plan, the principal assumed a coaching role and inquired about specific aspects of implementation; that is, he asked them to reflect forward on their anticipated work together. He asked questions like, "What are you going to do the first week of class?" "What are some of the common themes across your disciplines? For example, how is conflict evident in living systems and evident in written words?" The teachers had a great idea and they knew the results they wanted for students, but they had not yet figured out how to get started. Throughout the summer, the principal and teachers met every couple of weeks for a brief coaching session. The teachers created a more specific instructional plan, and classes were scheduled back-to-back so the students would be together for two periods.

The principal and teachers met four times during the first trimester. Coaching questions included, "How are you integrating the two content areas? In what ways are you learning about teaming together? What roles do each of you assume? What are some indicators that you are making a difference for the kids? In what ways do you see students making connections between biology and English? How are your relationships with your other colleagues?" At the end of the first trimester, the principal asked them about the outcomes of their interdisciplinary venture. The English teacher said he was now teaching composition using the scientific method, and the biology teacher said he was now teaching science using journaling. Sometimes magic happens when you are able to facilitate putting people together, and you let learning happen.

Coaching to Reflect Back, Then Forward

One day, a world language teacher asked the principal for an hour of his time. She said, "You always give me great ideas." He was surprised, especially because he speaks only English. He was trying to remember any idea he suggested and said, "What ideas have I given you?" After pausing, she said, "Well, all I know is that I come out of our talks with more ideas." The principal relaxed, knowing that he needed to ask reflective questions, not give ideas. Coaching supports others to come up with their own best ways.

The principal inquired about the year that had just finished. How did the results compare with what the teacher thought would happen? What influenced those results? What might make sense to work on next year? These types of questions provided an opportunity for the teacher to reflect backward, inward, and forward. It is important to emphasize again that the principal facilitated the reflection process by asking questions to help the teacher clarify her own thinking. In this situation, the coach's role was to ask questions that supported the teacher taking risks, generating new ideas, and reflecting on her practice.

Coaching to Expand Possibilities for Addressing Problems

In a junior high school, a course in coaching for reflective thought was being offered to the staff. The principal, who was the instructor, held an informational meeting before school started. The principal was enthusiastic when he heard that the head custodian was interested in attending. They knew each other from another building so trust was already established. The principal asked the custodian why he had signed up for coaching. The custodian said he had a lot of trouble controlling his temper (which the principal already knew and he valued him as a good worker) and he wanted to be seen by staff as a problem solver rather than someone who reacted to problems by becoming angry and yelling.

The principal and the custodian engaged in a coaching relationship for the entire year. They met formally about once each month. Informally, they interacted daily as principal and custodian around facility-related issues. These informal interactions helped to build a positive, trusting relationship. Some of the issues addressed in the formal sessions included, "What are options for responding to teachers who want everything NOW?" "How might requests for action from the principal's office be presented?" "When there are multiple priorities for immediate action, what are some of the factors that need to be considered?" The principal as coach also followed up on previous issues and asked what happened? What worked? What didn't? Have there been any new challenges? Any surprises? At the end of the year, the custodian said that teachers treated him differently because he had volunteered to be coached. He thought that the teachers respected him more and that they knew he was there to learn and improve, just as the teachers were. He did not say that his own self-respect had increased in the process, but this was evident in his actions and interactions. Relationships improved. Staff members remarked to the principal that the custodian was more helpful and congenial. Students felt noticeably better about him, too. The custodian accomplished a great deal that year by having the courage to reflect on his behavior, consider alternatives, and choose different actions.

PRACTICE EXAMPLE 5.2

CO-TEACHING: GENERAL EDUCATION, ENGLISH LANGUAGE, AND SPECIAL EDUCATION AT FARNSWORTH AEROSPACE 5–8 CAMPUS

Contributed by Jennifer Parker, English Language Arts Teacher, Matthew Palmer, English Language Teacher, Taylor Anderson, Special Education Teacher, Farnsworth Aerospace 5–8 Campus, Saint Paul Public Schools, Saint Paul, Minnesota

Context

Farnsworth Aerospace Upper Campus, a fifth through eighth grade school in the Saint Paul Public School District, is a magnet school. Our students come from across the district with a high proportion from the east side of Saint Paul (see Table 5.4). They are Hmong, Karen, Latino/a, White, Black, and Native American. They speak English,

Table 5.4 Demographic Composition of Students at Farnsworth School (2014–2015)

	Number of Students	Percentage of Student Population
Total Enrollment	667	
American Indian	8	1%
Asian American	373	56%
Hispanic American	82	12%
African American/African	132	20%
Caucasian	72	11%
	Number of Students	Percentage of Student Population
Free and Reduced Lunch	534	80%
English Language Learners	313	23%
Special Education	120	18%

Source: Minnesota Department of Education Data Center (2015).

(Continued)

(Continued)

White Hmong, Green Hmong, Spanish, Karen, Somali, and other languages. They are from single-parent homes and two-parent homes. They are from families that live far below the poverty line to families that are upper middle class. Some are homeless, some live in apartments, some live in houses. They receive language services, special education services, and social work services. They are friends, brothers, sisters, sons, and daughters. They want to be successful.

Our school has a seven-period day and offers both regular and co-taught English Language Arts (ELA) classes. Our eighth grade co-teaching teams include Jennifer (ELA teacher) and Matt, English Language (EL) teacher, who co-teach two periods each day, and Jennifer and Taylor, Special Education (SE) teacher, who co-teach three periods each day. In the co-taught general education GE-EL courses, about 33 percent of the students are English Learners. Most are second-generation immigrants where English is not the first language spoken at home. We use the WIDA Assessment to determine our students' language levels: Level 1 (entering), Level 2 (beginning), Level 3 (developing), Level 4 (expanding), Level 5 (bridging), and Level 6 (reaching). The students' language acquisition levels range from Level 2 (beginning) to Level 5 (bridging). In our GE-SE co-taught courses, about 25 percent of the students have disabilities, including learning disabilities, emotional-behavioral disabilities, other health disabilities, physical disabilities, and speech language impairments. The majority of these students qualify for both EL and SE services.

We entered into our co-teaching partnerships over the last few years, each with our own beliefs about students and their capabilities. As a result of our teamwork, we now believe that all students, without exception, want to learn, can learn, and want to be challenged. We believe that how we differentiate and scaffold instruction to match student needs, regardless of their current level, is the key for advancing their reading and writing to the next level. We believe that we cannot force (and should not try to force) our students to learn anything. Rather, we provide students with the rationale for learning and invite them to bring their best selves forward into the learning. We do not believe in doing the hard work of learning for our students; rather we construct lesson and activities to support our students in doing the hard work of learning for themselves. Together, our dream for our students is that they will . . .

- be fully prepared to take any ninth-grade-level English class of their choice: regular, accelerated, pre-AP (Advanced Placement), or IB (International Baccalaureate);
- leave us trusting their own thinking, writing, and reading skills;
- advocate for themselves and ask for assistance when they need it;
- come back from ninth grade to visit us and say, "My English class is easy. I already know everything" ;
- believe that their voice is important and desperately needed in this society; and
- believe that they have the power to change the world!

Sometimes we are asked, "When do you collaborate?" A more applicable question is "When *don't* we collaborate?" We work collaboratively on almost everything. This year, we are fortunate to have both a common prep and a common Professional Learning Community (PLC). (Our administrators work to develop the master schedule to have this level of alignment, but during some years both common prep and PLC is not possible.) We meet in the morning before school, during passing time before class starts, during prep periods, and from home over shared Google Docs, text messages, and e-mails. Sometimes, we even collaborate on weekends or weeknights over coffee. We do this because we know that it is making a difference for the students. We attend the same English Language Arts professional development so we have a common knowledge base to ground our work and incorporate the best practices into our lesson plans.

Our lesson planning process usually starts with us looking through the district's curriculum pacing guide and deciding how we can meet each learning objective for the respective state standard and how we will meet the end-of-unit product with our students. We routinely build in pretesting at the start of a unit, as well as formative assessments throughout the unit to continually guide our planning and flexible grouping. Flex groups are based on each student's learning needs, not his or her label. For instance, we often collect exit tickets at the end of the lesson looking to assess students' progress toward learning targets. The next day we follow with small group instruction that is tailored to the needs of each group based on what we learned.

It is significant to note that two years ago, we relied more on homogeneous flex groups based on skill levels. Our data showed little student growth regardless of a student's achievement level. After reflecting on the outcomes, we felt that students with lower academic proficiency had few oral role models for practicing higher level skills, while students with higher academic proficiency had fewer opportunities to model and apply their skills. In the end, neither group of students benefited from this strategy. Last year and this year, we created heterogeneous small groups to maximize use of academic language and concepts. For example, at the beginning of the year in the GE-EL co-taught classes, we looked at each student's state achievement and English Language proficiency test scores to create a seating chart. We strategically placed students with diverse academic and language development levels at each table. Each table had a student who scored higher in reading than the other students. We assured that the state achievement test score spread of the students at each table was not too wide, but that each group had at least one member who could model reading and writing well for the others. This student also served as a language model for others at the table. We did this to create rich turn and talk discussions, to be able to effectively use the think-pair-share strategy, and to support use of academic language. As the year progressed, we used both formative and summative assessments to determine how to regroup the flex groups to maximize learning.

Our co-teaching model is fluid. Our co-teaching roles change depending on the lesson and needs of the students. Each day, it may include large group instruction,

(Continued)

(Continued)

small group instruction, parallel instruction, or one-on-one conferring and support. It looks like shared responsibility and accountability. It looks awesome.

Day to day, our co-teaching also varies depending on the co-teaching pair. Flexibility and respect for each other is core to our work. Regardless of the way that the co-teaching plays out each day, it is equal and supportive. Each teacher leads the activities most aligned to their expertise. Sometimes one teacher takes the hard line to push students to perform at higher academic levels, sometimes both teachers do this. In all cases, both are present to provide the support needed to achieve the intended outcomes.

What might this look like during a teaching unit? In the GE-EL co-taught class, Matt (EL teacher) leads an initial mini-lesson on a topic to ensure that the EL students comprehend the reading material. For this mini-lesson, the focus is on the language objective and is usually the mentor text that the students will be referring to throughout the unit. Comprehending this content is important because it anchors the learning throughout the unit. It is important to acknowledge that this strategy supports all students to grasp higher-level concepts, increase vocabulary and build on academic language. On the following days, Jennifer (GE teacher) teaches the mini-lesson focusing more on the content objective of the unit. Or, in the GE-SE co-taught class, we parallel teach. Jennifer (GE teacher) teaches half the class and Taylor (SE teacher) teaches half the class. The identified groups are strategic and heterogeneous. Both teachers focus on the same lesson, but vary how they differentiate the instruction and/or the materials. An extremely important part of this design is that the two groups come together for the last segment of the class to share what they learned around the common learning target. We also carry out alternate teaching, where one person takes a larger group and another takes a smaller group focusing on a particular skill. We enjoy station teaching because we can differentiate instruction on many different levels to meet the diverse needs of the students. During individual or small group work time, we rotate through the class to work with or conference with individual students. We keep notes on the students with whom we have worked so that during our planning, we can share what we did and learned in our work with respective students. We have found that the instructional strategies that we integrate in our classes support all students whether they are GE, EL, or SE (e.g., re-teaching, pre-teaching, word walls, vocabulary, sentence frames, modeling, repeating directions/restating directions, small group work, check ins).

Put simply, our students have made incredible success with advancing their grade-level reading proficiency at Farnsworth. This growth reinforces the belief that we have in each student and their capabilities. We saw the growth through our pre- and post-unit assessments. Then last year, the eighth grade reading proficiency increased 19 percentage points (yes, 19!!) on the state achievement test. We also surveyed our students to hear their voice and to listen to their feedback about our classes and instructional approaches. Students answered anonymously. The results showed that our students feel safe. They feel respected. They feel challenged and supported. They believe that we expect them to treat each other with respect. Significantly, the positive results did not vary by a student's race, cultural identity, or disability. We get wonderful feedback from our students. We don't hear complaints from students about our co-teaching. We are more apt to hear sighs and complaints when one co-teacher is gone for the day.

Reflection is core to our work. We reflect individually and collectively. For Jenny and Matt, this is our fourth year of co-teaching together. For Jenny and Taylor, this is our second year of co-teaching. We are able to reflect on last year's lessons to make them even better this year. We never assume these results are guaranteed. We reflect on what is working and not working by analyzing formative assessments, student work, and class assessments. We make changes accordingly. Sometimes this means adjusting and modifying in the same class period. When students show that they do not understand a lesson, we know that we have to change how we are teaching. For example, when Jenny and Matt taught a lesson about themes in short stories, many students were unable to distinguish between theme and summary. Only a few students showed proficiency or understanding of theme. We knew we had to extend our teaching of this lesson until we had evidence that the students understood it. We sorted the work based on how much the students comprehended the concept of theme and formed groups accordingly. We extended their learning by having them compare themes in different texts that they had read during the short story unit.

What we have learned from experience is that our co-teaching makes a difference and it will continue to make a difference in students' lives, as well as our professional lives. We have shown that co-teaching with high rigor and support helps to close the achievement gap. We were not always sure about this. When Jenny first learned that she would be co-teaching she was nervous about another adult teaching with her every day, judging her lessons, her ideas, and her classroom management techniques. After having co-taught the majority of her school day for the last four years, she absolutely loves it. Why? Together everyone involved knows that they can meet the individual needs of all students through their collective partnership.

 Available for download at **http://resources.corwin.com/YorkBarrReflective**

Nurturing Reflective Capacity Beginning With Induction

Based on work by Jim L. Roussin, formerly of Big Lake, Minnesota, currently working as a Strategic Change Consultant and the Executive Director for Generative Learning

In a growing third ring suburban school district, there is a strong value in building and sustaining reflective capacity within the staff. Beginning with the initial interview, prospective teachers get a hint of expectations for reflection by questions intended to elicit reflection. For example, *when reflecting on your job performance, what are some of the main factors you consider?*

Once hired, teachers are required to participate in a two-day New Teacher Support Program where the seed for continuous growth and reflection is carefully and firmly planted. Each new teacher receives one of two resources. First year teachers are given Harry and Rosemary Wong's (1998) *The First Days of School*. Teachers with one or more years of experience are given Jon Saphier and Mary Ann Haley-Speca's (2008) *The Skillful Teacher: Building Your Teaching Skills*. Portions of these resources are revisited throughout the year by principals and district office personnel as one means of inviting reflection and growth for new staff.

The teachers also are introduced to Charlotte Danielson's (2007) work, *Enhancing Professional Practice: A Framework for Teaching*. The principals use this framework or a similar model not just as an evaluation tool, but also as a means to invite reflective conversations with the teachers about instructional choices and student learning. Principals are not just interested in how students behave, but in how they learn and how learning is assessed.

Systematic efforts to support reflective practice continue throughout the year with individualized cognitive coaching, small group mini-forums, and a full day workshop. Each of these induction components is described below.

Individualized Cognitive Coaching

The cognitive coaching component involves a minimum of one scheduled observation and coaching session between the teacher and a district coach who is not in a supervisory position. In preparation for the session, teachers complete a form that describes the student learning goals, evidence that would indicate reaching those goals, strategies or learning activities for engaging students, the teacher's personal learning focus for the lesson, and data the teacher would like the coach to collect when observed. (See Figure 5.2 for this new teacher cognitive coaching pre-conference form.)

Mini-Forums

The mini-forums are held every other month, August through June (total of six sessions), at the end of the school day for about ninety minutes. They are designed to provide a safety net for staff and a space for reflective dialogue. Although the structure is flexible to allow conversation about common issues that arise among the new teachers, there are predetermined topics, such as curriculum maps and secure outcomes, professional learning communities, cognitive coaching, and differentiated instruction. Of the six forums, three (the first, middle, and last) bring together all teachers who are new to the district. The intent is to convey the message that all K–12 teachers must work together to best serve the interest of students.

Figure 5.2 Questions to Prepare for Being Coached

Cognitive Coaching: Preconference Form

Staff member _____

Administrator _____ Coach _____

Grade/subject to be observed _____

Pre-conference date/time _____

Observation date/time _____

Post-observation date/time _____

Please complete this form and send a copy to the building principal who will be observing your lesson in the Cognitive Coaching cycle. The questions below will be the focus of the preconference session with your coach.

What are the **learning goals you are targeting** for the lesson/event that will be observed?

What **indicators or evidence will you collect** to know that you were successful in reaching your targeted learning goals?

What are the **strategies or learning activities** you will be implementing to engage and guide your students toward the identified learning goals?

What is a **personal learning focus** you have for this particular lesson?

What **data would you like the coach to collect** for you that could be helpful in supporting your own learning or success in reaching your targeted professional learning goals?

Is there anything in particular that you want the principal and coach to know prior to the lesson?

Source: Contributed by Jim L. Roussin.

 Available for download at http://resources.corwin.com/YorkBarrReflective

Mixing staff also creates the potential for better understanding and appreciation of varied roles and responsibilities. In the other three meetings, elementary and secondary teachers meet separately to delve more deeply into level-related topics.

December Workshop

All new teachers participate in a one-day workshop in December that explores cognitive coaching, ladder of inference, single loop and double loop learning, perception and how it affects attention, and trust. The purpose of the workshop is to expose staff to ways that we tend to limit ourselves as learners and to emphasize the need for continuous growth and examination of professional practices in order to effectively support learning for ALL students. After the December workshop, each teacher participates in a reflective conference that is embedded in the second observation by the building principal. As described earlier, the teacher meets with the principal *after* engaging in the reflective conference with the coach.

Reflective Practice in Paraprofessional Development and Teaming

Paraprofessionals frequently provide direct instruction to special education students, often with little or no preparation. In addition, paraprofessional training and supervision is now a common responsibility of many specialist teachers. The following example describes the efforts of one special educator to support paraprofessionals to become reflective in their work with students.

Evergreen is an urban high school with 1,850 students: thirty of whom have physical disabilities and are supported by three special educators and eleven paraprofessionals. The students attend general education classes and a special education support class. Their programs are individualized because of their complex needs and multiple services. The special education teacher implemented a job-embedded paraprofessional development plan that included reflection to enhance the knowledge and skills for supporting students, and to create a culture where inquiry and reflection were the norm, not the exception. She wanted paraprofessionals to (1) learn specific strategies for supporting individual students in their respective classroom contexts, (2) develop a sense of being a team member who shares responsibility for overall program effective-ness, and (3) embed the program vision and philosophy throughout the whole school day.

The core focus of the job-embedded paraprofessional development plan was student learning. The special educator met individually with each paraprofessional to discuss individual students, share student information and effective instructional strategies, and reflect on what was working well, what wasn't, and why. As specific training needs were identified, she arranged for appropriate staff members (e.g., occupational therapists) to meet with the paraprofessional to teach the information and skills. Reflective questions were continually woven into everyday conversations so that the paraprofessionals developed a set of shared values and goals that served as a foundation for making decisions about practice. Acknowledgment of the paraprofessionals' needs and showing respect for their input were significant influences in developing a new team culture built on trust. Small group meetings were held to discuss general instructional and support issues as well as specific student issues, as appropriate. One small group structure was the "Kid of the Day" where any teacher or paraprofessional could initiate a meeting if there was an issue or concern about a student that needed to be discussed by the team. To create time for these meetings, team members covered each other's assignments for short periods. The special educator also scheduled meetings with all of the paraprofessionals every two to three weeks. In addition to presenting individual topics, she facilitated discussions on the assumptions that the paraprofessionals held about students and student learning, about roles and responsibilities, and what showing respect for students and staff looks like.

As raising questions and learning together became the norm rather than the exception, the paraprofessionals asked more targeted questions about students, provided feedback on student programs, and shared ideas on how to work effectively with students. They facilitated student involvement and self-advocacy rather than simply "doing it" for the students. Modeling by the paraprofessional helped general educators learn how to work with individual students. Some paraprofessionals also became involved in buildingwide initiatives.

Schoolwide Dyads and Triads

A middle school principal, who was committed to coaching as a way to increase reflection, took a risk and asked the teachers in his building to form triads for the school year. His objective was for these small teams to talk about learning, teaching, students, and education. During workshop week, the staff members chose partners. In the beginning, most groups simply got together and tried to engage in learning conversations. Some just went through the motions of reflective practice. At the end of the school year, the principal asked whether the staff members would be willing to continue these conversations. One staff member declined, and everyone else said they would—as long as one change occurred. They explained that in the beginning, because they were unsure of what was going to happen, they partnered with their friends. The next year, they wanted to change reflection partners so that there would be a different grade level and discipline represented in each triad. The staff members felt they would learn more by having conversations with people from different perspectives rather than with their friends. High praise goes to that staff; learning requires trust.

By the end of the year, they were willing to take greater risks to learn more. This example illustrates the interwoven nature of the importance of trust (Chapter 2), courage (Chapter 4), communication, and time.

Weekly Reviews

As teachers begin to work more closely with one another in the design, delivery, and evaluation of instruction for students, they need more time together to plan and reflect. In many schools with diverse student populations, increasing numbers of general educators, special educators, and second-language teachers are co-teaching for some parts of the school day or week, frequently during language arts or math blocks of time. In order to teach together, they must come to know all the students, recognize and use their respective strengths as teachers, and plan for instruction together. In our work with teacher teams, Thursdays consistently emerge as the best day to meet, because the present week can be reviewed, and planning for the next week can begin. At one school, the principal and staff decided to leave every Thursday afternoon open, meaning that no other meetings could be scheduled after school on Thursdays. Early in the school year, meetings of instructional partners usually are consumed by planning units and lessons, determining co-teaching roles, and generally getting organized. Over time, the focus shifts to reflecting on individual students who are struggling, work samples from many students, and classroom performance as a whole, which results in regular grouping and regrouping of students. In other words, the emphasis and depth of the reflection evolves as the co-teaching relationship and experiences evolve. Regular reflection and dialogue can result in the discovery of new solutions, and in an ongoing differentiation of instruction to meet varied student needs.

Science Teachers Initiate
Conversations for Student Success

At an urban high school, two science teachers involved in a school-wide project focused on literacy reflected regularly during their lunch period. They did not share common students or a common prep, but did share an office. One teacher taught general science to ninth grade students. The other taught biology to tenth graders. During their lunch periods, they discussed students, ways of embedding new literacy strategies, pertinent schoolwide issues, and science activities. They also identified concerns about grading practices in the science department, which prompted them to initiate conversations with other members of the department. Key questions were discussed, such as why are so many students failing tenth grade biology? What could be done to help these students? How could we help teachers to prepare ninth graders for the content in upper-level classes? As an indicator of their value, these department conversations have continued.

Listening Practice

As collaborative ways of working and learning become more common and expected, intentional efforts to develop listening skills can greatly enhance reflection and communication. We describe here a listening activity developed by a colleague to help people experience and be mindful of what it is like to be heard as well as what it is like to be listened to. This experience is unique for many people. The activity is organized by forming dyads, with one person designated as the listener and the other as the speaker; or triads, with a listener, a speaker, and an observer. The speaker talks about a particular topic for three minutes. During this time, the listener just listens and does not talk. If used, the observer watches both the speaker and listener. At the end of three minutes, participants reflect on how it felt to be in their respective roles. They then switch roles.

Consider carefully the topics for this listening activity. Hot topics can reduce thinking by listeners and speakers. Emotion can take over the process. In one school, for example, there was controversy about the pullout method in special education services. Teachers tended to feel strongly one way or the other. Large group discussions had not been productive. The listening activity was used in two stages. First, partners took turns listening when the topic was of little consequence (e.g., a favorite family tradition). Afterward, they processed how that interaction felt and what each was thinking. Second, partners took turns listening to how each other felt about pull-out services and why. Afterward, they processed this listening session as well. Finally, the whole group processed their learning from both sessions, considering content and process. How did your listening and speaking differ in the different sessions? What accounted for the differences? What could help listening when the topics are more emotionally charged? Collectively, what did we learn how people view pull-out services? What might be some productive next steps?

REFLECTIVE PRACTICE WITH PARTNERS: MORE IDEAS TO CONSIDER

Many of the ideas that were shared in Chapter 4 for individual reflection are also well suited for use with partners. For example, reflecting on teaching portfolios and professional readings can be enhanced with another person supporting inquiry. Exchanging teacher narratives can provide insight into the thinking and practice of others, which prompts thinking about ourselves. In the next chapter, videotaping, book clubs, and teacher dialogues are described as ways to reflect and can also work well for partners. Here we offer a menu of ideas for reflective practice with partners. As you read, consider ideas you might find useful to enhance your practice.

Journaling the Old Fashioned Way: On Paper

Mini–Inquiries

In the context of a Professional Development School, Perry and Power (2004) employed several strategies intended to develop inquiring teachers, including a curriculum class focused on inquiry. This was an inquiry project in which interns developed questions and collected data from small group observations of mentor teachers, and mini-inquiries. Of particular interest was their use of mini-inquiries as "quick investigations of issues that get raised through professional readings, conversations or occurrences in classrooms" (p. 131). Sample questions were, "How do mentor teachers keep their classrooms running smoothly? What is appropriate technology of specific grade levels? How do teachers accommodate for special needs?" Some inquiries were intentionally aligned with the time of year, such as "How do teachers begin the year?" See Table 5.5 for an

Table 5.5   Sample Mini-Inquiry for Teacher Interns

Mini-Inquiry 1
How Do Teachers Begin the Year?

The early days of every school year offer new and experienced teachers exciting opportunities and challenges. The beginning of the year is hectic, at times overwhelming, AND crucial to setting the tone and day to day routines for the year.

In this first Mini-Inquiry please interview your mentor prior to the first day of school to find out what he or she does the first few days of school and why. The following questions to help you gather data have been created by mentors and former interns.

1. What lifelong values, skills, and attitudes do you hope your students will take away from your class this year and why?

2. What are examples of activities you do early in the year to support those goals?

3. How do you create classroom rules and why? How do you manage behavior problems and why? How do you communicate that to your students?

4. Early in the year, how far ahead do you plan?

5. Do your plans for this year differ from previous years? How and why?

6. How do you encourage risk taking and independence in students early in the year? Please give examples.

In addition while working in your mentor's classroom the first two days this fall, observe your mentor while reflecting on your interview.

Source: Reprinted with permission from Perry & Power (2004).

 Available for download at http://resources.corwin.com/YorkBarrReflective

example of a mini-inquiry used at the beginning of the school year. In preparing responses, interns made note of their observations, interviewed teachers, and read various materials. Importantly the "mini-inquiries provided a mechanism for the interns to question their mentors about teaching practices and goals, to delve into the mentor's reasoning behind their practices, and in doing so expand their own view of teaching" (p. 131).

Structured Reflection Logs

Finally, we offer an example of how special education teacher educators used structured reflective logs to better prepare preservice general education students for inclusive school and classroom settings (Kolar & Dickson, 2002). The authors offered examples of questions, question sets, scenarios, and video reflections to which the preservice teachers were expected to respond. Two sample question sets are provided here:

> Reflect on your experiences with individuals with disabilities. What experiences have you had with individuals with disabilities? This could be in elementary school, middle school, high school, or college. It could be with someone in your family or a friend. How have your experiences with people with disabilities influenced your understanding of them? How have your experiences influenced your expectations for working with students with disabilities in your classroom? (p. 396)

The preservice teachers viewed the reflective logs positively as tools for reflecting on their own experiences with individuals with disabilities, for expressing and formulating their thoughts and opinions about teaching students with disabilities, for making connections between prior experiences and the course content, and for developing a resource of ideas that could be valuable in future teaching. Not surprisingly, time was viewed as a constraint. As indicated previously, structured reflection through journaling seems well suited to foster critical reflection on issues of race and culture; so too is the case on issues involving students with disabilities.

Many of these examples relate to preservice teacher education, a context in which journaling and reflection can be, and often is, required. Regardless, the structures, interactions, and feedback offered through interactive journaling do foster reflective thought, and in some cases, influence practice.

Online Directed Journaling

Described for a cohort of advanced practice nurses engaged in community health clinical experiences, online directed journaling allowed the nurses to learn with and from one another as they practiced in different settings. *Don't skip this because you think it might not be relevant to your practice. Trust us, it is!* The specific intent was to foster discussion, mentoring, critical thinking, and socialization throughout the entire clinical experience.

All of the nurses had 24-hour access to a website discussion board and were expected to post at least one in-depth journal entry each week. In addition, they were expected to comment on at least two entries posted by other nurses. The clinical experience extended across

Table 5.6 Sample Topics for Online Directed Journaling by Advanced Nursing Students

Weeks	Topics
First Quarter	
Weeks 1 to 5	1. Practice philosophy of the preceptor
	2. Components, players, and roles of the political environment of the clinical site
	3. Barriers to advanced practice at the clinical site
	4. A legal issue encountered
	5. An ethical issue encountered
Weeks 6 to 10	1. Tools for practice and how they are used
	2. Problem in the targeted population not being addressed
	3. Resources to address the problem
	4. Process to secure the resources
	5. Physical and emotional effects of practice
Second Quarter	
Weeks 11 to 15	1. Preceptor role in decisions
	2. Preceptor role in policy development
	3. Types of data collected at the clinical site
	4. Data collection system
	5. Data not being collected that would be important to collect
Weeks 16 to 20	1. Challenge to implementation of selected intervention
	2. Preparation process for intervention implementation
	3. Easiest part of the intervention implementation
	4. Something unexpected that occurred
	5. Change in implementation design or implementation for the future

Source: Reprinted with permission from Daroszewski, Kinser, & Lloyd (2004).

twenty weeks. Five topics were posted at the beginning of the twenty-week period. Students could select which of the five topics they would respond to during each five-week period. This allowed flexibility to choose topics that were particularly relevant to each nurse in a given week. Table 5.6 lists the topics, many of which have direct application to educators as well.

Evaluation of the online journaling experience showed strong positive views, with an average rating of 4.7 on a 5 (high) scale. Comments were also positive with participants indicating that online journaling was user-friendly and fostered learning from the experiences and perspectives of other nurses. Overall, moving journaling from an individual to a shared reflection and learning modality was viewed as extremely valuable.

This reflective practice strategy holds great potential for educators as well, within and across sites and school districts. First year teachers or principals might be well supported as a cohort through use of online shared journaling. Teachers implementing a new curriculum (e.g., science teachers across a school district) or principals launching a new governance structure could benefit from an easy-to-access way of reflecting and communicating with colleagues. Ease of engagement, 24-hour access, prompts to elicit thinking, and simple guidelines (each person provide one entry and respond to one entry) seem to be key features for success.

Reflective Interviews

Again, most noted in the teacher preparation literature, but applicable for practicing teachers as well, is the use of interviews to prompt reflective thought about practice. In two studies, Pultorak (1996) and Dinkelman (2000), preservice teachers left alone to reflect gravitated to technical and practical dimensions of their practice almost exclusively.

In the Pultorak study, preservice teachers engaged in multiple forms of reflection at several intervals across a sixteen week period of time. The nature of the reflections varied with each form. Journaling every other day yielded entries that were predominantly technical and practical in nature, although between a quarter and a half of the comments tapped critical dimensions. Journaling every other week about overall teaching experiences of the past couple weeks yielded entries that were almost exclusively technical in nature, as did journaling after observing other teachers. When engaged in reflective interviews, however, critical reflection abilities increased substantially over time with just 4 percent of the students able to critically reflect in the semester, 43 percent by midsemester, and 77 percent by the end of the semester.

When the preservice teachers in the Dinkelman (2000) study were asked to identify the strongest influences on their reflections, journaling and being interviewed were ranked the highest, followed by observations, although observations did not elicit much critical reflection. Following are the questions used in the reflective interviews conducted in the Pultorak (1996) study. Note the first six questions are oriented toward reflection on technical dimensions of practice; the next two toward practical reflection; and the last two are more critically oriented.

- What were essential strengths of the lesson?
- What, if anything, would you change about the lesson?
- Do you think the lesson was successful? Why?
- Which conditions were important to the outcome?
- What, if any, unanticipated learning outcomes resulted from the lesson?
- What did you think about student behaviors?
- Can you think of another way you might have taught this lesson?
- Can you think of other alternative pedagogical approaches to teaching this lesson that might improve the learning process?
- How would you justify the importance of the content covered to a parent, administrator, and/or student?
- Did any moral or ethical concerns occur as a result of the lesson? (Pultorak, 1996, p. 285)

Structured Dialogue

The Pugach and Johnson study (1990), included in the previous two editions of this book, continues to be right on target for application in many schools today as the challenges referenced are ever present. They described the use of a structured dialogue process with general-education classroom teachers to promote reflection on how to more effectively support students with learning and behavior challenges in their classrooms. The goal was to increase the repertoire of effective interventions in the classroom and decrease referrals to special education. The teachers were provided with training about effective interventions and were then coached to engage in self-inquiry about actual classroom encounters involving students with learning and behavior challenges. Teachers were coached through the following four-step process: (1) Reframing the problem through clarifying questions; (2) Summarizing insights from the reframing process, including the identification of patterns of behavior exhibited by the student and specific variables over which the teacher has control; (3) Generating potential actions and predicting the outcomes of each; and (4) Developing a plan to evaluate the proposed change. What were the outcomes? When compared with a control group of teachers, those who participated in the structured dialogue significantly increased their tolerance of student behavior, shifted their attention from a student-centered to a teacher-centered problem orientation, and increased their confidence in dealing with classroom situations.

Framing Experiences From Practice Using Stories

Learning from practice at the preservice, inservice, or ongoing service levels requires learning to think critically about the meaning of real-world experiences. Schall (1995) presented a set of questions used to assist pre-service human services personnel in focusing and thinking critically about experiences in the field before presenting them to others for shared reflection.

- What prompts you to tell the story?
- What's the moral of your story?
- What's the specific point you are trying to convey?
- What is the generalized lesson of the story you or others might abstract?
- How could you generalize this lesson and test it?

This focusing process allows students to begin to make meaning from the "mess" of their experience at work. The appeal of this approach is its relative simplicity. It does not depend on a master teacher or require only gifted senior-level learners. (Schall, 1995, p. 214)

Reflection Structures to Foster Equity

Elliott and Schiff (2001) emphasize the importance of providing educators with opportunities to safely share their feelings about equity issues and of intentionally embedding reflection about equity into typical educational practices, which range from lesson plan design to curriculum reviews, and from personal to organizational practices. They propose structures and guidelines sharing experiences and feelings about equity issues, as well as for use in fostering reflection and learning about equity-related practices. The authors explain, "change in attitudes and beliefs occur as people are listened to and allowed to tell their own stories" (p. 40).

Guidelines offered to help to ensure safety and respect include allowing each participant equal time, assuring confidentiality, not allowing criticism, interruptions, analyses, or advice-giving. *Dyads* are considered relatively safe structures within which two people can take turns listening to one another about topics, such as the effect of school on one's confidence as a learner, the kinds of assets and gifts acquired from one's culture, or strategies that have proven helpful in creating bridges and alliances across racial lines. *Support groups* are suggested as a structure that works well for educators to talk about their experiences with bias. A third structure is referred to as *personal experience panels* in which three to five individuals take a few minutes each to talk about their experiences with a particular equity situation in curricular or extracurricular activities, for example, math expectations, competitive or cooperative instructional practices, school sponsored dances and athletics, and testing. After panel members share, then a facilitator can raise general questions about the focal topic to the entire group, not just to the panel members.

Practices that may be engaged in individually or with others include examination of instructional practices, informal assessments, scoring rubrics, student work, test results, and curricular choices to determine the presence of bias or culturally appropriate designs, strategies, and materials. Elliott and Schiff offer a set of questions to reflect on when reviewing curriculum:

- Are a variety of examples from various socioeconomic groups included?
- Are examples relevant to all socioeconomic groups?
- Do problem-solving strategies reflect cultural values other than the dominant culture?
- Are females, minorities, and people with disabilities shown in a variety of settings and environments as well as in a variety of behaviors, not those associated with stereotypes?
- Are representations of status and power distributed equally and fairly across diverse population groups?
- Do representations in curriculum material convey messages that differences are valuable?
- Are the messages accurate? (2001, p. 42)

The authors also suggest use of action research as a structure that allows teachers to ask questions of particular individual concern, such as, "Is my teaching culturally responsive? Are my attitudes and expectations responsive to cultural differences? Am I consistent, equitable, and individualized with each student and his or her needs?" (p. 42).

In closing, the authors remind us, "Everyone in America is influenced by societal messages that communicate biases related to race, ethnicity, gender, and economic status. No one escapes the negative influences of media and political institutions, one of which is the public school" (p. 42). So, too, the public schools are places where reflection on practice through an equity lens, followed by commitments and actions for improvement, can and must make a real difference in the lives of young people and the generations that follow.

Observational Learning

Taggart and Wilson (1998) explain,

Highly effective educators are often good observers. Observation is a skill that practitioners must possess to develop insights needed to make wise decisions. Observations should be ongoing, systematic, and developed to the point that a focus can be established, notes taken, and actions explored in a relatively short amount of time

with high effectiveness. Inferences and judgments are not components of the observation process, which makes the observation
skills difficult for many practitioners. (p. 58)

Observing peers is one way to learn more about students and teaching.
Systematic observations with a written documentation of events can serve
as the basis for reflection with partners. Written documentation can take
the form of a running record, a checklist, or an observational recording
form easily used in the flow of instructional routines. In the paradigm of
reflective practice, facts (descriptions) are shared; interpretation is a collaborative responsibility.

Gitlin (1999) offers an example of four teachers who took turns observing one another teach. Observations were followed by monthly dialogue.
Participation was voluntary and teacher directed. The teachers set the
agenda for learning. They valued this approach because it

allows questions and priorities of reform to emerge from the
teacher dialogue, [and] emphasizes the need for teachers to raise
critical concerns about each other's practice, including the taken-
for-granted aims, goals, and intentions that inform their work . . . [it]
helps to identify tensions between one's teaching philosophy and
practice. (p. 638)

As a result of this learning experience, teachers reported that reflection
had become more central in their teaching lives. "Now we talk constantly
about what is really important in terms of teaching. . . . This project has
[made me] realize that probably one of the best resources of knowledge are
the people you work with" (Gitlin, 1999, p. 641).

Classroom Coaching

An interesting twist on typical approaches to teacher observations was
introduced as classroom coaching by Black, Molseed, and Sayler (2003).
Instead of being observed just teaching one's own students, or observing
another teacher teaching their own students, this approach allowed a
classroom teacher to observe his or her own students as they are being
taught by a different teacher. In this case, the different teachers were visiting teachers from a nearby university center. (The visiting teachers, however, could be other teachers in the same school or district.) The classroom
teacher and coaches together watched and then discussed videotapes of
classroom instruction. Next, the classroom teacher taught their own class.
Then, each of the visiting teachers taught the classroom teacher's class on
subsequent days while the classroom teacher sat in the back of the room
observing. Debriefing addressed a range of interests, including curriculum, instructional strategies, student engagement and behavior, interactions, and overall classroom climate. The classroom teachers reported

great insights from being able to observe and reflect on their own students in their own classrooms. Not only did they observe varied instructional styles, but also observed how their students engaged with other teachers. This type of coaching model aligns with features advocated by Joyce and Showers (2002) described earlier in this chapter.

Action Research

One of the most widely recognized and researched ways to systematically reflect on and improve practice is action research. Action research is defined as "a disciplined process of inquiry conducted by and for those taking the action. The primary reason for engaging in action research is to assist the actor in improving and refining his or her actions" (Sagor, 2000, p. 3). Teachers are central in the action research process. Action research is a structured way to promote reflection on practice and contribute to the overall development of a professional learning culture in schools. Sagor (2000) describes a seven-step action research process, "which becomes an endless cycle for the inquiring teacher" (p. 3). The seven steps are (a) selecting a focus, (b) clarifying theories, (c) identifying research questions, (d) collecting data, (e) analyzing data, (f) reporting results, and (g) taking informed action. This process is similar to other reflection frameworks offered in this book. Important differences, however, are the emphases on formalizing research questions and systematically collecting and analyzing student data.

GETTING STARTED WITH REFLECTIVE PRACTICE PARTNERS

Reflection with a partner is a gift you can give to yourself as well as to a partner. Give gifts. Sometimes the gift is information, sometimes ideas, and the most meaningful gift is time. Always, when someone listens to understand, listening, too, is a gift. Adam Grant in *Give and Take* (2013) proposes that givers add the most benefit to the organization. Givers give, without expectation of a return, and are motivated by assisting everyone to move forward.

> When givers succeed: it spreads and cascades. When takers win, there's usually someone else who loses. Givers succeed in a way that creates a ripple effect. It's easier to win if everybody wants you to win. If you don't make enemies out there, it's easier to succeed. (p. 10)

We believe the goal of learning is that everybody wins, especially if everybody plays.

Most of us are driven to learn and improve, and a trusted partner can support our growth. In addition to the benefit of improvements in practice, a relationship is formed that is a valuable resource and support in many aspects of your work life. As you walk down the hallways, into a faculty meeting, or through the work room, you carry with you the assurance that at least one person knows and cares about you, your practice, and your desire to continuously improve. You are not alone. By reflecting with partners you can move from a congenial level of interaction to a more substantial and collaborative interaction, where commitments to improvement are shared.

Anaïs Nin names the potential that exists within friendships when writing that "Each friend represents a world in us, a world possibly not born until they arrive, and it is only by this meeting that a new world is born" (Nin, 1967). Her words may serve as inspiration for reflective practice with others. Some of our greatest insights have emerged from the relative safety of reflection with partners. So, too, have some of our most valued and long-term friendships that provide not only support, but also challenge our thinking and learning processes. How through our interactions with our reflective practice partners might new ways of thinking, doing, and being take root and grow?

To guide your thinking about moving forward with reflection as partners, we invite you to contemplate the following questions:

- What are my biggest questions about my teaching or leadership practice? What do I want to learn more about?
- Why am I drawn to reflecting with a partner or two?
- Who might listen well and guide my thinking? Who would offer a different perspective that could enrich my learning? Who would be interested in contributing to my growth as an educator?
- What type of environment is conducive to listening, exploring, and thinking?
- How often would I like to, or would it be reasonable to, get together?
- What would make our reflection time a real treat (e.g., coffee and good food)?
- What type of reflection framework, strategy, or protocol would support our learning together?

FINALLY, WHAT DO YOU DO WHEN NOTHING SEEMS TO WORK?

Here we offer a model, developed by Bill Sommers, one of this book's coauthors. He refers to his model as a *Continuum of Conversations*. Each of the conversations offers a strategy or approach that is aimed at moving forward through conversation. Sometimes, the result is success in moving forward. Sometimes, other options must be considered.

As you know, the main focus of our book is reflective practice. We know that most of the time, for most of the professionals this has the greatest impact on learning, both their learning and learning by their students. Embedding regular opportunities to reflect on practice and the impact of our practices informs how we move forward refining and growing our teaching repertoire. Learning our way forward is the means by which we continuously improve our practices and mindsets for successfully engaging the young people whose lives we affect every day.

When we work with administrators, teacher leaders, and learning coaches, we often are asked something like this, "Okay, but what about those who are not creating productive learning environments for kids?" Accordingly, we offer "The Rest of the Story," as Paul Harvey famously stated at the end of his radio spots.

Take a look at Figure 5.3, Continuum of Conversations, as a way to get clear about a range of options for engaging with teachers in attempts to advance their practice. As identified in the figure, the development emphasis of this book is on the left side of the continuum. For sure, growth oriented teacher practitioners often become well-grounded in the knowledge, skills, and dispositions for becoming reflective practitioners.

Figure 5.3   Continuum of Conversations

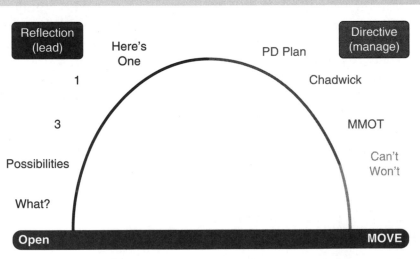

Source: Based on Sommers (2012).

 Available for download at http://resources.corwin.com/YorkBarrReflective

As we all know, we also encounter teachers who seem less growth-oriented and either don't know how to improve their practice or are resistant to do so, even when well-meaning, personalized, and private support is available and offered by administrators or teacher leaders. In these cases, more directive strategies often are warranted and used by administrators. Notice the right side of the Continuum of Conversations. That side includes directive approaches aimed at increasing clarity about focus, action, and results. Using the feedback from our colleague, Jane Stevenson, a high school principal and former special education teacher and lead teacher, the Continuum offers support options that range from least to most restrictive strategies. To be effective moving individuals, groups, and systems forward, leaders do well to develop practices and mindsets that offer flexible means of support, from the least to the most restrictive. Key questions:

- What are some ways we can support better results, using the most reflective and least intrusive coaching strategies?
- And, at what point is more directive coaching a better means for supporting progress and results?

This reminds us of the Buddhist philosophy on the "right use of power." In leadership positions, the key is using the "just right" amount of power or position to get the desired results. Overuse of power or position usually has a counterproductive result. So, with this in mind, we continue by developing and offering specific examples for each designated point along the Continuum of Conversations. One more caveat before we get started, this process works to support not only teacher growth, but also administrator and student growth as well.

The Reflective Side of the Continuum

Briefly, the left side starts at open-ended inquiry into the practices or mindsets being learned, and refined. For teachers, the focus is typically on growing instructional classroom practices that engage, accelerate, and sustain learning. The focus is on growing possibilities and making connections between what teachers are crafting and the corresponding responses by students. We are interested in what the teacher has in mind and what the teacher is intending to happen. We always want to "mine their minds" first, before offering any type of feedback or ideas. Find out what they already know.

In fact, feedback can have a demoralizing impact on teachers as it tends to elicit a sense of being evaluated or being the recipient of someone else's ideas, which can feel dismissive of one's own sense of empowerment and efficacy. As constructivists point out, the mind is not a blank slate. Always the starting point is to learn what people already know and can do, and build from there. Sound familiar? OK, this is the same process we want teachers to use with kids, isn't it? When it comes to learning, there are more similarities than differences in terms of what motivates and grounds both student and adult learning.

When an open-ended approach doesn't work, the coach, leader, mentor, or whatever the term is in your venue, tries to get some clarity about what the goal or outcome is by narrowing the options. Without a goal, we waste lots of time and energy, which are in limited supply.

The Directive Side of the Continuum

One Idea

Moving toward the directive side, a coach (leader, mentor) might say, "Here is one thing that I might suggest would be worthwhile discussing." Notice we are still suggesting using conditional language to encourage reflective thought. Another possibility is "Based on feedback you have received (or they have received) here is one thing we could work on." Assuming you get agreement, then continue the reflective process using open questions to invite the partner(s) to describe indicators of success and then corresponding practices that are likely to move students toward productive behavior and learning orientations in the classroom.

Professional Learning Plan

In those few cases, where we have not gotten momentum toward positive behavior, the coach (leader, mentor) could pursue crafting a professional development plan. On a side note, it is important to continue placing positive attention on development at this point, assuming progress can and will be made, avoiding a "gotcha" situation where the "coachee," if not successful, will bring with it more directive intervention. In Dr. Sommer's experience (as the principal among us), when he finally has to go to the most directive end of the continuum, the question he must answer first is "What did I do to try to help the situation?"

A professional development plan may include having a mentor teacher work with the teacher in the classroom, setting up opportunities for the teacher to observe other teachers in their classrooms, locating relevant and grounded professional development sessions, or tapping other resources available within or outside the school or district. Again, the coach has to be able to answer the question, "What did I do to try to help the situation?" Perhaps along with, "What other resources can I draw on to help bolster this teacher's practice?"

Chadwick Process

If what has been tried doesn't encourage the desired result, a next step is to move to a process learned from Bob Chadwick (2012), a master at moving from conflict to consensus. Unfortunately, Bob passed away this past year and his legacy lives on through the many people he trained to reduce conflict and confusion in the world. WE are grateful for his contribution to the world. The coach/facilitators can write down what the coachee says AND tell the coachee what the coach thinks about what was shared. Here is a tip: Use your computer to write your answers down first. It helps you prepare for the conversation and will make it easier to send a copy of the notes of the conference after the meeting.

1.   *Identify issues.* What do the meeting participants think is going on related to this issue at hand? Many times they provide fluffy answers. And, often, they answer by identifying external causes (e.g., the kids don't behave, kids don't want to learn, parents are not supportive). A key indicator of efficacy is when the person moves internally, indicating, for example, "When I do this, I get that." When you see or hear signs of efficacy, it means you are probably on a good path to make improvements. Teacher efficacy, which is the belief that you can do something positive, has been shown to be an important driver of student learning. Gain as much clarity as possible in order to identify the real issues.

2.   *Worst possible outcome.* For example, you might ask, "What is the worst possible outcome if you cannot solve this issue?" "What are the kids doing or saying that causes you to say they don't want to learn?" Get specifics. Generalities will not signal progress. I use additional tools here from the book *Influencing With Integrity* by Laborde (1987). It presents a great strategy called the "metal-model" to elicit specifics. Again, without specifics, we end up talking around a problem, not addressing it. Try to identify the current realities for the coachee. What is happening that they don't want to happen? What is not happening that they want to happen?

3.   *Best possible outcome.* Most people need time to vent or tell their story. Once they are done with that, as outlined above, you, as the facilitator of change, can shift the conversation. Many people stop at answering what they don't want. These questions are designed to shift the focus on what we do want. "What is the best possible outcome by solving these issues?" There may be a pause. You are causing a reflective shift to identify what they want. Listen carefully because this is the goal, or possible ideal behaviors they want to see and hear.

4.   *Strategies and actions.* It is not enough to have a goal or plan. Having a strategy should help identify what the participants are willing to do. A plan without actions will not lead to behavior change. When talk substitutes for action, change is just talk. Again, getting specifics will increase the chance of changing for better outcomes. What is outlined here will be the action plan to use in follow-up conversations.

5. *What will be the evidence?* This is the assessment criteria that can guide ongoing conversations. You can ask for short-term and long-term evidence. What will be the evidence that will indicate that you are making progress toward the desired outcome? From my experience, when the coachee takes some responsibility, it increases the chance of making progress.

This process is designed to shift questions from "what can't be done" to "what do we want?" Additionally, "what are we going to do?," and "how will we know if it is making a difference?"

OK, take a breath. You are now in very rare territory. This is certainly a point where instructional coaches, mentors are now finished. If this process has, so far, not yielded responses and behaviors that seem to improve the situation in the classroom or for the teacher to be successful, we need to try something else. To move forward, we think, requires an administrator with the proper license to monitor and evaluate staff. Be very careful having a person without positional responsibility move any further. It could decrease trust in the whole system of improving learning.

Managerial Moments of Truth

This is the last point on this Continuum of Conversations, one more try before closing the deal. One more try. Occasionally, someone will ask, "Why keep going?" One answer is, as the leader, each of us wants to be able to look in the mirror and say, "I gave this person my best and it just didn't change."

Managerial Moments of Truth (2011) by Bodaken and Fritz describes a strategy that can work when you are down to just a few options. It is a four-step process.

1. *Acknowledge the truth.* We are now assuming that this is one of many meetings on this issue, or a multitude of issues about teacher performance. There needs to be a history of interventions and positive assistance before moving to this step. The first step is to get acknowledgment of what happened. For instance, the teacher was supposed to contact the parents if a certain behavior occurred. The question: Did you contact the parents as we agreed? The teacher responds, "I couldn't because . . . (fill in the blank)." The question is "did you contact the parents?" You are waiting for a "NO, I didn't." If the teacher is not honest, there are probably few remaining options. The teacher has to admit reality. If you can't get admission, I recommend moving forward with the next step.

2. *Analyze HOW it got that way.* Once they admit reality, then move to what happened. Now they are ready to listen to the reasons, and they may or may not think the reasons are plausible.

3. *Create an action plan.* One last time, what is the action required? Period. No further comment needed.

4. *Establish a feedback system (What if?).* Begin with, "If this happens again, the next steps will be . . ." (e.g., letter of reprimand, suspension, termination). Typically, the response is "This will never happen again." It may not happen again, nevertheless it is important to lay out the specifics of what will happen if it does. Remember, you have already exhausted many prior steps trying to correct behaviors. I learned from my early days working in Chemical Dependency, promises are made, but without consequences, not much changes.

As you refer back to the Continuum of Conversations and the Managerial Moments of Truth (MMOT) and behavior has not changed, you may have reached the stage of either "can not" or "will not" change. At this point, you have a decision to make. What is the best alternative to continuing as is? Hopefully, you now feel more confident that even if you sent the person to numerous professional learning opportunities that it would not change their behavior, OR that the person simply will not change. The person might have put themselves in the "you can't make me" position. True, I can't make you change, BUT, I can change how and where you work. I can MOVE you:

M	Move to another assignment
O	Offer outplacement
V	Voluntarily leave
E	Exit them

Move to another assignment, offer outplacement services, the person can voluntarily leave, or . . . it may be necessary to terminate. Each of these possibilities is described in a bit more detail here.

Move to Another Assignment

As the administrator in charge, you have right of assignment. If the case for termination cannot be made, but you believe the staff member is hurting student learning and school culture, you can, metaphorically speaking, put them in a "box." This means you put them in a place of least potential to do harm. Sometimes, central office can assist you in determining a place. For example, permission might be granted to shift the teacher or administrator to a position of In-School Suspension Monitor. That becomes their position. They could also be assigned as a one-on-one tutor, or lunchroom or study hall supervisor. One administrator was moved and placed in charge of testing, security, transportation, and maintenance. They were formally in charge of curriculum, instruction, and scheduling.

Offer Outplacement Services

Business uses this as a strategy. There have been times when the person also feels trapped, but cannot develop a plan to get out of the situation. Outplacement counselors can provide pathways for the person to find another line of work.

Voluntarily Leave

Sometimes the person who is not as effective as they want to be understands the problem. Although rare, a person who takes this positive step is willing to admit the position might not be the right place for them and voluntarily departs.

Exit Them

Bottom line, students aren't learning and there has been little, if any, cooperation in trying to improve. Lest you be distressed after reading this, remember that you are dealing with very, very few people at this point. In over forty years of administration, Dr. Sommers has removed only four teachers before the end of the year. It just doesn't happen that often. Of course, there has to be administrative support in the central office to take this step.

On a positive note, your best teachers know that protecting inefficiency or incompetence does not help staff or students, and has the potential to harm a productive school community culture. The willingness to confront hard issues is good for the culture and learning in general. Use these strategies sparingly and wisely.

Using the Chapter Reflection Page (Figure 5.4) you can jot down what you recall as big ideas, insights, questions, and targets for future action. You may also want to write down something you wish to reflect on with a partner and a particular person with whom you might follow-up to begin the process.

Figure 5.4 Chapter Reflection Page

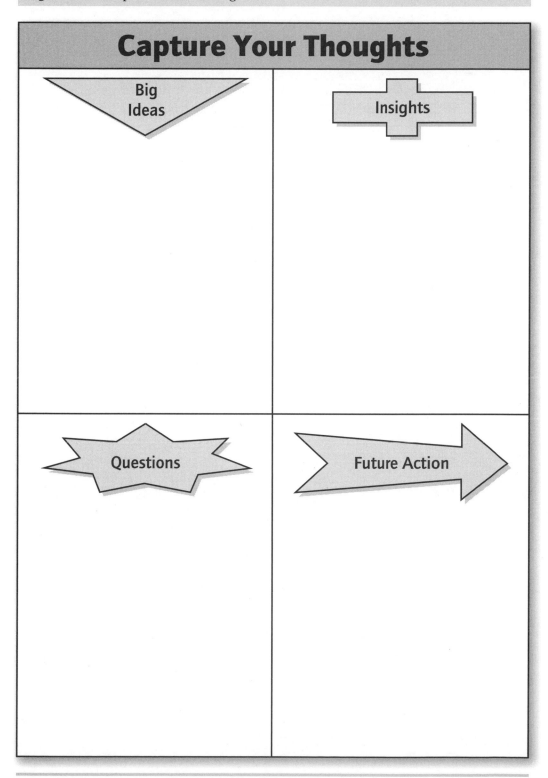

6

Reflective Practice in Small Groups and Teams

Reflective practice is vital for the swamp. It enables people to be present and it helps them and their organizations make meaning from what are generally complex, multidimensional experiences.

—Ellen Schall, *Learning to Love the Swamp: Reshaping Education for Public Service*, 1995

The opening quote derives its context from Donald Schön's metaphor, contrasting "the swamp" and "the high hard ground" of practice (Schön, 1983). The *swamp*, as described earlier in the book connotes the ambiguity, uncertainty, complexity, and oftentimes conflicting values that define the daily teaching context. "Swamp knowledge," therefore, describes the tacit knowledge teachers develop from construction and reconstruction of their swamp experiences.

Further, Schön contrasts *swamp knowledge* with *high hard ground knowledge* derived by researchers who may have been at one time creatures of the swamp, but typically have extracted themselves from the swamp. They are most often observers of practice and write about their observations. The vast majority of educators are swamp people, grounded in practice in schools with myriad young people. Reflection on practice in the swamp is what builds repertoire and expertise. It is practitioners who discern subtle and significant insights about how to tailor practice to engage a wide variety of students. Teachers engage in a type of research each and every day through their observations of subtle differences in the ways that students engage and respond to instruction. These observations expand their repertoire and deepen their expertise. What could be more important than work in the swamp?

Clearly, there are significant reasons for small groups and teams to meet in schools. Teamwork and collaboration are core resources in schools that continuously learn and improve. In a book by the Axelrods (2014), *Let's Stop Meeting Like This*, they list

> two criteria for determining whether to hold a meeting: (1) Is there a need to share information?; and (2) Does the information that needs to be shared require dialogue? The answers would determine whether or not to hold a meeting. Criteria for people who would attend a meeting are: people who have information or knowledge to share related to the decision, have decision-making authority, and are vital to the issue at hand. (p. 3)

For sure, learning meetings are vital for creating an energizing culture that attracts and retains learning-oriented and efficacious staff members who, together, improve learning for students. Most educators will attend meetings and contribute if they believe something worthwhile results. Often, however, educators comment that they are on "meeting overload." First and foremost, meetings must meet the "why?" criterion, meaning that the meeting purpose is clear and relevant to their practice. *Is the meeting purpose grounded in advancing teaching and learning so that teachers and students learn and improve their practice?* Assuming significant purpose, meetings are thoughtfully designed considering the specific participants and purposes. The specific "what" (content chunks) and "how" (reflection and learning processes) of a meeting are tailored based on purpose and participants. To create a conversational learning space, meeting participants must listen well to others, inquire respectfully and honestly, and create an inclusive and informative dialogue that grounds decisions that are understood, owned, and then honored by appropriate follow-up action. Examples of tailored group processes are presented later in this chapter. If you wish to begin with a clearer idea of what such processes might be like before you read on, skip ahead to the Eisenhower Elementary guided reading groups example (page 233) and the Harding High School inquiry group example (page 239). Among other things, you will notice the intentional design work reflected in the processes. Absent intentional focus and thoughtful design, conversations are usually less focused and outcomes more ambiguous.

Patrick Lencioni (2004) in *Death by Meeting* suggests different meeting structures for different goals: short meetings (5 to 15 minutes) for information exchange (e.g., schedule changes for the day, upcoming meetings, new "heads-up" information); longer meetings (1 to 2 hours) for teams working on issues, once or twice a month. This might include PLCs, vertical content teams, climate committees, and leadership teams; once a month for larger meetings like faculty or parent meetings. A fourth type, he suggests, are one to two day meetings for setting long-range visions, reviewing progress, and developing implementation plans.

While meeting in groups and teams is commonplace, the extent to which reflection and learning happens in such meetings is variable. The purpose of this chapter is to offer ways to craft small group conversations such that reflection, learning, and directions for future growth emerge. Such meetings serve not only the overarching organizational purpose, but also serve to renew and re-energize organizational members. Learning generates energy. To feel good about our work, each of us needs to see that our efforts matter and benefit our students. This is the starting place for building efficacy among educators. Efficacy is the belief, grounded in experience, that "what I do makes a positive difference," and efficacy inspires continued effort and enthusiasm for learning and improvement. This is not only true for adults, but also for students. Collective efficacy means that we are not only efficacious in our individual work, but that together we can learn more and achieve even greater good.

Face-to-face meeting time is perhaps the most valuable learning resource in schools. *The learning is in the conversation.* The vast majority of this time should be spent listening, reflecting, and learning together in ways that lead to actions, which positively impact school renewal and student learning. Recall the emphasis in Chapter 3 on the impact of different types of work at different levels in the systems. External knowledge and resources go only so far to support practice in particular contexts. Educators frequently have tasks that are open-ended, complex, and require collaborative inquiry to come up with new understandings, interventions, and plans appropriate to local contexts of practice. Educators must "work together to construct knowledge rather than to discover objective truths" (Cranton, 1996, p. 27) as a primary way of advancing practice. Thinking aloud together describing what seems to be working well and why it is working, along with what doesn't seem to be working well and why not, holds much potential for both advancing practice and for deepening connections among practitioners within a shared teaching and learning context. Members learn through experience that they don't have to figure things out alone. They learn that to *not* know how specifically to proceed in a given circumstance is not a sign of weakness, but a humble recognition that none of us knows how to do everything and our conversations can yield next best ideas of how to proceed. To share what is working and what is not working in their respective contexts expands practice possibilities. There is no need, nor do we want each professional to learn individually. "Teamwork is itself both a process and a principle [of adult learning]" (Vella, 1994, p. 19).

One of us, on her first day of school as a newly licensed professional, was warmly greeted by people who turned out to be her new core team. Here is what they said, "We are SO HAPPY to have you join us! We have a bunch of really interesting kids in this school and we meet at least weekly to share and learn together. You never have to figure out what to do all by yourself. It's really supportive, creative, and fun to work here!" It is hard to imagine anyone who wouldn't want to be welcomed, in earnest, with this same message. The message was clear: we can't know it all and we are not supposed to be alone in our practice. Naively, this newbie thought, "Wow, I had no clue this is what it was like to work in a school!" When she left this school, she learned it wasn't always this way in other schools. Grounded in this early career experience, she was drawn to work that focused on trying to help create that kind of supportive, collaborative, energizing learning context for everyone who worked and learned in schools.

In a study comparing teamed and non-teamed middle school teachers, Pounder (1999) found that teamed teachers (i.e., those whose jobs had a shared work-group emphasis) reported significantly higher levels of knowledge about students, skill variety in their work, helpfulness and effectiveness within their work group, teaching efficacy, professional commitment, and overall satisfaction and growth. Further, students were more likely to be held accountable to high and shared expectations by teachers who worked collaboratively. Reflecting on the overall findings from the study, Pounder suggested that "the most encouraging of these results may be the increased knowledge that teamed teachers seem to gain about students" (p. 338). The design of effective instruction begins with understanding the abilities, interests, challenges, and learning strengths of individual students. After all, sharing strategies that are working in our school about our students demonstrates what can work. Context matters. Practices often require tailoring.

Predictably, the journey toward reflection and learning in groups and teams is challenging. As a reminder, refer back to the Framework for Growing Reflective Practice Communites in Figure 2.2 in Chapter 2 (page 39) that makes visible skills, practices, and mindfulness required to become an authentic learning community. Listening is the core competency that undergirds all forms of communication, including establishing regular use of collaborative norms, growing collegial trust, engaging in honest dialogue that enhances discussion and decision making, and ultimately creating the potential to become a high functioning, supportive practice community. "Teamwork cannot be taken for granted. *People must learn how to work together efficiently*" (Vella, 1994, p. 20, emphasis added). Of course, we know this about our students, right? When we choose group work as the student learning structure, we have to teach them how to do this and allocate time for them to practice learning together. We often forget this "knowing" when it comes to becoming a vibrant team of grown-ups. Shaping such a collaborative culture is no less important and no less challenging with grown-ups. Keep in mind, it is likely that they have had many more years of practice not listening well, and not enacting collaborative norms that deepen learning. So, beware, allocating time to re-norming group conversations is often neither welcome nor valued, at least initially, when you step in to the thoughtful and interesting work of shaping productive group conversations and cultures. Keep at it. Most folks eventually see the value as they reap the rewards.

As described more fully in Chapter 2, one of the greatest challenges of growing high-functioning teams is establishing trust among team members. Contrary to the adage claiming safety in numbers, Osterman and Kottkamp (1993) remind us,

> Reflective practice in a group setting is a high-risk process. In most organizations, problems are viewed as a sign of weakness . . . to break this conspiracy of silence requires new organizational norms. To engage in the reflective process, individuals need to believe that discussions of problems will not be interpreted as incompetence or weakness. (pp. 44–45)

Intentional planning and skilled facilitation are almost always required in the early stages of group formation. In another study, Supovitz (2002) concluded:

> The communities that develop are often not communities engaged in instructional improvement. For teacher communities to focus on instructional improvement, communities need organizational structures, cultures of instructional exploration, and ongoing professional learning opportunities to support sustained inquiries into improving teaching and learning. (p. 1591)

In Chapter 2, we shared an important understanding about conversations based on the insights of Peter Block (2002) that were grounded in his experience coaching business leaders and also his ground-level work in local communities. Perhaps one of the most significant offerings from Block was to reframe "how" questions to "what" and "why" questions. "Why" questions get at the purposes that underline all the doing. If there is no meaningful "why," then the "hows" do not matter. Who cares? We have to care to exert the effort. A useful reflection routine is to continuously ask ourselves *why* are we doing these things, and *why* are we doing these things in these ways. Finally, we offer the reflective practice cycle (Figure 6.1), once again. The elements apply equally well to group reflective practices as they did to individual and partner reflection.

Figure 6.1   Reflective Practice Cycle

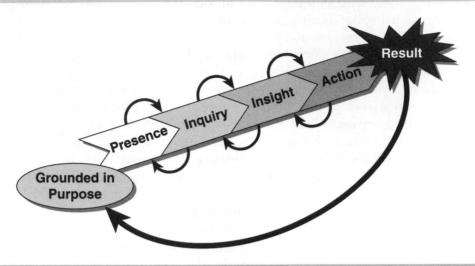

An introduction to reflective practice in small group and teams would be incomplete without some discussion of Professional Learning Communities (PLCs), which have emerged in many schools over the past couple of decades. Some have been an extremely valuable resource for sharing teaching repertoire that enhances student learning and builds a shared sense of community among educators. We continue to emphasize that the purpose of PLCs is *learning* so that practice continually improves (Hord & Sommers, 2008). The original purpose espoused by Hord, Louis, McLaughlin, and others was to focus on adult learning that results in higher student achievement. When it works, it is masterful. When it doesn't, PLCs become just another time-consuming meeting.

In the writing of *Leading Professional Learning Communities*, Hord and Sommers (2008) suggest four guiding questions that invite reflection and feedback on the process and outcomes of the PLC meetings. When educators call and say, we went to a training, but our PLCs don't seem to be working, our response is always the same.

Our *first question* is "What are you learning?" Generally, the person on the other end of the phone starts telling us what they are doing. For example, we meet on Tuesdays and plan. Our response is "What are you learning?" Their response is often something like, "We are doing a book study." Our response is "What are you learning?" If they can't tell us what they are learning, we don't believe they have a PLC. They have a meeting, not a PLC.

When educators tell us what they are learning, our *second question* is "Why are you learning that?" What we want to hear is some reference to data (e.g., findings from focused observations, results of formative assessments). Often we hear responses, such as "A group of students isn't learning," or "It is a topic that all our department members could finally agree on," or "The secondary administrators went to a conference and identified a new program for us to implement throughout the district." Multiple forms of student data, when strategically gathered and thoughtfully analyzed to inform practice, are extremely valuable. Data used to blame and shame students or staff will reduce engagement and send professionals into a protective mode.

Our *third question* is "How are you going to learn?" In response, we often hear structures for learning, such as a jigsaw book study, school visitations, workshops, or three early release days throughout the year. Any time allocated for staff learning can be enormously valuable, assuming the reflection and learning design is tailored for the purpose and participants. The reflection and learning design must be focused on the main thing: what works to engage the particular students in front of them and its corollary: How will we support teacher learning to achieve student engagement? We encourage educators to do their own collaborative action research. And, if they discover an intervention or practice that doesn't work, they will stop doing it. If they find that something is working, they should tell others what they did, how the students responded and why, specifically, they think it was successful. Share the wealth right where you are with colleagues who share your same practice context and student population. And, equally important, if not more so, is to make the learning process visible to the students. Here is a series of sentence stems you can use to invite reflection by your students: *Our question was . . . And so we decided to . . . Then we noticed that you responded by . . . So, can you tell us why that [strategy] helped you learn and understand the content? You are the expert on how you learn best, what else do you know about how we can teach well so that you can learn well?*

Students are empowered learners when they become aware of *why* and *how* what they are doing is working. They can be taught how to be researchers and informants. Often, they are more than willing to offer feedback. If you don't already invite this feedback, try to see how much *you* learn. When we leave students out of the reflection, we rob both them and us of deeper understanding. If teachers learn by reflecting on their practice, it makes sense that students do as well. Growing reflective learners early in life can only be good!

Our *fourth and final question* is "How is your learning influencing student learning?" Of course, this is the most important question. Shirley Hord and Stephanie Hirsh (2007) sums it up by stating,

Staff learning precedes student learning, and its [staff learning] focus is derived from the study of both student and staff data that reveal specific insights and needs. Thus the staff engages in intentional and collegial learning aligned with needs and goals determined by data. (p. 28)

SPECIAL CONSIDERATIONS FOR REFLECTIVE PRACTICE IN SMALL GROUPS AND TEAMS

Some educators have become skeptical, if not resistant, about being part of small groups, teams, and especially committees! Honestly? Grounded in their personal experiences, many have good reasons for their less than enthusiastic perspective. Through experience, they may have learned that working in groups can be frustrating, energy draining, inefficient, and unproductive. In short, meeting in groups has felt like a waste of their time. No value was added to their thinking or practice. Negative prior experiences makes it both more difficult and more important that efforts to promote reflection and learning in groups be carefully designed and facilitated for success. Sometimes a period of unlearning has to precede new learning. In other words, reluctant members must move through the stage of "prove to me that it is going to be different this time," before they will choose to expend energy and to risk exposure that can emerge in group reflection and learning. As much as people might want to believe positive change can happen, they won't *really* believe it until they experience it.

Recall from Chapter 3, the discussion of growing ownership and commitment around new practices (see Figure 3.4, page 102). This is a major consideration when designing and facilitating group learning experiences. Specifically, when facilitating groups whose members have not regularly experienced learning-FULL conversations, structures and processes must be intentionally designed such that reflection, sensemaking, and learning result. That type of meeting creates an energy boost. Again, we refer you back to Chapter 3, specifically Figure 3.5 (page 105), that suggests how leading reflective practice requires structure and nurture around an organizing force. The *force* is a meaningful purpose that inspires engagement, drawing educators more deeply into the work. An example might be creating level- or strategy-alike small reading groups for students so instruction is tailored to their particular learning needs. The *structure* is how the groups will be configured (e.g., small or large groups, alike roles, or mixed roles). An example of an alike group would be all the teachers from a grade level who share responsibility for all the students, or a subject area team, even though they do not share the same students. An example of a different or complementary role group is cross subject area high school teachers coming together to focus on ways to support student access to learning by an intentional focus on literacy across the content areas. The *nurture* ranges from crafting language that will support reflective conversations to offering a range of options for moving forward and allowing participants to deliberate about what they think makes the most sense. When participants begin to experience useful and informative learning conversations, grounded in relevant content and activated by earnest reflection for future practice, they are more likely to believe there is value in learning together and their practice community begins to take root.

Figure 6.2   Learning Structures and Processes at a Glance

Learning Structures

LEARNING DESIGN
- Purpose
- Opening, Closing
- Content, Process

GROUPINGS—Size
- Individual (on your own)
- Dyads
- Triads
- Small Group
- Whole Group

GROUPINGS—Mix of People
- Alike Groups (e.g., same level/school, same role)
- Mixed Groups (e.g., vertical levels, X-roles)

POSITION—Spatial
- Sitting (with or without tables)
- Standing
- Walking

Learning Processes

Reflective Practice

CONVERSATION
- **Every voice in the room**
- **Dialogue or discussion**
- **Norms of collaborative work ~ discussion**
- **Coaching/reflective conversations**

CREATE SOMETHING (e.g., posters, skits, slogans, 6-word essay)

PROTOCOLS/THINKING GUIDES
- **Grounding**

  Pick a quote (from reading)
  Something excited about today's session (after purposes stated)
  A positive "happening" in your classroom/school this past week

- **Multipurpose (e.g., readings, session reflection)**

  What? (description)
  So what? (meaning, importance)
  Now what? (implications)

- **Reflecting Back** ←

  What happened?
  What might be some reasons for this?
  Possibilities for future?
  Consideration and decision about next steps?

- **Reflecting Forward** →

  What would you like to have happen?
  What are some ways that might happen?
  What would success look like?
  What are some next steps?

- **Closing Reflections**

  Big ideas? Insights? Questions? Next steps? Learned? Affirmed?
    Challenged? Do?
  "Shapes" (e.g., question circling, point of interest, squares with beliefs)
  This session in-a-word (whip-around)
  Something to share with a colleague in your team/school

The Harding High example includes a detailed agenda (Practice Example 6.2) that embeds such reflective processes in small group conversation. Figure 6.2 is a resource that lists numerous structures and processes that can be employed to support engagement and learning for staff and students.

In this section, special considerations for designing reflective practices in small groups and teams are discussed. A list of all the considerations is provided in Figure 6.3 for easy reference. As you review this information, keep in mind there are no absolutes for design, only an array of possibilities and considerations on which to continuously reflect to determine appropriate applications in specific contexts and groups of people.

Figure 6.3   Considerations for Reflective Practice in Small Groups and Teams

You may wish to do a quick review of the Guidelines for Leading Reflective Practice, offered at the end of Chapter 3 (Table 3.2, page 107), and also the skills identified in the Framework for Growing Reflective Practice Communities (Figure 2.2, page 39)) and described more fully in the text that follows the figure in Chapter 2. And, as always, we urge you to continue affirming your pledge to "Go-eth not alone." Locate a reflection and design partner to bring more ideas, energy, and stamina to the design work.

What Can Be Expected in Terms of Group Development Over Time?

One significant influence on reflection and learning in groups is the nature of how groups develop over time. In the classic work of Tuckman (1965), four phases of group development were identified: forming, storming, norming, and performing (Figure 6.4). In the *forming* phase, group members begin to learn about one another and the work at hand. Typically interactions are courteous and cautious, if not superficial. This is a period of checking each other out. How do members connect with the group's purpose and with one another? They are scanning the environment, scanning to discern how safe is it here. What is our potential for doing real work? Can I learn anything from this experience? Do I have a contribution to make? Will this be worth my time and energy?

As group members come to know one another, begin to understand more about their charge and try to figure out how to proceed together, a

Figure 6.4 Phases of Group Development

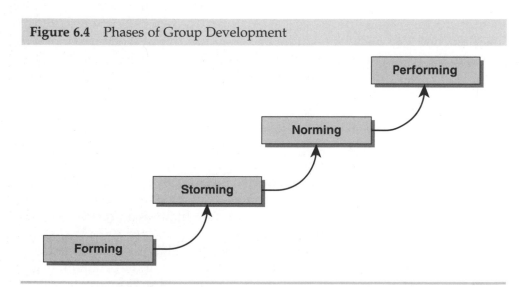

Source: Adapted from Tuckman (1965).

period of *storming* ensues; sometimes the storm is intermittent cloud bursts and sometimes it has hurricane force gales. The intensity of the storm often depends on the volatility of the topic and the potential for participants to feel blamed or exposed.

How does the specific work of the group become defined? What are some best ways to proceed? What is important to each group member? How are different perspectives heard and responded to? What are the sources of conflict, and which ones need to be addressed? Who participates, who doesn't, and why? It is during this *storming phase* of group development that many groups fall apart. Even if group members continue to attend meetings, they may psychologically disengage, or worse choose to behave in counterproductive ways. To move forward, group members must learn how to interact with one another respectfully and how to engage in effective group processes.

Occasionally, individual follow-up with members who seem less engaged is helpful to better understand their reasons for disengagement, and then together come to an agreement about productive ways to proceed. Our view on conversation topics, whether early in the forming stage or when groups have matured and are high functioning, is that topics always should be relevant. Conversation opportunities are too valuable to be frittered away. Having said that, early in group formation, topics that are meaningful but not volatile or requiring extensive deliberation are productive starting points. An objective for establishing or re-establishing effective group learning is to generate momentum for moving forward. False or feisty starts move participants away from the work, and sometimes away from each other.

Early topics may address "low-hanging fruit," such as ways to launch an upcoming lesson or considerations when forming student learning groups during whole group instruction. Ideas are generated by the group. Each teacher then decides what he or she thinks might work best in their respective classrooms. Everyone shares their thinking and related reasons. This itself sets a context for learning from one another's practice without forcing consensus about how, specifically, all the teachers *must* launch. This approach honors both the integrity of learning content and process, and the reality that each group of young people has its own particularities that likely require some context-specific accommodations. Just be sure to identify or pose initial topics that do not require absolute uniformity. Equally important is to be sure to return to these choices in a next gathering. This presents a perfect opportunity to structure a reflection-on-action opportunity, allowing participants to learn from their own practice, as well as the collective insights of the team.

With particularly stormy groups, an external facilitator who is considered more neutral may be a good option for skillfully guiding the group by using small conversation structures (e.g., dyads, triads) within the group, and by teaching listening and paraphrasing skills, both of which require concentration on what another person is saying. This diverts, at least temporarily, attention away from an individual tendency to quickly rebut and respond.

During early stages of group formation, the conversational processes, whether generating ideas, or deliberating about feasible options, or making decisions are slowed down to increase the possibility of members listening to others and being more observant (and less reactive) to what is happening. A well-structured and guided conversation has the potential to support new ways for members to talk, listen, learn, and make decisions together. Essentially, the typical way of "doing things around here" is being re-cultured. Slowing down the pace a bit often simultaneously slows down everyone's breathing and creates a more open space for thinking.

One seemingly small strategy that typically yields a significant positive impact is to pose a question and ask members to reflect on and then write their thoughts down on paper. When members are finished writing, in a round robin sequence each person shares what he or she wrote while others listen without commenting or questioning. Writing first provides the opportunity to clarify one's own thinking. Sharing round robin with no comments increases listening and consideration of varied perspectives. After each perspective is shared, members are asked to form dyads or triads (depending on how large the group is) and think together about what they heard and then how it connects with the work of the group.

A key principle brought to life in the example above is: *structure is your friend*. Without high structure, members who are the most comfortable speaking out, along with those who have strong opinions (sometimes these are the same people ☺), often take over and disrupt the conversational space. A structured process that creates space for breathing, thinking, and equitable participation is especially important early in group formation, as well as when tough issues likely to create conflict are addressed. When deemed necessary, high structure and skillful facilitation help to create a group culture in which presence, reflection, and trust grows. This lays the foundation for equitable voice, robust learning, productive deliberation, and mindful engagement around issues that raise conflict. Increasing mindfulness about one's own thinking and ways of responding lays the foundation for growing high functioning groups and teams. And, each of us has to learn to get over us. Meaning, what I think isn't the way it has to be for others. There are times, however, when common practices among teachers are highly beneficial for students. Learning content continually evolves. Many learning processes are effective across different contexts and content areas. If such processes become habituated by students, meaning they require less cognitive fuel to use, energy is conserved and can be focused more specifically on learning content.

You may wish to review the Framework for Growing Reflective Practice Communities in Chapter 2 (page 39) to identify different skill areas on which to focus to grow your group. Also consider revisiting the Perspectives on Designing and Facilitating Reflective Practice located at the end of Chapter 2 (page 79), along with Guidelines for Leading Reflective Practice located at the end of Chapter 3 (page 107).

When a group has successfully navigated the storming phase, they move into a period of relative calm and clarity referred to as *norming*. One bit of evidence that norming has emerged is the evenness of breathing and its postural counterpart of calm. Members have likely clarified their work and generated ways to collectively engage in their work. Members know one another better and they are both listening and learning more from one another. The "blustery" folks have likely settled a bit, and the quieter members, who often are the most observant, have found their voices. Individual strengths (e.g., focus, listening, humor, inquiry, paraphrasing) as well as group preferences (e.g., seating arrangements, reflection routines, learning supports, food) have emerged, been recognized, and increasingly used to leverage participation and improve the quality of the conversations. Most important, through experience members are beginning to view group membership as having the potential to increase their learning, which, in turn, has the potential to advance student learning. Ultimately, all these shifts contribute to more energy, effectiveness, and efficacy. They are moving from the norming to the performing stages of group development.

We offer here one note of caution. Sometimes when group members reach the performing stage and have become more comfortable with one another, it is easy for the intentional focus on student engagement and learning to slip away. Teams sometimes slip back to more congenial patterns of interaction. Be sure to maintain the focus on significant team learning that continues to positively impact teacher practice and its corollary, student learning. Sustaining focus on core work, that is, the continuous growing of one's craft as a teacher in service to the young people in front of them, requires vigilance and a strong team of colleagues.

When entering the work of intentional group development you may be well served by sharing Tuckman's group process development framework. It is simple and easy to grasp. And, it is helpful for members to be aware that developing well-functioning groups or teams develops with intentional design over time. This is true for grown-ups and students. Most people do not inherently know how to function well in a group learning context. Without an awareness of group development phases, members can interpret storming as a sign of ineffectiveness and incompatibility, instead of as an inevitable part of the messiness and the fits and starts of becoming a well-functioning group. Reframed in a personal context, most of us can relate well to this process. Recall times in your life when you and another person (e.g., sibling, roommate, partner, stepparent) took up shared residence. Remember the period of adjustment? At first, it may have gone smoothly, each person trying to accommodate. There is a reason this is called the "honeymoon stage." Learning about one another in new ways, observing different ways of doing things, noticing different degrees of tolerance for disorder can make it harder to remain graceful managing the differences. With good communication, you eventually learn and decide how to manage differences and to share responsibility for growing your relationship. Norms, expectations, compromises, agreements, and strategies are mutually figured out. The promise of being together becomes possible and more harmonious. So it is in teams. There is a growing sense that, together, making a substantial difference in the lives of young people is not only possible, but probable, especially when we can draw on the resources of a high functioning team. Making a difference is what attracted most of us to the field of education in the first place. It takes persistence and strategic design to move beyond the default culture of isolated practice to a more supportive, energizing, and effective culture rooted in collaborative practice. The possibilities of learning more, feeling more supported, and creating more good for students can be increasingly realized.

In What Ways Does Group Size and Composition Influence Teamwork?

Give a good idea to a mediocre team, and they will [goof] it up. Give a mediocre idea to a great team, and they will either fix it or come up with something better. If you get the team right, chances are that they'll get the ideas right. (Ed Catmull, President, Pixar Animation Studios, 2014, p. 315)

The following paragraphs offer considerations about group size and composition.

Group Size

Envision a third-grade team of five people and a fourth-grade team of nine. Considering just the variable of size, which group is more likely to have full participation and why? An optimal group size for working and learning together is considered to be four to six people (Johnson & Johnson, 1999). This size offers varied perspective and skills while still allowing, if not expecting, participation by all members. This size is also small enough or made small enough to promote trust and participation. Somewhat larger groups frequently are necessary in schools and can function well if relationships are developed and processes are well designed and implemented (Thousand & Villa, 2000). When groups are large, individual participation can still be achieved by breaking into smaller groups, as long as the entire collection of members from both groups come back together to share their thinking and work. We use this strategy often . . . very often. It offers a smaller and more participatory conversational space, and by having smaller groups share out, offers the significant benefit of hearing a broader range and/or significant commonalities of perspective. In general, groups need to be large enough to offer a variety of perspectives and to have sufficient resources for learning and for accomplishing the work. As discussed earlier in this chapter, early in group formation, smaller sub-groups within a larger group can create a context that feels safe and also allows for more participation in conversation. Trust also tends to be established more quickly, assuming members behave in trustworthy ways.

Group Composition

Achieving shared purposes of group work is significantly influenced by who specifically is part of a group. One consideration is the *same-versus-different view dimension*. You can have a very congenial group of like-minded folks, but this does not necessarily assure effectiveness. In general, you want all relevant perspectives, including diverse perspectives, to be part of the conversation. Without those views, plans can be doomed to fail even before they are conceived, either because of insufficient perspective or knowledge to come up with a workable plan, or because those not included have the power and influence to sabotage results. One question we frequently ask is "Given our meeting purpose, who is not at this meeting that should be?" Leaving people out, even if they have differing viewpoints, can reduce effectiveness and dampen implementation. Outliers, sometimes, become saboteurs. Each of us has a need for a certain amount of influence (think: power) and some of us come up with disruptive ways to influence the group if we are viewed or view ourselves as fringe. If there are valid reasons (and there often are) for keeping the group size contained, making the effort to connect individually with strategic others who were not included demonstrates interest and respect, and can alleviate attempts at sabotage.

Another consideration in determining group composition is the *heterogeneity-versus-homogeneity dimension* related to characteristics, such as gender, age, race, amount and type of experience, and disciplinary or content area background. Heterogeneity in groups has the potential to enhance learning, given the enriched pool of information, perspectives, and skills. Teams formed to explore integrated service models, for example, involve general educators, special educators, and language learning teachers. Groups formed to determine space use in a school include teachers from varying content areas and grade levels. Committees formed to provide leadership and oversight for professional learning should include teachers and administrators representing the many varied school and district constituents. Another reason to promote diverse group composition is to intentionally foster connections among people who rarely see one another. See the web of relationships in Figure 6.5 and consider the benefits that can be realized when a rich network of relationships extends throughout a school. Students are much less likely to fall through the cracks or break through the web.

Combinations of different groups of staff members learning together throughout the school can result in expanded and strengthened relationships among all staff members. In effect, a web of relationships forms to facilitate communication and connection throughout the school community (see Figure 6.5). This web of relationships serves several very important functions:

- *A safety net is created for students,* who are less likely to feel anonymous and fragmented because staff members are in better communication about students, especially those who are struggling in school
- *A rich network of resources*—people and information—is formed and any member of the school community can tap it; if someone in our immediate network does not know something, we are likely to be connected to someone in another network who may know
- When we are more tightly coupled with others in our work, there is a greater likelihood of more *comprehensive, effective, and rapid response* to schoolwide issues, ranging from safety concerns to adoption of new curricula

To enhance the web metaphor for school improvement, consider that the threads of weaver spiders are one of the strongest organic materials that nature produces. In laboratories, scientists harvest the threads and weave them into bulletproof vests. Thus the web is an apt metaphor for the durable and protective community that emerges and spreads from the spinning of many individuals.

To envision how the web of relationships can accomplish these important functions, look at Figure 6.5 and think of it as representing a well-connected and effective community of educators in a school. Now picture something falling onto the web. The specific something could be a student with unique challenges, a new program or curriculum, new teachers, or newly remodelled space. Because of all the interconnections, whatever falls onto the strands of

Figure 6.5 Visual Representation of the Relationship Web Among Staff Members, Strengthened by Reflective Practices

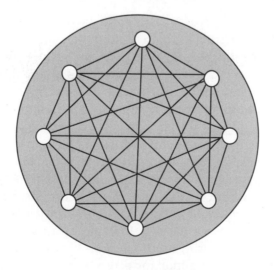

the web is caught. The web flexes to accommodate its presence, so it does not fall to the ground underneath. Every connection (relationship) in the web knows that something new has arrived and can offer resources and support. Without these connections, whatever lands in the school (web) falls to the ground and is on its own to stand upright and establish the connections needed to survive. A web of relationships can embrace a new presence, connect it to the broader community, and bring forth resources needed to effectively interact with or respond to the new presence in the web. Reflective practice is one significant means of forming and strengthening the relationships, which are the verbal, social, behavioral, and emotional connections that constitute the web. (A copy of the web of relationships is available on the companion website at http://resources.corwin.com/YorkBarrReflective.)

Having just promoted the value of heterogeneity, we now point out that at times a relatively homogeneous group composition is also appropriate and productive. For example, early in the process of becoming more reflective, educators may feel more comfortable examining their practices with colleagues whom they know well and who have similar experiences and perspectives, although this can also feel *more* risky because an "alike" colleague might view perspectives shared as off the mark of best practices. Another consideration is the *voluntary-versus-mandated dimension*. The value of voluntary or self-organized learning groups is easily understood. Initiation, interest, and self-direction tend to foster learning, ownership, and commitment. Mandated assignments are a reminder of the hierarchical organization of schools and can foster resentment. Unprofessional behavior sometimes results. When learning sessions are mandated, for example, there is often a significant number of people who are unhappy as they enter the room. Vella (1994) urges that people be allowed to choose "their own teams as often as possible, especially when the learning task is complex and difficult" (p. 18). Depending on the presence of highly structured facilitation, however, a counter argument is that an opportunity is created to begin re-norming an existing team's conversation space. When deciding to use alike or mixed groups, be mindful that the only type of participation that can be mandated is physical presence. Genuine engagement of the mind and heart comes only from the inside and is usually the outgrowth of intentionally designed and effectively facilitated conversational processes that engage group members. When a gathering is mandated is it best to acknowledge the mandate, articulate the importance and intended outcomes of the work, describe the processes that will be used and why, and express words of appreciation for presence and participation.

One final consideration related to group composition is the *existing-versus-reconfigured dimension*. Depending on the purpose of the group and the people whose voices are needed, existing groups could be used, existing groups could be reconfigured, or new groups might be convened. After groups have been together for a while, two threats to effectiveness can emerge: *groupthink* and *group expectations* (Fullan, 2001a). Groupthink is evident when there is nothing new going on—no inquiry, no new learning, no new generation of ideas, no new perspectives. Such groups fall into predictable patterns of congeniality—going along to get along. No one and nothing is growing. Eventually, the bell rings and they get to leave.

A saying attributed to Marshall McLuhan is "I don't know who discovered the ocean, but I know it wasn't the fish." When people work together for a long time there is an economy of time in the routines and structures in the organization. Normally strong leadership is developed over time. On the other side, new ideas or new ways of doing things are not addressed because of the successes of the past. When asked, "Why are you doing this?" a common response is "That is the way we do things here," which is a spot-on description of culture. A common dilemma for teams and staffs is: How do you keep the deep knowledge and leadership of experienced professionals while bringing in new people and ideas to keep current and to offer new energy to the learning conversations? If you really want to know about your system, ask someone who is new to your staff. Ask, what have you noticed? . . . what have you figured out about being here? . . . what are you wondering about? If they are secure enough and trusting, they may describe some of what they have observed and then inquire about purposes, processes, and outcomes. Take that as great feedback and answer the question. It may be time to change or at least check it out. If you have been in a particular culture (context) for a long time, you are like the fish in the sea, meaning you may not be particularly aware of the dominant culture. You have adapted and survived. It no longer needs to be conscious. If you are a different species of fish, or if you come from a fresh, not saltwater environment, what you experience may reveal a significant need for adaptation or inquiry to survive.

Liz Wiseman (2014), author of *Rookie Smarts*, suggests that "Perhaps the most important quality leaders can infuse into their organizations is a youthful metabolism and the ability to learn" (p. 12). New people or new combinations of people can have the effect of unfreezing thinking, routines, and expectations. Newly configured groups provide an opportunity to set new expectations, to consider new roles and patterns of participation, to establish a culture of learning and inquiry, to form new relationships before unproductive norms take hold and the refreezing process sets in. New people bring new potential and energy that can be put to good use with an intentional design to support learning and reflection. When existing groups have ceased to be functional, changing group composition, in addition to changing expectations and structures for interactions, can go a long way toward improving effectiveness. Facilitating reflective learning processes can grow content knowledge, relationships, and a community of practice.

Killion and Simmons (1992) make important distinctions between a training perspective and a facilitation perspective when working with groups. Trainers (sometimes referred to as presenters) are responsible for providing specific information and material to participants, for supporting the development of predetermined skills, and for accomplishing explicit outcomes. In contrast, facilitators are responsible for guiding groups through thinking processes to discover their own insights and outcomes. Training is an outside-in process, meaning someone "out there" has identified content (often comprehensive programs of some sort) to be learned by participants. The role of the trainer is to engage participants around the content. Facilitation is an inside-out process. It is also sometimes referred to as process consultation. In this type of process, facilitators serve as guides instead of experts. Often they are the ones who guide conversations so that materials and information presented in "training" are reflected on with an aim toward nuanced application within particular practice contexts. They ask open questions to support reflection, sensemaking, and application by participants. Of course, a person guiding group learning can include both training and facilitation elements. Offered in Figure 6.6 is a "job description" that captures the dispositions of people who make successful facilitators. Garmston and Wellman (1999) emphasize that the most important role in any group is that of *engaged participant*, a role for which each group member is responsible (Garmston & Wellman, 1999). In the absence of engaged participation by group members, nothing much is learned or accomplished. "In strong groups, engaged participants monitor their personal adherence to meeting standards . . . [and also] monitor the group's adherence to standards" (p. 82). Finally, at times there may be other roles assigned or assumed by group members, such as recorder, timekeeper, or observer. A word of caution related to designating roles. Often, participation decreases by the group members who takes on an additional role. As groups become skillful, recording key points and outcomes of conversation can easily be an inclusive closing activity in which all members can contribute. Similarly, members become more observant of balanced conversation, subtly inviting the perspectives of members who tend to speak less.

In *Covert Processes at Work*, Robert Marshak (2006) says, "One of the most important functions of process consultation is to make visible that which is

Figure 6.6   Reflective Practice Facilitator Position Description

Position Available:
Facilitator for Reflective Practice

WANTED

A person who has great confidence in others' desire for and capability for learning and trusts them to assume responsibility for their own learning; the facilitator will be sensitive to the needs and feelings of others, and at the same time be able to anticipate and provide information and resources to support learning. The facilitator is inherently curious; someone who doesn't have all the answers and isn't afraid to admit it; someone who is confident enough in his or her ability to accept challenges in a nondefensive manner, secure enough to make his or her thinking public and therefore subject to discussion; and a good listener. Experience desirable, but not as important as the ability to learn from mistakes.

Source: Reprinted with permission. Adapted from Osterman & Kottkamp (2004).

invisible" (p. xii). When educators come together a lot of time is spent developing trust, a working relationship, and the willingness to participate and contribute. If professionals are fearful of sharing their expertise, we fail to expand our group intelligence. Being able to verbalize FUDs (fears, uncertainties, and doubts) can strengthen emotions that sometimes are obstacles to high group functioning. As Marshak pointed out, if we can make issues visible or overt, we can appropriately acknowledge their presence, choose to put them aside, at least temporarily so that a shift in focus moves to learning and growth.

Who Facilitates?

In one school, fifteen teachers were trained in the Adaptive Schools Model (Garmston & Wellman, 1997, 1999) that focuses on how to develop high functioning groups and teams. After the learning sessions, participants decided to have department meetings facilitated by a teacher from a different department. A physical education teacher facilitated the Language department meetings. In the past, the French teacher, who was the department chair, facilitated the meeting. The language department indicated that when the PE teacher facilitated, they knew she had no stake in the budget or preconceived notions about what should happen. The department chair, therefore, was not privileged by positional authority. Ideas were more openly exchanged. There was increased emotional safety. It took pressure off the department chair and members. The external facilitator also was positioned to both solicit and share reflections about the group processes and group member conversations: What seemed to support the conversation? What did not work and what might be some reasons for that? How might you proceed? An interesting, if not somewhat unexpected source for post group reflections is the *After Action Review* strategy, popularized by the United States Army. To learn more, do an Internet search on *After Action Review*. It is relevant, interesting, and very worthy of consideration.

The advantages and disadvantages of the use of internal and external facilitators are listed in Table 6.1. Internal facilitators are usually more readily available, and they bring a better understanding of the context. As a facilitator, however, they may have difficulty remaining neutral (even when they are committed to neutrality). Further, they are not free to be a group participant and to share their views. Straus (2002), in his book *How to Make Collaboration Work*, states

> If you are a leader, manager, or chair of a group or organization, you should seriously consider not running your own meetings. I believe it's a conflict of interest for a leader to run a meeting when he or she has a large stake in the subject matter. (p. 118)

External facilitators bring a more objective perspective and may also bring more expertise as a facilitator. They offer the distinct advantage of allowing insiders to participate fully as group members. When group members have little experience, knowledge, or capacity for effective group learning or when group members do not interact well together, external facilitators can often shape more effective interactions using well designed and tightly structured processes. On the downside, external facilitators are often more costly and less convenient in terms of scheduling and communication.

There must be an intentional design to create a safe and productive learning environment. In considering safety, however, recall from the previous chapter that learning, particularly learning that involves reframing, involves periods of discomfort. "Safety does not obviate the natural challenge of learning new concepts, skills, or attitudes. Safety does not take away from the hard work of learning" (Vella, 1994, p. 6). Considerations related to the structures and processes for learning in groups are presented sequentially below: planning for groups, opening the group process, engaging in the core agenda, and closing the group process.

There are several examples of intentional group learning designs offered in this chapter. First, there is an example from an elementary school (Practice Example 6.1) that describes and shows how the first

Table 6.1 Potential Advantages and Disadvantages of Internal Versus External Facilitators

	Potential Advantages	**Potential Disadvantages**
Internal Facilitator	Knowledge of context can support facilitation design	Knowledge of context can result in bias
	Opportunity to foster or expand relationships internally	Personal or professional interest in the outcome
	Aware of group outcomes and needs	Role confusion for facilitator and participants
	Builds internal capacity for facilitation	May have less facilitation expertise than an external person
		Cannot participate as a participant, resulting in lost perspective or vote
External Facilitator	Little knowledge of context, better able to remain neutral	Little knowledge of context, less able to consider relevant context variables in facilitation design
	Expertise in facilitation and group-process skills	Must establish credibility with group
		May be less convenient or efficient in terms of scheduling, time, and communication
		May incur more cost

grade team uses a Promethian Board (Figure 6.10) to easily reflect on student progress across the grade level. This has been both efficient and effective for determining level- or strategy-alike guided reading groups, drawing students from across the grade level into appropriately focused small groups. To make this example work, the school level schedule for various support services personnel (e.g., special education teachers, Title 1 or supplementary services teachers, English learning teachers) had to be altered. This is an example of principals from different schools learning together in a PLC structure. There is also an example from a high school (Practice Example 6.2) showing a sample detailed agenda (Figure 6.11) for what they refer to as Inquiry Groups. These are small groups of teachers (typically five to seven members) from different content areas who learn together once a month about ways to support common literacy and engagement practices to support student learning. There are other examples, as well, a few of which were in the previous edition of this book, but remain current in terms of their usefulness in today's schools.

What Are Some Ways to Allocate Time to Meet?

Finding common times to meet is a major challenge. Specific strategies are offered later in this chapter (Table 6.2). In addition, one of the practice examples, Time for Team-Learning Task Force, describes a site-based, task force process focused on scheduling time for teams to meet. Before and after school are often convenient times but pose quality constraints. Before school, participants can be distracted by the impending start of the instructional day. After school, participants can be either drained or agitated. Time in the middle of the day has both problems. Release time provides the best quality advantage, as long as students do not incur instructional disadvantages. Depending on the nature of the task, half-day meeting blocks are desirable, and sometimes can be arranged using internal coverage. When meetings are held before, during, or immediately after the instructional day, an activity should be planned that assists members to transition from the fast-paced instructional day to more reflective learning time.

The physical arrangement of the meeting area also affects reflection and learning. When seated in a circle, participants can easily see one another; they are, in effect, more exposed. This presence tends to increase attention and reflection about what is being said and also what is being communicated through nonverbal postures and facial expressions. Recall from earlier chapters discussion about the powerful communication of nonverbal behavior in meeting spaces. In the book *Lame Deer, Seeker of Visions*, John Lame Deer (1994), a Sioux elder, eloquently describes the symbolism of circles (see Figure 6.7).

Figure 6.7   Symbolism of the Circle From the Perspective of a Sioux Elder

**A Reading From
John Lame Deer, a Sioux Elder**

We Indians live in a world of symbols and images
where the spiritual and commonplace are one. To you
symbols are just words, spoken or written in a book. To us they
are a part of nature, part of ourselves—the earth, the sun, the
wind, and the rain, stones, trees, animals, even little insects like ants
and grasshoppers. We try to understand them not with the head but with
the heart, and we need no more than a hint to give us the meaning . . .

To our way of thinking the Indians' symbol is the circle, the hoop. Nature
wants things to be round. The bodies of human beings and animals have no
corners. With us the circle stands for the togetherness of people who sit with
one another around the campfire, relatives and friends united in peace while
the pipe passes from hand to hand.

The camps in which every tipi had its place was also a ring. The tipi was a
ring in which people sat in a circle and all families in the village were in
turn circles within a larger circle, part of the larger hoop which was the
seven campfires of the Sioux, representing one nation.

The nation was only part of the universe, in itself circular
and made of earth, which is round, of the sun, which is
round, of the stars, which are round. The moon,
the horizon, the rainbow—the circles
within circles, with no beginning
and no end.

Source: Lame Deer & Erdoes (1994, pp. 108, 110–111).

As you read this passage,

- What words, phrases, and images stood out for you?
- What are some reasons these selections captured your attention?
- In what ways might the perspective communicated by John Lame Deer connect to life in our school communities?
- What are the circles in your life that sustain and energize you?

For us, powerful images of interconnectedness among people emerge. We are reminded that none of us is supposed to go alone, to be alone. We are meant to be in community with others. It is our interdependence that creates a strong web of connections through which care, protection, knowledge, and creativity can thrive.

Other circular imagery emerges. For example, the adage, "What goes around, comes around" has served us well as we reflect on our work and on how we aspire to show up in the world. The more good energy each of us puts out in earnest attempts to nudge forward a sense of interdependence among us, to do good by the young people we serve, the more likely they are to learn well and grow up to do good in the world. And the more likely *we* are to continue learning and making earnest attempts to do good. We are reminded that whatever perspective we hold dear, will enlarge. Through what we say and what we do, we can choose to "do good." Earnest attempts to do what is good, to grow what is good, and to continually reflect and improve our practice is good. Not one of us has the stamina to do this work of heart and spirit alone. We need a community. We need our own circles of care, support, learning, and creativity. We need our "circles within circles," an image offered by John Lame Deer. In a circle formation we are exposed to others as they are to us. As trust and learning grow, the sense of exposure begins to subtly shift to one of warmth, understanding, empathy, and support. We can be who we are. We can speak our truth. We can, together, go far.

Opening the Group Process

The way in which a group or meeting begins communicates to the participants the degree of safety, respect, preparation, and perceived importance of the time planned together. Each group gathering requires attention to supporting the transition of members from where they were before they entered the group setting to be settled and oriented in the group setting and learning work. Here are some other guidelines for initiating the group:

- *Seating.* Members should be seated so they can see one another. If necessary, take the time to rearrange the furniture so this happens without specific prompting or rearranging after participants have already chosen a seat. Seems this point should not have to be made explicit, right? We still observe, however, many team meetings where members arrive and sit in student desks that are arranged in rows and columns. Members need to see each other and speak into a common space, such as the middle of the circle.
- *Review and preview.* Reference an agenda (either posted or on handouts) and introduce the purpose of the meeting—both the BIG purpose (i.e., the long-term goal of the group) and the more focused purpose of the current meeting.
- *Grounding.* Members should be seated so they can see one another. Grounding is a strategy originally introduced through Bob Garmston's Adaptive Schools work (1999) and more recently described in his 2012 book, *Unlocking Group Potential*, which is an outstanding resource for group development. When groups meet for the first time, reflection prompts for the Grounding might be as follows.

- Please share your first name and your position or role. (Note: we advise that you not ask participants to share the number of years they have worked in the school. This risks setting up a perceived hierarchy of value, knowledge, or power that can serve to diminish participation by members with fewer years of experience.)
- How would you describe your relationship or connection to our topic?
- What are some things you are interested in learning more about related to our group's purpose?

- *Warm-up activities.* There are two types of warm-up activities often used in group work, relationship-building and on-ramp activities. Relationship-building activities are useful early in formation of the group, especially when groups will meet on an ongoing basis. These activities should be safe, but personal. For example, ask participants to share a little known fact about themselves, describe a favorite family ritual, inform the group about where they were born, or find out who travels the farthest to get to school every day. This provides an opportunity for participants to practice disclosure in a safe way (they determine what to share and what not to share) and offers another way to know each person in the group, which assists with remembering names. What participants choose to share varies greatly. One teacher shared that as a young child, she tried to teach her pet fish to walk. Another was afraid of elevators. This disclosure prompted a number of participants to join her using the stairs as a form of job-embedded exercise! A young teacher shared that just a few years ago, when he was in the best physical shape ever, he had a stroke. Each of these disclosures expands the understanding and connections among group members. Through stories of humorous events or personal challenges, individuals become connected in ways other than just work. This builds the relationships, which strengthens commitments to group purpose, participants, and process. One way to keep this type of connecting activities going is to rotate responsibility for leading an icebreaking activity at the beginning of each session. This also fosters shared responsibility for group development.
- *On-ramp activities.* On-ramp activities assist participants with getting oriented to the group task or purpose. To help reframe meetings as opportunities for learning, for example, a brief reflection activity might be inserted. We have a handout with reflective practice quotes and invite participants to read the quotes and share a quote that struck them as meaningful. To prompt thinking, you could share a story, or an abstract from a recent research article—each with carefully constructed questions to prompt reflection and conversation. These activities serve the function of bringing the thoughts and energy of group members into the present.

Group Norms and Expectations

Paying attention to norms and expectations at every session serves as a reminder of behaviors and dispositions that facilitate learning and working together. We frequently begin group sessions with the verbal or visual reminder that "we are all in the same room, but not in the same place" (anonymous as quoted by Garmston & Wellman, 1997, p. 29). This serves to acknowledge differences among individuals and to support an expectation that different perspectives will be shared. Norms and expectations can be provided, generated, or a combination of both. They should be posted in clear view. As presented in the Growing Reflective Practice Communities section in Chapter 2, we also suggest offering the seven norms of collaborative work developed by Bill Baker and formally articulated in the work of Garmston and Wellman (1999). "When the seven norms of collaborative work become an established part of group life and group work, cohesion, energy, and commitment to shared work and to the group increase dramatically" (Garmston & Wellman, 1999, p. 37). Figure 6.8 shows these norms along with visual reminders about dialogue, discussion, and suspension as tools for individual and group use.

This depiction, which we call the Tabletop Norms of Collaborative Work, has been formatted as a handout on the book's companion website at http://resources.corwin.com/YorkBarrReflective and can be sized for insertion in 5-by-7-inch self-standing acrylic picture frames to be placed on tables within the group. To be effective, norms and expectations must be regularly and intentionally revisited. One way is to invite group members to identify norms on which to focus at the start of each meeting.

Figure 6.8   Tabletop Norms of Collaborative Work

Source: Adapted with permission from Garmston & Wellman (1997).

 Available for download at http://resources.corwin.com/YorkBarrReflective

We would suggest adding one more addition to the Norms of Collaboration. This addition was originally proposed by Bill Baker: *Providing Data* (personal communication, 1993). This "data" norm helps to keep the focus on, "How do we know something is working or not?" "What should we pay attention to that will inform our use? How will we collect the information we find most valuable to us?"

Closing the Group Process

Specific attention to ending a group session affirms the importance of the effort. "People need to feel that the work of the group is meaningful if they are to take such activities seriously in the future" (Will, 1997, p. 37). Closing a session is a form of reflection-on-action that addresses both the content and process of the session. General questions might include a focus on the content, for example, "What were the most significant insights or outcomes of today's gathering?"; and a focus on process, for example, "What were strengths in terms of our overall group process and what might be some things to work on next time?" Use of metaphors and synectics (see the example on metaphors and synectics at the end of this chapter) also work well for closing and are described later in this chapter. A variety of reflection frameworks that can target both content and process are shown in Figure 6.9. Used most effectively, they would first involve asking participants to spend a few moments reflecting individually or with a partner before sharing with the whole group. Regardless of the specific method of reflection that is chosen, group capacity is enhanced when individuals and the group as a whole reflect on their contributions, learning, and outcomes. Consider again the assertion from Judi Arin-Krupp: "adults do not learn from experience, they learn from processing experience."

Here we share an out of field example on the significance of what we refer to as grounding. Atul Gawande, MD/MPH, is a surgeon, writer, and public health researcher. He wrote the book *Checklist Manifesto* (2009). In his book, Dr. Gawande identifies three types of problems: simple (e.g., baking a cake), complicated (e.g., sending a rocket to the moon), and complex (e.g., raising a child). The first two types of problems can largely be thwarted by the use of checklists. He described the challenge of extreme complexity that exists in medicine today, and specifically identified three potential sources of error during surgery: memory, attention, and omitting steps. He experimented with the use of "checklists" as a way to reduce errors during surgery. Before surgery, each member of the surgical team introduced herself or himself and identified their respective goals for the operation. A new rule also was put in place: "if doctors didn't follow every step, the nurses would have back-up from administration to intervene" (Gawande, 2009). The results were so dramatic that they weren't sure whether to believe them:

The ten-day line infection rate went from 11 percent to zero. They calculated that in this one hospital, the checklist had prevented forty-three infections and eight deaths, and saved two million dollars in cost . . . further, this reduced from 41 percent to 3 percent the likelihood of a patient's enduring untreated pain. (Gawande, 2009, audiobook)

He concluded: "Get the stupid stuff right!"

Figure 6.9   Sample of Closing Reflection Worksheets

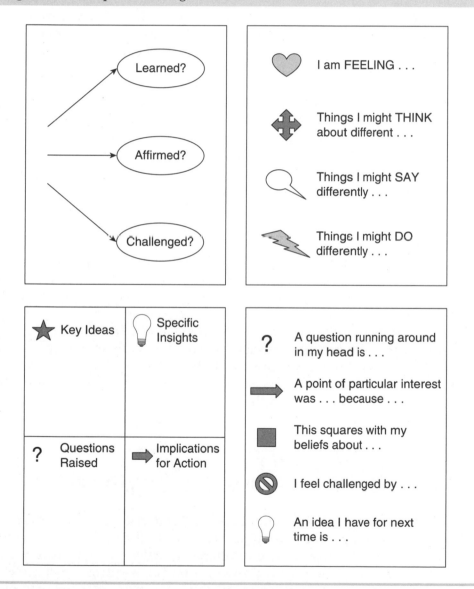

In What Ways Can Time Be Allocated for Learning Together?

Time is our most valuable non-renewable resource. Educators must make wise decisions about how time is best used in schools. School renewal and improvement efforts that occur on the fringes of the school day or school year are unlikely to become embedded dimensions of school culture (Speck, 2002). This means that embedding professional learning in the school day and throughout the school year must be a priority. Time has been consistently identified as an essential structural condition within organizations to support both individual and collective learning (Donahoe, 1993; Louis, 1992; Raywid, 1993; U.S. Department of Education, 1996; Watts & Castle, 1993). "If student achievement is to improve, then teachers need time to learn, practice, implement, observe and reflect" (Speck, 2002, p. 17). Although having time does not guarantee effective reflection and collaboration, not having time precludes even the possibility. Unless schools intentionally schedule collaborative time for professional learning, the dominant culture of isolated teacher work will continue (Adelman, 1998). Schein (2004) states that there is probably no more important factor in the analysis of an organization's culture than how it allocates and uses time. The pace of events, the rhythms of the building, the sequence in which things are done, and meeting agendas are all signs of what an organization or team values. "The perspective most needed . . . is that of time as a resource that can be shaped and reshaped to meet educational needs rather than as a straitjacket into which teaching and learning have to be stuffed" (U.S. Department of Education, 1996, p. 11).

Allocating time for collaborative learning has become a high priority for many schools across the country. A decision that such time is important must be followed up with efforts to make it happen. After clarifying specific reasons for meeting, decisions must be made about who needs to meet together, how often meetings should be held, and when and where to meet. In some of the cases below and also in the chapter that follows, we offer some examples for creating or allocating time for learning.

REFLECTIVE PRACTICE IN SMALL GROUPS AND TEAMS: PRACTICE EXAMPLES

Because of the many teams, committees, ad hoc and governance groups in schools, embedding reflective practices within these structures holds much potential for advancing educational practice. In this section, we describe numerous examples from work that is occurring in Minnesota. We begin by highlighting intentional decisions in the design of group learning. This is followed by examples from elementary, middle, and high school educators who engage in reflective practices as a part of addressing relevant issues in their respective practice settings. As you read these examples, we invite you to reflect on the following questions.

- In what ways have learning opportunities been intentionally designed?
- How does planning and design support participation by group members?
- How is reflection used to foster learning and monitor the group process and progress?
- What is the role of the facilitator? How do facilitators initiate and guide group learning and process? What are some examples of facilitators reflecting in and on action?
- What about a particular example do I want to remember and ponder further? Why?

PRACTICE EXAMPLE 6.1

COLLABORATIVE DATA CYCLES INCREASE TEACHER LEARNING, TAILORED INSTRUCTION, AND STUDENT LEARNING

Contributed by Mr. Tom Geisenhoff, Instructional Coach,
and Dr. Kari Rock, Principal, Eisenhower Elementary School,
Anoka Hennepin School District, Minnesota

The Anoka-Hennepin School District has a student population of approximately 45,000 students. It is the largest district in the state of Minnesota and encompasses residents from 13 suburban communities located north of Minneapolis. The school district has five high schools serving Grades 9 through 12, six middle schools serving students in Grades 6 through 8, and twenty-four elementary schools serving students Grades K through 5.

Eisenhower Elementary School currently serves approximately 636 students. About half (45.8 percent) of the students qualify for free and reduced lunch. The district had gone through a restructuring process, including closing of schools. The result for Eisenhower was an increase in student population from 404 to 617. Fifty-four percent (333) of students qualified for Free and Reduced Lunch; 12 percent were English Language Learners; and ethnic diversity was 68 percent Caucasian, 5 percent Latino, 13 percent African-American, 11 percent Asian/Pacific Islander, and 3 percent American Indian. One outcome of these shifts was a dramatically increased range of reading abilities in the classrooms. Teachers were required to deliver whole group and small group reading instruction. Whole group teaching involved using the

(Continued)

(Continued)

Figure 6.10 Differentiated and Flexible Reading Groups Across First Grade, Assisted by a Promethean Board

Time	Teacher 1		Teacher 2		Teacher 3	Teacher 4	Teacher 5
	Level 14		Level low 10		Level 8	Level 3	Level 10
	T/W		M-Th		M-F	M-F	M/W/F
10:20	Student Name Here	Level 16	Student Name Here		Student Name Here	Student Name Here	Student Name Here
to	Student Name Here	Th/F	Student Name Here		Student Name Here	Student Name Here	Student Name Here
10:40	Student Name Here	Student Name Here	Student Name Here		Student Name Here	Student Name Here	Student Name Here
	Student Name Here	Student Name Here	Student Name Here		Student Name Here	Student Name Here	Student Name Here
	Student Name Here	Student Name Here	Student Name Here		Student Name Here	Student Name Here	Student Name Here
		Student Name Here			Student Name Here	Student Name Here	
	Level 18	Student Name Here	Level 24				Level 12
	M		F				T/Th
	Student Name Here		Student Name Here				Student Name Here
	Student Name Here		Student Name Here				Student Name Here
	Student Name Here		Student Name Here				Student Name Here
	Student Name Here		Student Name Here				Student Name Here
	Student Name Here		Student Name Here				Student Name Here
	Student Name Here		Student Name Here				
	Level 3		Level 24		Level 6	Level 4	Level 8
	M-F		M		M-F	M-F	M-Th
10:40	Student Name Here		Student Name Here		Student Name Here	Student Name Here	Student Name Here
to	Student Name Here		Student Name Here		Student Name Here	Student Name Here	Student Name Here
11:00			Student Name Here		Student Name Here	Student Name Here	Student Name Here
	Student Name Here		Student Name Here		Student Name Here	Student Name Here	Student Name Here
	Student Name Here		Student Name Here		Student Name Here	Student Name Here	Student Name Here
			Student Name Here		Student Name Here		
			Level 6				Level 12
			T-F				F
			Student Name Here				Student Name Here
			Student Name Here				Student Name Here
			Student Name Here				Student Name Here
			Student Name Here				Student Name Here
							Student Name Here
	Level 6		Level 12		Level 12	Level 10	Level 4
	M-Th		M-W-F		M-W-F	M-W-F	M-F
	Student Name Here		Student Name Here		Student Name Here	Student Name Here	Student Name Here
11:00	Student Name Here		Student Name Here		Student Name Here	Student Name Here	Student Name Here
to	Student Name Here		Student Name Here		Student Name Here	Student Name Here	Student Name Here
11:20	Student Name Here		Student Name Here		Student Name Here	Student Name Here	Student Name Here
	Student Name Here		Student Name Here		Student Name Here	Student Name Here	Student Name Here
	Student Name Here				Student Name Here	Student Name Here	
	Level 18		Level 18/20		Level 20	Level 18	
	F		T/Th	Gappers	T/Th	T/Th	
	Student Name Here		Student Name Here		Student Name Here	Student Name Here	
	Student Name Here		Student Name Here		Student Name Here	Student Name Here	
	Student Name Here		Student Name Here		Student Name Here	Student Name Here	
	Student Name Here		Student Name Here		Student Name Here	Student Name Here	
	Student Name Here		Student Name Here		Student Name Here	Student Name Here	
	Student Name Here		Student Name Here		Student Name Here	Student Name Here	

Teacher 6	Teacher 7	Teacher 8	Teacher 9	Teacher 10	Teacher 11	Teacher 12
in 1A	in 1K	in 1D	in 1S	in 1CK	in 1S	in 1D
M-F	Level 4	Level 6				
Student Name Here	M-F	M-F				
Student Name Here		Student Name Here				
Student Name Here	Student Name Here	Student Name Here				
	Student Name Here	Student Name Here				
Student Name Here		Student Name Here				
Student Name Here						
		Level 6	Level 4			
M-F	M-F	M-F	M-F			
Student Name Here	Student Name Here	Student Name Here	Student Name Here			
Student Name Here	Student Name Here	Student Name Here	Student Name Here			
Student Name Here	Student Name Here	Student Name Here	Student Name Here			
Student Name Here		Student Name Here	Student Name Here			
	Student Name Here					
				Level 10	Level 10	
				M-Th	M-Th	
				10 min.	10 min.	
				Student Name Here	Student Name Here	
				Student Name Here	Student Name Here	
		Level 3	Level 8	Level 6	Level 8	Level low 10
M-F	M-F	M-F	M-F	M-Th	M-Th	DD 1 3 4 5
		Student Name Here	Student Name Here	Student Name Here	Student Name Here	Student Name Here
		Student Name Here	Student Name Here	Student Name Here	Student Name Here	Student Name Here
Student Name Here	Student Name Here	Student Name Here	Student Name Here	Student Name Here	Student Name Here	Student Name Here
Student Name Here	Student Name Here	Student Name Here	Student Name Here	Student Name Here		Student Name Here
Student Name Here	Student Name Here			Student Name Here		Student Name Here
	no Wed.					

(Continued)

(Continued)

Time	T1	T2	T3	T4	T5	T6	T7	T8	T9	T10	T11
10:15											
10:30											
10:45											
11:00											

Making Meaning trade book text and small group instruction was grounded in Jan Richardson's (2009) *Next Steps in Guided Reading*. In almost all of the classrooms, there were four small groups that met for fifteen minutes every day in an attempt to connect with all students below grade level at their respective instructional levels.

Two of the five first grade teachers initiated a focused action research project in which they shared students during the designated small group time. Four, fifteen minute groups a day in separate classrooms had been inadequate for addressing the range of student reading levels and also inadequate in terms of how much time was available to teach. By sharing their students, the teachers decreased the number of small groups that they had to meet with daily while still grouping students by reading level, and sometimes reading strategy needs. Each group was limited to six students per group. Results were significant in that a much larger percentage of students were provided a small guided reading group daily in those two rooms.

Having experienced success with this action research trial, the idea of expanding this small group design to the entire grade level was proposed. As with most changes proposed, there were some thoughtful initial questions and concerns, in particular regarding the issue of sharing students. After a number of thoughtful conversations with the grade level, several concerns surfaced about peers lacking relationships with students from other classrooms and what might be the focus when addressing the needs of those students. Other questions that arose focused on logistical issues, such as keeping track of data, determining groupings, and managing transitions.

Conversations began during the last few weeks of the school year about the advantages and struggles of sharing students across the grade level. Consensus was reached to move forward, on a trial basis, for the remainder of the year. The first grade team began to share students within the grade level. During the following year, a decision was made to do cross-classroom groupings for small group instruction in kindergarten and second grade as well.

At the start of the next school year, an outgrowth of this initial shift in practice was a review of reading data for all students in the grade level by all teachers in the grade level. More specifically, every six weeks the principal and/or site instructional coach met with the teachers to review the data that was to be used to inform grouping and re-grouping of students for small groups, and to include planning of strategy instruction. The teachers took ownership of this change with a focus on results. They deepened their conversations about students, learning, and their own practice. They frequently met before the six-week meetings to make changes to groups and their practice.

Each grade level's monthly review date was set for the entire school year. School-based professional learning focused on growing teacher understanding and effectiveness with strategy instruction. The specific teacher learning targets were not put on the professional learning calendar because the specific learning focus for each month was to be determined by what each respective teacher and grade level needed to learn about most that would best support the students within the specific guided reading plans they were using. In this way, learning was responsive to specific teacher and student learning needs.

(Continued)

(Continued)

A Promethean board (see Figure 6.10) served well to support conversations and decisions about student grouping. Time frames for the small groups were identified on the vertical axis of the Promethean board. Names of the grade level classroom and support teachers ran across the horizontal axis. Also across the horizontal axis were column headers indicating reading level or reading strategy focus for each respective group. Each teacher had a particular level or strategy focus under her or his name. The colors were added to quickly notice which students were receiving an extra scoop of service. All extra service was provided in the classroom environment instead of pulling students out of the room. When the entire team met, data were reviewed for each student. If changes in small groups were indicated, students were easily moved ("dragged and dropped") into a new place on the Promethean board. Some of the teachers, eventually, began using an Excel spreadsheet for this tracking.

The rest of the story... Eisenhower Elementary was designated as a Reward School by the Minnesota Department of Education in 2012, 2013, 2014, and in 2015 with the ninth highest Multiple Measurements Rating (MMR) Focus rating when compared to over 2,200 MN Title schools.

 Available for download at **http://resources.corwin.com/YorkBarrReflective**

This practice example offers several "gems" in terms of reflective practice. First, the team structure, whether dyads or the entire grade level, offer the opportunity to reflect, learn, and plan together around a shared interest: ensuring each student in a grade level receives instruction at a level or focused on a strategy specific to her or his learning need. Second, reflecting together also expands the insight and practice wisdom from a larger group of like professionals. Such collaboration, once teachers learn its value and let go of feeling like each must know everything, brings the invaluable resource of "just right" and "just in time" support. Third, using the Promethean board, or some other visual focus, is an example of going to "third point." In this case, the board serves as the focus of conversation. Teachers can look at it, point to it, interact with it, and yes, even talk to it! Focused on a third point, instead of sitting around looking at one another, lessens the interpersonal tension that can arise when team members are watching and looking at each other. Fourth, implementation design has become the initial focus with any structured building level initiative. Piloting a best practice idea with staff who are interested and then tracking results creates an internal acceptance (bottom up) rather than an external push (top down) for changing school practice. The outcomes of such shared practice reinforce the principle: "Go-eth not Alone." The work is too complex and energy consuming. Reflection and learning together is an enormous resource that keeps the energy growing to "do good."

PRACTICE EXAMPLE 6.2

FOUR LITTLE QUESTIONS GUIDE POWERFUL LEARNING DESIGN IN HIGH SCHOOL

Contributed by Louis Francesco and Luke Leba,
Reading Teachers and Coaches, Harding High School,
Saint Paul Public Schools, Minnesota

Winging it doesn't work, at least not for most of us. Even when we have designed, facilitated, and reflected on the outcomes of hundreds of gatherings, each new gathering has its own particularities to consider on the front end, so good things happen in the conversation. The four little questions are: Why? Who? What? How? In this case, we know *who* is involved. Therefore, this example is most focused on offering clarification about *Why?*, *What?*, and *How?*

1. *Purposes*, often stated by the facilitator and serving as an initial orientation to the learning ahead;

2. *Opening*, usually with an on topic grounding question that serves to get every voice in the room participating. This assists with the transition from teaching all day to the present;

3. *Going deeper* into the learning, usually by means of reflective questions, and sometimes moving to smaller configurations, such as dyads or triads to elicit more active participation and to allow for more conversation. In this particular example, the third page of the agenda offers a reflection guide for members to jot down notes before sharing; and

4. *Closing* which may take the form of sharing out ideas for follow-up in participants' classrooms and offering ideas for next month's conversation.

In Figure 6.11 you can review a sample agenda that was used for one of the Inquiry Group gatherings. You will notice there are four big chunks of the agenda: purposes, opening, core, closing. One additional feature to note: there are three pages to the Agenda. The first is for use by the facilitator. Notice that both the content and process columns have text. The second page is for the participants. Notice that the content column has text, but the second column has no text. This version was for the participants so they could make notes. Early in our Inquiry Group learning design, the participants received this same exact version of the agenda. As time went on, members suggested that the participants had a version absent the process so they could take notes as they went along. And so, this is what we did.

(Continued)

(Continued)

Figure 6.11 Sample Inquiry Group Agenda

Inquiry Group Meeting 4—November 20, 20XX—Sample

Purposes—Reflecting on Strategy Use—Individual and Collective Learning

1. Reflect on your use of a strategy, focusing on a specific student.
2. Identify what seemed effective and also ways you might refine use of the strategy in future teaching.
3. Share your "learnings" with Inquiry Group colleagues. Keep in mind your aim to support collective understanding and effective use of selected strategies.
4. Identify how this strategy (or how any of the learning from your Inquiry Group) might be useful in your PLC.
5. Decide on a learning focus for next month (e.g., stick with or change strategy focus? peer visits? other?).

CONTENT		PROCESS
1. **Opening** Purpose and agenda overview	**OPENING**	a. Provide members with agenda. b. State meeting purposes.
2. **Grounding (every voice in the room)** Q: *As you reflect on your strategy use this past month, what is one word that comes to mind?* (individual response)		a. Ask members to locate one quote of interest and think about why the quote was significant (1 minute). b. Each member shares round robin. Other members listen (no responding) to keep process moving.
3. **Describe and reflect on strategy use—focusing on one student.** (On the backside of this agenda there is a guide for these conversations, along with plenty of room to write.) • Step 1: Individual Reflection *Reflections on use of a strategy with focus on a specific student.* • Step 2: Sharing in a Dyad *Taking turns sharing and listening, to gain insights about strategy use.* • Step 3: Share-Back to the Group *Each dyad share insights or points of interest with the whole group.* • Step 4: Whole Group Reflection *Q: How might our Inquiry Group learning be useful in our PLCs?*	**CORE**	a. Ask members to pair up. b. Introduce the reflection work for the meeting: individual, followed by paired reflection, then sharing back key learnings to the whole group. Note: *A strong reason for dyad sharing is to provide an opportunity to delve more deeply into the use and response strategies being studied.* c. One dyad member shares responses to questions. Then, second member shares. Together identify points of interest to share with whole group. d. Each dyad shares their points of interest, building on or connecting to points from other dyads. e. Invite members to think of ways that the learning within this Inquiry Group might be useful or somehow "fit" into planning conversations that happen in PLCs.
4. **Closing Conversation** • What's our learning focus for next month?	**CLOSING**	a. Offer ideas, such as: staying with a focus on strategies (or chapters) already studied? Moving to a new focus? Schedule classroom visits with next month's learning focused on those? Other?

Inquiry Group Meeting 4—November 20, 20XX—Sample

Purposes—Reflecting on Strategy Use—Individual and Collective Learning

1. Reflect on your use of a strategy, focusing on a specific student.
2. Identify what seemed effective and also ways you might refine use of the strategy in future teaching.
3. Share your "learnings" with Inquiry Group colleagues. Keep in mind your aim to support collective understanding and effective use of selected strategies.
4. Identify how this strategy (or how any of the learning from your Inquiry Group) might be useful in your PLC.
5. Decide on a learning focus for next month (e.g., stick with strategy? change? peer visits? other?).

CONTENT		PROCESS
1. **Opening** Purpose and agenda overview	**OPENING**	
2. **Grounding (every voice in the room)** Q: *As you reflect on your strategy use this past month, what is one word that comes to mind?* (individual response)		
3. **Describe and reflect on strategy use— focusing on one student.** (On the backside of this agenda there is a guide for these conversations, along with plenty of room to write.) • Step 1: Individual Reflection *Reflections on use of a strategy with focus on a specific student.* • Step 2: Sharing in a Dyad *Taking turns sharing and listening, to gain insights about strategy use.* • Step 3: Share-Back to the Group *Each dyad share insights or points of interest with the whole group.* • Step 4: Whole Group Reflection *Q: How might our Inquiry Group learning be useful in our PLCs?*	**CORE**	
4. **Closing Conversation** What's our learning focus for next month?	**CLOSING**	

(Continued)

(Continued)

Inquiry Group Meeting 4—November 20, 20XX—Sample

Step 1: Individual Reflection: Identify one student who you paid attention to when you embedded use of a strategy we are learning into a recent lesson. Write some notes in response to the reflection questions below.

1. What is the student's first name and what was the strategy you were using?

2. What did you notice about ways the student engaged or responded to the strategy use?

3. How might you use or refine use of the strategies in the future, with this student or others?

4. Overall,

   . . . what did you learn about the strategy and about the student through these teaching opportunities?

   . . . what are you wondering about or questioning?

Step 2: Dyad Share: Form dyads—perhaps with a new conversational partner.

- As the "sharing" member, share your responses to all the questions.
- As the "listening" member, allow the sharing member to share responses to all the questions (without interruption).
- After the "sharer", the listener offers ideas about what seemed to be key insights or challenges of the story.
- Switch roles and repeat. Then identify points of interest to share with the whole group.

Step 3: Share-Back to Group: Each dyad shares your "something" with the whole group.

Step 4: Group Reflection: How might our Inquiry Group learning be useful in our PLCs?

 Available for download at http://resources.corwin.com/YorkBarrReflective

The specific example offered in Figure 6.11 presents a sample of the small group learning design for a schoolwide practice example presented in Chapter 7, Embedding Literacy Practice Schoolwide at Harding

High School. At Harding there are two schoolwide small group learning structures for teachers. One is Professional Learning Communities (PLCs) and focuses on content area teaching and learning practices. The other is Inquiry Groups, the focus of which is supporting teachers to learn about literacy practices, and specifically how to embed literacy practices as a standard part of their content area teaching. If you are interested in the buildingwide initiation and scope of this secondary literacy work, skip ahead to Practice Example 7.3.

PRACTICE EXAMPLE 6.3

PLCS ARE GOOD FOR ADMINISTRATORS TOO!

A high school administrative team was presented with a challenge question from their staff, "If we have to do PLCs, what are the administrators doing?" Yikes, suddenly modeling and authenticity trumped being busy. The administrative team chose the book *Unmistakable Impact* by Jim Knight (2011). Twice a month the team met. Each time they met, a chapter was required reading. As the team made progress through the book, the conversations centered on what they were seeing in real time in the school that was discussed in the book, and what they were not seeing that would also be helpful to their progress. The administrators used the book as a guide to determine what was happening in the school, what they wanted to see happen in the school for adults and students, and most importantly, how they could make the changes to increase the school's chance for success. Each member took on a challenge that would be helpful to themselves, as leaders, and what would be helpful to the school.

Goldberg and Pesko (2000) initiated teacher book clubs, based on a belief that literacy instruction would improve if teachers themselves were involved in reading and reflecting on literature. The selections were pleasure reading, not professional reading. This re-created an opportunity to personalize the experience of literature and better understand the range of reading styles and reading responses of students. "We read and discuss literature, analyze our personal preferences for reading, reflect on classroom practices, and modify classroom practices on the basis of what we have learned" (p. 39).

 Available for download at http://resources.corwin.com/YorkBarrReflective

PRACTICE EXAMPLE 6.4

MIDDLE SCHOOL TEACHERS FACILITATE LEARNING WITH PEERS

Contributed by Sarah Holm and Gary Aylward,
Richfield Public Schools, Minnesota

This teacher-led learning example was initially presented in the previous edition of this book. Ten years later, it is no less relevant. Two middle school teachers invited their colleagues to form a collaborative group to learn more about research-based instructional strategies. They chose the book *Classroom Instruction That Works: Research-Based Strategies for Increasing Student Achievement* (Marzano, Pickering, & Pollock, 2001) to guide their learning. The teacher leaders articulated the following objectives: to practice using norms of collaborative work during group interactions; to read about research-based instructional strategies; to implement one research-based strategy in the classroom and share that experience with group members; and to identify strengths and applications for all the instructional strategies studied. Six teacher colleagues representing the core areas (math, social studies, science, and language arts) decided to join them.

The teachers who led this effort developed a schedule where one instructional strategy was the focus of each learning session. A unique feature of this study process was that in addition to reading about the instructional strategies, participants were each expected to select one instructional strategy and practice using that strategy with their students before the group was scheduled to talk about it. The teachers viewed this as a form of action research.

[Recall the 4-step process from Chapter 4 included the following reflection prompts: what happened? (description); why? (analysis and interpretation); so what? (overall meaning); and now what? (implications for action).]

During the last collaborative group session, the teacher leaders asked participants to evaluate the group learning experience by responding to the following questions.

Content Questions

- Was the book selected relevant to what you wanted to accomplish in the classroom? Did you have adequate time to practice and reflect on the strategy you selected? How will what you learned be useful to you? In what ways will you be able to apply what you learned?

Process Questions

- Was the collaborative group format helpful to your learning . . . if yes, how? Was the group facilitator prepared? Were the goals and objectives clearly specified when you began?

Context Questions

- Was the meeting room setting conducive to learning? Were you provided with treats that you really wanted to eat? ☺

In reflecting on the sessions and on the responses to the evaluation, the teacher leaders concluded that participants were mostly positive about the learning process, the action research, and using the selected book. Participants had indicated feeling proud that they were already using many of the instructional strategies in their daily lessons. Participants also indicated that allocating time to meet within the school day was positive and important.

Reflecting on their roles as learning facilitators, the teacher leader pair shared that initially responsibility for leading a peer group felt a little scary. Sometimes they felt pressure to put on a "dog and pony show." They created a mental picture, however, that helped support them in their new roles as facilitators. They envisioned serving as a *guide*. They envisioned the role of a guide as assuming responsibility for gathering and reflecting on collective wisdom and then for determining specific paths to take. These teachers decided they could do that. Overall, assuming roles as facilitators and participants, the teacher leaders felt that taking time out of their busy schedules to study collaboratively was worthwhile and that they grew as facilitators. For them, the most gratifying aspect of all was that the participants indicated having grown as teachers.

 Available for download at **http://resources.corwin.com/YorkBarrReflective**

PRACTICE EXAMPLE 6.5

TIME FOR TEAM-LEARNING TASK FORCE AT PLAINS ELEMENTARY

This practice example describes one adaptation of a scheduling process that two of this book's authors have used in multiple schools to create time for interdisciplinary team members who support a common group of students to reflect, plan, and learn together.

Plains Elementary School, a K–6 urban school with about 650 students, was developing collaborative instructional models to support its diverse student

(Continued)

(Continued)

population. Recognizing that time to meet is a key factor for successful collaboration, a task force was formed with the charge of finding time for teams to meet. Task force members reflected on readings about scheduling options. They examined current school schedules and considered the impact of various scheduling options. They also solicited feedback from other Plains faculty throughout the process.

The task force participants were a representative group of ten teachers, including teachers from primary and intermediate grades, special education, English language learning (ELL), fine arts, the teachers' union, and two teachers with prior experience developing schoolwide schedules. The principal, as an ad hoc member, was kept abreast of the task force progress. Representative membership was intended to ensure that schoolwide perspectives were heard and that task force recommendations would be well conceived and well received.

Early on, half- or full-day meetings were held off-site, but nearby to keep participants focused on the work and to eliminate interruptions. Initial meetings were scheduled three to four weeks apart to allow time for participants to reflect on the options, questions, and directions that resulted from the meetings. This schedule also allowed participants to obtain feedback from staff not involved in the meetings. When the task force process shifted from learning and brainstorming to decision making and planning, the meetings were scheduled closer together to sustain the momentum necessary for accomplishing their task. A brief summary of the task-force process follows.

Meeting 1: Reflecting on Beliefs, Practices, and Research

Participants reviewed research about why team meeting time was important and how other schools had created blocks of time for teachers to meet and learn together. Through dialogue, participants considered how the various time strategies might apply in their school. The process was intentionally kept open to consider a variety of options. No decisions were made.

Meeting 2: Identifying Principles for Decision Making

Typical of most complex learning, there were points of confusion and tension. In particular, as task force participants considered how time to meet might work into the school schedule, they recognized that before figuring out a schedule, they had to determine how teams would be configured. Some were uncomfortable with this expanded dimension of their work. To move forward, task force members decided on two principles to guide decision making: (a) program coherence and consistency for students, and as much as possible for staff; and (b) regular meeting times for grade level instructional teams to reflect on curricular, instructional, and student performance issues.

Meeting 3: Updating the Principal

Task force members updated the principal by sharing posters that summarized the work of the previous meetings. It became apparent to all that despite the challenges substantial progress had been made. The principal agreed with the summary principles and encouraged the group to continue.

Meetings 4–6: Developing Specific Schedule Options

Using paper cutouts of all staff members (color-coded by position), task force members spent a day brainstorming ways that staff might be reorganized into grade-level teams composed of classroom teachers, specialists, and assistants. The cutouts were arranged and rearranged amid much conversation of advantages and disadvantages of different configurations. The purposes of the activity were to identify who needed time to meet and then brainstorm scheduling options that supported both short weekly and long monthly blocks of time for team reflection and planning. Two short follow-up meetings (meetings 5 and 6) were held to fine-tune the two scheduling options. Table 6.2 outlines the options proposed by the task force.

Table 6.2   Time for Reflection and Learning: Strategies and Examples

Strategy for Finding Time	What Is it?	What Have Schools Done?
Freed-Up Time	Temporary blocks of time were created for teachers through the use of substitutes, volunteers, or creative use of staff.	• Hired substitutes to release groups of teachers to meet every other week. • Scheduled special performances or assemblies so grade-level teams were free to meet during this time. • Arranged for a licensed staff member without regular classroom assignments to cover a classroom so that the classroom teacher had time to observe a peer teaching, or to meet with a team member. • Created a reflection pool: teachers volunteered to give up their prep time to cover a colleague's class allowing the colleague time for reflection. In exchange, the freed-up colleagues then placed their names in the pool in order to cover other colleagues' classes.

(Continued)

(Continued)

Strategy for Finding Time	What Is it?	What Have Schools Done?
Purchased Time	Schools found creative ways to find and fund professional time, including use of early retirees, foundation funding, or contractual compensation. These strategies can be temporary, transitional, or institutionalized by building it into contracts.	• Negotiated teacher contracts that lengthened the teachers' day by one hour after students leave, creating time for teachers to meet. • Schools on year-round schedules dedicated two to three paid days during intersessions for teacher meetings and staff development. • Offered compensatory pay for summer meetings and learning together times. • Teachers stayed later one day a week to meet in reflective practice groups in exchange for being able to leave at the same time as students on another day. • Negotiated two hours a month for each special education paraprofessional to engage in team meetings and/or building staff development.
Common Time	Schools developed team or grade-level schedules to create a common planning period or lunch period.	• Created brown-bag lunch groups that met once a week to reflect on their practice. • In schools with a ninety minute block schedule, sixty minutes of one planning period were dedicated to reflection on student learning, and thirty to daily business. • Targeted an available period of time, such as a common prep period, for embedding staff development into the day.
Restructured or Rescheduled Time	Schools formally altered the school calendar or teaching schedule on a permanent basis.	• Specialists (e.g., art, music, gym) developed a series of half-day programs to periodically free up each grade-level team to meet. • Banked time by arranging for students to attend school several extra minutes on four days a week and to be released early on the fifth day, creating a block of time for teachers to meet during the school day. • Created a longer block of time by scheduling grade-level, common planning periods or special events immediately before or after a team's lunch period. Then rotated the schedules so that all grades had one extended lunch period every two weeks.

Strategy for Finding Time	What Is it?	What Have Schools Done?
		• Teachers met in individual study groups after school throughout the school year in exchange for not having to attend a scheduled staff development day. • Organized community service opportunities for all students for one-half day a week to create a block of time for teachers to meet. • Once a week, teachers arrived early at school and students started later to create a block of time for teachers to meet.
Better-Used Time	Staff examined current practices to see how schools are using the time they currently have to meet. When we meet, what do we meet about? Is our meeting time aligned with what we want to create and accomplish? How can we best focus our time together on instruction and professional development?	• Refocused weekly faculty meetings so that school business was discussed once a month and reflective practice groups met the other three weeks to focus on students, curriculum, instruction, assessment, and other teaching and learning topics. • Used alternative communication formats (e.g., memos, e-mail, voicemail) to dedicate more faculty meeting time to issues and discussions requiring broad input. • Explored ways in which technology could be used to develop collegial networks within and across buildings (e.g., e-mail, online discussion groups).

Source: Framework from Watts & Castle (1993); also used by North Central Regional Educational Laboratory (1994).

Meetings With the Rest of the Staff: Soliciting Feedback

Task force members decided to meet separately with each grade-level team to summarize the task-force process, share the decision-making principles, propose two scheduling options, and solicit feedback. The task force facilitator and selected members led these meetings. No decisions were made.

Making Final Recommendations

After gathering and reflecting on the feedback from the grade-level teams, task force members made two recommendations. First, they recommended that general

(Continued)

(Continued)

education and special services teachers be formally reconfigured into grade-level instructional teams. These teams would meet once each week during a common prep period. Second, they recommended a schoolwide schedule with monthly "double preps." This meant that once a month students in each grade would attend two consecutive prep periods, thereby freeing up grade-level teams to meet for an additional 100-minute block of time. The principal and the faculty accepted both recommendations with implementation to begin the following school year.

 Available for download at **http://resources.corwin.com/YorkBarrReflective**

PRACTICE EXAMPLE 6.6

SPACE ALLOCATION AT NEWBURY HIGH SCHOOL

**Contributed by Jane Stevenson, Formerly a
Special Education Teacher in Minnesota**

Similar to many high schools, space allocation was a volatile topic. Historically, administrators made decisions about space and many staff did not trust their decision-making process. Some teachers were known to effectively maneuver for better space. It was no coincidence that new teachers were the "floaters" who taught in several rooms. Further, space allocation was based on short-term needs instead of long-term department and school needs. This resulted in a predictable cycle of putting up walls one year and tearing them down the next.

One teacher at Newbury was particularly bothered by this annual cycle and sought to design a more inclusive and equitable process. She proposed that a volunteer committee study schoolwide space issues and make specific recommendations to department chairpersons. The chairpersons would then make final decisions. Her proposal was accepted and a committee was formed, including an assistant principal, thirteen staff who volunteered from a variety of departments, and key individuals specifically invited to participate (e.g., custodian, athletic director, police liaison). Described below are the major components of the committee's process.

Developing Committee Norms and Expectations

Committee members agreed on general expectations: interactions would be respectful, all members would be heard, and reflection and learning would be an essential part of the process. To achieve this, they adopted the seven norms of collaborative work (refer back to Figure 6.8; Garmston & Wellman, 1999). The norms were reviewed and monitored, especially during tense conversations. Differences between dialogue and discussion were described and ways to engage in both forms of conversation were reviewed. A ritual, referred to as Rumor of the Week, was established that invited members to share rumors they had heard about the committee's work. This kept the committee in touch with staff perceptions and also created opportunities to teach and model direct yet respectful ways to dispel rumors. As a result, trust in the committee members and the committee process developed.

Clarifying Values for Decision Making

All teachers at Washington were surveyed to identify values to serve as the basis for space utilization decisions. Using the survey results, department chairs facilitated conversations with their members to rank order the values. Space committee members then compiled this feedback and identified four values for decision making: (a) use of space for instruction had priority over use of space for non-instructional purposes; (b) every teacher should teach in space that is conducive to student learning; (c) special consideration should be given to classes with unique instructional needs (e.g., art, science); and (d) teachers who taught five classes a day should have one classroom for the whole day.

Determining Short- and Long-Term Space Needs

Committee members intentionally designed a process to press teachers into thinking beyond their own realm of practice to consider the space needs of all staff. Using an open-ended survey, each staff member was asked to describe his or her space needs, including how the space would be used. These results were compiled to focus conversations within departments about their short- and long-term space needs. Next, the committee took a walking tour of the school to refresh their memory about the physical layout and specific facilities so they had current knowledge of space for making decisions.

(Continued)

(Continued)

Engaging in Dialogue

As they moved into dialogue, committee members were given: (a) the values for decision making; (b) each department's short- and long-term needs; (c) the master schedule, including details about staffing assignments; (d) a map of the building; and (e) a database of current room usage. Members then proceeded to talk about space use, room by room, floor by floor, and period by period. They made an effort to ensure understanding about why specific uses were suggested as well as the inherent trade-offs with different options. They created a color-coded map that visually displayed all staff or program changes. The facilitator continually archived information to document the decision trail for future reference.

Presenting Recommendations

After extensive dialogue, a space allocation plan and accompanying rationale for each decision were presented to the administration and department chairs. The plan was reviewed. The committee was asked to revisit a few issues that had been raised by staff. Ultimately, the plan was unanimously approved. Afterwards, the facilitator solicited input from the committee members and the department chairs about the decision-making process. No changes were recommended. The committee process of studying the issues, soliciting input and feedback, clearly articulating values for decision making, and providing a rationale for each decision became accepted practices for space allocation. Even though all staff members did not agree with every decision, they trusted the process and honored the outcome.

Reflecting on the Space Allocation Process

Committee members learned to think organizationally as they examined issues that affected the work of all staff and students. In doing so, they learned more about what other staff members do and how their work contributes to the high school as a whole. New relationships were established that supported movement away from self-interest and "turf culture." Committee members learned to develop, organize, and participate in a fair and ethical process in which dialogue was a valued means of interaction. Agreed on public norms and values fostered adherence to effective and professional interactions.

 Available for download at http://resources.corwin.com/YorkBarrReflective

REFLECTIVE PRACTICE IN SMALL GROUPS AND TEAMS: MORE IDEAS TO CONSIDER

Reflective Planning for Differentiated Instruction

Given the increasing variety of students in today's classrooms, teachers are becoming more and more adept at differentiating instruction to effectively match student learning interests, styles, and abilities. Kronberg and York-Barr (1998) developed a framework to guide individual teachers and teacher teams in a reflective planning process for differentiating teaching and learning opportunities in specific courses or curricular units. The seven step framework, along with a sampling of questions to prompt thinking about each step, is presented in Table 6.3 and is also available online at http://resources.corwin.com/YorkBarrReflective. For more information and examples about this differentiation framework, go to http://www.ici.umn.edu, and search for *Differentiated Teaching and Learning*.

Table 6.3   Reflective Planning Framework for Differentiating Instruction

Step 1: Identify key concepts, standards, guiding principles or essential questions, and desired outcomes.

Sample reflective question: What do I want students to know (e.g., concepts, facts, vocabulary words) and understand (e.g., generalizations, links with prior knowledge or experiences) at the end of this unit?

Step 2: Differentiate levels of student understanding.

Sample reflective questions: Given the core concepts, relevant applications, key generalizations, and critical skills that I want all students to learn, how can I extend the knowledge and skills for those students ready to move further? How can I ensure that students needing a more basic level also receive enriching opportunities to learn about the key concepts?

Step 3: Determine which skills are important for the students to learn, review, and apply.

Sample reflective questions: What do I want students to be able to do at the end of this unit? What new skills will students need to learn for this unit? What opportunities are present for students to review and apply skills they have already learned?

Step 4: If relevant to your particular context, identify which district objectives and/or state standards might interface with the unit or topical area.

Sample reflective question: In context of the intended learning from this unit, how can I blend district objectives and/or state standards?

(Continued)

Table 6.3   (Continued)

Step 5: Given the range of student needs, abilities, strengths, and experiences, determine how students can best learn about the identified concepts, principles, or essential questions.

Sample reflective questions: What activities can be used that will maximize student strengths, interests, abilities, and experiences? What do students already know about this topic? What additional support needs will some of the students have? How can the activities best accommodate those additional support needs? How best can I group students for the activities in this unit?

Step 6: Select product options that will encourage students to apply their learning from the unit as well as integrating the knowledge and skills from the unit with previous knowledge and experiences.

Sample reflective questions: What kinds of products will allow students to demonstrate what they have learned relative to the key concepts, principles, or questions? What products would show integration and application? How can individual student strengths be used to guide demonstrations? How might student choice be incorporated into product selection? In what ways can students best share what they have learned?

Step 7: Select formative and summative assessment approaches that can be used throughout the unit to provide helpful feedback to both students and staff.

Sample reflective questions: How can I best assess what students already know about the topic? What kinds of feedback do I want throughout the unit to help me determine the effectiveness of the lessons and activities? How can I best design assessment tools that will be sensitive to varied levels of student proficiency? How can I actively involve students in self-assessment? (p. 34).

Source: Adapted from Kronberg & York-Barr (1998).

 Available for download at http://resources.corwin.com/YorkBarrReflective

Reflective Protocols for Collaborative Examination of Student Work

Table 6.4   Protocol for Collaboratively Examining Student Work

1. Get started and study the student work. (15 minutes)

    - Group members identify the learning goal correlated with the student work.
    - Group members individually look at student work and make notes about the strengths and weaknesses evident in the work.

2. Describe the work: what do you see? (20 minutes)

    - Group members describe what they see in the work.
      a. What are the specific skills and understandings evident in the work?
      b. What don't students know as evidenced in the work or what is missing from the work?

3. Identify next steps for instruction. (20 minutes)

   • Everyone is invited to share ideas for the next instructional steps to improve achievement toward and beyond lesson objective:

      a. How have group members approached these skills and concepts in the past? What instructional strategies did they focus on since the last session?
      b. How can group members build on the skills/concepts evidenced in the work?
      c. What will each member of the group do within his/her instructional setting to improve learning in this area?
      d. What ideas does this generate for the group or the school?

4. Reflect on the experience and identify next steps for staff development. (5 minutes)

   • Group discusses how the protocol process is working.
   • Group identifies any needed professional development or resources.
   • Group schedules next review of student work and determines the learning goal on which to focus and the type of work to bring.

Source: Developed by Nancy Nutting, consultant from Minneapolis, Minnesota, and Cindy Stevenson of the Lakeville Public Schools, Minnesota; adapted from the Student Work Initiative at the Intermediate District 287 PREPCenter, Plymouth, Minnesota. More information about the two protocols described here and others is available from the Looking at Student Work Collaborative at http://www.lasw.org.

 Available for download at http://resources.corwin.com/YorkBarrReflective

Photographs to Prompt Sharing, Understanding, and Critical Reflection

A team of middle school teachers developed an "urgent curiosity" about the intersection of their teaching practices and six students considered at risk for being lost within the education system or worse, or possibly leaving school (Kroeger et al., 2004). They developed an action research project that employed two strategies, open-ended interviews and Photovoice (Wang & Burris, 1994), in an attempt to understand their students better and to develop stronger bonds. Here we focus on the use of Photovoice, which involves taking photographs to document various aspects of one's life and using the photographs to prompt sharing stories about one's life.

The six students were provided disposable cameras and asked to "take pictures that depicted their lives as learners" (p. 51). Once developed, the students selected and titled photographs to be placed in an album. Before the photographs, conversations were largely teacher directed. Students were reluctant participants. Once the photographs became part of the conversations, the balance of interaction shifted dramatically. "[Students] eagerly shared their photographs and the stories that accompanied them. On the basis of the photo prompts, students—individually and as a group—interpreted, explained, and even re-explained the meaning and context of the photographs" (p. 51). The enthusiasm was palpable.

Listening to students tell their stories revealed more about their real interests and also about their experiences and reflections about school. The teachers developed a heightened awareness about how most of school is explicitly conceived and directed by teachers. Student voices are rarely heard, valued, or acted on. This prompted more in-depth reflection around Paulo Freire's view that the recurring themes of education should come from the experiences and perspectives of the individuals being oppressed.

The team of middle school teachers offered the following final thoughts.

> When, we teachers, we reach that place where we no longer understand the struggling student, when we hear ourselves saying, I've tried everything—or worse—Nothing is working, it is then that we need to take a step back and listen. We listen to the student. We listen to the environment. We listen to ourselves and then we reflect on our practice. While the simple act of reflection does not guarantee critical insight, it is the place to begin. (Kroeger et al., 2004, p. 56)

What types of possibilities for learning may grow from efforts like this, when students and adults engage in inquiry together? What else might we learn from the children? In what ways are we already listening to children in our current work? In what ways can we do better?

Metaphors and Synectics

Metaphors (also described in Chapter 3) offer a way to give meaning to an experience or object symbolically. "Metaphor is a transfer of meaning from one object to another on the basis of perceived similarity" (Taggart & Wilson, 1998, p. 188). Hagstrom and colleagues (2000) used metaphor to write about their experiences as teachers. They completed the sentence stem, "Teaching is like . . ." with responses that included the ocean, making bread, and geology. Then they wrote short essays to further explain their metaphor choice. Shared use of metaphors enriched their individual and collective understanding of life as a teacher. This process "resulted in some of the most joyful and most thought provoking writing we have ever done" (p. 25).

A specific type of metaphor, referred to as *synectics*, can be an effective and fun way to close a group session by eliciting higher-level thinking and application. Specifically, invite your small groups to write down four nouns—for example, cat, chocolate, bicycle, bus. Then ask that they select one of the nouns to complete the following sentence: X is like X because X. Here are two examples: (a) Dialogue is like chocolate because it is rich, you share it with people who are close to you, and you want it to last a long time; (b) Co-teaching is like riding a bicycle because it takes two strong wheels working together to get anywhere.

A final idea for the use of metaphors in groups is to capture both current and desired future states. For example, during initiation into reflective practice, a team of teachers was asked to identify a metaphor for how reflection felt very early in the learning process, and then how they hoped it would feel by the end of the year. Here is a sample response: "Reflective practice now feels like an elephant because it is big, heavy, bulky, and slow.

In the spring, I hope it will feel like a monkey—flexible, flowing, responsive, and moving between different levels."

Talking Cards

Talking Cards is a strategy for obtaining full, but anonymous participation in a group context. Each member is provided with index cards and the same color felt-tip pen or marker. A question is posed to the group, and members write their responses on index cards (one idea or response per card). All the index cards are then collected and laid out for group members to see and sort the cards into clusters or themes to make sense of all the ideas shared. The group then labels each cluster. This results in a comprehensive presentation of group members' collective perspectives that can be used to understand issues and make well-informed decisions.

We use this strategy regularly with groups of teachers and often with an entire faculty contingent. For example, we used a variation of this process to help teams of general educators, special educators, and English language teachers to reflect on their first few months of team teaching. First, they were asked, "If you were to explain your team teaching approach to another school, what features would you point out?" Their descriptions were outlined on poster paper, posted, and explained to the other teams.

Second, each teacher was asked to respond to four questions, individually and anonymously, using a different-colored index card for each question. This prompted perspective sharing about how well the team teaching was working or not. The questions were:

- What have been the advantages of team teaching for students? (Green cards)
- What have been the disadvantages of team teaching for students? (Pink cards)
- What have been the advantages of team teaching for the adults? (Yellow cards)
- What have been the disadvantages of team teaching for the adults? (Blue cards)

The teachers could contribute as many responses as they wanted for each question. They simply wrote each response on an individual card. When all the teachers finished writing, the cards were collected, sorted by color, displayed on the table or floor, and sorted into clusters. The clusters were then labeled. For example, cluster labels that were related to advantages for students included "modeling from peers" and "closer relationships with classmates." Cluster labels for adult team-member advantages included "learning ideas from other teachers" and "feeling more connected to team members."

Lastly, each group inquired about what this means, the so-what and now-what aspects of the reflection process. Questions included, "What is our overall assessment of how things have been going? What strengths do we want to maximize? How might we reduce the disadvantages? What might be our next steps for improving how we teach and learn together?" The card responses can also be typed to provide a record for more reflection at a later point. The conversation that occurs in the sorting, clustering, and inquiry aspects of this process is invaluable. This is when the individual and collective group learning occurs.

E.X.P.L.O.R.E.

Pierce and Kalkman (2003) present a directed reflection strategy called E.X.P.L.O.R.E that they use to increase students' recognition and understanding of their own and others' views and to then seek alternative and external views. Here is their description of the strategy:

- *Examine* opinions. Initially students are presented with a controversial statement and asked to commit themselves to a position relative to that issue.
- Create *Pairs*. People who agree with the statement raise their right hands, while people who disagree raise their left hands. Class members stand and walk up to someone with whom they can grasp opposite hands.
- *Listen.* Each member of a pair takes a turn explaining his or her position. The other member is instructed to listen effectively enough to be able to summarize what was just stated so that the speaker can agree that the summary was accurate.
- *Organize.* When both people's positions have been heard accurately, they organize the information into a compare/contrast matrix.
- *Research.* Each member of the pair conducts research to determine what the literature says about the conditions under which either approach to the issue could be correct.
- *Evaluation.* Members of each pair share their findings and agree on research-based statements. (Pierce & Kalkman, 2003, p. 129)

This strategy or specific steps within this strategy could be easily adopted for use in practice settings, such as departmental or schoolwide considerations of existing practices or proposed initiatives. Instead of members from each of the many pairs independently engaging in the steps—organize, research, and evaluate—all of the steps could be considered collaboratively in each group. Further, there would be practice situations where decisions would need to be made about a common direction for proceeding. Understanding alternative views, considering external information (e.g., research) would serve as part of the dialogue that all members engage in prior to moving forward into decision making. Regardless of the specific decision made, this type of approach ensures recognition and consideration of multiple perspectives.

Video Clubs

Videotapes, and more recently, video recordings using tablets provide an "objective record of what actually takes place" in a specific instructional context (Wallace, 1991, p. 8, as cited in Bailey, Curtis, & Nunan, 1998, p. 553).

Sherin (2000) explains that video clubs "are opportunities for teachers to review their classroom interactions in ways that are different from their standard daily practices" (p. 36). Groups of four teachers gather monthly to watch and then converse about short segments (ten minutes) of videotaped teaching. The purpose is to specifically examine and reflect on instructional practice, *not* to evaluate. Use of video allows teachers to narrow their view of classroom interactions. Unlike being in the act of teaching, the teacher does not have to attend the entire group. Individual or small groups of students can be observed more carefully. Teachers can also observe how they responded, then consider why they responded in that way and examine alternatives. A significant finding was "teachers reported not only increased understanding when reflecting on video, but also paying more attention to student responses during instruction" (Sherin, 2000, p. 37). In a study of inservice and preservice teachers, 87 percent stated that "seeing themselves on videotape had made them aware of habits and mannerisms that they were now trying to change" (Wallace, 1979, p. 13). This indicates that reflection-on-action subsequently increased reflection-in-action.

Video conferencing is being used more and more effectively. In his book *Focus on Teaching: Using Video for High-Impact Instruction* (2014), Jim Knight presents very useful video conferencing techniques. Administrators are using this strategy for several reasons. First is trust. The videos are being done on the teachers' own iPads and iPhones. The teacher retains control of the video. Second is accuracy. Rather than depending on recall, scribbled notes, and differences of opinion, the video becomes a third point of reference. In the discussion about instruction, both the administrator and teacher can replay the video and see what happened. Third, the teacher can review the video to see opportunities to change what did not work as well as planned. This personal reflection leads to professional self-modification. Fourth, the videos can be used by PLCs or instructional team meetings as exemplars and as feedback for what is working and not working. Finally, this kind of vulnerability deepens the focus on learning rather than looking good. This is all good.

Reflection Roundtables

We began the use of reflection roundtables as a way of gathering medium-size groups of teachers within our partnership schools to engage in conversations about a variety of issues and topics. Early in our work with one school, we needed a schoolwide perspective about how general and special educators worked together, the strengths and challenges in their present way of providing services to students with disabilities, and the areas or ideas for improvement that would make a difference for students. We did not want to hear from only a handful of teachers, or a few lead teams. We also did not want to interact with the entire faculty at once. We wanted the interaction to be a reflection and learning opportunity for all those involved. We held a series of three roundtable conversations, each had a mix of eight to twelve teachers and lasted about ninety minutes. These roundtables increased our understanding and the understanding of all the teachers engaged in the conversation. It also was the start of trust and relationship building. The reflection roundtable continued to be used as a way to solicit input, feedback, and ultimately decision making about new directions for service provision.

Another use of reflection roundtables occurred in a school that had successfully piloted a general educator and special educator co-teaching model of instruction during language arts and math. In the spring of the pilot year, the entire faculty needed to be involved in a conversation about implementation and outcomes of the co-teaching model. A series of round-table conversations were held with small groups of teachers, this time homogeneously grouped. We sat around small tables and asked partici-pants what they wanted to know about the pilot. We shared what the co-teaching looked like in each of the pilot classrooms, what the teachers thought about it, and how the students had responded. We were careful to disclose a balanced view of the process and outcomes. Participants asked questions and expressed concerns and offered special considerations. The cumulative learning and perspectives offered during the roundtable con-versations were then (anonymously) shared during an extended faculty meeting. The faculty talked further in small groups during the meeting and ultimately made the decision to expand co-teaching in specific ways and with specific cautions.

Reflection roundtables have been an effective means of sharing, learn-ing, understanding, and relationship building that support decision mak-ing. They offer opportunities for dialogue before moving toward decision making. They have been effective because of the relatively small group size, intentional group composition (heterogeneous or homogeneous depending on purpose), high degrees of participation, an initial focus on reflection and inquiry through dialogue, and multiple gatherings and con-versations before decision making.

Interactive Reflective Teaching Seminars

Seminars that included preservice teachers, cooperating teachers and principals, and college faculty members provided a means for interactive reflection on teaching practice (Diss, Buckley, & Pfau, 1992). "Reflective teaching is an introspective process of examining one's own teaching behavior" (p. 28). The focus of reflection was the instructional decision-making process of the teachers to gain insight about decision making in action. "Reflective teachers identified the strengths and weaknesses of their instructional decisions through inquiry, observations, peer interac-tion, and analysis to improve classroom decision making" (p. 28). The interactive seminars occurred four times in a semester. In addition to attending the seminars, preservice teachers observed experienced teachers for a total of sixteen hours over the course of a semester. Prior to the obser-vations, they identified specific questions about teaching that guided their observations. In the words of the authors, participants' reactions to the program were extremely favorable. Teachers reported that the seminars contributed to their professional growth by: (a) increasing their awareness of the need to think critically and creatively about decision making; (b) broadening their teaching repertoires; (c) providing confirmation of their effective teaching methods; and (d) reinforcing the value of ongoing reflective teaching. (Diss et al., 1992, p. 30)

Teachers rarely talk together about their practice, which made the interactive design of the program especially valuable. Also valued was the mix of preservice and experienced teachers.

GETTING STARTED WITH REFLECTIVE PRACTICE IN SMALL GROUPS AND TEAMS

We opened this chapter with the observation that many educators feel they are on meeting overload. We then offered a review of key considerations in working together as a team, and ended the chapter with numerous practice examples of small groups and teams engaged in meaningful reflective learning experiences. As a way to further understand the place of face-to-face meeting time in schools, we asked graduate students in a collaboration course to create a list of groups (e.g., teams, committees, PLCs) that meet in their respective schools. We then asked them to estimate the amount of time spent in meetings and to identify groups that seemed to be effective. Their findings were, not surprisingly, disappointing and enlightening. Disappointing because few groups meet about teaching and learning, and because very little learning occurs for group members—enlightening because of the clarity that emerged about the need to shift priorities in how face-to-face time is used in schools.

When reflecting in groups or teams, there is potential to influence more broadly the educational practices within and throughout the school. This potential significantly increases when multiple groups and teams embed reflective practices in their work, and when efforts expand to include the vast majority of individuals and groups in a school. The sustainability of groups depends on four factors: a meaningful and continuing purpose; positive and productive working relationships; the opportunity for learning, growth, and contribution; and the outcomes realized by students. These factors provide a framework for evaluating the effectiveness or likelihood of effectiveness in schools. We invite you to keep these factors in mind as you read Chapter 7, which more carefully examines issues of expanded and sustainable schoolwide reflective practice. One particularly useful framework for clarifying group learning purposes, content, and processes is located in Chapter 7. Figure 7.4 (page 283) shows a diagram of the core components of a Reflective Practice Planning Framework. The accompanying text describes each component and offers reflection questions to help spark planning and design.

Figure 6.12   Chapter Reflection Page

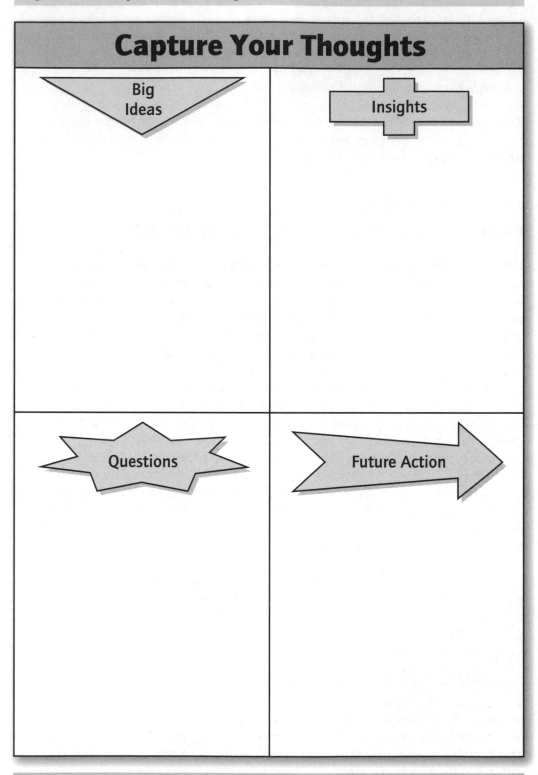

7

Schoolwide Reflective Practice

If you look at the way we meet in organizations and communities across the country you see a lot of presenters, a lot of podiums, and a lot of passive audiences. This reflects our naiveté in how to bring people together.

—Peter Block, as quoted in Axelrod & Axelrod,
Let's Stop Meeting Like This, 2014

Over the past couple of decades, there has been an increasing emphasis on improvement efforts that are schoolwide, instead of just individual or team-based. Small, often isolated, efforts, such as initiatives taken on by individual teachers, teachers at a grade level, or subject area teachers, typically result in isolated improvement. Spread of beneficial practices to other groups of students is unlikely. This is one reason for the emergence of efforts intended to re-create schools as professional learning communities in which members collectively and actively participate in ongoing learning for improvement. Fullan (2000b) explains, "The existence of collaborative work cultures (e.g., professional learning communities) makes a difference in how well students do in schools . . . we now have a much better idea of what is going on inside the black box of collaborative schools" (p. 581).

Hord (1997) summarized findings from numerous studies to identify outcomes for students and staff when schools organized themselves as professional learning communities. Students had lower rates of absentee-ism, a reduced dropout rate, and cut fewer classes. In some cases, larger academic gains were noted in math, science, history, and reading. In smaller high schools, increases in learning also were shown to be more equitably distributed throughout the school, with smaller achievement gaps among students. For staff, outcomes were documented related to improved practice and professional conditions for teaching. Also reported for teachers were higher levels of satisfaction, morale, and like the students, lower rates of absenteeism.

This reinforces efforts to maximize the *learning* for adults and students. As discussed in Chapter 3, growing a set of common learning routines and practices, that is, the "how" of learning, throughout a school helps to create a more coherent learning context, which in turn allows students to use their cognitive fuel to pay more attention to the "what" of their learning. The business world refers to this experience as scaling up.

Growing authentic learning communities requires members who reflect together, recognizing that varied perspectives are an asset for understanding complex issues of practice, for informing actionable possibilities, and for advancing practice to achieve shared goals for student learning. Depending on the issue at hand, such teams might include instructional staff, students, parents, support services personnel, administrators, and community members at large. In possibility generating conversations, *knowledge*, specifically what we already know or what we think we know, is both important AND insufficient for addressing complex problems of practice. Reflective practice, supported in a community whose members reflect the diversity of the school community, is a powerful resource for learning and creating possibilities to move forward. Possibilities that are widely informed, understood, and owned by those who will be affected hold strong possibilities for advancing practice as well as deepening purpose and connection among members. The issue has always been and will continue to be content AND process.

Laszlo Bock (2015), Director of Human Resources for Google, said that when they are looking to hire, they are not looking for high GPA or SAT scores. They are hiring, *first*, for learning ability. Yes, learning ability. Whether you are going to be a teacher, electrician, auto mechanic, principal, or banker, you will have to continually learn. Things change, will you? *Second*, Bock identified collaboration skills. As the saying goes, "No one is as smart as all of us." Surowiecki (2004) in *The Wisdom of Crowds* says decisions made by a crowd are 90 percent better than the decisions made by experts on a subject. Why? Hearing, viewing as valid, and negotiating shared meaning can be both challenging and enlightening. Mostly, each of us knows only what *we* do, and therefore we view our respective organization from our particular place and experience in the organization. Broadening our understanding of the work throughout the organization increases the potential for making well-informed, well-vetted, and well-supported decisions that support organizational purpose.

Most schools, for example, have widely differentiated staffing (e.g., clerical, administrative, direct service licensed professionals with different areas of content or linguistic expertise, direct service paraprofessionals, building support and maintenance personnel). Inviting perspectives grounded in differentiated work domains is likely to expand both understanding about a challenge and commitment to implementing whatever possibilities for improvement that emerge. As discussed in Chapter 3, persons who will be part of supporting changes in practice must both understand and feel ownership of the changes in practice.

In brief: sharing, thinking, and learning with and from others increases the likelihood of creating ways to move forward that may actually work. As we get better at bringing people together and at ensuring that each voice is heard, we begin to create a culture where all members feel more connected to one another in support of their shared organizational purpose: to successfully grow the next generation of grown-ups whose lives we influence every day. This can and does happen, but rarely without substantial effort in the design and facilitation of conversations that matter.

As asserted in Sanborn's (2006) book title, "You don't need a title to be a leader," greater influence for the greater good has the potential to happen when people show up together. Roland Barth (1990) said "the crucial role of the principal is as head learner" (p. 46). Noel Tichy (1997) in *The Leadership Engine* said that leaders need to serve two functions: one, be a learner, and two, develop other leaders. Often in our field, we bring in external consultants to offer advice or introduce practices. This may be helpful *and* it may be limited. As emphasized throughout this book, context—each student, group, class, team, school—is particular. What is likely to work in each particular context must be informed by the observations, conversations, inquiry, and possibilities generated by those who know it best. Often the support needed is right next door or down the hall. What might be some ways to tap and extend the practice wisdom located where you work and learn?

One of the resources that has caused us to reflect on what we have learned about schoolwide reflective practice is a book by Sutton and Rao (2014) titled *Scaling Up Excellence.* In the preface they say, "There was always some excellence—there just wasn't enough of it." There are pockets of excellence in every school we have been associated with, even schools with low test scores. This gives rise to the question: What are some ways to expand the reflective process to increase learning among students, colleagues, and all community members? The ultimate goal of schoolwide reflective practice is continuous improvement of organizational, team, and individual teacher and student practices so that *all* students learn well.

One lesson from Sutton and Rao is to stop looking for the *silver bullet.* Trying to clone precisely what has worked in other places probably won't work in the same ways in your venue. No doubt we can learn from others who have been successful, but most programs are not totally transferrable. Why? You already know what we are going to write: because every context is somewhat alike, *and* also discernibly different. There is never a 100 percent match. There is a Yiddish proverb: "Beware of the prophet who carries only one book." Multiple ideas are needed to work on multiple problem areas. We have never found one process that fits every situation, school, or district. The continuous reflective process helps to keep up with an ever changing environment. Take whatever you can from existing examples and mindfully adapt them to your situation. Accordingly, be assured that this also holds true for the examples we offer in this book. Learn from your successes and failures. Keep the best and change the rest.

A second lesson from Sutton and Rao they call the "problem of more." Years ago, Larry Lezotte, an American educational researcher said, we need "prioritized abandonment." Sometimes when there is an identified problem, leaders start throwing program after program at the problem, which in addition to being largely ineffective, costs dearly in terms of money and time. When everything is important, nothing is important. Abrahamson (2004) coined the term "repetitive change syndrome." Continual change keeps us thinking we are doing something to try to improve. Often we are doing something and probably not seeing results fast enough so we change course before *full implementation* occurs. The ideas and logic of new practices make sense as we learn *about* them. Learning how to do them, however, requires much cognitive effort and repetition before we become reasonably proficient with new practices until they become habitual. Learning new doings is big work—intellectually and pragmatically. Well grooved routines are tough to shift.

So, where do you start? Initiating and sustaining momentum is not easy. You can start growing reflective practice by modeling it and inviting others to do the same. Formal leaders have positional authority that compels a certain degree of engagement by staff members. However, informal leaders, such as highly respected teachers and support personnel, serve as daily points of horizontal influence among colleagues. As Reeves (2006) points out, the most powerful influence in organizations is within networks, which are largely horizontal, meaning among people who work closely together on a daily basis. Multiple informal leaders who model respectful and open conversations and also who model ongoing reflection on their practice to learn and improve are essential resources for school-wide learning and development. Modeling is the first teacher. Know that people are watching. Who you are, how you show up with others, and ways you invite and model inquiry hold much potential to influence . . . for the good.

Costa and Kallick (2000b) suggest that "every school's goal should be to habituate reflection throughout the organization—individually and collectively, with teachers, students, and the school community" (p. 60). Indeed, the greatest potential for reflective practice to renew schools lies with the collective thinking, inquiry, understanding, learning, and action that can emerge from schoolwide engagement around a compelling purpose and an inspiring vision. However, designing and facilitating reflective practices at the organizational level is much more complex than at the individual, partner, or small group levels. Even though organizational purpose is common among staff, contributions toward achieving collective purpose is differentiated among the varied staff positions. For reflective practice to be meaningful for participants, it must be connected to their work.

When we carve out time for meaning-FULL conversation, educators frequently emerge feeling re-grounded and re-energized. Teachers often share that reflective conversations about teaching and learning bring them to a deeper level of understanding practice and also affirm their desire to truly make a difference in the lives of their students. Together, it seems more possible to accomplish those important goals. When the pace of practice feels like "just get it done" and "just get me through this day," exhaustion can settle in as a routine part of the daily work. Margaret Wheatley (2009) asks, "Will we have the courage to reclaim time to think?" Our view? If we do not claim the time, we do so at our own peril . . . and, indirectly to the detriment of the current generation of young people in front of us. We must create time and space to reflect and learn, just as we must also create time and space for the students in front of us to do so.

Alex Pentland, in *Social Physics* (2014) writes

> What is the basis of the collective intelligence we uncovered? Unexpectedly, we found that the factors most people usually think of as driving group performance—i.e., cohesion, motivation, and satisfaction—were not statistically significant. The largest factor in predicting group intelligence was the *equality of conversational turn taking*; groups where a few people dominated the conversation were less collectively intelligent than those with a more equal distribution of conversational turn taking. The second most important factor was *the social intelligence of group members,* as measured by their ability to read each other's social signals. Women tend to do better at reading social signals, so groups with more women tend to do better. (p. 88)

This is why group cohesion and collaboration are critically important, as suggested by the Block quote cited in Axelrod and Axelrod (2014) at the beginning of the chapter. What matters most is creating opportunities for members of the same community of practice to reflect, learn, and re-energize together. AND, as reinforced by Pentland, what matters most is the equality of conversational turn-taking. Recall from Chapter 6 the emphasis on intentional conversational design structures and processes that help to shape equitable conversation in which every voice is heard. This supports a fundamental understanding of how to grow reflective practice communities: *The learning is in the conversation.* Having partnered in creating the conversational design of many, many, many learning sessions, we can state as fact that the amount of time required to design the conversations . . . including intentionally crafting specific group structures (e.g., size, composition), language structures (e.g., questions, directives, multiple options), and products to emerge from the work . . . is *at least* twice as much time as the learning sessions themselves. *And*, it takes design partners who know the context well. The good news? Many people find this work to be totally energizing, both because it matters so much for the engagement and results and because the learning is so rich for members of the design team. When it is "go time," meaning the learning session starts, facilitators need to feel well grounded in the "why," "what," and "how" of the session—not only to be well prepared and ready to go, but also to be well positioned to make adjustments when what you thought would happen doesn't.

Consequently, a core focus of the design work is an intentional blueprint for how the conversation happens, including structures (e.g., individual, partners, small groups, full group) and processes (e.g., write then share, reflect in partners then share, speak words, or write words to share; you may wish to refer to Figure 6.2 on page 211). One quick idea you can put to immediate use: if the energy is low, ask participants to stand up, find a partner they rarely get to talk with, and while remaining standing take turns sharing your respective views. Standing requires a bit more energy, and ironically offers a bit more energy. Clearly, intentional efforts are warranted to ensure equitable voice so that perspectives that both honor individual perspective and reflect a range of perspectives within the community of practice are heard. The wisdom generated within local communities of practices offers fuel for renewal and reconnection. Pay careful attention to structures and processes on the quality of the conversation. Over time, you will grow very adept at design work. You also become very adept at noticing ways participants respond to the design and facilitation. Nudging along productive conversations requires ongoing reflection-in-action to figure out which groups are moving, which could use some gentle nudging along, and which are stuck and would benefit from stronger guidance to reflect and learn. Reflecting-in-action provides feedback to the facilitator that informs next moves to support skillful productivity. Skilled facilitators are always observing participant responses—verbal and nonverbals—in order to notice whether participation seems even within a group or if they are stuck, or if conversation is dominated by particular members. With intentional practice, most groups develop conversational norms that ensure every voice is heard and that result in a more inclusive, informative, and productive use of meeting time.

SPECIAL CONSIDERATIONS FOR SCHOOLWIDE REFLECTIVE PRACTICES

We start with a story: A principal who was new to a building arrived at a faculty meeting several weeks into the school year and announced, "Please put on your coats and meet me in the parking lot." Somewhat perplexed, the faculty complied with this request. As soon as everyone reconvened in the parking lot, the principal explained that in his short time in the building, he had noticed that the real meetings among faculty occurred in the parking lot. He wanted to have a real meeting, one in which faculty members actively participate in face-to-face sharing, listening, and inquiry. The point was made. Regardless of where the faculty meetings were held, they can provide an opportunity for learning. What topics of interaction inspire ongoing reflection and inquiry on a school-wide basis? What conditions promote honest open exchanges among staff members? Who leads the process? Where do you start? One place to refresh a bit is to review the Guidelines for Leading Reflective Practice located at the end of Chapter 3 (page 107) in Table 3.2. Also, take a look at Table 2.2, Perspectives on Designing and Facilitating Reflective Practice, located at the end of Chapter 2 on page 79.

In strong creative and participatory cultures, people are open to speaking and listening to ideas of others. If a culture either verbally or nonverbally shuts people down, then they are not inclined to contribute much. Nobody wants to be ridiculed or lose face in front of others. As discussed in Chapter 2, trust grows in conversations that are grounded in listening with the intent to understand along with collaborative group norms. Trust maximizes learning and co-creation of next ways forward.

We worry that PLCs will become another "here today, gone tomorrow" initiative of small consequence unless the grown-ups' focus is unequivocally on learning such that meaningful and substantial improvements result for students. The challenge becomes one of how to have these words "professional learning community" truly reflect meaningful learning that happens among professionals intentionally committed to learning together. Michael Fullan (2001b) explains, "Educational change depends on what teachers do and think. It's as simple and complex as that" (p. 115).

To create an environment that invites and enhances honest conversations about learning and teaching requires leadership and trust. The following two quotes summarize key findings from research about the necessity of strong leadership support for developing practice communities whose members learn with and from one another, doing good for the young people they serve.

> Leadership is second only to classroom instruction among all school factors that contribute to what students learn at school. (Leithwood, Seashore-Louis, Anderson, & Wahlstrom, 2004, p. 3)

Leadership that is shared among principals and teachers is increasingly recognized as a core feature of successful school renewal and improvement initiatives. (Bryk, Camburn, & Louis, 1999; Camburn, Rowan & Taylor, 2003; Lambert, 2005; Leithwood, Seashore-Louis, Anderson, & Wahlstrom, 2004; Marks & Louis, 1999)

One of our concerns is how leaders remain healthy. The demands on school leaders continue to escalate. If leaders are emotionally drained, it is likely that their learning, and the learning of others who they serve, will suffer.

A study by two researchers at the Graduate School of Social Work at Boston College found that a child's sense of well-being is affected less by the long hours their parents put in at work and more by the mood their parents are in when they come home. Children are better off having a parent who works into the night in a job they love than a parent who works shorter hours but comes home unhappy. (Sinek, 2009)

We think this statement is true of educators, both formal leaders and also teachers who lead the learning of students every day. How do we sustain and deepen the love of teaching? One way is to have conversations that confirm positive impact on students. Another way is to help educators understand their impact by engaging in reflective conversations that bring attention to what is working, in addition to what we often focus on, which are the areas in need of improvement. Spend time talking about what matters most and surround yourself with positive proactive peers whose good energy can help sustain you in the work. Administrators and teachers who make sure they continually have learning conversations show more satisfaction with their profession.

PRACTICE EXAMPLES OF SCHOOLWIDE REFLECTIVE PRACTICE

We now shift our focus to offer examples of ways that the "why," "what," and "how" of reflective practice can look when engaging members throughout a school. Starting this work, it is important to recognize that participants may not know one another well . . . *yet*. First we offer some quick examples of "why" members might work across their typical work boundaries, and "who" might show up together. We then offer more extensive practice examples.

Here are some quick examples. An *entire school staff* may be involved in cross grade level or content area learning groups on a common topic. For example, secondary teachers from different content areas or grade levels might learn together about literacy skills for content area instruction, or about ways to create authentic performance assessments. Interdisciplinary groups might form to exchange disciplinary perspectives to create a set of integrated student outcomes that would be addressed within each discipline. Teachers from a common subject area might gather to create common assessment structures and processes for use across all sections of designated courses. Teachers from common subject areas but different grade levels might work together to create a progressive sequence of subject area concepts and skills. Such cross grade level groups also might examine ways to more effectively support students transitioning between grades. Science teachers might ask that math and literacy teachers participate in the selection of teaching and learning resources appropriately suited for students. A schoolwide or districtwide curriculum adoption process might involve *teachers from across grade levels* to work together, identifying where standards show up and how they are addressed.

Before a collection of individuals begin walking together on the path of shared work, it is helpful (if not, essential) to know more about one another, especially in relationship to the group's work. Depending on the amount of time allocated to meet and the anticipated complexity and duration of the development work, the entire first gathering could easily and beneficially be spent *grounding* (described more fully in Chapter 6). Grounding is an activation strategy that requires each member to bring their voice "into the room" by responding to a few on-topic questions (or invitations), such as:

- Please share your name, position, and the type of work you do.
- What are some connections you have to [group's purpose]?
- What seems especially important to you about the work we will be doing?
- What questions or wonderings do you have? And what would you like to learn?
- What might be a "best possible outcome" for our work?

After the questions are introduced, provide time for each member to reflect on the questions and write their responses. This "think-write-share" strategy serves two important purposes. First, writing offers each person an opportunity to clarify her or his own thoughts on paper. Second, with responses already written, participants can listen more fully to what others say. We were introduced to Grounding through Bob Garmston and Bruce Wellman's (2013) Adaptive School's work. More recently, Bob Garmston expanded on this work in his 2012 book, *Unlocking Group Potential to Improve Schools.* This has been an incredibly valuable resource in our teaching and also in our school learning and development work.

Next, we offer three recent practice examples. Some are relatively brief, some are extensive, all have been thoughtfully crafted and generously given to us to share with you, in hopes you will find them informative. Given the complexity of schoolwide reflective practice, we also offer additional extensive examples in an effort to describe more fully the structures and processes designed to support reflection. The examples are offered in the text and also can be located on the accompanying website (http://resources.corwin.com/YorkBarrReflective) for ease of access and use in your practice contexts.

As you consider these examples and contemplate ways to design the deepening of reflective practice in your school community, you may wish to review Table 2.2, the Perspectives on Designing and Facilitating Reflective Practice in Chapter 2 (page 79). Also revisit Table 3.2, Guidelines for Leading Reflective Practice (page 107), in Chapter 3, and some of the strategies for growing small groups and teams, along with Figure 6.2 (page 211), that presents numerous possibilities for learning structures and processes, located in Chapter 6.

PRACTICE EXAMPLE 7.1

FOCUS, COHERENCE, AND REFLECTIVE PRACTICE CONVERSATIONS BOOST STUDENT LEARNING

Contributed by Catherine Rich, Principal, and Michelle Brown-Ton, Academic Coach, Phalen Lake Hmong Studies Magnet School, Saint Paul Public Schools, Minnesota

At Phalen Lake Hmong Studies Magnet (PLHSM) 86 percent of our students are designated as English Learners (ELs). Our students' linguistic diversity presents both opportunities and challenges with respect to the development of their academic language. Based on principal walkthrough observation data and a thorough analysis of student assessment data, the staff identified three priority needs for these students:

1. If students are to acquire academic language they need to use academic language.

2. To ensure instructional equity, the use of specific instructional routines needs to become habituated practice in every classroom.

3. Students must be actively engaged in their learning because whoever is doing the work *and* talking about the work is doing the learning. Teacher talk and student talk must be balanced.

To meet these identified needs, staff members collaboratively engaged in cycles of reflective practice. More specifically, they reflected during their teaching by observing the extent to which students engaged, and if indicated, re-taught or made adjustments to scaffold connections for students. They reflected back on their teaching, often through partner or team conversations, to identify what successfully engaged students and also areas for refinement or greater differentiation. As shown in Figure 7.1, there are numerous staff learning structures in place at PLHSM. Three key structures for staff learning, reflection, and data-driven decision making are:

1. *Job-embedded professional learning,* with a *focus on students using academic language.* Grade level teams, including general education, English learning, and special education teachers, meet weekly for seventy-five to ninety minutes. In addition to analyzing student performance data, the teams engage in reflective conversations for the purpose of aligning instruction to standards, differentiating instruction to ensure all students engage in the content, and reflecting on their practice. [Refer back to Chapter 5 to locate the Learning Conversation templates shown in Figures 5.1a and 5.1b that are used to support individual teachers reflecting on their practice with a partner whose role is to prompt reflection by asking open questions and not offering advice.] An initial outcome of this team-based professional learning was that all instruction would incorporate use of sentence stems, allowing all students the opportunity to actively participate in classroom learning. This resulted in a substantial, positive impact on student achievement. Work in this team learning structure continues to focus on next steps for increasing academic language in literacy and mathematics.

2. *Extended monthly staff meetings* (ninety minutes) serve as another structure providing *all staff* the opportunity to *engage in focused learning, reflective practice, and equity conversations.*

3. *Grade level teams* also meet trimonthly as a part of a focused Math or special content area PLC using a six-step data team process to *track student proficiency and make data-based instructional decisions.*

One deceptively simple structure that has contributed substantially to the continuous improvement in our schools is the use of what Jim Knight (2011) in the book *Unmistakable Impact* refers to as a *Target Page.* He writes, "If a school is going to become an Impact School, a school that is passionately committed to dramatically improving professional learning, everyone must have a clear understanding of the goals and how to get there" (p. 9). More specifically, he advocates a one-page *Instructional Improvement Target.* "A simple plan with clear goals, makes it easier for everyone in a school to work together to dramatically improve teaching."

The Leadership Team developed the first PLHSM Target Page five years ago. This Target Page is a one-page document that explicitly states teacher practices in four development areas: instructional planning, delivery of instruction, student assessment, and professional learning intentionally designed to advance practices in these other areas. The Target Page grounds the schoolwide instructional *focus* and *coherence* that has *accelerated student learning.*

(Continued)

(Continued)

Figure 7.1   Staff Learning Structures

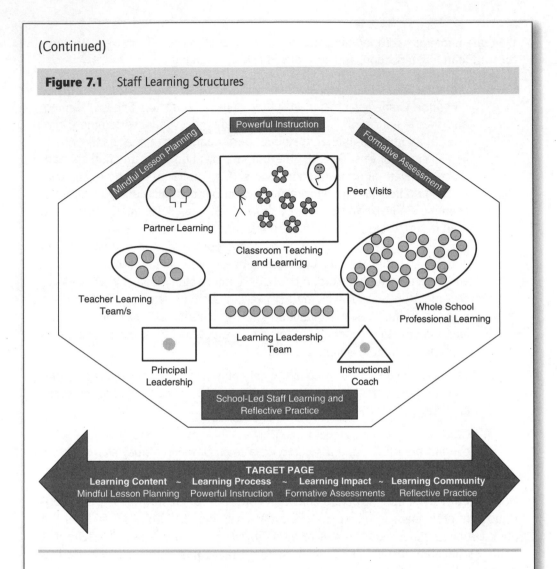

The creation and implementation of the Target Page continues to be a shared endeavor, revised and implemented annually with significant staff involvement. It is a living and breathing document that guides our work and supports our school's success. This document is the cornerstone of who we are. It has carried us through our *transformation* from a *Focus school* to a two time *Celebration Eligible* school. Two significant and enduring outgrowths from the use of the Target Page have been:

- Teams working collaboratively to establish agreed on implementation of an instructional practice. An example is the use of explicit feedback for both teachers and students. John Hattie's seminal work (2009) ranks "feedback" as number ten out of 138 instructional practices affecting student achievement.

Table 7.1   2015–2016 Instructional Target Page for Phalen Lake
Hmong Studies Magnet School

Phalen Lake Hmong Studies Magnet 2015–2016
A community in which all students and staff members are learners
Students receive exceptional instruction and are engaged learners every day in every class

Learning Content: Mindful Lesson Planning Through a Racial Equity Lens

- All teachers intentionally plan expected learning, building from students' linguistic and cultural strengths in all content areas
- All teachers' lessons are standards-based, focused on critical skills with intentional scaffolds and lesson closure
- All teachers intentionally create a range of higher order questions that support students speaking in multiple sentences using academic language
- All teachers intentionally plan opportunities for students to engage in a variety of cooperative routines throughout the lesson
- All teachers identify and plan for the language students need to meet content objectives

Learning Process: Powerful Instruction Through a Racial Equity Lens

- Teachers post and state the lesson focus for the expected student learning and revisit the focus throughout the lesson
- Teachers help students identify their strengths and foster a growth mindset
- Every student does the work, every student does the learning

  All students use identified academic language
  All students participate in a variety of cooperative routines
  All students respond to higher level questions
  All students engage in collaborative activities that scaffold the targeted learning from the concrete to the abstract
  All students are given the opportunity to solve authentic problems and wrestle with big ideas

Learning Impact: Ongoing Analysis of Assessments Through a Racial Equity Lens

- All teachers collaboratively analyze data from core reading assessments and common formative math assessments to make instructional decisions
- All staff analyze data from walkthroughs, target surveys, peer visits, and video reviews to determine instructional impact on student achievement
- All teachers provide timely and consistent feedback to students

Learning Context: Creating a Racially Conscious Professional Community

- Every voice is heard
- Reflective practice and learning conversations are embedded in our professional learning
- Professional development focused on: Growth Mindset, Developing Racial Consciousness and Culturally Relevant Teaching, Higher Order Questioning, Math and Literacy Instruction

(Continued)

(Continued)

- Creating a culture of trust as staff members engage in reflective practice through learning conversations focused on instruction, including peer visits and video-taped lessons, based on the work of Jennifer York-Barr et al.(2006) in *Reflective Practice to Improve Schools*. [Refer to Chapter 5 to learn how PLHSM uses what they refer to as learning conversations to reflect back on practice in order to inform future practice.]

We include the 2015–2016 PLHSM Target Page in Table 7.1 to illustrate specifically the connections between evidence-based practices and student outcomes. Also shown are the staff learning practices that are the means by which practice continues to improve and the interdependence deepens. We also include Figure 7.1 that shows the array of differentiated structures that deepen learning and reflective practice at PLHSM focused on implementation of practice priorities identified on the Target Page.

To illustrate more specifically, we offer an example here. The English Learning (EL) Team at PLHSM collectively reviewed data to inform decisions about ways to increase student learning and achievement in literacy. A deep analysis of district reading assessment data showed EL student reading proficiency remaining at a transitional reading level in Grades 3 through 5. The EL team, then, increased the focus of their instruction on the language structures found in higher level texts to better support students acquiring the language of those texts. This emphasis was also aligned with the schoolwide focus for all students to increase their use of academic language. As a result, all staff were involved through conversations in job-embedded professional learning, staff-led professional learning sessions, and co-teaching partnerships.

An example from the 2014–2015 school year involved the third grade team's job embedded in professional learning tailored to deepen understanding of third grade math standards and strategies to support student learning, with an emphasis on all students using manipulatives. Instructional strategies included implementation of the researched-based model of concrete-representational (visual/pictorial)-abstract (CRA). This work was a contributing factor to the third grade proficiency in Math increasing *from 25 percent in 2014 to 49 percent in 2015,* as well as an 8 percentage point increase in all students' proficiency in Math from 2014 to 2015.

Additionally, in 2014, 54 percent of our EL students were on track for success. *In 2015, the percentage of ELs on track for success increased to 68 percent.* Further, from 2014 to 2015, *59 percent of all our students at PLHSM made high growth* on MCA Math and 27 percent made medium growth. Clearly, multiple and aligned forms of staff conversation and learning advanced both teaching practice and student learning.

 Available for download at **http://resources.corwin.com/YorkBarrReflective**

PRACTICE EXAMPLE 7.2

KEEPING THE LEARNING OPPORTUNITIES VISIBLE

Contributed by Dr. Kari Rock, Principal, and Mr. Tom Geisenhoff,
Instructional Coach, Eisenhower Elementary School,
Anoka Hennepin School District, Minnesota

At a different school, the variety of learning structures used to support reflection on and for practice are kept visible with the help of a large whiteboard wall calendar (www.Flex-A-Chart.com). Each learning focus or structure is assigned a different colored 1½-by-1-inch self-stick note. For example: leadership team meetings are designated with a *blue* note; staff meetings are *yellow*; grade level meetings are *pink*; PLCs are *orange*; one of the new learning initiatives (EnVOY) was *bright green*; another (Cultural Competency) was *bright yellow.* At this school, the large whiteboard calendar was mounted in the principal's office (see Figure 7.2). She and the instructional coach met there regularly and could quickly look back on previous learning gatherings and reflect ahead to upcoming designated staff learning blocks to begin reflecting on both "what" and "how" to design the learning. Sometimes, upcoming blocks designated for specific learning would be switched out given more pressing needs in the building. The calendar of learning opportunities served to both focus and reground reflection on

Figure 7.2   Wall Calendar

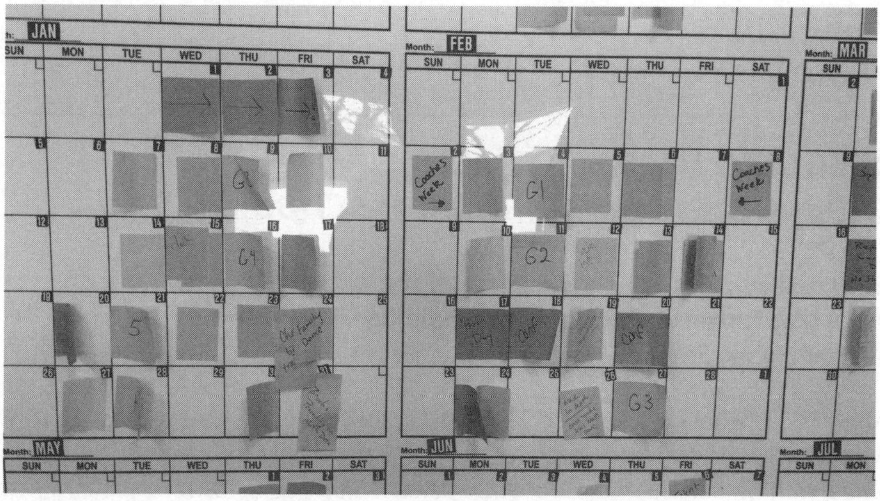

(Continued)

(Continued)

what had happened (reflecting back) in previous learning sessions and what are next development moves (reflecting forward). Essentially, it served as what Michael Grinder, a nonverbal communication expert, would call a *third point* in the conversation. Might sound like a small or insignificant point and . . . having a third point often simultaneously eases the conversation and makes it more productive. Oriented to the calendar, participants look at it, reflect on it, pointing to it, talking to it, and moving self-stick notes around on it. This practice allows thinking to be shared both visibly and audibly.

The size of the calendar, the color-coding, and the use of self-stick notes makes it easy to switch around and for everyone to contribute to creating a very productive conversational space for reflection, focus, organization, planning, and, as appropriate, change. Adjacent to the giant calendar were full-sized pieces of paper, color-coded to match the respective color of the notes on the calendar. The full-sized paper was used to note learning that had already occurred for each respective focus and sketched ideas for upcoming learning. In another school, this type of calendar is located in the staff room, making it readily accessible for all staff in the building. Structure, augmented in these situations by color, reinforces the reflection and planning guideline, "Structure is your friend."

 Available for download at http://resources.corwin.com/YorkBarrReflective

PRACTICE EXAMPLE 7.3

EMBEDDING LITERACY PRACTICE SCHOOLWIDE AT HARDING HIGH SCHOOL

Contributed by Louis Francisco and Luke Leba, Literacy Coaches, and Douglas Revsbeck, Principal, from Harding High School, Saint Paul Public Schools, Saint Paul, Minnesota

Harding High School currently serves 2,140 students on the east side of Saint Paul, Minnesota. The student body represents a rich variety of language and cultural backgrounds, with 52 percent Asian, about 24 percent Black, 13 percent Hispanic, 8 percent White, and 2 percent American Indian. Harding has a strong schoolwide commitment to literacy, with a team of six reading teachers who may co-teach with core content area teachers, in addition to teaching their own reading classes.

About five years ago, Harding launched Inquiry Groups, a schoolwide small group learning structure, which serves as a complement to the other small group learning structure of Professional Learning Communities (PLCs). Harding PLCs are formed around content areas with an intentional focus on the "what" of instruction. The Harding PLC Self-Assessment Rubric guides the PLCs with attention paid to team dynamics, use of data to guide instruction, and a focus on their impact on instruction and learning.

The Inquiry Groups are designed to offer a space for facilitated small group interdisciplinary conversations related to shared practices and effective practices. The Inquiry Groups provide for a more differentiated professional development focused on the "how" of instruction, thereby deepening the knowledge and use of "best" instructional practices to meet the needs of Harding's diverse learners.

The Inquiry Groups' focus is deepening and expanding literacy teaching practices in all classes, not just the reading classes; use of formative assessment to guide instruction, and learning the most effective instructional practices to meet the needs of the large number of English language learners. The work of the Inquiry Groups was an intentional outgrowth of the literacy focus that Harding had identified as critical for student success, which has been an ongoing focus for over eight years.

Inquiry Groups were formed by organizing teachers into cross-curricular learning groups (about nine teachers in a group) based on a shared interest in using the same book as the text for learning. Prior to the inquiry meetings each month, the Inquiry Group leaders (teachers and literacy coaches) meet to talk about the current chapter or strategy, create or revise the learning agenda, and problem solve any anticipated challenges their group may encounter.

During these monthly planning meetings, the inquiry facilitators have the opportunity to reflect on their successes and struggles, share ideas that have worked to engage their members in reflective conversations, and learn from one another how to facilitate hard conversations.

The monthly Inquiry Group learning cycle is to read, reflect, and implement new ideas or strategies. Prior to the monthly meeting, participants read the chapter, annotating or highlighting significant ideas. During the monthly meeting, teachers talk with one another to make sense of the reading, plan ways to implement new practices in their own classrooms, and learn from reflecting on their own practice and hearing from others' experiences.

At the end of each meeting, time is spent setting up the expectations for the next meeting and addressing specifics on implementing the new practice into classrooms. As the years progressed and trust grew within the Inquiry Groups, classroom visits and observations began to become more common with teachers intentionally visiting one another's classroom to see the new practices in action. Schoolwide showcases were scheduled twice a year to share the best practices that emerged from the monthly inquiry meetings.

(Continued)

(Continued)

After the Inquiry Groups' first year, the staff learning focus was aligned with the specific needs of the students. Led by Harding's literacy coaches, high leverage literacy practices were aligned with current student performance data and literacy standards, and then inquiry book choices for the year were identified to align with student practices. This alignment helped teachers identify their learning goals for the year and use this as their primary criteria for book choice and meetings for the upcoming year.

To clarify how this might look, the literacy coaches developed a backward design model (Four Block Learning Design) (see Figure 7.3). The first block, Student Outcomes, identified the skills that were critical for student success based on student data. The second block, Teaching Practices, identified the teaching practices that support students learning these outcomes and related directly to the book choices for learning for the year. The third block, Professional Learning, showed all of the professional learning structures at Harding. The fourth block, Leadership, identified the formal leaders for the professional learning.

Figure 7.3   Harding High School Learning Design

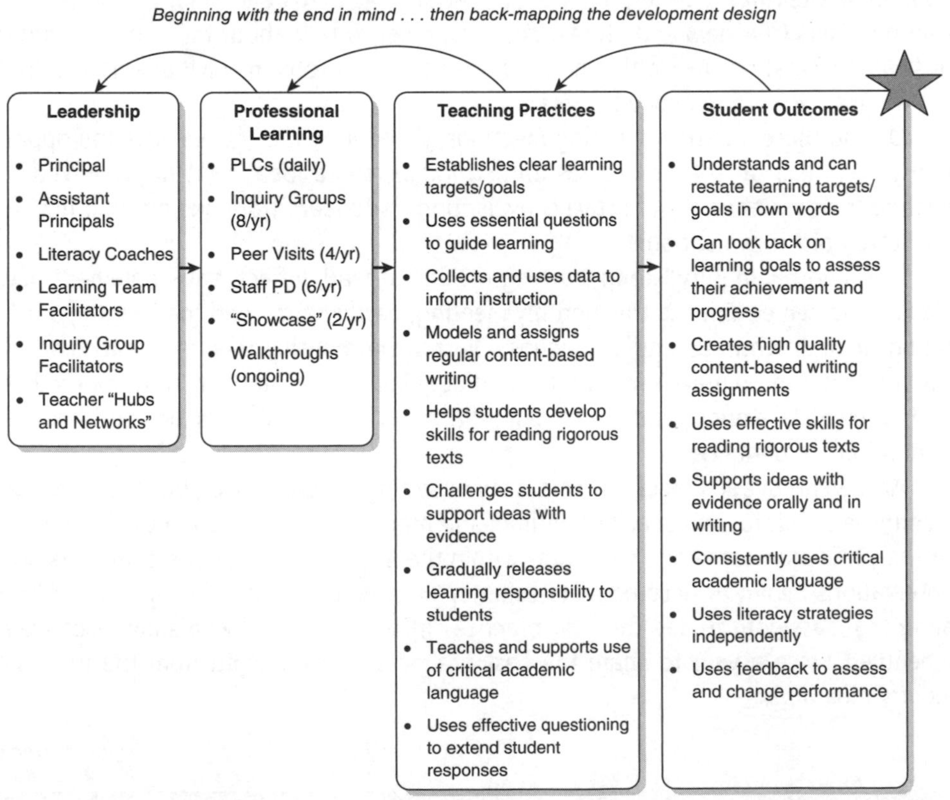

Beginning with the end in mind . . . then back-mapping the development design

Leadership	Professional Learning	Teaching Practices	Student Outcomes
• Principal • Assistant Principals • Literacy Coaches • Learning Team Facilitators • Inquiry Group Facilitators • Teacher "Hubs and Networks"	• PLCs (daily) • Inquiry Groups (8/yr) • Peer Visits (4/yr) • Staff PD (6/yr) • "Showcase" (2/yr) • Walkthroughs (ongoing)	• Establishes clear learning targets/goals • Uses essential questions to guide learning • Collects and uses data to inform instruction • Models and assigns regular content-based writing • Helps students develop skills for reading rigorous texts • Challenges students to support ideas with evidence • Gradually releases learning responsibility to students • Teaches and supports use of critical academic language • Uses effective questioning to extend student responses	• Understands and can restate learning targets/goals in own words • Can look back on learning goals to assess their achievement and progress • Creates high quality content-based writing assignments • Uses effective skills for reading rigorous texts • Supports ideas with evidence orally and in writing • Consistently uses critical academic language • Uses literacy strategies independently • Uses feedback to assess and change performance

Harding's Learning Design clearly maps out the high priority learning that is needed for student success, identifies the learning structures, and identifies the individuals who lead any learning priority at Harding. In this case, you can see *Inquiry Groups* as the designated monthly learning opportunity, and *Literacy Coaches* and *Inquiry Group Facilitators* as the designated guides for this work. As most people know, without learning opportunities and leadership for development initiatives, the work stalls. (Note: A sample inquiry group agenda was provided in Chapter 6 in Figure 6.11.)

 Available for download at http://resources.corwin.com/YorkBarrReflective

GETTING STARTED WITH SCHOOLWIDE REFLECTIVE PRACTICE

As one tugs at a single thing in nature, he finds it is attached to the rest of the world. (Attributed to John Muir, conservationist)

Getting started with reflective practices on a schoolwide basis is inspiring, courageous work, and requires much stamina. Changes in culture (that is, how we do things around here) do not happen in the fast lane and are typically not widely embraced. The proverb "Go slow to go fast" captures both the reality and the depth of the work. Once you step into the work, you are taking the long view of creating enriching possibilities, while simultaneously keeping a close watch on how the growth unfolds. To commit to the work reflects an optimistic view of educators, of schools, and the potential for meaningful and sustained change . . . for the good.

Moving toward reflective practice at the schoolwide level also is courageous in that the territory is vast and context-specific pathways are largely uncharted. Clearly, a commitment to ongoing reflection on, in, and for practice is required, as are learning and development partners. As emphasized previously, to change how we "do things around here" takes a lot of mindful work. The energy required to learn new ways to *do* and new ways to *be* can be hard to muster. To bolster your energy as you go, hold onto the vision of ongoing, meaningful learning that energizes staff to continually advance practices that result in higher levels of student learning. Make no doubt about it, individually and collectively, you are among the most powerful influences on today's young people. The very same people who—when they are grown-ups—will be making decisions about how our world will be, including how *we* (all of us current grown-ups) will spend our later years in life. Hmmm . . . now that catches our attention, yes?

We are inspired and energized by this work because we learn so much along the way about how to tailor the learning and development processes, and because we get to learn alongside an amazing array of educators deeply committed to the work of creating schools that are authentic communities of practice; their deep commitment to learning cannot be overstated.

Before we offer a framework for planning template to support your design work for schoolwide reflective practice, we offer a few more ideas about this work.

The greater the number and variety of people who will be learning about reflective practices and how to embed such practices in their daily work in schools, the greater the need for intentional design (structure) *and* ongoing support (nurture). Schoolwide initiatives require a team of people who understand the school context and culture. They are essential for informing, designing, supporting, and at least informally leading the schoolwide development process. Who will join you in this work?

Colleagues who strive to continually refine and expand their practices serve as authentic models in this work and are likely partners. Authenticity is a powerful attractor. High levels of trust and commitment also are needed—commitment to the shared leadership work of the team, to the growth and development of colleagues and of the school, all of which are grounded in the aspiration to do well by the students whom you serve. Such shared and worthy commitments help to keep proactive and countercultural initiatives like reflective practice on the front burner. As mentioned earlier in the book, work in schools is "hot action" (Eraut, 1985), making it especially easy for proactive development work to fall by the wayside as urgent issues create pressure and demand attention. A committed team that takes the long view helps sustain a proactive stance.

In the beginning, the questions and wonderings can feel overwhelming: What are we trying to create and why? What's our plan for getting started? Who will be involved? What skills or capacities will need to be developed or expanded? Which structures will support opportunities for meaningful collaborative reflection and learning?

To guide your thinking about advancing schoolwide reflective practice, we offer the Reflective Practice Planning Framework shown in Figure 7.4. As you can see, we identify key elements of a learning system, all of which interact in support of reflection, learning, and renewal. The elements are *purpose, people, design (reflective practice and learning structures and processes),* and *resources.* Below we offer descriptions of each element along with related questions to support reflection and planning. The questions are not ordered in a linear sequence. They are intended to prompt a potpourri of ideas for your planning (i.e., reflecting forward) conversations. The questions also can guide reflecting back on what happens as you step into the active work of implementation. One more upfront consideration: Given that much of schoolwide reflective practice begins in the context of small groups and teams, we encourage you to review the extensive set of design considerations in Chapter 6. In addition, refer to Practice Example 2.1, Cascading Equitable Practices in an Urban District (page 70). This offers a comprehensive application of the planning framework presented here.

Figure 7.4   Reflective Practice Planning Framework

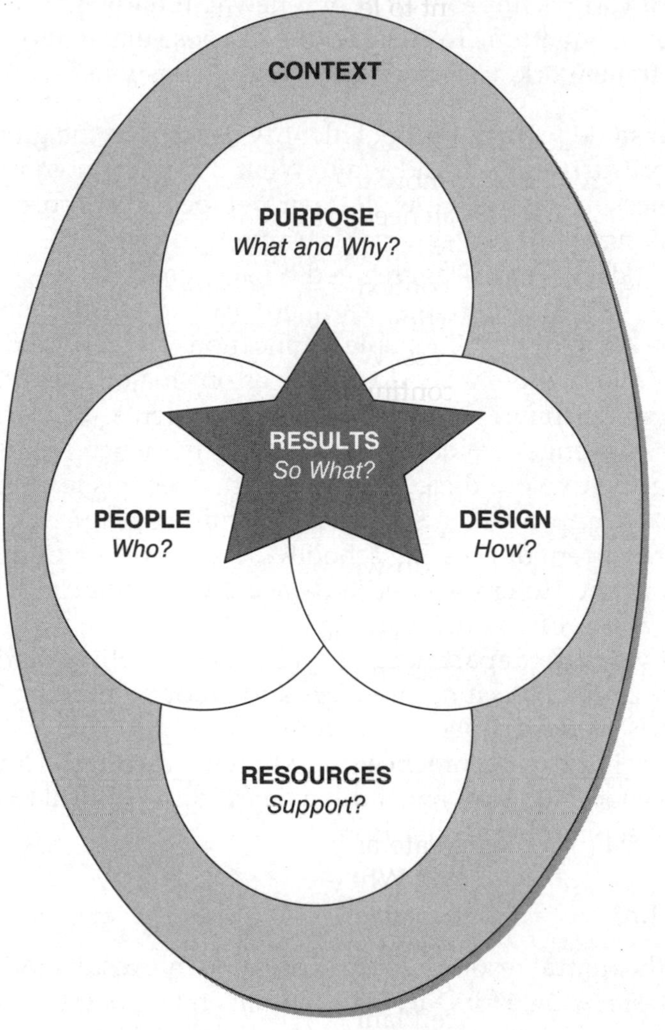

CONTEXT

PURPOSE
What and Why?

RESULTS
So What?

PEOPLE
Who?

DESIGN
How?

RESOURCES
Support?

Source: York-Barr, Ghere, & Sommerness (2003).

 Available for download at **http://resources.corwin.com/YorkBarrReflective**

Purpose . . . What and Why?

Purpose is the foundation on which effective schoolwide initiatives are built. The purpose is the reason for getting started in the first place. It is what gives meaning for participants. It is what drives motivation and effort. *Why?* Primary motivators for educators are student growth and opportunities to learn and grow in their individual and collective practice and effectiveness. Purpose is operationalized by articulating compelling outcomes or goals for students, which inspire engagement, and ultimately action. Too often, participants are not clear about or connected to the purpose or hoped for outcomes of various improvement or renewal initiatives. This results in drag instead of momentum. To consider the purpose element of the reflection planning framework, we offer the following questions:

- What do students in our school identify as some of the greatest challenges or frustrations? And why? What are their most meaningful experiences in school? How do their perspectives inform our decision making about professional learning priorities?
- If student data were disaggregated by age, gender, race, or primary language, what would we learn about our effectiveness? What might be some of the actionable implications of these findings?
- Looking schoolwide, what do we see as our major strengths related to student learning? In what areas are students experiencing the greatest challenges? What is the range of evidence we use to substantiate and explore these claims? Where does this lead us in terms of targeting improvements in teaching and learning?
- Are there current or pressing schoolwide goals or issues that present an opportunity to embed and advance our capacities for reflective practice and professional learning?
- In what ways do department or grade level meetings and committee work impact teaching practices and student learning? How are the efforts of departments and committees throughout the school related to improving practice and student learning? How can we support a focus on staff and student learning as central to team conversations, planning, and action?

People . . . Who?

People are the central resource for realizing positive results for any initiative. The greatest resource for learning is within and among the individuals who reflect, create, and work together. Involvement increases ownership and a sense of responsibility for outcomes. Joined by common purpose, strong relationships, and complementary strengths, participants leverage the capacity to accomplish great works. In reflecting on the people element of the reflective planning framework, consider the following questions:

- Who would be centrally involved in the design, leadership, and facilitation of a schoolwide initiative? Who would be supporting players? Who and how many among the entire staff would be participants?
- In what ways will we be sure to foster trust, relationships, and learning?
- Who are the highly respected teachers that could serve as instructional leaders?
- How might their capacities be tapped? What conversations would inspire and support their central involvement in a schoolwide development initiative?

- How will we continually model and foster the value of inclusivity? In what ways will we continually invite and encourage authentic participation by all members so that collective contributions are leveraged?

Design . . . How? What Learning Structures and Processes Will Support Reflective Practice?

Design encompasses the intentional design of reflective practice structures and processes, and the orchestration of structures and strategies is intended to support participant engagement. Structures include designated time for professional learning and specific determinations of group composition. Strategies include more specific procedures and skills for guiding interactions, reflection, and learning by participants. The knowledge, skills, and dispositions of participants will influence the design. Highly knowledgeable and skilled participants often need a lesser degree of design than those who are less knowledgeable or skilled. Design work is complex, interesting, and critically important. Reflect on the following questions as you consider the design element of the reflective planning framework:

- How well are opportunities for professional learning embedded into the daily and weekly schedules, and the annual calendar?
- What is the level of inquiry in our building? How skilled are our staff members with reflective practices? Are there sufficient numbers of people skilled in facilitation, communication, and group process skills to ensure productive use of group time?
- What would be effective ways for staff members to learn together? Vertically? Horizontally? New and experienced mixed? Same or cross subject areas?
- Would assigning or rotating specific group roles result in more productive interactions? Are external facilitators needed to get learning groups off to a strong and successful start or to build the confidence and competence of internal facilitators?
- In what ways can we support continuity and accountability within and between groups?

Resources . . . Support?

As used here, *resources* are viewed as the tangible supports, other than people, for initiating and moving the process forward. Such resources include space, time, equipment, materials, and refreshments. Questions for considering resource needs for schoolwide efforts to develop reflective practices are listed here.

- How much time will be allocated for engaging in reflective practices and professional learning? In what ways can we support embedding opportunities into existing schedules and activities?

- Can group members easily access one another at times other than face-to-face meetings, by means of physical proximity, voice mail, or e-mail, for example?
- Are there equipment or materials (e.g., books, handouts, media, refreshments) needed to support the development of reflective practices? Is there a budget to support this work?

Context . . . Where?

Context refers to the surrounding conditions or logistics in which the reflective practices and professional learning take place. It includes elements such as school culture, supportive and shared leadership, power, and politics. Too often, context is overlooked because it is viewed as existing outside the boundaries of core work and learning of educators. To the contrary, surrounding context deeply affects the accomplishments and sustainability of professional learning. The context (as depicted in Figure 7.4) surrounds the more operational or core elements of the framework. This is because it can either constrain the core work, squeezing and constricting the development efforts; or, it can enlarge and undergird the core work. Even highly effective learning groups can hit a ceiling if their work is not supported in the larger school context. Here are some questions for considering the context in which reflective practices and professional learning are being fostered and its potential influence on this work:

- In what ways does the work align or conflict with high profile school or district agendas or goals?
- Are administrators and informal school leaders supportive of the goals and proposed means of accomplishing the goals? How is this support communicated?
- How might key individuals who oppose or block the work of the team be engaged?
- Is there is a history of failed improvement attempts or of punishing initiation? Such a culture dissuades participation. How can inviting nurturing conditions be put in place?
- How can our school become a place where innovation and creativity are valued, modeled, and actively encouraged?
- What stories do people tell about our school? What kind of culture is reflected in these stories? What kind of stories reinforce the positive and hopeful views?

Results . . . So What?

Results are the products and outcomes of reflective practices and professional learning. Results are what sustain the interest and energy of participants. Results are both intrinsic and extrinsic, including student, educator, group, and school level outcomes. Reflecting on the following questions can assist in gauging progress toward results:

- How have students and student learning been affected by our reflective practices? Have we learned to think more creatively and optimistically about influencing the learning and lives of our students, all of them? Are we making progress toward these outcomes? How do we account for progress being made or not?
- Do students notice the effects of our work? Has our professional growth re-created the learning atmosphere for students in positive ways? What might students say about how we learn and work together? Why might this matter?
- Have our groups grown in their capacities for learning and working effectively? Have working relationships improved? What have we noticed as indicators of progress?
- Have individual participants grown and been renewed by their participation? Have dispositions and practices been enhanced?
- How will we know whether reflection, learning, and improvement are taking hold? What evidence would we expect to observe, hear, or collect? How will we obtain and examine feedback about the progress we are making?

Are more people choosing to engage in and support reflective practices? Is there more interest and confidence in our work by colleagues, administrators, and board members?

The absence of any one of the six elements in the reflection planning framework inhibits effectiveness. We invite you to use the Chapter Reflection Page (Figure 7.5) to write down your thoughts in response to these questions. You may also wish to skim through earlier chapters to be reminded of other ideas and strategies you view as significant. In the next and final chapter, we present lessons learned from our work of embedding reflective practices in the work of individual and school improvement and renewal. These lessons concisely capture a vision for reflective practice and may provide additional insight for the design and ongoing support of schoolwide reflective practice initiatives and efforts. And, in the final chapter we offer some personal reflections on hope, possibility, and renewal in our work as educators.

As educators join together to learn and advance practice, their sense of professional efficacy and collegial support seems to increase. This is a critical capacity in the development of schoolwide reflective practices. Teachers must believe that positive and significant change is possible. As they join together, they begin to realize that others, like themselves, are interested in and committed to significant and positive improvements in the teaching and learning process. Together, improvement is possible. Alone, it seems unlikely.

CLOSING

Over the last decade, the term *Learning Catalyst* has stuck for us. *Catalyst* is an energy source that sparks an event of some kind *without* getting used up. A *Learning Catalyst* is a person who sparks learning and we don't want them used up. We have adopted this term as we see evidence of it everywhere. In the examples provided above, catalysts were both formal and informal leaders, administrators, and teachers, and teams. Collectively they created, vetted, and continually adapted the reflective practice designs (both content and process) to engage entire staffs, team, and partner learning conversations.

Leaders of reflective practice also must be lead learners, not only for the purposes of "practicing what they preach," but also to continue learning and improving their own practice as lead learners and respected colleagues. *Learning catalysts* spark meaning-FULL and enriching conversation wherever they show up. Learning catalysts ignite learning for themselves and those around them. They are masters at shifting the energy of a conversation in productive ways. Each of us gets to choose how we show up and what we intentionally try to grow. How do you choose to show up? However you choose, it will influence your community of practice. In what ways could you show up as a learning catalyst? And, significantly, what are some ways you re-energize?

Taking the role of the learning catalyst requires listening, asking questions, and helping learners, young people or grown-ups, create a plan they believe will work. AND THEN, the learning catalyst helps the learner reflect on the event thereby learning from the experience. Only the learner is going to know what is possible in their context. This is why it is important to "work with" rather than "do to" others.

Reflecting on our own practice regarding the work of changing practice and culture, we have learned much. And undoubtedly will continue to learn more. Here we offer three of our most significant lessons.

First, some words of caution, what works now may not work in the future. Does anyone believe there will be less diversity, less demand for creativity, and less need for ongoing learning? Reflection is a process of continual re-examining of what is working and what is not so that we can hone our understandings and practices to achieve the desired results.

Second, learning, as life itself, is messy. General Eric Shinseki said, "If you don't like change, you are going to like irrelevance even less." Donald Schoen, an esteemed elder, now deceased in the field of organizational learning, including reflective practice, used the metaphor of the high hard ground versus the swamp. Envision someone standing on an embankment looking down into a swamp. On this high hard ground certain observations about the surface conditions and activity of the swamp are possible. Contrast this to being immersed in the swamp trying to make sense of the activity below the surface. With all due respect, most of you and most of us are "swamp creatures." Somewhere along the line we learned that a surface look does little to inform ways forward. So, colleagues, put on your boots and step into the swamp. Therein lies the essential learning about how life in the swamp is . . . what happens, why that might be the case, and how could life in the swamp become richer for all who live there. Perspective from the high hard ground won't get us where we need to be.

Humans, young and old, are not machines, nor are they always predictable. They are complex. Each of us is a unique "piece of work" and on any given day, we hope a work in progress. We live in a dynamic world where a certain amount of uncertainty is inevitable. This means that we have to get better and better at continuous learning, grounded in our practice, paying careful attention to the ways that students respond to what we do and how we do it so that we can learn to do it better. That's the bottom line. We just have to keep getting better. Learning is our way . . . learning with others is even better. Remember the perspective of Lazlo Bock: the first consideration for hiring at Google is learning ability. Learning from our practice and learning from shared practice offers a growth enhancing pathway forward.

Finally, as previously mentioned, we need people at all levels and in all corners reflecting, learning, and enhancing the learning. As one of our spouses said years ago, "Is there any end to the workshops you go to?" The answer was, and still is, "NO." There is always something new to learn about and to learn how to do. When what we are doing doesn't work, we have to adapt or be willing to accept the results we are getting. When asked what the answer is, we say: (1) there is no one right answer; and (2) if it isn't working, try something else. Working together, administrators, teachers, and the rich variety of direct service staff in schools, in partnership with students and families, can find, create, and sustain successful efforts to improve teaching and learning. Together, we can generate the capacity in ourselves and our systems to ensure every child is supported to learn well during their years in Pre K–12 education. We wish you well as you, too, join with your colleagues and community to grow this generation of young people. Just remember, "Go-eth not Alone." We all need partners in our work and in our lives.

Figure 7.5   Chapter Reflection Page

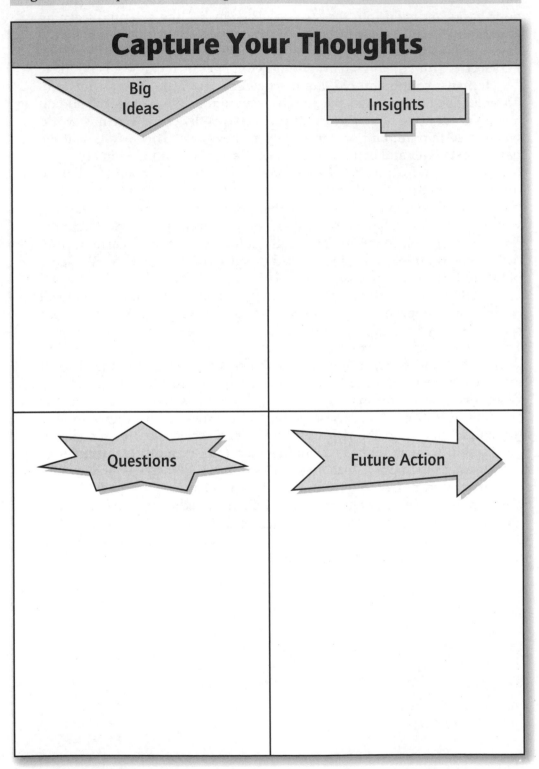

Moving Forward With Reflective Practice . . . in Hope and Possibility

You must become the change you want to see in this world.

—Attributed to Gandhi

To become the change you want to see in your world of teaching and leading means making a commitment to continuously learn and improve your practice. After all, modeling is the first teacher. We have learned from brain research that mirror neurons have an important role in facilitating others to learn. As Roland Barth (1990) said years ago, "the crucial role of the principal is as head learner" (p. 46). It means being a reflective professional. Beginning with yourself, you become a fractal of the larger organization. Then, with others, grow and expand reflective practices toward the outer rings of the reflective practice spiral. Modeling is still one of the best teachers. "Organizations ultimately learn via their individual members" (Kim, 1993, p. 37). It is the collective reflection and learning, the establishment of a professional learning community that holds the greatest potential for positively affecting student learning and lifelong learning capacities.

Wenger (1998) describes the rich learning opportunities available when individuals come together in a community of practice. He specifically emphasizes the strengths of a community where members with varied degrees of experience intentionally choose to learn together across levels and areas of the organization. New members learn from and contribute to the culture of practice as they participate more fully in the community. Three key features in Wenger's depiction of communities of practice are mutual engagement, negotiated meaning through dialogue, and a shared repertoire to enhance the system—in other words, joining together, learning together, and then acting together.

In a recently published book, *Rookie Smarts* (2015), author Liz Wiseman writes about ways to bring new people into our system, learn from them, and help them contribute to the existing system to achieve more positive results. Modeling reflective practice will accelerate teaming, increase understanding by remaining open to new ideas, and spread the growth of successful strategies.

As human beings, we have an internal drive for learning and growth. We are also social beings who naturally seek connections to others; to be and to be connected, not just to do. Establishing communities of practice focused on learning is one way to satisfy our human needs to grow and belong, in addition to our collective purpose of improving educational practice and life opportunities for young people in schools.

A desirable and possible future for our schools is that they become a *place of attraction* to which community members are drawn because of the opportunities to learn, to connect with others, and to make a difference in the lives of children, families, and communities. Creating a place of attraction requires intentionally developing both the intellectual and pathic capacity of the school by promoting inquiry, seeking multiple perspectives on issues of practice, examining both internal and external knowledge, and nurturing connectedness and care. It is likely that school communities that are most successful in establishing norms of reflection and continuous learning will be rewarded with long-term, enthusiastic commitments by staff members.

A teacher who participated in seasonal retreats facilitated by Parker Palmer (1998), author of *The Courage to Teach*, and focused on what it means to be a teacher commented how remarkable it was to be "treated like a plant to grow, instead of a machine to be fixed." This means supplying nutrients, caring for the relationships, and achieving good results. Reflective educators who are committed to lifelong learning and improvement will be looking for communities of practice that encourage their values and commitments, that engage their intellectual and social capacities, and that support their growth . . . all of which also help grow the young people they have chosen to teach.

As stated in the preface to this book, we believe strongly in the positive intentions and commitments of today's educators. We also view educators as having knowledge and expertise that is largely untapped and underutilized. We know that well-designed and implemented opportunities for reflection and learning together result in new insights about practice and renewed energy for teaching and learning. Questions incumbent on school leaders to keep ever present in their minds are, "How do we create and nurture schools that are authentic communities in which all members, young people and adults, continue the journey of learning and continuous renewal?" And, how do we continue growing and deepening a schoolwide culture that supports meaningful learning in genuine communities of practice?

In this final chapter, we once again share our reflective practice cycle, but expand considerations related to both its application and also the consequences when it is absent. Possibilities and questions about this particular model are put forward, with an emphasis on applications and connections with educators. Then, we offer some additional lessons learned about establishing reflective practices to promote learning and improvement in schools. Our R-E-F-L-E-C-T-I-O-N mnemonic synthesizes and clarifies some of our learning over the past few decades. Next, we highlight some of the paradox inherent in the ongoing design, implementation, and evolution of reflective practices. The last section of the chapter includes a story, along with strategies about hope, possibilities, and renewal for our work as educators. In this final section, we reflect on the ways that hope and possibility are critical dispositions for work in schools and communities.

We offer this chapter as inspiration and encouragement in your journey of becoming a more reflective educator who in turn inspires and encourages others. Together we can and, most days, we do make the world a more inclusive, joyful, compassionate, connected, and *learning-full* place. And then, we rest up to perform the same thing again tomorrow.

Of all the chapters in this new edition of our book, this one has undergone the least amount of change. It has been updated, but not substantially changed. At first, this was a source of discomfort and then it occurred to us that the tenets and practice of reflection are thousands of years old. (See the historical timeline, Significant Contributions to the Thinking About Reflective Practice, located in the accompanying website at http://resources.corwin.com/YorkBarrReflective.) Why then, in the space of mere decades, would the groundings and practices substantially change? What has changed is the context in which educators work. As emphasized in Chapter 1, "hot action" is an apt term. There is more testing and more technology, which has both supported and intensified teaching, learning, and learning about teaching. So, we kept intact much of what was our favorite chapter in each of the first two editions, and which remains so in this third edition. This chapter speaks to our hearts and minds as educators, and inspires hope and the possibility for much good to grow in years to come. We are delighted and honored to share our thinking and our practices with you, kindred spirits . . . for the good.

REVISITING THE REFLECTIVE PRACTICE CYCLE

The growth of understanding follows an ascending spiral rather than a straight line. (Joanna Field [1934] as quoted in Maggio, 1992, p. 331)

As our reflective practice team gathered to consider how we might bring this third edition of our book to a close, we spent a lot of time in dialogue about the reflective practice cycle presented throughout the book. We revisit this cycle in this last chapter to share some of our—your authors—deliberations on reflective practice. As depicted in Figure 8.1, the reflective practice cycle doesn't stand alone. It is embedded in a messy context that represents the world of practice; as mentioned previously, this is

Figure 8.1   Theory as a Catalyst for Asking More Questions

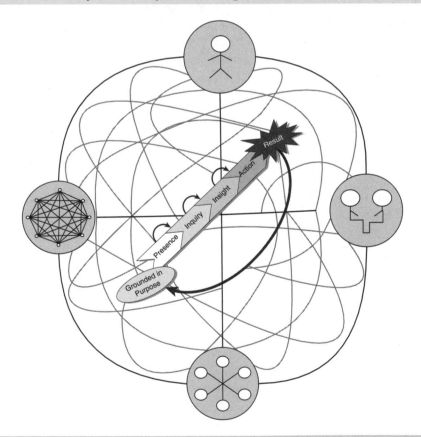

what Donald Schön (1983) refers to as the "swamp," and it can be used to guide reflective practice within each ring of the reflective practice spiral, as represented by the individual, partner, small group and team, and schoolwide symbols.

Theory as a Reframing Tool

The reflective practice cycle is also aptly viewed as a theory of action for reflective practice. It is just one way to think about reflective practice. Know that what appears to be a linear presentation is deceptively oversimplified. Just as Joanna Field said in the above quote, we know that learning does not follow a straight line, and that an ascending spiral image better represents the learning process. In learning, we do not return to the same place on the same plane. Learning involves change. If we learn something, we usually change, or tweak, our practice. If we change something, we usually learn from the change. Therefore, Change = Learning; Learning = Change.

One member of our team suggested that the progression of the elements orient downward instead of upward to reinforce the idea of moving deeper into the complexities and understandings of practice. Another member thought we should rearrange the elements in a more random order to illustrate that the components do not necessarily occur in the order presented. We all agreed, however, that regardless of position or orientation, each of the elements indicates an important dimension of reflective practice. As initially introduced in Chapter 1, the absence of any one element of the reflective practice cycle can disrupt the flow of reflective thought. To illustrate this point more clearly, we describe here what can result when any one of the elements is absent.

> Without *purpose*, there is little reason to invest and commit one's energy. Why bother?

> Without *presence*, reflective thought, multiple perspectives, and listening are often absent;

> Without *inquiry*, there is no wondering about why our practice had the impact it did or did not;

> Without *insight*, nothing new is learned or reinforced, making it unlikely changes in practice will result;

> Without *action*, nothing changes and neither participants nor students benefit.

One purpose of a theory or framework is to assist in understanding or explaining something about the world. In our case, this particular framework (reflective practice cycle) grew out of our need to put some order and structure around what seemed core components of reflective practice that could yield new understandings and practices that resulted in improved student learning. Knowing that *the learning is in the conversation*, we also have deliberated extensively about how to structure a reflective, learning-full conversational space. Do we begin and end our team gatherings by creating space for every voice to be heard and considered? When topics of conversation require more in-depth consideration, do we maximize participation and idea generation by forming small conversational structures (e.g., dyad or triads) before having a whole group conversation? As facilitators, what do we pay attention to that informs moves that will clarify purpose and support processes that privilege reflection? When members interact in guarded ways, suggesting that trust is not yet established, how do we tailor reflection structures, topics, and processes so they feel safe? One idea we often use is for participants to write their thoughts anonymously on cards. Everyone writes on cards that are the same color and size and everyone uses the same color marker. Then, we collect the cards and they collectively sort them into categories they identify as meaningful. This requires conversation around getting the task done, but maintains anonymity in terms of participant responses to the task. In what ways do we model inquiry-based learning among staff members as one way to support their use of inquiry approaches to teaching and learning? What questions spark inquiry and reflection? Here is an example: What are some practices or actions I am hoping to change so that my students engage more deeply? How can we work on this together? What might be some ways to assess our effectiveness?

Theory as a Catalyst for Asking More Questions

The process of creating this third edition of our book served as a catalyst for asking deeper questions. One conversation focus was about the presence of "choice" in reflective practice processes. Human beings are largely autonomous: "I am in charge of me!" Further, the "egg carton" structure of schools, used as a metaphor for how schools are typically organized as a bunch of separate spaces (i.e., classrooms) with one teacher in each space, reinforces autonomy of practice, such that few other school peers, except the students, know how any of us teach. This reminds us that "the times they are a-changing." Since the publication of our previous edition of this book, there has been a positive, discernible revitalization of co-teaching between subject area or grade level teachers and support services teachers (e.g., language learning teachers and special educators). Our observation is that this trend has generated more energy, support, and reflection for teachers, as well as produced more tailored personalized instruction for students. If you have not yet read the co-teaching practice example located in Chapter 5 (page 173), it's not too late to go back and take a look!

For the most part, a commitment to reflect, learn, and grow begins with each of us. Each of us chooses how we show up each and every day in our work as teachers, learners, and colleagues. What do you choose?

- *Do I choose* a learner stance?
- *Do I choose* to be open and to ask questions of myself?
- *Do I choose* to take the risks involved in examining my thinking, my teaching, and my collegial practices, along with the effects of my practice?
- *Do I choose* to take action to improve and to seek out others to support my growth?
- *Do I choose* to regularly seek out partners with whom I can reflect, and whose reflection I can support?
- *If I choose* these stances and disposition and actions, what is it that compels me to do so?
- *What are my choices* that reinforce and engrain these patterns of being, doing, and learning?

There are educators among us who never choose a growth disposition. There are educators among us who begin the process of reflection and learning, but never move to action, individually or collectively. Of course, this is sometimes true of each of us as well. To be sure, traditional norms of isolation in schools can make it difficult to choose a reflection connection with a colleague. But, if we don't choose the connection, we do so at our own peril. We deprive ourselves of the energy and partnership that grows when we dare to learn with others. From daring to engage in partnerships, much good can grow.

We are thrilled that over the past decade, there are many fewer schools that do NOT have time to collaborate, reflect, and learn built into the schedule. Because of the equal parts demanding and equal parts exhilarating work involved in our field, we have grown to know that we need each other to learn, to be more effective, to build stamina, and to not be alone. Moving more deeply into collaborative forms of teaching, learning, and reflective practice can feel risky and vulnerable, but it is a rare professional who can continue to practice well without the energy and ideas that grow within an authentic community of practice. Remember from earlier chapters, we are not supposed to go alone in this work.

The reflective practice cycle prompts us to raise new questions about intention and choice making in the learning process, and also poses numerous questions as we think about enacting components of the cycle relative to our experiences.

- How and why do we move beyond connection and insight to action?
- What conditions can we create such that action is expected, anticipated, and embraced as part of the process?

- Without action there is no authentic feedback from which to determine effectiveness. Is it reflective practice if there is no action?
- What compels us and what detours us from action?
- Might there be important changes happening even when evidence of behavior change is not readily apparent? Do we sometimes act without knowing that our actions have in fact been influenced by the thinking and learning that arise from a reflective process?

These are just some of the many questions that remain elusive about reflective practice. We encourage you to create your own reflective practice cycle or theory of action in conversations with colleagues and to raise your own questions. Take out a pencil and make additions, subtractions, or any other changes that fit for your thinking about learning, growth, and change. Make your own theory of practice, just be sure that inquiry remains a central element. Remember, it is questions that spark reflection and thinking. We believe the laws of physics hold true equally well in the context of professional practice as they do in physics. Bodies at rest tend to stay at rest; bodies in motion tend to stay in motion. It may seem ironic that we urge action given our emphasis throughout the book on taking time out from daily doings to engage in reflection and learning. Time out to reflect is one of the greatest influences on improved action. Our individual and collective purpose is to do our best to grow young people who learn both subject area content and ways to be a good human, student, friend, and colleague. Never doubt that how you show up every day has an impact! Who you are and how you are also serves to teach young people. These young people are the very same people who will be making decisions about how we live when we grow old.

LESSONS LEARNED ABOUT REFLECTIVE PRACTICE

A Mnemonic Strategy to Synthesize Key Learning

We now shift gears to offer lessons learned through our experiences and study of reflective practice. We developed a *R-E-F-L-E-C-T-I-O-N* mnemonic (see Figure 8.2) as the way to share these lessons. These lessons grew from reflecting on our own experiences as reflective practitioners and in conversation with one another over time. Be sure to create some rest stops along the way with your colleagues to reflect and learn together.

R: Relationships are first. Establishing positive working relationships focused on student learning is an essential foundation for reflective practice. Relationships are the means by which information is communicated within a system. Relationships are the means for exploring who we are, what we believe, and how we might act. Relationships are the building blocks for any

Figure 8.2   Reflective Practice Mnemonic: Lessons Learned

Relationships are first

Expand options through dialogue

Focus on learning

Leadership accelerates reflective practice

Energy is required for any system to grow

Courage is needed to reflect and act

Trust takes time

Inside-out

Outside-in

Nurture people and ideas

Available for download at http://resources.corwin.com/YorkBarrReflective

system (Wheatley, 1992). Webber (1993) advises that when you want to understand how an organization works, map the relationship flow, not the formal organizational structure. Wheatley (1992) writes, "The time I formerly spent on detailed planning and analyses, I now spend looking at the structures that might facilitate relationships" (p. 36). How can a web of interconnected relationships among staff members be woven throughout our school?

E: Expand options through dialogue. Much knowledge about practice is inside the minds and hearts of educators. Conversations and dialogue are a way to "discover what they know, share it with their colleagues, and in the process create new knowledge for the organization" (Webber, 1993, p. 28). The value of time to reflect together cannot be overemphasized. Through dialogue, understanding is increased, assumptions are made explicit, possibilities are explored, and options are expanded. Creative and divergent thoughts emerge as colleagues inquire and share their perspectives and interpretations about events, circumstances, and experiences. Creativity is one of our most valuable resources as education moves forward in the new millennium. An open exchange through dialogue allows community members to participate in the creative process of shaping future directions and moving forward with important work. Ownership, responsibility, and commitment increase. In what ways might educators gather together to know one another, to remain open to other points of view, and to engage in dialogue that results in greater insights and expanded options for practice?

F: Focus on learning. The purpose of reflective practice is to improve staff and student learning. If educators are not focused on learning, it is hard to imagine why students would be. At the core of reflective practice are the desire and commitment to continuously learn so that practices improve and students learn at higher levels. A focus on learning requires a certain amount of humility. When we let go of needing to be right, we acknowledge that we do not and cannot know everything. We are open to learn more. Ultimately, "enlightened trial and error outperforms the planning of flawless intellects" (Kelley as cited in Webber, 2000, p. 178). Reflection on practice involves learning through planning and reflective trial and error. Such learning transforms events, experiences, and information into the tacit knowledge and wisdom of distinguished educators. Opportunities for learning are limitless. *How can learning become a more intentional focus of staff conversations?*

L: Leadership accelerates reflective practice. Leadership by the formal and informal leaders in schools is an essential organizational resource for reflective practice and improvement. Leadership is influence and action, not position. No one knows everything; everyone knows something. Leading the growing of reflective practice communities must be shared practice by administrators and teachers with the common goal of learning. Without that premise, the commitment of resources and the commitment by people can waiver. The values and actions of the principal strongly influence the engagement of staff. Without teachers also leading, however, ground level collegial relationships and energy that are essential for continuous improvement are less likely to be activated. The rich learning that emerges from the first-hand knowledge of student engagement in classroom contexts will not be part of the conversation. Teacher leaders understand the inner workings and relationships within a school and can access those relationships as resources to positively influence both staff and student learning. To support educators' learning, schools must be structured to encourage the intellectual stimulation that fosters continuous development (Stewart, 1997). It is the job of the leadership team to create and model the conditions necessary for fruitful conversations about practice to happen (Webber, 1993). *In what ways do, or could, formal and informal leaders work together to create an environment that promotes conversations about learning?*

E: Energy is required for any system to grow. Living systems require energy to grow. Energy in schools emerges from people who are meaningfully engaged in teaching, leading, and learning processes. Reflection creates energy by leading to new discoveries and insights about practice. Reflection with others creates even more energy as discoveries and insights are shared and channeled through relationships among educators throughout the school. Without positive energy that is productively channeled, systems die. Living systems cease to function when they do not have, or cannot make use of, the critical ingredients that create energy for life.

Without supportive leaders and cultures, reflection and learning will not be defining elements in schools. Without educators reflecting and learning, schools will die. *How do we harness and multiply the positive energy that already exists in our school?* Learning is a renewable energy source.

C: Courage is needed to reflect and act. Courage is the internal grounding that supports taking action, despite knowing the inherent risks. Making a commitment to reflective practice on a personal basis is a courageous act because it means opening ourselves up to honest consideration of multiple perspectives and ways of doing things. It means critically examining our assumptions and our behaviors. It means taking responsibility for our own learning and growth as professional educators, and modeling this valuable way of practice among peers. Making a commitment to support reflective practice in groups or teams and throughout the school is a courageous act because it means going public with our commitments. It means being part of something that runs counterculture to the strong norms of constant doing rather than learning and doing. It means trying to walk the talk of being a reflective practitioner . . . listening, being open, sharing, learning, questioning, and holding ourselves accountable. *In what ways can we develop, demonstrate, and sustain the courage it takes to critically examine our practice and to make our learning public?*

T: Trust takes time. Trusting relationships are the foundation for learning together. In a trusting relationship, we allow ourselves to be vulnerable—a requisite for learning. We can be open to exploring our assumptions. We choose to take risks, confident that we will not be punished or embarrassed if we make mistakes.

> Learning requires tolerating and learning from people who make mistakes. Learning requires inefficiency. Learning requires tolerating failure. Learning requires letting people try things that they've never done before, things that they probably won't be very good at the first time around. (Webber, 2000, p. 176)

Fear and control, which is the opposite of trust, is way too prevalent in some schools today. Webber (2000) points out that everyone seems interested in organizational learning, but no one is much interested in allowing individuals to learn. Mistakes and inefficiencies are inevitably part of the learning process, but too often are not gracefully accepted. Educators will not choose to learn, at least not publicly, unless they are in a reasonably safe environment. Trust is difficult to build and easy to destroy. *How do we foster a high trust culture of learning in schools? How might each of us increase our own trustworthiness?*

I: Inside-out. Becoming a reflective educator is a process of inside-out change. Reflection is an internal capacity that is tapped by a genuine desire to learn and grow, not by external mandates. In the words of Michael Fullan (1993), "You can't mandate what matters" (p. 125). What matters most for teaching and learning is what is in the minds and hearts of educators. It is this inner capacity that connects educators with children, and children with learning. Becoming a reflective educator involves figuring out our own identity—who we are as people, as teachers, and as learners. We can teach only who we are (Palmer, 1998), and by extension, we can only lead who we are. As we become more reflective, we can inspire an interest in others to become more reflective and to take the risks involved in continuously learning from and improving practice. Actions, including spoken words, reflect beliefs and values. "What you do speaks so loudly no one can hear what you are saying" (quote attributed to Ralph Waldo Emerson). *What space can we create in our own lives to begin or to expand our commitment to reflective practice and personal change?*

O: *Outside-in.* Becoming a reflective educator also requires being open to outside influences, such as colleagues with different views, findings from research, experiences of other schools and systems, and concerns expressed by the public and by policy makers. What are the external "triggers" that cause us to learn or cause us to hide (Goldsmith, 2015)? We must be willing to ask for input as well as to receive it. None of us is an island; none of our schools are islands in the community. We are influenced individually and organizationally by our surrounding context and must pay attention to it. Sometimes, change happens only when forces from the outside press in. Everything is connected to everything else. Open systems that engage with the environment grow and evolve (Wheatley, 1992). If we ignore external influences, we do so at our own peril. Closed systems eventually devolve. This principle holds whether the system is a person, a partnership, a team, a school, a district, or a community. Reflection is a process for making sense of both internal and external influences and for determining priorities for action. *What helps us to remain continually aware of and open to our surrounding environments?*

N: *Nurture people and ideas.* Be inclusive. Show your caring side. Create a culture of attraction in which educators are drawn into a school community because their needs to learn, to create, and to make a difference in the lives of children are met. Nurture their creativity and their spirit by allowing them to bring their unique contributions and gifts to the teaching and learning process. Teaching and learning are highly interpersonal. Effective educators vary greatly in their approaches and styles. For educators to bring their best to their work with children, they must be in places that nurture their growth, support their creativity, and offer feedback in the context of a trusting, professional learning community. Continue to invite people into the community of reflective educators. It is the collective energy that emerges from reflection and learning by many people that has the greatest potential for sustained and widespread improvement in educational practice. *How might we be more inclusive and nurturing of the people in our school communities?*

Paradox of Reflective Practice: More Lessons Learned

To light a candle is to cast a shadow. (Le Guin, 1968, as quoted in Maggio, 1992, p. 237)

Pathways to school renewal and improvement are less specific and more ambiguous than was once thought. The dynamic interplay among internal factors, combined with the influence of external factors, does not lend itself well to prescriptions for improvement. As emphasized in Chapter 3, the work of advancing teaching and learning is different among levels of practice (e.g., school board, central office, school administration, teaching and learning in schools). Partnerships among levels and places in the system can go a long way toward creating development plans that have a good likelihood of being supported. And . . . even with well-informed plans, often the best we can do is to remain clear about purpose, stay grounded in principles and not specific steps, and commit to ongoing reflective practice with key development partners—only the direction and design can be controlled, not the outcomes. Additionally, even the design must constantly evolve in response to feedback that emerges with implementation, changing context variables, and new insights. Experimenting with reflective practice as one means of supporting school renewal has raised as many questions as answers about how to do this kind of work. Our work has heightened our understanding about paradox within reflective practice. Paradox can be thought of as tension that exists around ideas that seem both contradictory and true at the same time. This is the nature of our world as a whole and also in our field of education. Both the light and shadow are a part of the experience of a lit candle. The universe is one of randomness as well as pattern. Reflective practice requires both clarifying one's own voice and being open to other viewpoints. Schoolwide renewal may be fed by both inside-out and outside-in energy. Areas of paradox that become evident in our reflection and analyses are shown in Figure 8.3.

For reflective practices to be initiated, grown, and expanded, *there must be* enough vision and direction for participants to know where the initiative is headed and why, as well as enough flexibility to allow participants to shape the initiative to make it personally meaningful and contextually relevant. *There must be* enough design and structure for the process to get underway, as well as enough flexibility and creativity to allow ongoing adjustments that support implementation. *There must be* enough support and encouragement for participants to feel safe, as well as enough pressure and challenge to focus and promote divergent thinking and action. At a personal level, individual teachers must constantly attend to their own wholeness—keep their oxygen masks on first—and teachers and schools also must be focused on the well-being of all members of the community. *There must be* both care of self and care about others. *There must be* acknowledgment of the uncertainty, ambiguity, and value of practice in the

Figure 8.3   Paradox of Reflective Practice

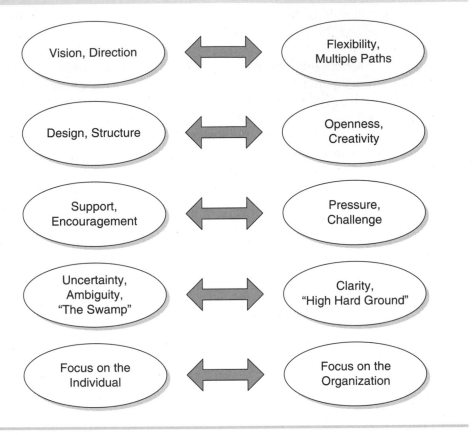

"swamp," as well as consideration of the clarity found in "high-hard-ground" knowledge reported in research literature. *There must be* enough focus on individual learning and growth needs, as well as attention to the learning and growth needs of the organization. *There must be* sustained attention around student needs since this is ultimately why we are teaching, as well as persistent attention toward the adult learning needs within a community since when the adults stop growing, student learning becomes vulnerable as well.

Again, we present our Paradox of Reflective Practice visual (Figure 8.3) with the hope that it becomes another seed for reflection and inquiry. How much is enough planning, and yet the process still remains open enough? How do we discover the balance between the points of tension? It's hard to tell until you get underway. What's important is to know that these areas of apparent contradiction are actually inherent tensions. Imagine launching a reflective practice initiative without any direction or aim. Why would anyone be compelled to participate? Imagine only the presence of support and encouragement, without pressure and challenge. How would new thinking emerge? Imagine a commitment to reflective practice without a design or structure to support it. How would you start? The nature of paradox is the coexistence of multiple and seemingly contradictory truths. The work of reflective practice rests solidly within "both/and" thinking instead of "either/or" thinking. If you notice the presence of paradox, it is an invitation for more learning, and not something to be feared or to run away from.

FOSTERING HOPE AND RENEWAL

In this final section of the book, we once again return to a focus on hope and renewal. What is hope? In Scott Sanders's book (1998) *Hunting for Hope*, he shares, "I have discovered that the words *hope* and *hop* come from the same root, one that means to leap up in expectation" (p. 20). Further, he adds, "Memory grips the past; hope grips the future" (p. 22). Hope involves expectations. In *The Impossible Will Take a Little While: A Citizen's Guide to Hope in a Time of Fear* (2004), Paul Loeb suggests that believing that we have options and seeing abundance in our world are ways to move toward hope and not descend into despair. He writes,

> Whether the challenge is political or personal, effective remedies differ from individual to individual. But solutions always involve altering perspective, replacing tunnel vision with an expanded view that lets in more light, more possibility. And possibility is the oxygen upon which hope thrives. (Loeb, 2004, p. 19)

Although Sanders and Loeb do not use the term *reflective practice*, their ideas of expectation, options, possibilities, and abundance resonate with the work of reflective practice and connect this work to a broader context. Consider these six strategies illustrated in Figure 8.4 to nourish your spirit of hope, possibility, and renewal on your reflective practice journey.

Why is hope so important? Current studies on hope and optimism have shown that more hope results in higher grades, higher graduation rates, and higher attendance in schools. Professionals do teach content, but just as important is the modeling and teaching of hope; hope that situations can improve, and that life can be better. It is the meta-curriculum that we rarely talk about. We do more than teach content. Hope can be a gift to students with long-term positive consequences. Whatever your position is in education, one of your jobs is to "keep hope alive."

Figure 8.4   Strategies for Hope, Possibility, and Renewal

Ask questions, listen well

Shift to an abundance mindset

Listen and learn from the children

**Hope
Possibility
Renewal**

Remember your past

Acknowledge despair and fear

Express your vision and values

As Shane Lopez (2014), in *Making Hope Happen*, says, hope requires a goal, specifically, where we want to go, what result we want, and how will we behave while pursuing our goal. Then, to feel hope, we have to believe we have the ability to make things happen. Finally, hope requires a plan to get to our outcome. When these three things coalesce, we begin to see progress.

Ask Questions and Listen Well

A dual focus on both inquiry and listening is key to reflective practice in schools and to an overall orientation of fostering hope. Questions bring in new perspectives and possibilities. Questions help create a "crack" that lets the light in, replacing tunnel vision with an expanded view. Questions help reframe, create possibilities, and develop new pathways for positive behaviors. Listening—deep listening—suggests deepened understanding, and new insights that can grow from considering new possibilities. Listening requires a deliberate pause, a slowing down, a focus on seeking to understand one's own voice and other voices. Listening might be one of the most important skills. People feel validated as a human when someone listens to them. To feed hope, ask questions and listen well. In other words, be reflective.

Acknowledge the Despair and Fear

Many educators feel pulled and squeezed. Many experience a narrowing of the curriculum and are concerned about movement toward less relevant and lifeless school experiences. There are changes that we fear. There are students and families with difficult lives. The budget cuts and loss of staff positions are painful. There can be points of despair in our work. We believe that part of nourishing hope involves finding ways to understand and constructively address despair and fear, not pretending that fears and concerns don't exist. Parker Palmer, a renowned educator, and Pema Chodron, a well-known western Buddhist nun, both describe the benefits of moving into and through fear, instead of following an instinct or tendency to run from it (Chodron, 1994; Palmer, 1994). Administrators and teacher leaders can be role models for dealing with fear and despair in constructive ways. We think that it can be hard for teachers to move on to hopeful actions if fears and moments of despair are never validated. This book holds insights and strategies for naming and learning from fears and concerns—so do you!

Shift to an Abundance Mindset

An abundance paradigm feeds hope and possibility. Abundance is reflected in beliefs, such as *everything that we need is right here . . . we have enough . . . the answers exist within, we just have to find them*. Abundance is sometimes contrasted with a paradigm of scarcity: *we don't have enough . . . you have what I need . . . I won't be ok until I get x, y, or z*. We acknowledge the genuine scarcity of resources in schools, such as staff, chairs, reading books, paper, computers, and assistive technology for students with disabilities. This is real. We also challenge ourselves to focus on a paradigm of abundance, abundance of ideas, creativity, and capacities within for growth and renewal. This is also real. An abundance lens looks to name the progress; notices what is and not just what is not; celebrates the movement forward, even when it seems like baby steps; says "wow . . . look at that"; nurtures and renews the garden instead of doing a complete overhaul; and celebrates the points of light. A friend of one of the authors says:

"There's a crack in everything—that's how the light gets in." The paradigm of possibility, of abundance, is "the oxygen upon which hope thrives" (Loeb, 2004, p. 19).

Remember Your Past

Consider historian Howard Zinn's words:

What we choose to emphasize in this complex history will determine our lives. If we see only the worst, it destroys our capacity to do something. If we remember those times and places—and there are many—where people have behaved magnificently, this gives us the energy to act, and at least the possibility of sending this spinning top of a world in a different direction. (As quoted in Loeb, 2004, p. 71)

So we ask ourselves: Who has inspired my development as an educator and as a person, and how? What magnificent people do I want to remember in my journey as an educator and human being? And, in looking at our history as reflective practitioners, we savor the present voices of knowledge and inspiration from Schön, van Manen, Sparks, Langer-Colton, Chodron, and Palmer, to name just a few. And then we stretch back to Dewey. And then we stretch much farther back in time to Socrates, Buddha, and Lao Tze. We are not the first and we will not be the last in this quest to create reflection in our work and in our lives. This instills hope, knowing that we are a part of an important sustainable idea—reflective thought.

Listen to and Learn From the Children and Youth

Ultimately, what may give many of us the most hope is in continuing to find ways to listen and learn with and from our children and youth. Why are we teaching? The children. Why are we trying to improve ourselves as teachers? The children. Who can hold deep insights and excellent questions about learning and life? The children. The power and possibilities that emerge from our youth are astounding.

Express Your Vision and Values

A final strategy for building hope and renewal involves keeping vision and values alive in our daily work. Naming, showing, asking, drawing, telling a story, expressing our beliefs as educators through our daily actions. What are the non-negotiables for me as a teacher when it comes to how to teach and what I teach? What feelings and experiences do I want each child to have when entering this learning community? What matters most in our school, and how do we express this? Vision as a verb brings hope to our work by inspiring us to reach to our ideals.

Located in Table 8.1 is a story about vision from Walter Olsen and Bill Sommers's (2004) book titled *A Trainer's Companion: Stories to Stimulate Reflection, Conversation, and Action.* We invite you to consider the hope and possibilities within this and other stories that speak to your hearts and settle your mind about the good within you, your families, your communities, and your communities of practice. We believe that this story challenges us with a vision that many educators and citizens would like to see permeate all communities. Many agree that we are not doing enough for the children in the world. Together, we can do more.

Table 8.1   A Story of Hope and Possibility

A Masai Story: How Are the Children?

Among the most accomplished and fabled tribes of Africa, no tribe was considered to have warriors more fearsome or more intelligent than the mighty Masai. It is perhaps surprising then to learn the translation of the traditional greeting that passed between Masai warriors. "Kasserian ingera," which means "and how are the children?"

It is still the traditional greeting among the Masai, acknowledging the high value that the Masai always place on their children's well-being. Even warriors with no children of their own would always give the traditional answer, "All the children are well." This meant, of course, that peace and safety prevail, that the priorities of protecting the young, the powerless are in place, and that the Masai people have not forgotten their proper functions and responsibilities and their reason for being. "All the children are well" means that life is good. It means that the daily struggles of existence, even among a poor people, do not preclude proper caring for its young.

I wonder in our own culture, how it might affect our consciousness or our own children's welfare if we took to greeting each other with the same daily question: "And how are the children?" I wonder if we heard that question and passed it along to each other a dozen times a day, if it would begin to make a difference in the reality of how children are thought of or cared for in this country.

I wonder if every adult among us, parent and non-parent alike, felt an equal weight for the daily care and protection of all children in our town, in our state, in our country. I wonder if we could truly say without hesitation, "The children are well, yes, all the children are well."

What would it be like? If the president began every press conference, every public appearance, by answering the question, "And how are the children, Mr. President?" If every governor of every state had to answer the same question at every press conference. "And how are the children, Governor? Are they well?" Wouldn't it be interesting to hear their answers?

Source: Olsen & Sommers (2004).

 Available for download at **http://resources.corwin.com/YorkBarrReflective**

Leap up in expectation.
Grip the future.
Be reflective.
Nurture relationships, nurture the garden.
Choose to learn. Choose to pause. Choose to act.
Take risks. Be daring.
Find a crack to let the light in.
Be aware. Be kind. Be human.
Leap up in expectation. Hop. Hope.

CLOSING

The world is round and the place which may seem like the end may also be only the beginning. (Ivy Baker Priest, 1958, as quoted in Maggio, 1992, p. 28)

In coming to the end of the book, we acknowledge the blur between beginnings and endings, and also our belief in wholeness, cycles, and connections. Learning and reflection is a never-ending cycle of making sense of our worlds and trying to find our way in it . . . our way to contribute to something larger than ourselves . . . something like doing good for the young people in our communities . . . because they are the ones who will, at our end, be the decision makers. The circle of life never ends.

Our wish for you the reader is to "end" the book with not only a greater understanding of reflective practice concepts, skills, and strategies, but also a sense of renewal, new beginnings, and recommitment to the possibilities that exist in our work with children in our schools. We also realize that some readers may never "end" the book, since perhaps you are the type that skims and pokes through various parts of the book that look the most relevant and you're always starting new or continuing on.

Still, embedding reflective practice in education is about creating significant cultural change in schools. It is messy. It is complicated. There are no certain paths. The outcomes, however, can significantly and positively affect both educators and the students whom they serve. As you move through a process of becoming more reflective as an individual and with your colleagues, reflection-in-action, reflection-on-action, and reflection-for-action will provide the feedback needed to make ongoing adjustments. Use the Chapter Reflection Page (Figure 8.5) to write down ideas from this chapter that you may find worthwhile for future reference as you continue your work in this area. Future practice and study about reflective practices for professional development and school renewal will increase our understanding about how to move forward. For now, congratulate yourself on beginning the process, or on this new beginning of sorts!

Feel confident that your choice to reflect on your practice will result in changes in thought and action that positively influence learning and growth for you, your students, and your communities of practice. Remember that the objective is progress, not perfection. Keep clearly in mind that

> To reflect on action is to be a lifelong learner. To be reflective is a choice that is made against the background of beliefs and values. To be a constantly developing performer or to remain an expert performer requires the constant input of energy to do the work of reflection and learning with commitments to action. This energy source is inside the self; it is released by enabling understandings within a worldview. Quality performance is the outcome of a belief in quality. (Butler, 1996, p. 280)

What do you think you might do first as a result of reading this book? In what ways could you use this information tomorrow? Who else might work with you to expand reflection and learning in your school? If your school were a place where students and staff continuously learned and had fun doing so, what would that look like? What would a desirable future school be like for you? How might you be part of that vision? How might you be part of making that vision a reality?

We leave you here to begin. We leave you in the spirit of hope and possibility. What better time than now to leap up in expectation of a future in which the importance of teaching and learning is transparent to students, is appreciated by our communities, and is validated through the continued goodwill and good works of educators. Such a future is possible as individual educators join together, join with students and families, and join with their communities to create places where reflection, learning, growth, and action are anticipated, honored, and valued. Our collective futures are in our hands. The children and young adults whom we serve today will be serving the world tomorrow. We must do what we can to teach them well, to help them realize their potential, to instill in them a sense of connection, curiosity, and a drive for learning that will be so very much needed in tomorrow's world—the world they will lead.

Never deprive a person of hope. It may be all they have.

—H. Jackson Brown, author

Figure 8.5   Chapter Reflection Page

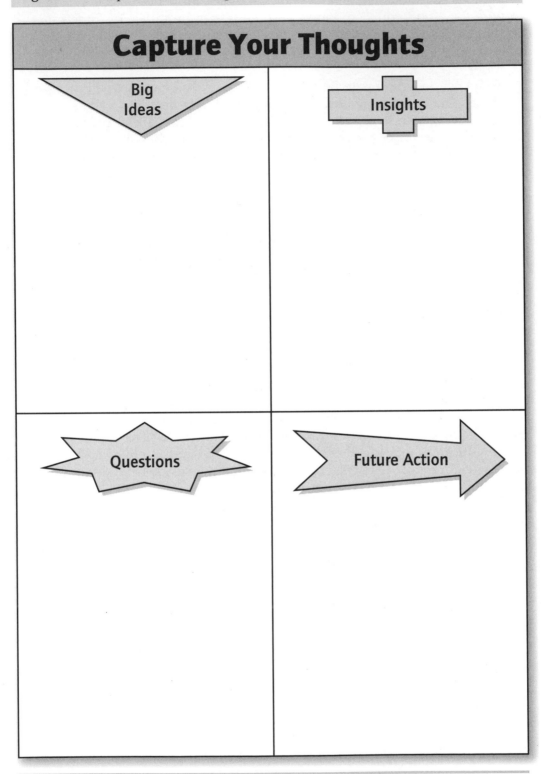

References

Abrahamson, E. (2004). *Change without pain*. Boston, MA: Harvard Business Press.

Adelman, N. (1998). *Trying to beat the clock: Uses of teacher professional time in three countries*. Washington, DC: Policy Studies Associates.

American Psychological Association. (1997). *Learner-centered principles: A framework for school redesign and reform*. Washington, DC: Author.

Arin-Krupp, J. (1982). *Developing adult learners*. ASCD workshop. Minneapolis, MN.

Arrien, A. (1993). *The four-fold way: Walking paths of the warrior, teacher, healer, and visionary*. New York, NY: Harper Collins.

Ash, D., & Levitt, K. (2003). Working within the zone of proximal development: Formative assessment as professional development. *Journal of Science Teacher Education, 14*(1), 23–48.

Axelrod, D., & Axelrod, E. (2014). *Let's stop meeting like this*. San Francisco, CA: Berret-Koehler.

Bailey, K., Curtis, A., & Nunan, D. (1998). Undeniable insights: The collaborative use of three professional development practices. *TESOL Quarterly, 32*(3), 546–556.

Baker, B. (1993). *Providing data*. [Personal communication at Cognitive Coaching Advanced Training workshop. South Lake Tahoe, CA.]

Barth, R. (1990). *Improving schools from within*. San Francisco, CA: Jossey-Bass.

Bergsgaard, M., & Ellis, M. (2002). Inward: The journey toward authenticity through self-observing. *Journal of Educational Thought, 36*(1), 53–68.

Black, R., Molseed, T., & Sayler, B. (2003). Fresh view from the back of the room: Coaching in their classrooms offers teachers more points of view. *Journal of Staff Development, 24*(2), 61–65.

Block, P. (2002). *The answer to how is yes: Acting on what matters*. San Francisco, CA: Berrett-Koehler.

Block, P. (2009). *Community: The structure of belonging*. San Francisco, CA: Berrett-Koehler.

Bocchino, R. (2015). *Studies in advanced leadership*. Baldwinsville, NY: Heart of Change.

Bodaken, B., & Fritz, R. (2011). *The managerial moments of truth*. New York, NY: Free Press.

Bohm, D. (1989). *On dialogue*. Ojai, CA: David Bohm Seminars.

Bohm, D. (1999). *On dialogue* (L. Nichol, Ed.). New York, NY: Routledge.

Bonder, N. (1999). *Yiddishe kop: Creative problem solving in Jewish learning, lore, and humor*. Boston, MA: Shambhala.

Brandt, R. (1998). *Powerful learning*. Alexandria, VA: Association for Supervision and Curriculum Development.

Bright, B. (1996). Reflecting on "reflective practice." *Studies in the Education of Adults, 28*(2), 162–184.

Brookfield, S. (1992). Why can't I get this right? Myths and realities in facilitating adult learning. *Adult Learning, 3*(6), 12–15.

Brown, H. J. (1997). *The complete life's little instruction book*. Nashville, TN: Thomas Nelson.

Brown, J. D., & Wolfe-Quintero, K. (1997). Teacher portfolios for evaluation: A great idea or a waste of time? *Language Teacher, 21*, 28–30.

Brown, R. (1998). The teacher as a contemplative observer. *Educational Leadership, 56*, 70–75.

Bryk, A., Camburn, E., & Louis, K. S. (1999). Professional community in Chicago elementary schools: Facilitating factors and organizational consequences. *Educational Administration Quarterly, 35* (Suppl.), 751–781.

Bryk, A. S., & Schneider, B. (2002). *Trust in schools: A core resource for improvement*. New York, NY: Russell Sage College, The American Sociological Association's Rose Series in Sociology.

Burch, P., & Spillane, J. (2004). *Leading from the middle: Mid-level district staff and instructional improvement*. Chicago, IL: Cross City Campaign for Urban School Reform.

Burley-Allen, M. (1995). *Listening: The forgotten skill*. New York, NY: John Wiley.

Butler, J. (1996). Professional development: Practice as text, reflection as process, and self as locus. *Australian Journal of Education, 40*(3), 265–283.

Caine, R. N., & Caine, G. (1997). *Education on the edge of possibility*. Alexandria, VA: Association for Supervision and Curriculum Development.

Camburn, E., Rowan, B., & Taylor, J. E. (2003). Distributed leadership in schools: The case of elementary schools adopting comprehensive school reform models. *Educational Evaluation and Policy Analysis, 25*(4), 347–373.

Canning, C. (1991). What teachers say about reflection. *Educational Leadership 48*(6), 18–21.

Carlson, R. (1997). *You can be happy no matter what: Five principles your therapist never told you* [CD]. Novato, CA: New World Library.

Carlson, R. (2006). *You can be happy no matter what: Five principles your therapist never told you*. Novato, CA: New World Library.

Carlson, R., & Bailey, J. (1997). *Slowing down to the speed of life: How to create a more peaceful, simpler life from the inside out*. San Francisco, CA: HarperCollins.

Carse, J. P. (1986). *Finite and infinite games*. New York, NY: Ballatine Books.

Catmull, E. (2014). *Creativity, Inc.* New York, NY: Random House.

Chadwick, R. (2012). *Finding new ground: Beyond conflict to consensus*. Terrebonne, OR: One Tree.

Chaleff, I. (1995). *The courageous follower*. San Francisco, CA: Berrett-Koehler.

Chaleff, I. (2015). *Intelligent disobedience*. Oakland, CA: Berrett-Koehler.

Chodron, P. (1994). *Start where you are: A guide to compassionate living*. Boston, MA: Shambhala.

Costa, A. L., & Garmston, R. J. (2015). *Cognitive coaching: Developing self-directed leaders and learners* (3rd ed.). Lanham, MD: Rowman & Littlefield.

Costa, A. L., & Kallick, B. (2000a). *Activating and engaging habits of mind*. Alexandria, VA: Association for Supervision and Curriculum Development.

Costa, A. L., & Kallick, B. (2000b). Getting into the habit of reflection. *Educational Leadership, 57*(7), 60–62.

Covey, S. (1989). *The seven habits of highly effective people*. New York, NY: Fireside.

Cranton, P. (1996). Types of group learning. In S. Imel (Ed.), *Learning in groups: Exploring fundamental principles, new uses, and emerging opportunities*. San Francisco, CA: Jossey-Bass.

Danielson, C. (2007). *Enhancing professional practice: A framework for teaching*. Alexandria, VA: Association for Supervision and Curriculum Development.

Darling-Hammond, L. (2006). *Powerful teacher education: Lessons from exemplary programs*. San Francisco, CA: Jossey-Bass.

Daroszewski, E. B., Kinser, A. G., & Lloyd, S. L. (2004). Online directed journaling in community health advanced practice nursing clinical education. *Educational Innovations, 43*(4), 175–180.

Dewey, J. (1933). *How we think*. Boston, MA: D. C. Heath.

Dewey, J. (1938). *Experience and education* (6th ed.). New York, NY: Macmillan.

Dilts, R. (1996). *The new leadership paradigm* [NLPU online forum]. Santa Cruz, CA: Author. Retrieved from http://www.nlpu.com/Articles/article8.htm

Dinkelman, T. (2000). An inquiry into the development of critical reflection in secondary student teachers. *Teaching and Teacher Education, 16*, 195–200.

Diss, R. E., Buckley, P. K., & Pfau, N. D. (1992). Interactive reflective teaching: A school-college collaborative model for professional development. *Journal of Staff Development, 13*(2), 28–31.

Dobson, M., & Singer, D. (2000). *Managing up!* New York, NY: AMA.

Doidge, N., MD. (2007). *The brain that changes itself*. New York, NY: Penguin.

Donahoe, T. (1993, December). Finding the way: Structure, time, and culture in school improvement. *Phi Delta Kappan, 75*(3), 298–305.

Drago-Severson, E., Blum-DeStefano, J., & Asghar, A. (2013). *Learning for leadership: Developmental strategies for building capacity in our schools*. Thousand Oaks, CA: Corwin.

Elliott, V., & Schiff, S. (2001). A look within: Staff developers use structures, inquiry and reflection to examine feelings about equity. *Journal of Staff Development, 22*(2), 39–42.

Eraut, J. (1985). Knowledge creation and knowledge use in professional contexts. *Studies in Higher Education, 10*(2), 117–133.

Fendler, L. (2003). Teacher reflection in a hall of mirrors: Historical influences and political reverberations. *Educational Researcher, 32*(3), 16–25.

Fenwick, T. (2006). Learning as grounding and flying: Knowledge, skill and transformation in changing work contexts. *Journal of Industrial Relations, 48*(5), 691–706.

Ferrace, B. (2002). Renewing the teaching profession: A conversation with John Goodlad. *Principal Leadership, 3*(1), 31–34.

Fisher, R., & Ury, W. (1981). *Getting to YES: Negotiating agreement without giving in*. New York, NY: Penguin Books.

Fisher, R., Ury, W., & Patton, B. (2011). *Getting to YES: Negotiating agreement without giving in*. New York, NY: Penguin Books.

Forde, C., McMahon, M., McPhee, A., & Patrick, F. (2006). *Professional development, reflection and enquiry*. London, UK: Paul Chapman.

French, J., & Raven, B. (1960). *Five forms of power.* Holland, MI: Hope College.

Fullan, M. G. (1993). Why teachers must become change agents. *Educational Leadership, 50*(6), 12–17.

Fullan, M. G. (2000a). The three stories of education reform. *Phi Delta Kappan, 81*(8), 581–584.

Fullan, M. G. (2000b). The return of large scale reform. *Journal of Educational Change, 1,* 5–8.

Fullan, M. G. (2001a). *Leading in a culture of change.* San Francisco, CA: Jossey-Bass.

Fullan, M. G. (2001b). *The new meaning of educational change* (3rd ed.). New York, NY: Teachers College Press.

Fullan, M.G. (2005). *Leadership and sustainability.* Thousand Oaks, CA: Corwin.

Fullan, M. G. (2010). *Motion leadership: The skinny of becoming change savvy.* Thousand Oaks, CA: Corwin.

Garet, M. S., Porter, A. C., Desimone, L., Birman, B. F., & Yoon, K. S. (2001). What makes professional development effective? Results from a national sample of teachers. *American Education Research Journal, 38*(4), 915–945.

Garmston, R. (2012). *Unlocking group potential to improve schools.* Thousand Oaks, CA: Corwin.

Garmston, B., & von Frank, V. (2012). *Unlocking group potential.* Thousand Oaks, CA: Corwin.

Garmston, R., & Wellman, B. (1995). Adaptive schools in a quantum universe. *Educational Leadership, 52*(7), 6–12.

Garmston, R., & Wellman, B. (1997). *The adaptive school: Developing and facilitating collaborative groups.* El Dorado Hills, CA: Four Hats.

Garmston, R., & Wellman, B. (1999). *The adaptive school: A sourcebook for developing collaborative groups.* Norwood, MA: Christopher Gordon.

Garmston, R., & Wellman, B. (2009). *The adaptive school: A sourcebook for developing collaborative groups.* Norwood, MA: Christopher-Gordon.

Garmston, R., & Wellman, B. (2013). *The adaptive school: A sourcebook for developing collaborative groups.* Norwood, MA: Christopher-Gordon.

Gawande, A. (2009). *The checklist manifesto: How to get things right.* New York, NY: Metropolitan Books.

Gitlin, A. (1999). Collaboration and progressive school reform. *Educational Policy, 13*(5), 630–658.

Goldberg, S. M., & Pekso, E. (2000). The teacher book club. *Educational Leadership, 57*(8), 39–41.

Goldsmith, M. (2015). *Triggers.* New York, NY: Crown.

Goldstein, J., & Kornfield, J. (1987). *Seeking the heart of wisdom: The path of insight meditation.* Boston, MA: Shambahla.

Grant, A. (2013). *Give and take.* New York, NY: Viking.

Gruenert, S., & Whitaker, T. (2015). *School culture rewired.* Alexandria, VA: ASCD.

Guskey, T. (1986). Staff development and the process of teacher change. *Educational Researcher, 15*(5), 5–12.

Haberman, M. (1995). *Star teachers of children in poverty.* Indianapolis, IN: Kappa Delta Pi.

Hagstrom, D., Hubbard, R., Hurtig, C., Mortola, P., Ostrow, J., & White, V. (2000). Teaching is like . . . ? *Educational Leadership, 57*(8), 24–27.

Hall, G. E., & Hord, S. M. (2014). *Implementing change: Patterns, principles, and potholes* (4th ed.). Boston, MA: Allyn & Bacon.

Hargreaves, A. (1994). Guilt: Exploring the emotions of teaching. In A. Hargreaves (Ed.), *Changing teachers, changing times* (pp. 141–159). New York, NY: Teachers College Press.

Harvey, O. J. (1967). Conceptual systems and attitude change. In C. Sharif & M. Sharif (Eds.), *Attitude, ego involvement and change.* New York, NY: Wiley.

Haslam, S. A., Reicher, S. D., & Platow, M. (2011). *The new psychology of leadership.* New York, NY: Psychology Press.

Hattie, J. (2009). *Visible learning: A synthesis of over 800 meta-analyses relating to achievement.* New York, NY: Routledge.

Hatton, N., & Smith, D. (1995). Reflection in teacher education: Towards definition and implementation. *Teaching and Teacher Education, 11*(1), 33–49.

Hawkins, M. R. (2004). Researching English language literacy development in schools. *Educational Researcher, 33*(3), 14–25.

Heath, C., & Heath, D. (2010). *Switch: How to change things when change is hard.* New York, NY: Broadway Books. Available at http://www.schoolbriefing .com/wp-content/uploads/2010/11/November-2010-Main-Interview-Transcript.pdf

Heifetz, R., Grashow, A., & Linsky, M. (2009). *The practice of adaptive leadership.* Boston, MA: Harvard Business Press.

Hock, D. (1996, October/November). Dee Hock on management. *Fast Company,* 79.

Hord, S. (1997). *Professional learning communities: Communities of continuous inquiry and improvement.* Austin, TX: Southwest Educational Development Laboratory.

Hord, S., & Hirsh, S. (2007). Making the promise a reality. In A. Blankstein, P. Houston, & R. Cole (Eds.), *Sustaining professional learning communities* (Chap. 2). Thousand Oaks, CA: Corwin.

Hord, S., & Sommers, W. (2008). *Leading professional learning communities.* Thousand Oaks, CA: Corwin.

Ingvarson, L., Meiers, M., & Beavis, A. (2005). Factors affecting the impact of professional development programs on teachers' knowledge, practice, student outcomes and efficacy. *Education Policy Analysis Archives, 13*(10). Retrieved from http://epaa/asu.edu/epaa/v13n10/

Isaacs, W. (1999). *Dialogue and the art of thinking together.* New York, NY: Currency.

Jackson, Y. (2011). *Pedagogy of confidence: Inspiring high intellectual performance in urban schools.* New York, NY: Teachers College Press.

Jay, J. K., & Johnson, K. L. (2002). Capturing complexity: A typology of reflective practice for teacher education. *Teaching and Teacher Education, 18,* 73–85.

Johnson, D. W., & Johnson, R. T. (1999). *Learning together and alone: Cooperative, competitive, and individualistic learning* (5th ed.). Needham Heights, MA: Allyn & Bacon.

Johnston, M. (1994). Contrasts and similarities in case studies of teacher reflection and change. *Curriculum Inquiry, 24*(1), 9–26.

Joyce, B., & Calhoun, E. (2010). *Models of professional development.* Thousand Oaks, CA: Corwin.

Joyce, B., & Showers, B. (2002). *Student achievement through staff development* (3rd ed.). Alexandria, VA: Association for Supervision and Curriculum Development.

Jupp, B. (2012, January 18). *Homeroom: The official blog of the U.S. Department of Education.* Washington, DC: United States Department of Education. Accessed at http://www.ed.gov/blog/2012/01/join-ed-and-teachers-for-a-teachtalk-discussion-on-twitter/

Kahn, W. A. (1992). To be fully there: Psychological presence at work. *Human Relations, 45*(4), 321–349.

Keating, C. N. (1993). Promoting growth through dialogue journals. In G. Wells (Ed.), *Changing schools from within: Creating communities of inquiry* (pp. 217–236). Toronto, Canada: Ontario Institute for Studies in Education.

Killion, J. P., & Simmons, L. A. (1992). The Zen of facilitation. *Journal of Staff Development, 13*(3), 2–5.

Killion, J. P., & Todnem, G. (1991). A process of personal theory building. *Educational Leadership, 48*(6), 14–17.

Kim, D. (1993, Fall). The link between individual and organizational learning. *Sloan Management Review,* 37–50.

Kinchloe, J. L. (2004). The knowledges of teacher education: Developing a critical complex epistemology. *Teacher Education Quarterly, 31*(1), 49–66.

Klein, G. (1998). *Sources of power: How people make decisions.* Cambridge, MA: The MIT Press.

Knight, J. (2011). *Unmistakable impact: A partnership approach for dramatically improving instruction.* Thousand Oaks, CA: Corwin.

Knight, J. (2014). *Focus on teaching: Using video for high-impact instruction.* Thousand Oaks, CA: Corwin.

Knight, J. (2015). *Better conversations.* Thousand Oaks, CA: Corwin.

Knowles, M. (1984). *Andragogy in action.* San Francisco, CA: Jossey-Bass.

Kolar, C., & Dickson, S.V. (2002). Preservice general educators' perceptions of structured logs as viable learning tools in a university course on inclusionary practices. *Teacher Education and Special Education, 25*(4), 395–406.

Koszalka, T. A., Grabowski, B. L., & McCarthy, M. (2003). Reflection through the ID-PRISM: A teacher planning tool to transform classrooms into web-enhanced learning environments. *Journal of Technology and Teacher Education, 11*(3), 347–375.

Kouzes, J., & Posner, B. (2007). *The leadership challenge* (4th ed.). San Francisco, CA: John Wiley.

Kroeger, S., Burton, C., Comarata, A., Combs, C., Hamm, C., Hopkins, R., & Kouche, B. (2004). Student voice and critical reflection: Helping students at risk. *Teaching Exceptional Children, 36*(3), 50–57.

Kronberg, R., & York-Barr, J. (Eds.). (1998). *Differentiated teaching and learning in heterogeneous classrooms: Strategies for meeting the needs of all students.* Minneapolis, MN: University of Minnesota, Institute on Community Integration.

Kruse, S. D., Louis, K. S., & Bryk, A. (1995). An emerging framework for analyzing school-based professional community. In K. S. Louis & S. D. Kruse (Eds.), *Professionalism and community: Perspectives on reforming urban schools* (pp. 23–42). Thousand Oaks, CA: Corwin.

LaBorde, G. Z. (1987). *Influencing with integrity.* Palo Alto, CA: Syntony.

Ladson-Billings, G. (2000). *The dreamkeepers: Successful teachers of African-American children.* San Francisco, CA: Jossey-Bass.

Lambert, L. (2003). *Leadership for lasting school improvement.* Alexandria, VA: Association for Supervision and Curriculum Development.

Lame Deer, J., & Erdoes, R. (1994). *Lame Deer, seeker of visions.* New York, NY: Washington Square.

Langer, G. M., & Colton, A. B. (1994). Reflective decision-making: The cornerstone of school reform. *Journal of Staff Development, 15*(1), 2–7.

Lee, P. (1995). *Creating collaborative work cultures: Effective communication*. Drake, CO: Changing Points of View.

Leithwood, K., Seashore-Louis, K., Anderson, S., & Wahlstrom, K. (2004). *How leadership influences student learning*. Minneapolis: University of Minnesota, Center for Applied Research and Educational Improvement; and Toronto, Ontario: Ontario Institute for Studies in Education.

Lencioni, P. (2004). *Death by meeting*. San Francisco, CA: Jossey-Bass.

Levin, B. B. (1995). Using the case method in teacher education: The role of discussion and experience in teachers' thinking about cases. *Teaching and Teacher Education, 11*(1), 63–79.

Lindsey, R. B., Roberts, L. M., & CampbellJones, F. (2005). *The culturally proficient school: An implementation guide for school leaders*. Thousand Oaks, CA: Corwin.

Loeb, P. (Ed.). (2004). *The impossible will take a little while: A citizen's guide to hope in a time of fear*. New York, NY: Basic Books.

Lopez, S. (2014). *Making hope happen*. New York, NY: Atria.

Louis, K. S. (1992). Restructuring and the problem of teachers' work. In A. Lieberman (Ed.), *The changing contexts of teaching: 91st yearbook of the National Society for the Study of Education* (Vol. 1, pp. 138–156). Chicago, IL: University of Chicago Press.

Lunenberg, F. (2012). Power and leadership: An influence process. *International Journal of Management, Business, and Administration, 15*(1).

Maggio, R. (1992). *The Beacon book of quotations by women*. Boston, MA: Beacon Press.

Marcus, S., Jr. (2011). *Pure group*. Available at https://th-th.facebook.com/PureGroupDFW/

Marks, H., & Louis, K. S. (1999, December). Teacher empowerment and the capacity for organizational learning. *Educational Administration Quarterly, 35* (Suppl.), 707–750.

Marshak, R. (2006). *Covert processes at work*. San Francisco, CA: Berrett-Kohler.

Marzano, R., Boogren, T., Heflebower, T., Kanold-McIntyre, J., & Pickering, D. (2012). *Becoming a reflective teacher*. Bloomington, IN: Marzano Research Laboratory.

Marzano, R., Pickering, D., & Pollock, J. (2001). *Classroom instruction that works: Research-based strategies for increasing student achievement*. Alexandria, VA: Association for Supervision and Curriculum Development.

Maxwell, J. (2007). *The 21 irrefutable laws of leadership: Follow them and people will follow you*. Nashville, TN: Thomas Nelson.

Miller, G. (2002). *Peace, value, and wisdom: The education philosophy of Daisaku Ideda*. Amsterdam, Netherlands: Rodophi.

Milner, H. R. (2003). Teacher reflection and race in cultural context: History, meaning, and methods in teaching. *Theory Into Practice, 42*(3), 173–180.

Murray, A. L. (2013). *An exploratory study of teacher leaders who work between the central office and schools*. (Submitted to the Graduate Faculty of the University of Minnesota in partial fulfillment of the requirements for the degree of Doctor of Philosophy). Advisor: Jennifer York-Barr.

National Education Goals Panel. (2000). *Strategies for meeting high standards: Quality management and the Baldridge criteria in education*. Washington, DC: National Education Goals Panel. Retrieved from http://govinfo.library.unt.edu/negp/reports/strategies.pdf

Nhat Hanh, T. (1993). *Interbeing: Fourteen guidelines for engaged Buddhism.* Berkeley, CA: Parallax.

Nin, A. (1967). *The diary of Anaïs Nin, Volume 1: 1931–1934* (G. Stuhlmann, Ed.). New York, NY: Harcourt Brace Jovanovich.

Norton, B. (2000). *Identity and language learning: Gender, ethnicity, and educational change.* Essex, England: Pearson Education.

Nyberg, D., & Farber, P. (1986). Authority in education. *Teachers College Record, 88*(1), 4–14.

Olsen, W., & Sommers, W. (2004). *A trainer's companion: Stories to stimulate reflection, conversation, and action.* Baytown, TX: AhaProcess.

Osterman, K. F., & Kottkamp, R. B. (1993). *Reflective practice for educators: Improving schooling through professional development.* Newbury Park, CA: Corwin.

Osterman, K. F., & Kottkamp, R. B. (2004). *Reflective practice for educators: Professional development to improve student learning* (2nd ed.). Thousand Oaks, CA: Corwin.

Palmer, P. (1998). *The courage to teach.* San Francisco, CA: Jossey-Bass.

Pappas, C. (2013, May 9). *The adult learning theory—Andragogy* [Web log post]. Retrieved from http://elearningindustry.com/the-adult-learning-theory-andragogy-of-malcolm-knowles

Pentland, A. (2014). *Social physics.* New York, NY: Penguin.

Perkins, D. (1992). *Smart schools.* New York, NY: Free Press.

Perry, C. M., & Power, B. M. (2004). Finding the truths in teacher preparation field experiences. *Teacher Educator Quarterly, 31*(2), 125–136.

Peters, T., & Waterman, R. (1982). *In search of excellence.* New York, NY: HarperCollins.

Phelan, K. (2013). *I'm sorry I broke your company.* San Francisco, CA: Berrett-Koehler.

Pierce, J. W., & Kalkman, D. L. (2003). Applying learner-centered principles in teacher education. *Theory Into Practice, 42*(2), 127–132.

Pounder, D. G. (1999). Teacher teams: Exploring job characteristics and work-related outcomes of work group enhancement. *Educational Administration Quarterly, 35*(3), 317–348.

Pugach, M. C., & Johnson, L. J. (1990). Developing reflective practice through structured dialogue. In R. T. Clift, W. R. Houston, & M. C. Pugach (Eds.), *Encouraging reflective practice in education: An analysis of issues and programs* (pp. 186–207). New York, NY: Teachers College Press.

Pugh, S. L., Hicks, J. W., Davis, M., & Venstra, T. (1992). *Bridging: A teacher's guide to metaphorical thinking.* Urbana, IL: National Council of Teachers of English.

Pultorak, E. G. (1996). Following the developmental process of reflection in novice teachers: Three years of investigation. *Journal of Teacher Education, 47*(4), 283–291.

Raelin, J. A. (2002). "I don't have time to think!" versus the art of reflective practice. *Reflections: The SoL Journal, 4*(17), 66–75.

Rappolt-Schlictmann, G., Daley, S., & Rose, T. (2012). *A research reader in Universal Design for Learning.* Cambridge, MA: Harvard Education Press.

Raywid, M. (1993). Finding time for collaboration. *Educational Leadership, 51,* 30–34.

Reeves, D. B. (2006, May). Of hubs, bridges, and networks. *Educational Leadership,* 32–36.

Reiman, A. J. (1999). The evolution of social role-taking and guided reflection framework in teacher education: Recent theory and quantitative synthesis of research. *Teaching and Teacher Education, 15*(6), 597–612.

Richardson, J. (2004). *From the inside-out: Learning from positive deviance in your organization*. Oxford, OH: National Staff Development Council.

Richardson, J. (2009). *The next step in guided reading*. New York, NY: Scholastic.

Robinson, D. N. (1997). Socrates and the unexamined life. In *The Great Ideas of Philosophy*. Springfield, VA: The Teaching Company.

Rockler, M. J. (2004). Ethics and professional practice in education. *Phi Delta Kappa Fastbacks*, 521.

Rodgers, C. (2002). Defining reflection: Another look at John Dewey and reflective thinking. *Teachers College Record, 104*(4), 842–866.

Rogers, C. (1986). Carl Rogers on the development of the person-centered approach. *Person-Centered Review, 1*(3), 257–259.

Sagor, R. (2000). *Guiding school improvement with action research*. Alexandria, VA: Association for Supervision and Curriculum Development.

Sanborn, M. (2006). *You don't need a title to be a leader*. New York, NY: Doubleday.

Sanders, S. R. (1998). *Hunting for hope*. Boston, MA: Beacon Press.

Sanford, C. (1995, September/October). Myths of organizational effectiveness. *At Work*, 10–12.

Saphier, J., & Haley-Speca, M. A. (2008). *The skillful teacher: Building your teaching skills* (7th ed.). Carlisle, MA: Research for Better Teaching.

Schall, E. (1995). Learning to love the swamp: Reshaping education for public service. *Journal of Policy Analysis and Management, 14*(2), 202–220.

Schein, E. (1993). On dialogue, culture, and organizational learning. *Organizational Dynamics, 22.* Retrieved from http://www.journals.elsevier.com/organizational-Dynamics

Schein, E. (2004). *Organizational culture and leadership* (3rd ed.). San Francisco, CA: Jossey-Bass.

Schein, E. (2009). *Helping—how to offer, give, and receive help*. San Francisco, CA: Berrett-Koehler.

Schein, E. (2013). *Humble inquiry—the gentle art of asking instead of telling*. San Francisco, CA: Berrett-Koehler.

Schön, D. A. (1983). *The reflective practitioner: How professionals think in action*. New York, NY: Basic Books.

Schön, D. A. (1987). *Educating the reflective practitioner: Toward a new design for teaching and learning in the professions*. San Francisco, CA: Jossey-Bass.

Scott, S. (2002). *Fierce conversations*. New York, NY: Penguin Putnam.

Seidel, S. (1991). *Collaborative assessment conferences for the consideration of project work*. Cambridge, MA: Project Zero, Harvard Graduate School of Education.

Senge, P. (2012). *Schools that learn: A fifth discipline fieldbook for educators, parents, and everyone who cares about education*. New York, NY: Crown Business.

Senge, P., Cambron-McCabe, N. H., Lucas, T., Smith, B., Dutton, J., & Kleiner, A. (2012). *Schools that learn: A fifth discipline fieldbook for educators, parents, and everyone who cares about education*. New York, NY: Currency, Doubleday.

Senge, P., Sharmer, O., Jaworski, J., & Flowers, B. S. (2004). *Presence: Exploring profound change in people, organizations and society*. New York, NY: Currency.

Sergiovanni, T. (1992). Moral leadership: *Getting to the heart of school improvement*. San Francisco, CA: Jossey-Bass.

Sherin, M. G. (2000). Viewing teaching on videotape. *Educational Leadership, 57*(8), 36–38.

Sinek, S. (2009). *Start with why: How great leaders inspire everyone to take action.* London, UK: Penguin.

Sinek, S. (2013). *Simon Sinek why?*[Video file]. Retrieved from http://www.bing .com/videos/search?q=ted+talk+simon+sinek+why&FORM=VIRE1#view= detail&mid=3A95274017FC2CC800443A95274017FC2CC80044

Singleton, G. (2012). *More courageous conversations about race.* Thousand Oaks, CA: Corwin.

Singleton, G. (2015). *Courageous conversations about race: A field guide for achieving equity in schools* (2nd ed.). Thousand Oaks, CA: Corwin.

Slap, S. (2010). *Bury my heart at conference Room B.* New York, NY: Penguin.

Smyth, J. (1989). Developing and sustaining critical reflection in teacher education. *Journal of Teacher Education, 40*(2), 2–9.

Sparks, D. (2003). The answer to "when?" is "now": An interview with Peter Block. *Journal of Staff Development, 24*(2), 52–55.

Sparks-Langer, G. M., & Colton, A. (1991). Synthesis of research on teachers' reflective thinking. *Educational Leadership, 48*(6), 37–44.

Speck, M. (2002). Balanced and year-round professional development: Time and learning. *Catalyst for Change, 32*(1), 17–19.

Steffy, B. E., Wolfe, M. P., Pasch, S. H., & Enz, B. J. (2000). *Life cycle of the career teacher.* Thousand Oaks, CA: Corwin.

Stewart, T. A. (1997). *Intellectual capital.* New York, NY: Doubleday-Currency.

Straus, D. (2002). *How to make collaboration work: Powerful ways to build consensus, solve problems, and make decisions.* San Francisco, CA: Berrett-Koehler.

Supovitz, J. A. (2002). Developing communities of instructional practice. *Teachers College Record, 104*(8), 1591–1626.

Surowiecki, J. (2004). *The wisdom of crowds.* New York, NY: Anchor Books.

Sutton, R., & Rao, H. (2014). *Scaling up excellence.* New York, NY: Crown Publishing.

Suzuki, S. (1982/1970). *Zen mind, beginner's mind: Informal talks on Zen meditation and practice.* New York, NY: Weatherhill.

Taggart, G. L., & Wilson, A. P. (1998). *Promoting reflective thinking in teachers: 44 action strategies.* Thousand Oaks, CA: Corwin.

The Socratic method and doctrine. (n.d.). *20-20 Site.* Retrieved from http:// www.2020site.org/socrates/method.html

Thousand, J. S., & Villa, R. (2000). Collaborative teams: Powerful tools for school restructuring. In R. Villa & J. S. Thousand (Eds.), *Restructuring for caring and effective education* (2nd ed., pp. 254–291). Baltimore, MD: Paul H. Brookes.

Tichy, N. (1997). *The leadership engine.* New York, NY: HarperCollins.

Tschannen-Moran, M. (2004). *Trust matters: leadership for successful schools.* San Francisco, CA: Jossey-Bass.

Tuckman, B. W. (1965). Developmental sequence in small groups. *Psychological Bulletin, 63,* 384–399.

Tushman, M. L., & Scanlon, T. J. (1981). Boundary spanning individuals: Their role in information transfer and their antecedents. *Academy of Management Journal, 24,* 83–98.

U.S. Department of Education. (1996). *Breaking the tyranny of time: Voices from the Goals 2000 Teacher Forum.* Washington, DC: Government Printing Office.

Valli, L. (1997). Listening to other voices: A description of teacher reflection in the United States. *Peabody Journal of Education, 72*(1), 67–88.

van Manen, M. (1977). Linking ways of knowing with ways of being practical. *Curriculum Inquiry, 6*(3), 205–228.

van Manen, M. (2002). The pathic principle of pedagogical language. *Teaching and Teacher Education, 18,* 215–224.

Vella, J. (1994). *Learning to listen, learning to teach: The power of dialogue in educating adults.* San Francisco, CA: Jossey-Bass.

Vogt, E., Brown, J., & Isaacs, D. (2003). *The art of powerful questions: Catalyzing insight, innovation, and action.* Mill Valley, CA: Whole Systems Associates.

Vygotsky, L. (2003). *Vygotsky's educational theory in cultural context.* Cambridge, UK: Cambridge University Press.

Wahlstrom, K., & York-Barr, J. (2011). Leadership: Support and structures make the difference for educators and students. *JSD Standards for Professional Learning* (theme issue). *JSD, 32*(4), 22–25, 32.

Wallace, D. (1996). Journey to school reform: Moving from reflection to action through storytelling. Washington, DC: National Education Association Library Publication.

Wallace, M. J. (1979). *Microteaching and the teaching of English as a second or foreign language in teacher training institutions.* Edinburgh, Scotland: Moray House College of Education, Scottish Centre of Education Overseas.

Wang, C., & Burris, M. A. (1994). Photovoice: Concept, methodology, and use for participatory needs assessment. *Health Education and Behavior, 24*(3), 369–387.

Watts, G. D., & Castle, S. (1993, December). The time dilemma in school restructuring. *Phi Delta Kappan, 75*(3), 306–310.

Webb, G. (1995). Reflective practice, staff development and understanding. *Studies in Continuing Education, 17*(1 & 2), 70–77.

Webber, A. M. (1993, January/February). What's so new about the new economy? *Harvard Business Review,* 24–42.

Webber, A. M. (2000, June). Why can't we get anything done? *Fast Company, 35,* 168–170, 176–180.

Weiner, N. (1998). *The human use of human beings.* Boston, MA: Da Capo Press.

Wenger, E. (1998). *Communities of practice.* Cambridge, UK: Cambridge University Press.

Wheatley, M. (1992). *Leadership and the new science.* San Francisco, CA: Berrett-Kohler.

Wheatley, M. (2009). *Turning to one another: Simple conversations to restore hope to the future.* San Francisco, CA: Berrett-Kohler.

Will, A. M. (1997, Winter). Group learning in workshops. *New Directions for Adult and Continuing Education, 76,* 33–40.

Wilson, E. O. (1992). *The diversity of life.* New York, NY: W.W. Norton.

Wiseman, L. (2014). *Rookie smarts: Why learning beats knowing in the new game of work.* New York, NY: HarperCollins.

Wolfe, P. (2010). *Brain matters: Translating research into classroom practices* (2nd ed.). Alexandra, VA: ASCD.

Wolfe, P. (2015). *Brain matters: Translating brain research to classroom practice.* Workshop presented July 2015 in Minnetonka, MN.

Wong, J. K., & Wong, R. T. (1998). *The first days of school.* Mountain View, CA: Author.

York-Barr, J., & Duke, K. (2004). What do we know about teacher leadership? Findings from two decades of scholarship. *Review of Educational Research, 74*(3), 255–316.

York-Barr, J., Ghere, G., & Sommerness, J. (2003). What's working and what's not for your team? In T. Vandercook, J. York-Barr, & V. Gaylord (Eds.), *IMPACT: Feature issue on revisiting inclusive education* (pp. 14–15). Minneapolis: University of Minnesota, Institute on Community Integration.

York-Barr, J., Sommers, W., Ghere, G., & Montie, J. (2006). *Reflective practice to improve schools* (2nd ed.). Thousand Oaks, CA: Corwin.

Yukl, G., & Fable, C. M. (1990). Influence tactics in upward, downward, and lateral influence attempts. *Journal of Applied Psychology, 75*(2), 132–140.

Yukl, G., & Fable, C.M. (1991). Importance of different power sources in downward and lateral relations. *Journal of Applied Psychology, 76*(3), 416–423.

Zeichner, K. M. (1993). Connecting genuine teacher development to the struggle for social justice. *Journal of Education for Teaching, 19*(1), 5–20.

Zeichner, K. M., & Liston, D. P. (1987). Teaching student teachers to reflect. *Harvard Educational Review, 57*, 23–48.

Zeichner, K. M., & Liston, D. P. (1996). *Reflective teaching: An introduction.* Mahwah, NJ: Lawrence Erlbaum.

Index

NOTES

NOTES

NOTES

A SAGE Publishing Company

CORWIN HAS ONE MISSION: to enhance education through intentional professional learning.

We build long-term relationships with our authors, educators, clients, and associations who partner with us to develop and continuously improve the best evidence-based practices that establish and support lifelong learning.

Solutions you want. Experts you trust. Results you need.

AUTHOR CONSULTING

Author Consulting

On-site professional learning with sustainable results! Let us help you design a professional learning plan to meet the unique needs of your school or district. www.corwin.com/pd

INSTITUTES

Institutes

Corwin Institutes provide collaborative learning experiences that equip your team with tools and action plans ready for immediate implementation. www.corwin.com/institutes

ECOURSES

eCourses

Practical, flexible online professional learning designed to let you go at your own pace. www.corwin.com/ecourses

READ2EARN

Read2Earn

Did you know you can earn graduate credit for reading this book? Find out how: www.corwin.com/read2earn

Contact an account manager at (800) 831-6640 or visit **www.corwin.com** for more information.